LANCASHIRE
TURF
WARS

LANCASHIRE
TURF
WARS
A FOOTBALL HISTORY

STEVE TONGUE

First published by Pitch Publishing, 2018

Pitch Publishing
A2 Yeoman Gate
Yeoman Way
Worthing
Sussex
BN13 3QZ
www.pitchpublishing.co.uk
info@pitchpublishing.co.uk

A CIP catalogue record is available for this book
from the British Library.

ISBN 978-1-78531-435-3

Typesetting and origination by Pitch Publishing
Printed and bound in India by Replika Press Pvt. Ltd.

Contents

and *Everton's Dean; Bolton's chaotic Wembley debut and 1920s FA Cup treble before north-west's worst-ever season; Blackburn take Villa down with them; City at Maine Road – the champions relegated; United's grim '30s; Blackpool's Jimmy Hampson tragedy; slow decline of Oldham; Third Division North for Rochdale, Tranmere and others; but only briefly for Nelson, Stalybridge and Wigan Borough; from South Liverpool, a new New Brighton.*

Interlude I: War **150**
The three-match season of 1939/40; ban on organised sport quickly lifted but with restrictions; goalscorers cash in; emergence of Liddell, Finney and Mortensen; Stanley Matthews a most welcome guest for powerful Blackpool, who join Preston and Bolton as War Cup winners; prisoners of war at Deepdale; United bombed out for eight years.

5. Stan and Tom and Nat – and Matt (1946–1960) **155**
Matt Busby revives United before the tragedy of Munich; Matthews and Finney build the Blackpool-Preston rivalry – but only one of them wins any medals; Burnden Park disaster and the Lion of Vienna; Merseyside pair swap fortunes and First Division place pre-Shankly; City's familiar ups-and-downs; Burnley unfashionable champions, Blackburn's ten years below stairs; plenty of Third North and Fourth Division strugglers; New Brighton voted out of league.

6. Swinging (1961–70). **193**
Goals and wages up, crowds down and reform rejected; divide begins between big cities and the rest as Preston, Bolton, Blackburn, Blackpool are all relegated; Everton and Liverpool lay down a powerful Mersey beat; Allison boasts he'll overtake United, who win the European Cup four days after City's league title; Burnley runners-up and European competitors before slow decline; Bury's eventful decade; Ken Bates's great plans for Oldham; Tranmere, Southport, Stockport turn to 'pay-night football'; Rochdale reach a League Cup final; but Accrington collapse in mid-season.

Acknowledgements

Many thanks to all who have helped with queries, memories and memorabilia, notably Tony Bugby, Cliff Butler, Roy Calley, Sarah Collins, Tony Coombes, Dr Graham Curry, Louise Gwilliam, Ian Herbert, Mark Iddon, Hyder Jawad, John Keith, Julian Lillington, Andy Mitchell, Gail Newsham, David Pugh, John Roberts, Paul Rowley, Catherine Tongue, Peter Wadsworth and Steve Wilson.

To Duncan Olner and Graham Hales for design and to Paul Camillin, Jane Camillin and Derek Hammond of Pitch Publishing.

Introduction

*'We suggest that Lancashire holds a very honoured
and exalted place in the football world.'*
History of the Lancashire Football Association 1878–1928.

AS the Lancashire FA approached its 140th anniversary in
2018, Liverpool were competing in the Champions League
Final, and the top two teams in the Premier League season
just finished were old enemies Manchester City and Manchester
United, the latter having also played in the FA Cup Final. Burnley
and Everton, founder members of the Football League in 1888,
made it five teams from the red rose county in the top eight.

That 'honoured and exalted place' in football had not only been
maintained but enhanced, all the more so since the inception in
the 1950s of European competition, in which Lancashire clubs can
boast 15 major trophies.

Much earlier on, the county's leading clubs had been
prominent in the two great innovations of the late 19th century,
professionalism and league football. Preston North End opened
the way for the former after openly admitting paying their players,
and the world's first football league was equally divided between
teams from the north-west and the midlands.

Preston's 'Invincibles' triumphed in that first competition,
adding for good measure the FA Cup that two different Blackburn
clubs had already won, and soon the great teams of Merseyside
and Manchester were winning trophies too. Blackpool, Bolton
Wanderers, Burnley, Bury and Oldham all made their mark before

the First World War and a new crop joined them when the Third Division North was born in 1921.

Local rivalry adds spice but can make for difficulties too, if there are too many clubs and too few people to sustain them. Early pioneers like Darwen, Blackburn Olympic and Bootle failed to maintain their momentum. Oldham Athletic, like Rochdale and two Wigan clubs, have always had local rugby league rivals to contend with.

So turf wars had to be fought not only on the pitch but off it, most famously with Everton leaving their Anfield home, spawning another huge club and the most local of rivalries (killing Bootle in the process), while Manchester United, like Woolwich Arsenal in London, moved from one side of town to the other (and beyond) in search of support and better facilities.

The 1921 intake have only ever progressed briefly above the lower divisions and mostly found the going hard. Stalybridge Celtic, Nelson and Wigan Borough lost their Football League places before 1939, then New Brighton, Accrington Stanley and Southport did so afterwards. Yet Stanley, once the butt of comedians' jokes, showed it was possible to fight their way back and aim high again. So did Tranmere Rovers, victims of automatic relegation to non-league football introduced in 1987, and Stockport County, like Southport, would love to emulate them. But the same system has allowed clubs like Fleetwood and Morecambe the chance to carry the name of their towns further afield.

Below them many more flourished at non-league level, their deeds marked here in the Interludes, also including sections on women's football and the war years.

Clubs, of course, need people and the north-west has been home to many of the greatest players, managers and administrators in English football as well as occasional scandal and tragedy interspersing the often glorious triumphs contained within these pages.

Note: For the purposes of this book, the broad definition of Lancashire has been taken to include the metropolitan counties of Greater Manchester and Merseyside created under the 1972 Local Government Act. Thus clubs like Stockport and Tranmere receive nothing less than their due share of recognition.

Chapter 1
Beyond Cottonopolis (1860–87)

*Central Lancashire, the first northern football powerhouse,
initially around Turton, Darwen, Bolton, Blackburn and
Accrington; Manchester, a huge cotton centre but still a rugby
city; Darwen, the first to make an impact in early FA Cups,
quickly followed by Blackburn rivals Olympic and Rovers as
supremacy of the southern amateurs is quashed; accusations
of payments to players unconvincingly denied before professionalism legalised in 1885; early days of Everton, Bootle and
Manchester clubs before Football League begins.*

MODERN northern powerhouses they may be, but when
Lancashire first began to rewrite the story of football in
England, Manchester and Merseyside were a footnote so
small as to be barely legible.

There can be no doubt as to the importance of both centres in
commercial terms to the cotton industry that thrived from the mid-
19th century. Manchester, with its 100 mills and more rejoiced in
the title of 'Cottonopolis' and has been described as 'the workshop
of England' and 'the world's first industrial city'; it had been linked
to the port of Liverpool by rail from as early as 1830 largely to
service that industry.

Yet despite the two areas having large populations of mainly working-class employees, football did not take off to any significant degree as it was already doing in other provincial centres like Sheffield and Nottingham. In 1875, with the London-based Football Association (FA) already a dozen years old and the FA Cup four years into its existence, *Athletic News*, newly created in Manchester, was bemoaning the fact that no clubs of significance existed in its home city. When the Lancashire FA (LFA) was founded in 1878 there was not a single Manchester representative among the 28 clubs; a Manchester FA did not emerge until six years afterwards, and as late as 1886, the LFA informed Everton, the best team on Merseyside, and founder members of the Liverpool FA (1882) that they were not considered good enough for the Lancashire Senior Cup and had to play in the Junior Cup.

It was further north that football first flourished, above all in a tight little line running roughly down the A666 the dozen miles from Blackburn to Bolton via Darwen and Turton, around which so many of those 28 teams were clustered. As the Bolton historians Peter Swain and Robert Lewis have put it, 'The cradle of Association football in the North West of England centred on Bolton, Darwen and Blackburn, with Turton FC being the centre of innovation in the diffusion of the game. Manchester was a rugby city until the late 1880s and early 1890s.'

Manchester Football Club, founded in 1860, was of the rugby variety; records of games for the Manchester team Hulme Athenaeum exist from 1865 to about 1873, although it is unclear which of the many variations of rules of that time they were using.

The FA may have been founded with the principal aim of 'settling a code of rules for the regulation of the game' but even **Turton**, established eight years later in December 1871, were still accepting handling as late as 1873 in the sense of outfield players catching the ball and claiming a 'mark'. That was one of the Harrow Rules adopted by the club's founder, headmaster and Old Harrovian, John Kay, from his *alma mater*. At least tripping, pushing and the hacking or 'shinning' beloved of the Blackheath contingent who had broken away from the FA a decade earlier to play rugby, were no longer part of the game.

In 1872 Turton played both Brookhouse Mills (from Blackburn) and Darwen under a mixture of Harrow and association rules and in August two years later they formally agreed association rules with no handling; it cost them a few members who wanted to play catch and left to join the rugby code, with clubs like the already established Preston Grasshoppers.

The name of Turton lives on to this day in the West Lancashire League, and the original ground at Tower Street in Chapeltown is still used by Old Boltonians, the old boys of Bolton School, giving it claims to be one the very oldest in continuous use anywhere.

Turton were a force until the early 1880s; in 1879 they began competing in the FA Cup for a run of four seasons, twice reaching the third round but losing in the last of those campaigns in the first round to Hurst (now Ashton United), one of the clubs finally emerging around Manchester. From then on they began to drop into the lower ranks, winning the Lancashire Junior Cup four times between 1900 and 1905.

The club also supplied Lancashire football with one of its most influential figures. John Bentley, son of a Chapeltown grocer, went on from his days as the club captain to become president of the Football League, having enjoyed considerable power in recommending which clubs should join the inaugural competition in 1888.

In September 1877 *Athletic News* wrote that while rugby was still dominant in the county, there were 'indications that the "dribbling" sport is making an unmistakeable headway'.

Twelve months later, establishing a Lancashire FA proved the point, and the list of clubs enrolling as founders illustrates where the greatest enthusiasm for the sport lay. The key meetings were held in South Turton and then Darwen, and the 28 who signed up, paying just over ten shillings (50p) each were: Astley Bridge, Blackburn Rovers, Blackburn Christ Church, Livesey United (Blackburn), Blackburn Park Road, Blackburn St George's, Blackburn St Mark's, Bolton Emmanuel, Bolton North End, Bolton Wanderers, Bolton St George's, Bolton Rovers, Bolton St Paul's, Church, Cloughfold, Darwen, Lower Darwen, Darwen Grasshoppers, Darwen Rangers, Darwen Lower Chapel, Darwen St James, Eagley, Enfield, Great Lever, Haslingden Rangers, Haslingden Grane, Myrtle Grove and Turton.

No Manchester, no Merseyside; but 28 leading teams drawn exclusively from Blackburn, Bolton, Darwen, Church (near

Accrington), Haslingden and Rawtenstall. There was not more than 15 miles between any of them, which helped build local rivalries at a time when transport was improving and players and spectators alike were looking for relief from grim hours in the dark satanic cotton mills.

For some time the greatest of these rivalries would be between the neighbouring towns of Blackburn and Darwen, only four miles apart, which produced the finalists in the first Lancashire Senior Cup of 1879/80 from 40 entries, and before long had helped change the face of football forever.

* * * * *

Of the six different clubs from **Darwen** among the LFA's founding members, the one that became the most famous was that which simply bore the name of the town and would carry it far and wide. The local cricket club dated as far back as 1845 and a football version started in early 1872 with a match against Brookhouse Mills (who won it 3-1) and then Turton. The following year the cricket and football clubs amalgamated at the Barley Bank ground in the middle of town.

As the number of clubs proliferated, the most ambitious of them began to desire not just local turf wars but more widespread battles and also the sort of competitive football which had begun in England on 11 November 1871 with the first four matches ever played in the FA Cup; effectively a Home Counties competition that admitted only two of its original 15 entries from north of Hertfordshire.

One of them, Donington School from Lincolnshire, scratched without playing a match. The other, significantly, came from as far away as Scotland, where Queen's Park (founded 1867) were first and foremost among the growing number of clubs and supplied all 11 players for the world's first international match, against England in Glasgow on 30 November 1872.

Difficulties with dates and the cost of travel meant that Queen's regularly withdrew, even when once given a bye to the semi-final, but relationships with northern clubs in England were easier to forge. On New Year's Day 1876, for instance, Partick (not Partick Thistle, who succeeded them) played at Darwen, emphasising the difference in class between the two by winning 7-0 and then 5-0 in a return game the following year. The link was William Kirkham, who played for both teams and may inadvertently have helped bring about the whole controversy surrounding professionalism; of which much more shortly.

It was not uncommon for players to appear for more than one team and it was a Darwen man, John Lewis, who proved instrumental in setting up the club that would become their greatest rivals. **Blackburn Rovers** may sound like the cloth-cap working class rivals to the southern toffs dominating English football's early years – providing every FA Cup finalist for the competition's first dozen seasons – but that was not the case. The meeting at the St Ledger Hotel in the town on 5 November 1875 featured well-educated and well-connected folk like Lewis and his fellow founder Arthur Constantine. There were a number of Old Malvernians in the club and Cambridge Blue was chosen for the quartered shirts, the first match being a 1-1 draw at Church on 11 December 1875, with both Lewis and Constantine in the side.

Lewis, born in 1855, is such a significant figure that when his grave was discovered in Blackburn Municipal Cemetery in 2008 and refurbished, the club agreed to maintain it from then on. As the son of a Methodist preacher, he was a churchgoer and campaigner against the demon drink; but he loved football. His playing career having been ended by a skating accident, he took up refereeing with such success that he was in charge of three FA Cup finals in four years from 1895–98. In all, Lewis was reckoned to have officiated in more than 1,000 games and given all his match fees to charity.

Having retired and become something of a football missionary in South Africa and Australia, he was still called on to take charge of the Olympic Games final of 1908 and then, aged 65, in 1920. When he sent off a Czech player in the latter match against host country Belgium, the rest of the team left the pitch in disgust and Lewis was forced to abandon proceedings before Belgium were awarded the gold medal.

Back to November 1876, when **Darwen**, undismayed by their second heavy defeat against Partick, overcame Blackburn Rovers 4-0, one of the results that encouraged them to enter the FA Cup the following season.

A small piece of history was made when they were drawn against fellow debutants Manchester FC from Eccles, enabling Darwen to stage the county's first FA Cup tie. The visitors were handicapped by two players arriving late and John Lewis – still playing for Darwen despite having co-founded the Rovers – scored an early goal before they made it on to the pitch. His team added two more and went on to face one of the few other northern sides among the cup's 40 entries that year, Sheffield. It proved to be a controversial tie in which the Lancastrians protested that the home team's only goal was offside, failed to convince the referee and walked off. An official protest to the FA failed and Sheffield were awarded the tie.

That was one of only two games Darwen lost in a highly successful season, leading the local paper to predict with heady optimism that with a bit of practice in the summer they would next season have a team to meet the famous Wanderers (who had just completed a hat-trick of FA Cup wins) in the final. Darwen would not go quite that far but would cause a stir way beyond the county borders and offer an early indication of the way the wind was blowing and how the times were changing in a momentous season for football.

After a difficult summer of industrial unrest and riots as employers attempted to cut piece-rates for weavers, football resumed to cheer up the town with the arrival of forward Jimmy Love and then full-back Fergie Suter, two Scots who would become known as the first of the professionals outraging the establishment by infiltrating English football. Both had appeared before in Lancashire, playing for Partick in their New Year's Day game against Darwen in 1878 (losing 3-2) and the following day against Blackburn Rovers, a 2-1 defeat that inaugurated the Alexandra Meadows ground.

Right-back Suter then appeared for Turton when they won the Turton Challenge Cup that year, and according to a club history was paid out of the winnings. He was originally a Glaswegian stonemason, though how much stone he ever cut in Lancashire is unclear. Respected journalist J.J. Catton wrote some years later that 'members of the club contributed a little each week to keep him in necessaries'.

October 1878 was a notable month in which the LFA began to function, with Darwen's Tom Hindle as its secretary, and a floodlit game was played at Barley Bank between Darwen and Blackburn XI, only the second anywhere.

Meanwhile Darwen went into their FA Cup campaign on the back of a 6-2 win over Accrington in which Suter made an impressive debut. After a walkover in the first round when Manchester's Birch scratched, they were held to a goalless draw at home by Eagley, from near Bolton, but won the replay 4-1 with Love scoring at least two goals; some reports gave him a hat-trick.

After losing the now traditional New Year's Day fixture against Partick 7-0, with Suter and Love in opposition to their brother and cousin respectively, Darwen now found their horizons growing even broader with a long trip down south for the third round to play the modestly named and apparently short-lived Remnants, who were based in Slough. The *Darwen News* launched a campaign to fund the train fares and an overnight stay but they still turned out in cast-off kit for a game refereed by none other than Charles Alcock, the FA secretary and founder of the competition.

At 2-2, Darwen having twice been behind, the home side agreed to an extra half-hour in which Jimmy Love got the winner. It was gleefully celebrated but meant another expensive trip, because all ties from the quarter-final onwards were played at that time at Kennington Oval; something that would change as a result of Darwen's exploits.

The opponents would now be the Old Etonians, beaten finalists in 1875 and 1876, who had knocked out the mighty Wanderers 7-2. For the game on 13 February 1879 England test cricketer Alfred Lyttleton was unavailable but fellow committee member Lord Kinnaird was one of four internationals in the side captained by Francis Marindin, FA president, founder of the Royal Engineers and a full-back for them in two of the first three FA Cup finals, but now playing in goal. Alcock was again referee, thus ensuring that many of the leading FA bigwigs of the day were present to see what would become one of the competition's most significant early matches.

Playing with a strong wind, the Old Boys soon went 3-0 up and by half-time led 5-1, future England centre-forward Harry Goodhart completing a hat-trick. An own goal then gave some encouragement to Darwen and to general astonishment the Etonians wilted. Love headed in for 5-3, an anonymous scorer in a scrimmage made it 5-4 and with five minutes remaining Love went through to equalise. Marindin, no doubt as bewildered as anyone by this turnaround, declined to play extra time.

Unable to replay in London the following day because of a LFA match, Darwen offered their opponents a substantial sum of £40 to play at Barley Bank. They refused, handing over £15 towards expenses, to which the FA added £10. So three weeks after the original game, an unchanged Darwen team headed back down south, seen off by 300 well-wishers at the station. Twice they went behind, only to earn another draw (the names of the scorers are disputed) and another refusal by the home side to risk either extra time or an away replay.

For the third game the following Saturday, Darwen travelled overnight after working all day. Trailing 3-1 at the interval despite Suter's goal, weariness overtook them in a 6-2 defeat, Tommy Marshall also scoring for the visitors. Old Etonians went on to beat Nottingham Forest in the semi-final, then Clapham Rovers 1-0 in the final, taking the trophy for the first time.

The southern amateurs had won the day but as a breed they were worried. Questions were being asked about what finance some of these northern players were receiving and within a day of the first Oval match, Old Harrovians were reported in the Darwen press to have tabled a motion for the FA's annual general meeting effectively proposing that only amateurs should be allowed to play in the FA Cup and that clubs should not be allowed to import outsiders specifically for cup games.

* * * * *

Sport in general was wrestling with these questions. Rugby league's split from rugby union was not far off and cricket had long paid some of its players while maintaining a rigid distinction between so-called 'gentlemen' and players that somehow lasted until the 1960s. In fact Tommy Marshall, a Darwen scorer at The Oval, was a professional sprinter and team-mate Ralph Crookes was a paid cricketer.

Further financial controversy soon followed. On Easter Saturday, **Blackburn Rovers** won 2-1 at Darwen, believed to be the latter's first defeat by any Lancashire side. Now the rivalry was really on, heightened when the *Darwen News* concluded its report by stating baldly that Hugh McIntyre, Rovers's Scottish half-back and captain, 'is engaged as professional'. The Rovers secretary issued a furious denial at this 'very nasty slur' and McIntyre had a letter published in *Athletic News* the following year emphatically denying it and claiming he had only ever received 'my bare railway expenses' and a gold watch with chain as an unexpected gift.

Yet on Easter Monday, two days after defeat by Rovers, Darwen played Blackburn Olympic and used the £40 gate money as a benefit for their players. A benefit match was one way of rewarding them and not just for long service. Later that month Darwen played at Turton watched by 2,000 paying spectators as a benefit for Love (whose last game it proved to be) and Suter, who would cause further uproar with his next move.

In November 1879 Rovers entered the FA Cup for the first time and to their delight knocked out Darwen in the second round before going down 6-0 to Nottingham Forest. Revenge was extracted 12 months later with a 3-0 Darwen victory in the first Lancashire Senior Cup Final, by which time Suter had switched to Rovers.

Cynicism is hardly required to imagine that financial inducement was involved. From then on he was well looked after, as he admitted in a newspaper interview some years after retirement, 'We had no settled wage, but it was understood that we interviewed the treasurer as occasion arose. Possibly we should go three weeks without anything, and then ask for £10. We never had any difficulty.'

His defection further strained relations between the two clubs and during a friendly in his first season a clash with Marshall prompted Darwen supporters in a Blackburn crowd estimated at 10,000 to invade the pitch, some kicking out at Suter, which caused the match to be abandoned. The Rovers secretary wrote to his opposite number cancelling the return fixture in February because of Darwen's 'disgraceful and ungentlemanly' behaviour; both clubs were expelled from the Lancashire Senior Cup and for a time Rovers even resigned from the LFA, clubs then being asked not to arrange matches with them.

The FA in London could not resist using the incident as an example of money being the root of footballing evil, claiming that 'the gate' had become all-important and that 'the subject of professional players will require the earnest attention of those on whom devolves the management of Association football'. It would occupy those good people for some time to come.

Without Suter, **Darwen** still achieved the longest FA Cup run in their history that season, with big wins over Brigg Town, Sheffield FC, The Wednesday and then Romford (15-0), scoring 33 goals in the process, to earn a return to Kennington Oval and a semi-final against Old Carthusians. Darwen took the lead through Marshall but had their protests about two disputed goals ruled out by Marindin, the Royal Engineers full-back/goalkeeper-turned-referee, and were beaten 4-1 by the eventual cup winners.

They would remain a strong cup team at least until the Football League began but by the start of the 1880s another local rival had emerged in the Lancashire town that would soon provide FA Cup finalists for no fewer than five successive seasons.

* * * * *

Blackburn Olympic, flying then dying within a dozen years, were the town's real working-class club, backed by local foundry owner Sydney Yates. In February 1878 clubs called Black Star, based at Mill Hill, and James Street joined up under the new name chosen by captain James Edmondson. Early that month the first game brought a 2-0 win over St John's at the home of Blackburn Cricket Club. Successful from the start, they won their first trophy in a local knockout competition organised by Livesey United.

The first derby against Rovers took place in February 1879, Olympic's 3-1 away win shocking their more established neighbours in what the local *Times* newspaper called 'one of the fastest and finest games ever played in Blackburn'. Olympic, the reporter suggested, were already 'one of the best if not the best in town'. A 0-0 draw that April suggested the pair were well matched, though not yet as strong as the Darwen of Love and Suter, who spoilt the season's record of one previous defeat in 15 games by drubbing them 8-2 and 3-1.

Darwen's efforts against the Old Etonians that winter inspired the Blackburn clubs too and encouraged other employers like Yates to become football benefactors.From the second full season of 1879/80 they played at a ground popularly known after the pub next door as the Hole i' th' Wall, where conditions were often poor, opponents finding the going difficult in clinging mud. That season

Olympic suffered an 8-2 defeat away to Rovers (after leading 2-0) but won 1-0 at home only a fortnight later. In January a 2-1 win over Darwen showed their potential, maintained in starting the following season with wins of 8-0, 9-1 and 12-0 before a lively FA Cup debut against Sheffield FC at Bramall Lane, lost 5-4.

Derbies with **Blackburn Rovers** could depend on the respective strength of teams put out; Rovers won all three meetings in 1880/81 and the first four the season after, offset by Olympic's success in defending the Blackburn Association Trophy. A further guide to the respective strength of the two teams – and Darwen's too – was that in October 1881 Olympic lost 3-1 in the FA Cup to Darwen, who then saw off Accrington and Turton with similar scorelines but found Rovers too good on the way to the first of four finals in five years.

Blackburn had been honoured in February 1881 when the first England home game to be staged outside London was played at Alexandra Meadows, where some 4,000 turned up to see Wales win 1-0. By the following season four of the town's teams were competing in the FA Cup. Newcomers Blackburn Law, a team of law students, lost to Bootle at the same first round stage as Olympic's defeat by Darwen but Rovers pulled off a series of local triumphs against Blackburn Park Road (9-1), Bolton Wanderers (6-2) and Darwen (5-1) to reach the quarter-final. Wednesbury Old Athletic, who had knocked out Aston Villa, were seen off 3-1 before a semi-final against The Wednesday that went to a replay; Suter and his fellow Scottish import Jimmy Douglas then got on the scoresheet in a 5-1 romp.

Before the final against Old Etonians, Rovers were unbeaten in all friendlies that season and won the Lancashire Senior Cup (beating Accrington at Turf Moor) but disappointment awaited at the Oval, where England international Reginald Macauley scored the only goal early on. The *Preston Herald* said of Rovers in a report of some 4,000 words, 'The form they displayed during the play thoroughly justified their reputation and the interest they have evoked,' adding that 'the occasion was indeed an important one in football annals'.

Neither the paper nor anyone else could have realised how much so, although the signs were growing. Lord Kinnaird in his eighth final may have celebrated victory with a headstand but northern clubs were now turning football on its head. A further example came in the same month as the FA Cup final, when the England trial match at Bolton became southern public school 'Probables' v northern 'Improbables' who included five Olympic players and forced a 4-4 draw.

Only once more in FA Cup history would any of the southern amateurs reach the final and when Old Etonians did so the following year, **Olympic** took Blackburn's revenge.

With former England captain Jack Hunter signed from Sheffield as player-coach, they went into the most memorable season in their short history as holders of the East Lancashire Charity Cup, having defeated Rovers in the final. When the FA Cup came along in November, Rovers lasted only two rounds, thrashing Blackpool St John's 11-1 but losing 1-0 at Darwen, who then lost a replay to Church. Olympic, favoured with a home draw in every round, twice scored eight in beating Accrington, Lower Darwen, Darwen Ramblers, Church and the Welsh Cup holders Druids to reach the semi-final.

Amusingly, the *Blackburn Times* forecast their demise before almost every round. 'Too much to prophesy any further victories for Olympic' was a typical prediction for the Church match, despite a 5-2 victory over them in a Christmas Day friendly. The tie finished 2-0 to Olympic.

Pessimism before the semi-final at Whalley Range, Manchester against Old Carthusians was perhaps understandable. There was still a belief in some quarters in the superiority of the old boys teams (not least among those teams themselves) and the Charterhouse chaps were the holders, who had won their five ties in defence of the trophy by 27 goals to seven, with a number of players from the previous year's victory over Old Etonians.

The forward-thinking Hunter now instigated a plan that would become a cliche of cup football for decades to come: a training trip to the seaside. Yates paid £100 towards costs of the week in Blackpool while supporters chipped in and employers, more surprisingly, were persuaded to allow the players time off in the interests of prestige to the town.

Preparation began each day at 6am with two raw eggs and a walk along the sands. The team ate well but kept in shape, and arranged two matches against local opposition on the South Shore pitch. Then on Saturday they took the train to Manchester, and hansom cabs to the ground. The majority of the crowd, defying an unseasonal snowfall, were backing Olympic, who shocked the opposition with the force of their play, creating chance after chance and taking two of them by half-time. In the second half they added two more for an emphatic 4-0 win and arrived back home to be greeted by cheering crowds and celebrations all over town; Rovers had beaten Bolton the same afternoon to reach the Lancashire Senior Cup Final.

Ahead of the final against Old Etonians, who had beaten Notts County in their semi-final, another Blackpool trip was arranged, this one over Easter weekend. It went well but could unfashionable Olympic avenge Rovers and overcome the toffs? 'A stupendous task,' as the ever pessimistic *Blackburn Times* put it. The Old Boys team showed only one change from the previous year, with five English internationals plus Scotland's Kinnaird as captain, and a top scorer in Goodhart, who amassed almost 30 FA Cup goals over half a dozen seasons.

Of the 8,000 crowd those reckoned to have made the trip from Lancashire numbered around 700, who saw Goodhart score with a fierce low shot, but forwards John Yates and Alf Matthews hit the bar and post respectively; and after seeing off a flurry at the start of the second half Olympic began to dominate. To Lancastrian roars George Wilson fed Matthews for an equaliser. The Etonians looked wearier and were reduced to ten men by an injury to England forward Arthur Dunn (who has had the national Old Boys cup competition named after him from 1903 to the present day).

They were unable to avoid extra time as they once had against Darwen, and it was no surprise given the run of the play and the respective fitness levels when Jimmy Costley (described in most contemporary reports as W. Crossley) took Tom Dewhurst's pass and scored the winner. In a new development the trophy was handed over on the day. FA president Major Marindin, not refereeing this time, gave it to skipper and full-back Sam Warburton, a plumber by trade, and handed a gold medal to every member of the winning team.

News of the result, relayed to the offices of the *Blackburn Standard* on Church Street, was received, the paper reported, 'with great incredulity'. On the same day Rovers beat Darwen 3-2 for the second of their four successive Lancashire Senior Cup wins (1882–85). The tide had turned. Football would never be the same again.

FA Cup Final 1883: Blackburn Olympic 2 Old Etonians 1
Blackburn Olympic: Hacking; Ward, Warburton, Gibson, Astley, Hunter, Dewhurst, Matthews, Wilson, Costley, Yates.
Old Etonians: Rawlinson; French, de Paravicini, Kinnaird, Foley, Dunn, Bainbridge, Chevallier, Anderson, Goodhart, Macauley.

* * * * *

Press comment even suggested that the north and midlands might now get a fairer crack of the footballing whip in terms of respect, international recognition and committee representation. The FA and the southern amateurs nevertheless remained suspicious, with some justification, of the effect money was having.

From the time of Olympic's seaside trips until professionalism was finally legalised two summers later, the debate about money and who was paying it to whom intensified. A year earlier, in October 1882, a *Manchester Courier* journalist who asked the LFA about players being paid was told the committee had no official knowledge of it. The word 'official' was significant. Looking back from a safer distance, players, officials and journalists were happy to recount case after case; some trifling, some not so.

Turton's James Haworth must have envied Fergie Suter his £10 every three weeks; Haworth openly told an LFA inquiry that he was on a shilling a week, which bought him 'six pints'. Olympic's Costley recounted meeting Rovers officials who promised him a share of the gate money from a game against Notts County and also said they could use their influence on the LFA and international committees to get him county and England recognition.

A Burnley official pointed out that during the club's first season, 1882/83, 'we did not pay a single player, and nobody came to see us', and it was revealed that many clubs kept duplicate books to avoid detection in any official inspection. As 'Olympian' of the *Bolton Evening News* wrote in the LFA's official history in 1928, 'Lancashire clubs came to the conclusion that it would be far better to acknowledge professional players than to encourage the deception which was rife.'

Accrington were disqualified from the FA Cup for two seasons running, in 1883 and 1884, after complaints from other teams, and Preston's chairman Major William Sudell was instrumental in bringing matters to a head during his club's first season in the competition. Accused by Upton Park of payments to players after a drawn fourth-round tie at the London club's ground in January 1884, he openly admitted as much and seemed surprised when the FA kicked North End out.

Dissent spread in Lancashire and the midlands, and nine months later an initial meeting of nine clubs in Bolton to discuss forming a breakaway professional British Association led to 60 more, spread from Sunderland to Birmingham, attending a conference in Manchester. An FA sub-committee then recommended accepting professionalism and after two meetings early in 1885 at which the necessary two-thirds majority was not achieved, a smaller meeting on 20 July voted 35-5 in favour, having been heavily influenced by such Lancashire stalwarts as John Bentley, Tom Hindle and LFA secretary Dick Gregson. The trio's only defeat was in failing to move FA headquarters to Manchester.

Illegal payments previously meant it was difficult for clubs to keep their best players. In 1883 Warburton, captain of cup-winning **Blackburn Olympic**, left for Darwen and centre-forward Wilson departed for ambitious Preston, recruiting hard under Major Sudell. Desperate to prevent further defections, holders Olympic persuaded first round opponents Darwen Ramblers to accept £10 to bring forward the game, cup-tieing other players. It worked and Olympic won 5-1 to start another run which took them to the semi-final, where the draw kept them apart from their neighbours Rovers to offer the prospect of a historic all-Blackburn final.

Gate money from the cup run was more than welcome as the Hole i' th' Wall was now a 'hole i' th' stand', the grandstand having blown down in a gale; a crowd of 6,000 turned up nevertheless for a return game billed as the Championship of Great Britain against Scottish Cup holders Dumbarton; 6-1 winners on their own ground in August, the Scots left Lancashire beaten 4-3 in a thriller.

Another Scottish giant, Queen's Park, would dispute that either of those clubs were Britain's best, and now they had the chance to prove it. Seven times Scottish Cup winners in the first 11 years of the competition and conquerors of four English sides, including

Villa 6-1 in the fourth round, Queen's Park lined up against the holders Olympic for the 1884 semi-final at Trent Bridge.

A huge crowd of 16,000 – the largest ever to watch the Blackburn team at that point – spilled on to the pitch more than once and saw the Scottish amateurs open the scoring after half an hour and double the lead early in the second half. As the game wore on Olympic's best hope appeared to be an abandonment for repeated crowd incursions, which hampered their traditional wing play. After a 4-1 defeat they handed a formal protest to the referee, the ubiquitous Charles Alcock, but the margin of defeat left little room for argument and the FA predictably ruled that conditions were the same for both sides.

Notts County also failed to have their semi-final defeat overturned after claiming that **Blackburn Rovers** forward Jock Inglis, who was still working in Glasgow, was being paid to play. He was able to take his place as one of the two central attackers, although it was local man Joe Lofthouse who scored the only goal. So Rovers qualified for the first of what would be two successive finals against the same opposition – still the only time such a thing has happened.

Slowly it was dawning on London that huge crowds of provincial football fans coming up for the cup was a phenomenon they would have to get used to. The 1884 final produced a famous article in the *Pall Mall Gazette,* the writer's tongue not entirely in cheek, which began, 'London witnessed an incursion of northern barbarians on Saturday – hot-blooded Lancastrians, sharp of tongue, rough and ready, of uncouth garb and speech. A tribe of Sudanese Arabs let loose in the Strand would not excite more amusement or curiosity. We can only say a word to the wise: Keep away from the Oval on occasions of this sort.'

Olympic's followers the previous season, it was claimed, had drunk every railway station dry en route and worse, broke the glasses and the windows, refused to pay, and 'struck horror into the usually complacent bosoms of the presiding goddesses.'

Whether or not the Rovers had a better class of follower, press reports praised their behaviour and sympathised on account of the 'ridiculously insufficient' arrangements for controlling the first five-figure crowd for a final, estimated to be between 12,000 and 15,000. They saw the Lancashire side, with Suter one of five players from the final two years earlier, struggle at first with the Scottish dribbling and passing but settle down and take a two-goal lead through Joe Sowerbutts and James Forrest. Shortly before half-time Queen's retrieved one goal but Rovers held on comfortably enough to keep the cup in Blackburn.

FA Cup Final 1884: Blackburn Rovers 2 Queen's Park 1
Blackburn Rovers: Arthur; Suter, Beverley, McIntyre, Forrest, Hargreaves, Brown, Inglis, Sowerbutts, Douglas, Lofthouse.
Queen's Park: Gillespie; MacDonald, Arnott, Gow, Campbell, Allan, Harrower, Smith, Anderson, Watt, Christie.

Rubbing in their sense of superiority, Rovers then beat their neighbours in a replayed Lancashire Senior Cup Final. But Olympic found any hopes of revenge the following season initially thwarted when a letter was received from the Rovers secretary asking them 'to remove our name from your list of fixtures for 1884/85'. Although they refused to make their reasons public, allegations of attempted poaching had gone down badly, but with relations at an all-time low the inevitable happened: the teams, FA Cup winners for the past two seasons, were drawn against each other in the second round of the competition.

The most eagerly anticipated of all Blackburn derbies took place on 6 December at Leamington Road, Rovers' home since 1881. It was watched by some 11,000 who saw the home side fall behind 2-1 but equalise from what Olympic were convinced was an indirect free-kick. The furious visitors began to leave the field and were only reluctantly persuaded back, their mood changing from black to worse when recent signing Harry Fecitt scored the winning goal.

It proved to be the holders' most difficult tie, including the final itself. In the semi-final at Trent Bridge, Old Carthusians were brushed aside 5-1 in what proved to be the last appearance at such a late stage of the competition for any of the southern amateur clubs.

At the Oval Blackburn fielded eight of the previous year's finalists, Queen's Park six. The Glaswegians were coming to the end of their southern sojourns (they would play only two more matches in the competition after being banned by the Scottish FA from taking part) and had won only one of their matches on the way to the final by more than a single goal. 'It can be stated without contradiction that the better side won,' reported the *Sunday Times* of the victory that Rovers earned with goals by Forrest in the first 15 minutes and new captain Brown just before the hour.

Confirmed as the leading club not only in Blackburn and the north but the whole of Britain – and it is tempting to say further afield – Rovers must soon have begun thinking of an FA Cup hat-trick in the first season of official professional football, 1885/86. After some close ties against teams like Clitheroe (2-0), Oswaldtwistle Rovers (1-0), Brentwood (3-1) and Swifts (2-1), the last side standing in their way were West Bromwich Albion, formed in 1879 and one of the strongest midlands clubs, but beaten quarter-final opponents the year before.

For the first time, the final was a goalless draw, Rovers declining to play an extra half-hour because, as the local paper reported, 'they were so unaccountably out of form' and full-back Dick Turner was suffering from a heavy ankle knock. Turner was fit for the replay a week later at Derby, where an April snowstorm threatened a postponement before Albion were beaten 2-0 with a degree of ease, the scorers being the reliable pair Sowerbutts and skipper Brown. The three-time winners were not allowed to keep the trophy but were given a silver shield instead.

There would not be a fourth success in a row, however. In December 1886, after 23 unbeaten FA Cup games, a 2-0 defeat by Scottish club Renton, local rivals of Dumbarton, ended the run. It was all the more of a surprise in that this was a home game after forcing a 2-2 draw in a game played amid widespread interest at Hampden Park. The *Blackburn Standard's* long factual account of the replay barely acknowledged the historic significance of the result, commenting only that 'the Rovers showed very indifferent form in the latter half, especially the forwards'. Renton, playing their only season in the FA Cup, lost to Preston in the third round.

Overall, however, Rovers' achievement had been timely, coming as it did shortly before the idea was mooted of starting a league competition. For several years the rivalry with Olympic had been good for both, but now the success of one came at the expense of the other, all the more so once only one club per town was allowed into the Football League.

* * * * *

For **Olympic**, like Darwen, professionalism brought problems and their demise was the quicker of the two. Initially players like Dewhurst, little Joe Beverley and Costley all remained loyal, Beverley refusing blandishments which reportedly included 'his wife adorned with a new dress at the expense of a noted Blackburn club'. Experienced goalkeeper Tom Hacking, a dentist, stayed amateur but Jack Southworth, converted from striker to keeper after a knee injury, took over the jersey. He became the subject of controversy when Church, beaten 4-2 in the FA Cup in October 1885, got the result annulled because a J. Southworth had played for Chester earlier in the season. Southworth claimed it was his brother James but was disbelieved and suspended for four months. After another draw the Accrington club went through with a 3-1 away win.

Contriving to lose a Lancashire Cup tie 11-2 to Bolton soon afterwards meant the rest of Olympic's season was devoted to friendlies with the exception of the East Lancashire Charity Cup, which brought another dispiriting defeat by Rovers. A small profit the previous season soon disappeared in wages and when the club reduced the money they paid to barely a fifth of what a club like Preston were offering, three key players went on strike, two of them never playing for the club again.

The same pattern kept repeating itself: early defeats in the two major cup competitions, a long diet of friendlies and modest results as players left, with only the visits of Rovers or Darwen drawing much of a crowd. In November 1887 the 5-1 FA Cup defeat by Rovers was followed by an 8-2 derby hammering at the Hole i' th' Wall and the regular Charity Cup defeat. It could still not be imagined that the season beginning 1 September 1888 would be the club's last, just as football was taking a huge step forward with Lancashire to the fore.

Passed over by the Football League's founding fathers, Olympic joined the Combination – not so much a league as a loose fixture circle – and again had no luck in the cups: expected to defeat Higher Walton in the county competition, they succumbed to a 2-1 home defeat with barely 300 people present and suffered a home defeat too in a qualifying round of the FA Cup by Oswaldtwistle.

Only four Combination games were played, Olympic not winning any of them and losing heavily to Bootle 4-0 and then 6-0 in what proved to be their last competitive fixture. From the end of January 1889, the decision was taken to dispense with professionals, using amateurs only, which helped explain the poor results from then on.

Eleven of the final 13 matches were lost, the last of them a 6-1 defeat by Everton, who had earlier signed Jimmy Costley. The last derby against Rovers was a 6-1 away defeat in which they were allowed to take all the gate money; too little too late. In August 1889 a final attempt to keep going foundered through lack of financial support, 11 years and six months after the club's foundation. Blackburn Railway Clerks took over the ground, and the innovative Jack Hunter became a trainer at Rovers.

* * * * *

Bolton Wanderers, already mentioned in passing, had begun as Christ Church, a Sunday school team, in 1874 although as with many other clubs of the time there is some confusion over precisely which code was played; a mixture seems likely. The first opponents are believed to have been Farnworth, played at Smithfield, the club settling at Pikes Lane near the Cross Guns pub. Meeting at a succession of local hotels made them happy wanderers, adopting that name as well as that of their town from August 1877.

Peter Parkinson, a local mill manager, became an influential backer the following year when they entered the Turton Challenge Cup won by Eagley and then in 1879 the inaugural Lancashire Senior Cup, losing to Blackburn Rovers.

More accurate records are available from a Christmas defeat by Turton that year, followed by fixtures against a range of local clubs including Great Lever, Eagley, Bolton Olympic, Accrington, Blackburn Olympic and Darwen, with reasonable results.

After moving to a different Pikes Lane ground in 1881 for £35 annual rent and starting to charge for admission, Wanderers joined the trend for Scottish imports by signing full-back John Devlin (Arbroath) and centre-forward William Struthers (Rangers) but acquired Welshmen like Jimmy Trainer, later goalkeeper of Preston's 'Invincibles', after playing Druids in the FA Cup. Entering the competition for the first time in 1881/82 they beat Eagley following a 5-5 draw before losing to Rovers in the second round, but enjoyed a good run in each of the next two seasons.

In 1882/83 Merseyside clubs Bootle and Liverpool Ramblers were beaten before three matches against Druids, who eventually came through 1-0; the following year it was the fourth round before narrow defeat by Notts County in a replay after special training at Blackpool. Perhaps success was down to new white shirts with garish red spots 'to make men appear much larger'; or perhaps not.

In between times Wanderers faced possible expulsion from the LFA as recommended by the FA in London after referee Sam Ormerod was not only 'hooted from the field' but, rather more seriously, followed from the ground and assaulted on his way to the station. Not for the first or last time the LFA backed one of their founder members against London and decided on no further action. They might have been less sympathetic had they known that an FA delegation inquiring into illegal payments were fobbed off by being presented with a false set of records immaculately written out by the club secretary.

Like many of their neighbours and rivals, Wanderers were paying players and they became among the keenest to legitimise it. It was in Bolton at the Commercial Hotel in October 1884 that Wanderers president Parkinson suggested a British FA, prompting London to grasp the nettle at last. The following year, when professionalism was finally accepted, John Bentley from Turton became club secretary and a hugely influential figure in Lancashire and then English football.

On the field, meanwhile, the club continued to make significant strides, winning the Lancashire Senior Cup for the first time in 1885/86 and following up as holders by beating Wigan 14-0.

Not that the legalisation of wages solved all disputes. For some time there were still restrictions like players having to live within a six-mile radius of the ground and Bolton were one of many caught up in these eligibility rules. In 1885/86 they benefited twice, when the FA disqualified opponents Rawtenstall and then Preston (who had beaten them), only for Wanderers themselves to be banned before the next round against Old Westminsters. Two years later there were even greater complications: having beaten Everton 1-0, Bolton had a player declared ineligible and had to play again. Two draws followed, then an Everton win after which the Merseysiders were disqualified for the same offence. Bolton, reinstated, promptly lost 9-1 to Preston.

If that did not bode well for league football, Wanderers did at least make the cut, their cause hardly hindered by having Bentley to make their case.

* * * * *

Preston North End, destined to become the first stars of the Football League a year after recording the largest victory in FA Cup history, did not see the light of day until after almost all those clubs they would conquer as The Invincibles.

True, the name North End had been adopted by a cricket club as early as 1867 at Moor Park in the north of the town. The first game under football rules, however, is dated no earlier than 5 October 1878, a week after the inaugural meeting of the LFA, its clubs concentrated as we have seen further to the east.

William Sudell, president of the cricket club and another benevolent mill manager, was in the team for that first game, a 1-0 defeat to Eagley. Two years later it was decided to join the county FA and change the name to the long-winded Preston Athletic Society and North End Cricket and Football Club.

A town with a population not far short of 100,000 was certainly capable of supporting a major club, although there were some understandably difficult games when taking on already renowned Lancashire clubs. The local press reported the 'first game of real importance' as being against the well-established Darwen, who won it 14-1, and an early loss to the equally experienced Blackburn Rovers was worse: 16-0. Then a first Lancashire Cup tie was lost 6-0 to Turton.

By 1882/83 Sudell, the key figure behind the scenes, had begun an ambitious and largely illegal recruiting policy, as well as effecting a tactical change from the standard 2-2-6 formation to a 2-3-5. Glaswegian James McDade became the first of many Scots to represent the club and early in 1884, as we have seen, Sudell helped change the whole face of British football with his admission following the club's fourth round FA Cup tie at Upton Park that Preston were paying players. They had earlier knocked out Great Lever (4-1) and Eagley (9-1) and following a 1-1 draw against the Londoners, with six Scots in the side, Sudell told an FA committee that every leading northern and midlands club was breaking the rules, that professionalism was the way forward and that 'wherever there is a crowd at any sport there is professionalism'.

The *Football Field* newspaper, compiling a merit table based entirely on goal average, made Preston the leading Lancashire club, from Bolton Wanderers, Great Lever, Blackburn Olympic, Accrington, Blackburn Rovers, Church and Burnley.

Among the notable Scots were defender Nick Ross, given a job as a slater, and his brother Jimmy, an inside-forward. Jack Belger was the principal goalscorer for a club now threatening to become the equal of Rovers, who they beat 3-2 at Deepdale, the club's home since the start. The standard was confirmed by having the better of teams like Aston Villa (7-2 and 5-1) Notts County, The Wednesday and Wolves.

A crowd of 12,450 turned up to watch the visit of Bolton Wanderers, although with some gates much smaller, a high percentage of games were played away, as North End proved popular opponents.

In 1885/86 with professionalism now legalised they went on an astonishing run, unbeaten in more than 50 games until losing at Accrington in late April. The final record was 59 wins from 65 games and 318 goals; Jimmy Ross and centre-forward John Goodall, signed from Great Lever, both passed a half-century.

Sudell's team – he was manager in all but name – would have fancied their FA Cup chances that season but ran into trouble again: after Bolton were beaten 3-2 in the third round, the versatile Scot George Drummond was ruled ineligible and Wanderers, as mentioned above, were reinstated, only to fall foul of the regulations themselves.

It was a formidable North End team. In 1886/87 they beat Queen's Park 6-1, the heaviest defeat the Scots had suffered at the time, as well as knocking them out of the FA Cup before losing a semi-final to West Bromwich. Blackburn, still celebrating their cup hat-trick, were thrashed 6-1 and then 7-1, the latter game in the Lancashire Senior Cup, which North End went on to win for the first time, beating Witton 12-0 and then Bolton in the final.

The following season began with a 2-1 defeat away to Hibernian, the Scottish Cup holders, in a match hyped as the unofficial world championship. North End then reeled off 42 wins on the trot with plenty of high-scoring encounters, including a new mark that remains to this day and put **Hyde FC** into the history books.

Hyde, formed in 1885, ambitiously invited Blackburn Rovers for a friendly early in the 1886/87 season and lost 8-0, which did not deter them from entering the following season's FA Cup. They received another warning about the possible quality of opposition when Bolton beat them 8-1 in a friendly, and the draw for the first round could hardly have been worse: Preston, away.

The *Preston Guardian* reporter who said he would eat his hat if Hyde won was never in any danger of indigestion. It was 12-0 by half-time and North End were sympathetic enough to allow a replacement to come on for the Hyde player who injured an arm – the first recorded FA Cup substitute.

The referee, rather than cutting short the visitors' misery, then lost track of the time and played anything between five and 15 minutes extra, during which North End took their victory margin to 26-0.

Charles Bunyan, the poor Hyde keeper, was praised for his efforts and told journalist J.J. Catton some years later that Preston might have scored 40. As it was, reporters did well to keep count of the total and scorers, crediting Jimmy Ross with eight, and Jack Gordon and Sam Thomson with five apiece. One of the many oddities of that extraordinary day in October 1887 was that Goodall, a year later the top scorer in the first Football League season, managed precisely one 26th of his team's goals.

The following day *The Times* – newspaper of record, though clearly not of records –placed the historic game only fifth in line of its 39 match reports, soberly observing, 'A most overwhelming defeat was sustained by Hyde at Preston, the North End winning by 26 goals to none'. Rossendale, beaten 11-0 at Accrington, were able to console themselves with not having suffered the worst defeat of the first round by a long way.

North End went on their merry way with a 6-0 win over Everton, who were disqualified anyway; and Bolton, who replaced them, were sent packing 9-1, Jimmy Ross adding a double hat-trick to his eight against Hyde. He finished the cup campaign with a record of 19 (plus one in the void game against Everton) that is highly unlikely ever to be broken. His goals in every round also helped Preston past Halliwell, Villa, The Wednesday and Crewe for a first place in the final, where over-confidence may have proved their undoing. They famously requested a photograph with the trophy before kick-off against West Bromwich, the regular referee Major Marindin suggesting they might need to win it first.

Behind from the eighth minute, North End then had the better of the game for a long spell and Albion, beaten finalists for the previous two years, appealed in vain against Fred Dewhurst's equaliser seven minutes into the second half. The cup's return to Lancashire, where the Blackburn clubs had held it from 1883–86, seemed likely, but a dozen minutes from time England international George Woodhall beat Dr Robert Mills-Roberts in North End's goal and Albion had managed to avoid a hat-trick of defeats.

It was a bitter blow for a side that had played 200 games in three seasons, scoring 930 goals. They may have regarded themselves as the strongest club in the country but as the *Birmingham Daily Post* pointed out without undue bias, the 'shabby little cup' conferred on its winners 'the championship for the year of English football'.

It would, however, be the last time that claim could be made. On the eve of the final, seven clubs, including Blackburn Rovers and Burnley, met in London and invited five more – Accrington, Bolton, Derby, Everton and Preston – to join them in contesting a league competition the following season (See Chapter 2).

Preston could have had the consolation of another Lancashire Cup win but for a stubborn stance. They had beaten Accrington, their opponents in the final, twice in friendlies, but were unhappy with Blackburn as the choice of venue for the final, claiming they had been subjected to unsporting behaviour by the locals on previous visits; knocking Rovers out 4-3 in one of them. Preston simply refused to turn up and Accrington were awarded the trophy despite losing 4-0 on the day to Witton, their semi-final opponents, who had been asked to attend on the day in case North End did not. The LFA duly suspended them for the rest of the year, which could have had serious consequences for what would become the Double season; but the FA overruled them and history was eventually made. With nobody to give the second set of medals to, Witton then beat the other semi-finalists Darwen Old Wanderers 2-0 and were officially named runners-up.

* * * * *

Only Preston among English league clubs can claim to have been at their present home for as long as **Burnley,** who in February 1883 accepted an invitation from the local cricket club to move to Turf Moor; all these years later fans still refer to the Cricket Field End, whichever sponsors may have adopted it.

A few months earlier Burnley Rovers had been born out of a rugby club playing at Calder Vale, playing a first competitive game in October 1882 against Astley Bridge of Bolton in the Lancashire Challenge Cup, which was lost 8-0. At Turf Moor, having already dropped the Rovers appendage, they began with a 6-3 defeat by Rawtenstall on 17 February 1883. By the following year there was a stand seating 800 and a reported 12,000 turned up for a local derby with Padiham.

The club were among those who threatened a breakaway that year and won the day. Entering the FA Cup for the first time in 1885, however, they were not allowed to field their many Scots like the outstanding Alec Brady from Renton Thistle and put out a reserve team that was beaten 11-0 by Darwen Old Wanderers.

Losing barely a quarter of their other games that season, they were gaining a reputation, as well as discovering, like Bolton, that legalisation of professionalism was far from solving all disputes. A second season in the national knockout competition ended in disqualification after a protest by Astley Bridge following the teams' two draws; and the following year the Old Wanderers, beaten 4-0 this time by Burnley's first team, were awarded a replay but scratched instead, after which Burnley lost 3-2 to Accrington.

The nickname 'Clarets' was some way off, shirts of that shade not appearing until 1910, and the club became known as the Royalites after playing host to the first member of the royal family to deem a football match worthy of their attendance. Prince Albert, Queen Victoria's son, who was in town in October 1886 to name Burnley's first hospital after his mother, turned up for the first half of the game against Bolton.

* * * * *

Accrington, another of the Lancashire half-dozen who would make the inaugural Football League, were an entirely separate club to the better known Accrington Stanley, who were not formed until 1893.

The Old Reds were another team with connections to an existing local sports club, playing at Accrington Cricket Club's ground in Thorneyholme Road, where overseas players as distinguished as Shane Warne, Wes Hall and Bobby Simpson have all appeared as resident professionals.

Accrington played their first game against neighbouring Church on 28 September 1878 and met them again under electric lights two months later, with 3,000 in attendance. They made rapid enough progress to become second winners of the Lancashire Senior Cup in 1880/81and the following season entered the FA Cup for what should have been a prestigious tie against Queen's Park. As usual at that time, however, the Scots scratched, and Accrington went out 3-1 at Darwen in the next round.

In the following season's competition they lost 6-3 at Blackburn Olympic before running into problems familiar to a number of other teams in the area over the issue of professionalism. They were expelled by the FA for offering an inducement to a player, but were backed up by the LFA, pointing out that a club could only face such drastic action at a special general meeting.

The FA had their revenge by throwing them out of the FA Cup in both 1883/84 and 1884/85, having won matches each time. Not surprisingly they were part of the 1884 revolt and in 1885 with professionalism legal, finally won a legitimate tie by beating Witton 5-4, then going out to Darwen Old Wanderers. In the autumn of 1887 they thrashed Rossendale 11-0 in the first round and then impressively beat Burnley 3-2 to improve their credentials as Football League applicants.

As described above (see Preston) they would also go into the league as Lancashire Senior Cup winners.

* * * * *

The influence of organised religion on early Merseyside football can be seen from the list of the 12 clubs who came together to form the Liverpool FA in 1882; St Benedict's, St George's, St Mary's and St Peter's were all there. Everton had originally been called St Domingo's, after the Methodist Sunday school from which they sprang and their great rivals as the best of the crop, Bootle, were originally Bootle St John's.

The others who formed their local FA at a meeting at the Tarleton Hotel were Anfield, Birkenhead, Liverpool Ramblers (still going strong in Crosby), Liverpool Stanley, Rovers and Wirral.

Everton were therefore typical in their origins, from the newish church on Breckfield Road North. In 1876, seven years after the church's foundation stone was laid, a new minister, the Rev. Ben Chambers, set up a cricket team and two years later younger members expressed a desire to play football.

Keen to expand and attract non churchgoers, they soon adopted the name Everton and amid the 100 acres of Stanley Park, opened eight years earlier, played a first match under that name in December 1879, beating St Peter's 6-0 and following up by winning the return 4-0 a month later.

Later in 1880 they joined the Lancashire FA, entering its cup competition with what new research shows to have been a 1-0 defeat away to Great Lever, after which Everton successfully protested that 'the Referee was a Member of the Great Lever Club, and was therefore biased in their favour'. The LFA upheld the appeal and ordered a replay, again in Bolton, where the Merseysiders were heavily beaten. 'The Great Lever men were rather riled at having to play again, and showed their temper most unmistakably,' reported *Athletic News*.

Having begun in blue and white stripes, the club earned the nickname The Black Watch by dyeing their shirts black and adding a vivid scarlet sash; colours changed every other season in the manner of a modern club, though for less obvious reasons, and it was not until 1895 that they settled for the famous blue shirts and white shorts, albeit initially of a lighter shade.

For a couple of seasons from 1880 results were outstanding and in March 1882 the decision was taken to move from playing in a public park and changing in the Sandon Hotel to rent a field off Priory Road and charge admission. In that final season in Stanley Park, the fixture list extended further afield and results suffered in defeats by teams like Blackburn Rovers (8-0 in the Lancashire Cup), Turton (7-0), Bolton Wanderers (8-2) and Wrexham (7-3).

A first trophy, the Liverpool Cup, arrived, however, in 1883/84. Having lost to main rivals Bootle in the 1883 semi-final, Everton drubbed them 5-2 at the same stage and then beat Earlestown 1-0 in the final.

Increasing popularity and crowds meant that the owner of the new ground wanted them out, so on 27 September 1884 came a first match at Anfield Road, where Earlestown were beaten 5-0. It was owned by a friend of John Houlding, a Tory councillor, self-made man and eventual lord mayor, who owned the Sandon Hotel and would later be a key figure in the split that gave birth to Liverpool.

Signing the club's first official professionals was another statement of intent. They included full-back George Dobson (Bolton) and forward George Farmer (Oswestry), who promptly knocked in eight goals in his seven games.

The 1885/86 fixture list was the longest yet, including for the first time some renowned midlands names like Aston Villa and Derby as well as visits from Corinthians and Ulster and all the leading Lancashire sides, including Blackburn's two FA Cup-winning clubs. For four successive seasons they reached the final of the Liverpool Cup, winning three of them – perhaps insulted and inspired by the diktat that they could not enter the Lancashire Senior Cup 'until they show proof of their ability'.

In 1886 they felt strong enough for a tilt at the FA Cup itself, although the competition brought a series of mishaps, mainly over the thorny question of eligibility. Drawn against Rangers for their debut, Everton, knowing some of their players were ineligible, played what they claim was a friendly, losing 1-0, despite official FA records having it as a cup result. (The Glasgow club, in their only season in the competition, went on to a semi-final defeat by Villa).

The following season, as already recounted (see Bolton), Everton were disqualified, with seven of their team declared ineligible, though they had lost 6-0 to Preston anyway. In addition the club were suspended for the month of December 1887 and the Liverpool FA took their cup back as a further punishment. Finally, in 1888/89 the draw brought an away tie with Ulster, which Everton decided was too far to go on a day they had what was now considered a more important commitment: a Football League game – to the envious disgust of their greatest rivals, Bootle.

* * * * *

It was appropriate that the first fixture played by **Bootle** was less than three miles away against Everton, whom they quickly came to challenge as the strongest team on Merseyside. Exactly like their neighbours, Bootle owed their existence to a sports-minded clergyman, in this case the young Rev. Alfred Keely, a public school and Cambridge University man who arrived at St John's Bootle in 1879.

Not only did he turn out in goal for the team's first-ever match as Bootle St John's, a 4-0 win away to Everton in Stanley Park on 20 October 1880, but his brothers Edwin and Sam shared all four goals. The Rev. Keely then demonstrated his versatility by playing an outfield role in the first home game at their Bibbys Lane pitch and scoring twice in a 3-0 win over Birkenhead.

Ambition was high, quickly bringing entry to the Lancashire Cup, with a 3-1 defeat by the oddly named Num Nook of Accrington, as well as fixtures against Newton Heath and Blackburn Olympic.

Within 12 months, having dropped the 'St John's' suffix, the newcomers were competing in the FA Cup, several years before Everton did. On Guy Fawkes Day 1881 they defeated Blackburn Law 2-1 in the first round (as well as playing Preston in a drawn Lancashire Cup tie later the same day). The second round brought a trip to the much more established Turton and a 4-0 defeat after three players missed their train to the match.

Losses of a different sort occurred in the following summer when the Rev. Keely moved to a new parish in London and a number of former Eton and Harrow old boys left the club and formed a football section of the Liverpool Ramblers cricket club (see Non-league chapter). Results suffered for a while, not helped by Bootle's tendency to turn up, like the worst organised Sunday morning park team, a man or two short. The ground, meanwhile, had moved to Marsh Lane, where Everton were beaten on their first visit in December, losing again in Stanley Park a month later.

'Between the Bootle and Everton teams a great deal of rivalry is springing up,' reported *Athletic News* on 24 January 1883, adding that Merseyside football as a whole was benefiting. 'The dribbling rules in the Liverpool district are becoming popular. A few more games like that of Saturday are sure to infuse a lot of life in the Associationists, for a better-contested match has not been witnessed in that part of Lancashire before ... settling the matter for the present that Bootle is the best team in the district.'

The rivalry continued when the sides were drawn together in the Liverpool Cup no fewer than six seasons in succession. In

March 1883 Bootle won 3-1 and went on to win the final against Liverpool Ramblers; but Everton won for the next five seasons, including the 1886 final.

By that time the Anfield side normally had the better of the derbies, and their larger attendances had a bad effect on Bootle crowds when the clubs both played at home.

For what would turn out to be the critical season of 1887/88, the last before league football began, Bootle secured some significant new players including the Scottish international full-back Andrew Watson, son of a British Guyanese mother and believed to be the first black international footballer. Teams like Preston, Blackburn Rovers and Bolton reflected the club's growing importance by sending their strongest XIs to the Hawthorne Road ground, home since 1883.

The FA Cup brought the best run to date, beginning with a 6-0 home win over Workington. In three successive away ties Blackpool's South Shore, Higher Walton and Great Bridge Unity from Smethwick were all beaten to earn a place in the last 16 away to Old Carthusians, Unity having protested in vain that Watson and others were professionals and therefore not eligible.

At Kennington Oval, Bootle were not disgraced in a 2-0 loss. They went on to win the Liverpool Cup after Everton had beaten them in an earlier round then been expelled. The most crushing defeat, however, came with confirmation that it was their great rivals who would represent Merseyside in the new Football League competition the following season.

For Bootle (see next chapter) it would be the Combination and Football Alliance instead, until a Second Division was formed in 1892.

❋ ❋ ❋ ❋ ❋

Further up the coast, **Southport** began life as Southport Central with a first match in November 1881 against Bootle reserves after switching from rugby. Like Bootle, they progressed quickly enough to gain admittance to the FA Cup within a year, holding Liverpool Ramblers in October 1882 before losing the replay, and continued to enter for another three seasons.

Being drawn away to Blackburn Rovers in the autumn of 1883 brought a not unexpected heavy defeat (7-0) but the following season they benefited from Accrington's expulsion after losing to them and won a tie for the first time before another heavy defeat, 10-0 to Church.

After merging with the Southport Athletic Society, the club was effectively taken over in the summer of 1886 by Southport Wanderers, who then dropped the Wanderers name, before reverting to Southport Central two years later.

* * * * *

By the end of the 1880s Manchester was still playing catch-up, not quite in time, unlike Merseyside, to earn a place in the first Football League. Even the County FA acknowledged in its centenary brochure of 1984 that 'in the early years of the Association, the predominant game in the Manchester area was Rugby Football'.

Records exist from 1863–73 for the **Hulme Athenaeum** club, though it is not clear which rules they were playing to. Some of the personnel then appeared with Manchester FC, founded in November 1875 and playing early games against a Liverpool students team and Northwich Victoria.

There was a significant pair of matches in December 1876 and February 1877 between Manchester and the provincial stronghold of Sheffield, the Lancashire side apparently confused in the return match by local interpretation of offside, which did not totally explain the margin of their defeat by 14 goals to nil. Later that year in November, Manchester FC became the first from the city to play in the FA Cup, losing 3-0 at Darwen.

The same year **Birch** rugby club created its own football team and then played the noted Scottish adventurers Queen's Park in April 1878, losing 6-0 in front of an estimated 2,000 spectators and entering the following season's FA Cup, only to scratch without playing a game.

Just as Ardwick/Manchester City would do six years later, Birch relaunched by incorporating the name of the city itself and styling themselves Manchester Wanderers, proving their potential by beating Blackburn Rovers; and in 1879 they merged with Manchester FC, becoming the first Mancunian club to join the LFA, whose cup competition they entered, reaching the fourth round.

In December 1883 they became the first English team to play an FA Cup tie in Scotland – losing 15-0 to Queen's Park with no excuses this time about the offside rule or anything else.

A year before, Manchester was chosen as host for an important conference of the four home nations, which paved the way for the International Football Association Board, the sports international law-making body, to be formed two and a half years later.

Hurst, who would much later become Ashton United, defeated Turton in their first FA Cup tie in October 1883, then scratched before their second round tie with Irwell Springs could be replayed, but were one of four clubs from their district among the 16 who founded the Manchester County Football Association in 1884. The full list was: Manchester, Manchester Arcadians, Dalton Hall, Eccles, Greenheys, Haughton Dale, Hurst, Hurst Park Road, Hurst Brook Olympic, Hurst Clarence, Levenshulme, Newton Heath LYR, Pendleton Olympic, Thornham, West Gorton and West Manchester.

Newton Heath, beaten by Hurst in the first Manchester Senior Cup final that season, and West Gorton were the two most significant names among the 16, as supporters of Manchester City and Manchester United are likely to know.

* * * * *

The rivalry between Manchester's two most famous football clubs even extends to which existed first. Contemporary reports suggest there was quite possibly no more than a single week between their first games, in November 1880, with City's forerunners St Mark's ahead by seven days. What the blue portion of the city cannot dispute, however, is that **Manchester United** in their earliest incarnation made the greater impression in the first decade.

The appendage LYR of the original club stood for Lancashire and Yorkshire Railway, whose employees it was in the Carriage and Wagon Works that started a team playing on North Road, Newton Heath. It is nowadays named Northampton Road, where Moston Book High School stands on the site. The pitch on the edge of a clay pit was owned by the Manchester Cathedral authorities, although it was the railway company who took the club's rent.

The Heathens played their first recorded match, wearing the railway colours of green and gold, in a 6-0 defeat by Bolton

Wanderers reserves on 20 November. Almost a year later, on 12 November 1881, the first derby against the St Mark's (West Gorton) team that would become Manchester City took place, attracting a reported 3,000 to see the Heathens win 3-0.

As founder members of the Manchester and District FA in 1884 they entered the Challenge Cup (later Manchester Senior Cup) and over the next few years went on to demonstrate their strength as one of the city's very best clubs by reaching the final five times in the first six seasons, losing the inaugural one 3-0 to Hurst but winning the trophy in 1886 and then from 1888–90.

Once professionalism was allowed in 1885, Newton Heath took advantage not by recruiting Scots, like so many other clubs, but by engaging a number of Welshmen who were able to work for the railway. By 1888 they were fielding five Welsh internationals, including full-back and club captain Jack Powell, who became an important figure, and the Doughty brothers Jack and Roger, both signed from the Druids club.

Jack Doughty scored the club's first ever FA Cup goals when they entered the 1886/87 competition, drawing 2-2 at Fleetwood Rovers but rather perversely refusing to play extra time; as a result, the tie was awarded to their opponents.

The Heathens, miffed, did not enter for the next two years and when they did lost 6-1 at Preston, who were on their way to winning a second Football League title. Manchester, from its slow start, had ground to make up.

* * * * *

Manchester City were another of countless clubs in Lancashire and beyond whose origins were as a church team, in their case in the West Gorton area around the Hyde Road.

In the 1870s it was a tough area with numerous local gangs, where valuable social work was done by local churches. St Mark's formed a cricket team in 1875 and five years later took up football to fill the winter months (and keep local youths out of mischief). The first-known newspaper report, from the *Gorton Reporter* says that on 13 November 1880 St Mark's (West Gorton) played the Baptist Church (Macclesfield) in 'a very pleasant and exciting game' and lost by two goals to one, James Collinge from Heywood being credited with the young team's first goal.

Collinge also scored two in achieving a first victory for the club in what has been recorded as their ninth and last game of the season, away to a depleted Stalybridge Clarence side.

For the second season, a better-quality ground than the one on Clowes Street was found at Kirkmanshulme Cricket Club near the Belle Vue Zoological Gardens for a campaign in which a dozen matches included the first derbies against Newton Heath. After their 3-0 defeat in November, St Mark's won 2-1 in the return.

Another season, another ground; variously known as Queen's Park or Clemington Park but still less than a mile from St Mark's, it became home for the 1883/84 season, when the club appear to have merged with Belle Vue Rangers under the name of West Gorton, before becoming plain Gorton. They played in an unusual kit of black shirts with a large white Maltese cross that possibly signified greater links with local masons than the Church.

Joining the Manchester & District FA brought a first match in the Challenge Cup and defeat by Dalton Hall, but Gorton were not ready for the FA Cup, which others like West Manchester, Birch, Hyde, Denton, Heywood Central and Newton Heath all entered.

Those clubs were ahead of Gorton at the time, as was emphasised by an embarrassing defeat to their greatest future rivals in the Manchester Senior Cup of 1886/87, when Newton Heath dealt out an 11-1 thrashing; still the biggest margin in any derby between the pair.

In 1887 came an important move from the latest ground on Reddish Lane and a further change of name. Ardwick was chosen because of the new district in Bennett Street off Hyde Road, close to the Manchester-Crewe railway line although still not far from St Mark's church; the waste ground formerly used for bare-knuckle and bare-chested fighting needed a summer of hard graft to make it fit for football. Some doubted whether they had achieved it and Hyde were allowed to replay a local cup tie after protesting at the state of the pitch.

There was an unfortunate beginning when opponents Salford failed to turn up for a supposedly grand opening on 10 September. So it was a week later that the ground was christened when a Denton club, Hooley Hill, won 4-2.

Blue and white stripes now replaced black shirts and with church influence diminishing, club headquarters was the Hyde

Road public house and the nickname was the Brewerymen after the support of Chester's, who helped fund a new stand holding 1,000 patrons. Like Newton Heath they were on their way but still not ready for league football at any level.

* * * * *

A little further north **Bury** were founded in April 1885 at the White Horse Hotel and found a suitable venue on Gigg Lane, known as Mr Barlow's Field. Little Lever provided the first recorded opposition on 5 September 1885, with a first home game the following week when Wigan were beaten 4-3 and gate receipts were £1 16s (£1.80).

Struggling financially in early days, by 1887 they could just about afford to expend £50 on a first covered stand, which was in place in time for the visit of the mighty Blackburn Rovers for what should have been a first FA Cup tie in October that year (the previous season they had missed entry by applying too late). Knowing a number of players would be ineligible, Bury played the game without apparently admitting to spectators that it was now only a friendly. Rovers won 10-0 and Bury are officially recorded as having scratched.

The cup would bring them glory soon enough and long before Manchester's finest had had a sniff of it. But it was the revolutionary concept of league football that now demanded Lancashire's attention.

Chapter 2

The draper's dream (1888–1900)

Lancashire's six form half of the world's first football league, dominated by Preston's 'Invincibles'; contrasting fortunes of Blackburn pair; Burnley's scandalous bore war ends relegation test matches; Bolton to Burnden; Everton leave Anfield and spawn greatest rivals, then take on new ones along the Ship Canal; Manchester's big two on the rise but shaken by Bury; twin towers of Blackpool and New Brighton; Bootle, Darwen and Halliwell can't live McGregor's dream.

A S proud regional newspapers in Blackburn and the midlands were apt to point out, up until 1888 the FA Cup winners could reasonably call themselves national champions; just like Queen's Park or any other of the Scottish Cup winners since 1874, and indeed the Welsh Cup holders from 1878. With professionalism having been formalised, football was developing but clubs needed a regular income; national and local knockout competitions, while prestigious, offered no guarantees that the best teams would either win or, crucially, earn more than one game's worth of gate money.

Hence the letter written on 2 March 1888 by Aston Villa committee man William McGregor. A heavily bearded Methodist and Liberal Party member who had moved from Perthshire to Birmingham, where he ran a draper's shop, he had never played football other than as a young boy. He would go down, however, as one of the great administrators of all sport for suggesting that '10 or 12 of the most prominent clubs in England combine to arrange home-and-away fixtures each season'.

McGregor initially contacted four other clubs as well as his own: Blackburn Rovers, Bolton Wanderers, Preston North End and West Bromwich Albion, telling them, 'I should like to hear what other clubs you would suggest.' Blackburn, Bolton and Preston were clearly regarded as the three major north-western sides, with Villa and West Brom (FA Cup winners in 1887 and 1888 respectively) in no way inferior. These were the 'big five' of the late 19th century.

Who would make up the '10 or 12' to complete this brave new world? The decisions caused considerable angst. John Bentley, unexpectedly deposed as Bolton secretary for a year, then re-instated, proposed Notts County, Stoke and Wolverhampton Wanderers from the midlands as well as Accrington and Burnley (all of whom were eventually accepted) plus Bolton's neighbours Halliwell, Mitchell St George's from Birmingham and even the southern amateurs Old Carthusians, who were not.

A preliminary meeting of clubs was held on the eve of the 1888 FA Cup Final at Anderton's Hotel in Fleet Street, London and followed up on 17 April at the now defunct Royal Hotel, Manchester (on the corner of Mosley Street and Market Street), at which Everton and Derby County were invited to complete the chosen dozen. Whether by accident or design, an even north-midlands balance was thus achieved for the grand opening of the 1888/89 season with six from each region.

The final selection was not without controversy. Only one club was admitted from each town or city, which meant Bootle missed out despite considering themselves at least as good as local rivals Everton (and going on to beat both Accrington and Burnley in pre-season). Sharing a cricket ground while Everton were ensconced at Anfield Road may have counted against them. *Athletic News*, hinting it seemed at Accrington and Notts County, pointed out that one or two of those included 'have been knocked into smithereens' by some of those missing out.

The oldest provincial strongholds of the game, Sheffield and Nottingham, were upset at having only one representative between them. The Wednesday, who had expressed reservations about the cost of home and away fixtures, were rejected, leaving the whole of Yorkshire without a club; as well as Bootle, others falling foul of the one-team-per-town rule included Nottingham Forest, Bentley's suggestions Halliwell and Mitchell St George's, plus Blackburn Olympic, FA Cup winners five years earlier.

The chosen 12 were pressing on, said *Cricket and Football Field* on 21 April, 'without a care for those unhappily shut out in the cold', although almost from the start there was talk of a possible 'second league' and play-offs between the bottom four and a second division's top four (which would appear within four years, furthering the geographical spread). By June, *Athletic News* had changed its tune somewhat, predicting even before any fixtures were formulated that 'the coming season will be of the most brilliant and successful character'.

League rules included a £15 guarantee to the away team (rather than the 50-50 split McGregor proposed) and until a second division emerged, the bottom four clubs – one-third of the league – would have to apply for re-election. Teams should field their strongest side and league games took priority over cup matches or friendlies. Blackburn still managed to miss the historic opening day, because of a pre-arranged friendly away to Newton Heath, but Stoke and Notts County found themselves fielding reserve teams in the FA Cup qualifying rounds in that first season, while Everton, as mentioned earlier, scratched from a tie away to Ulster in order to play Villa in the league.

As for the name, McGregor suggested the Association Football Union, an echo of the Rugby Football Union founded in 1871 after that sport's breakaway from association football. Although the word 'league' carried political echoes that some did not like, Preston's William Sudell won the day with his choice, the Football League. 'English League' might have been more obvious but McGregor had not given up hope that some of his native Scottish clubs might eventually be included.

Sudell became treasurer, Harry Lockett, the secretary-manager of Stoke, was secretary and stayed for 14 years, running it from the Potteries; and McGregor became chairman. 'I really believe that the game would have received a very severe check, and its popularity would have been paralysed once and for all, if the league had not been founded,' he said later.

A fixtures meeting, postponed in Birmingham at the start of May, eventually took place in the Royal Hotel on 23 July and set Saturday, 8 September as the earliest date for matches. Ten teams duly turned out on that historic afternoon, Notts County and Blackburn having to delay their entry for a week. The results, with estimated attendances were:

Football League
Saturday, 8 September 1888
Bolton Wanderers 3 Derby County 6 (3,000)
Everton 2 Accrington 1 (10,000)
Preston North End 5 Burnley 2 (5,000)
Stoke 0 West Bromwich Albion 2 (4,500)
Wolverhampton Wanderers 1 Aston Villa 1 (3,000)

The *Sporting Life* reported, not entirely logically, 'The weather Saturday was delightfully fine, the sun shining brightly all the afternoon, and, as consequence, most of the games played were late in starting.'

Varying kick-off times have led to some dispute about who can claim to have scored the first goal in league football. The honour was previously understood to have been no honour at all, being an own goal by Villa's Gershon Cox; that, however, was based on the mistaken assumption that the game in Wolverhampton had started half an hour earlier than the others. Jack Gordon of Preston has also been credited with getting the goals rolling, but contemporary reports say that his game did not start until ten to four because of Burnley's late arrival. So the credit has been given to James 'Kenny' Davenport of Bolton, scoring inside two minutes against Derby. In fact, Wanderers scored three times in five minutes of an extraordinary game before the visitors, possibly unsettled by also having arrived in a rush, recovered so well that they led 4-3 after half an hour. The home defence suffered further damage in the second half and a clear defeat.

The following Saturday, Everton, playing at home again, achieved another 2-1 victory as Notts County made their bow, and Blackburn's debut produced a sensational game in which ten goals were shared with the under-rated Accrington, who had led 4-3 at half-time.

Exciting it may have been for the 4,000 spectators, with Rovers equalising in the final few minutes, but some critics were scathing about the quality, notably Manchester's *Cricket and Football Field,* whose reporter called it 'one of the worst expositions of football ever seen, both sides playing like novices'.

Aston Villa, Everton, Preston (with nine goals) and West Brom won both opening matches while Bolton and Stoke lost both. Bolton's start was particularly unfortunate; for the second week running they lost 4-3 at home after leading 3-0. Visitors Burnley, it was reported, 'were even later than usual' and then had to disappear for a change of shirts because of a clash. Burnley's inside-forward Bill Tait, unconcerned, scored the first league hat-trick and after the team overdid their victory celebrations he was suspended with two defenders and played only three more games before returning to Newton Heath.

Oddly, the points system was not formally worked out until 21 November, about halfway through the scheduled programme. Bentley successfully proposed two points for a win and one for a draw although West Brom wanted no points for draws. At that stage Preston, with 22 points from a dozen games, already led by seven from Villa, with Blackburn and Wolves on 14, while Derby and Stoke, with only three wins between them, were struggling at the bottom.

* * * * *

Preston, with William Sudell's aggressive recruiting of players, and no local town close enough to seriously rival them, looked like favourites from the start; a table of results up to the end of January 1888, a month before McGregor's initial letter of invitation, had them winning all 28 games to date, scoring 157 goals, with only Aston Villa (31 wins from 34 games) remotely comparable. Even Sudell, however, could hardly have foreseen two successive titles and then three runners-up places in the first five seasons.

The team played with three half-backs helping the forwards to the extent that Preston going forward had eight attackers. In John Goodall, 'Johnny All Good', they also had the player who would become leading scorer for the whole league, a Golden Boot winner long before such a concept was dreamt up.

England were able to claim him for internationals (12 goals in 14 games) even though he had Scottish parents, as his actual birth took place in London. He moved to Kilmarnock with them at a young age but returned south to play for the Bolton club Great Lever and then from 1885 for Preston. Later in his career, having moved to Derby County, he made a couple of appearances in first-class cricket with Derbyshire and even wrote one of the first books by a footballer. In it he suggested that Preston succeeded as a result of teamwork and never knowing when they were beaten – which for a long time, of course, they were not.

Team-mate Jimmy Ross, born in Edinburgh, became a close rival to Goodall as leading scorer. Small and slight, he would surely have played for Scotland but for the policy of ignoring those with English clubs. Together with Fred Dewhurst, John Gordon and George Drummond the pair made up an especially dangerous forward line. North End began the campaign as they were destined to carry on. They started with six wins before Accrington held them 0-0, which was one of four draws. On 10 November Villa became the only side to hold them at Deepdale, 1-1, Goodall scoring early before his brother Archie, an Irish international centre-half who had become the first player transferred during the league season, set up the visitors' equaliser.

There were inevitably other close shaves. North End were 2-0 down at lowly Derby before winning 3-2, and were later held in derbies at Burnley and Blackburn, but there was never much doubt about who would become the first official English champions. On Boxing Day, still seven points clear, Preston produced one of their most sparkling performances in winning 5-0 away to West Bromwich to exact revenge for the FA Cup final defeat nine months earlier. The title was secured as early as the first week of January with a 4-1 win over Notts County on the same day as Villa were heavily beaten by improving Burnley.

From there the task was to remain unbeaten in the last three games. The 2-2 draw at Blackburn was the closest of them, Rovers believing they had scored a late goal, which was disallowed. A 2-0 win at Everton in mid-January set up a grand finale at Villa Park against second-placed Villa. On a snowy February day two goals by Dewhurst in the second half completed a record of 18 wins and four draws, with goals of 74-15. Goodall claimed 21 of them, Ross 18 and the Accrington game was the only time in 27 league and cup matches that Preston failed to score.

The *Athletic News* correspondent suggested they were now 'the cleverest Association team in the world'. 'Superlatively fine individual and collective work,' commented the *Birmingham Daily Times*. Villa were good enough to finish runners-up, but 11 points in arrears, having lost five times.

A week before the final league game, North End began their FA Cup campaign by beating Bootle 3-0. Victories over Grimsby and Birmingham St George's followed, then holders West Brom in the Sheffield semi-final, a game watched by up to 25,000, whose incursions on to the pitch almost caused the tie to be demoted to a friendly. Half-back David Russell scored the only goal.

The one team left standing between Sudell's team and a historic Double were Wolves, who had prevented what could have been an epic local derby by knocking out Blackburn Rovers in the other semi-final. They had finished third in the league but lost both games to North End, 4-0 in September and 5-2 at Deepdale the following month. The favourites duly came through by 3-0, equalling the highest victory margin in the 18 finals to date.

Interest was naturally immense and the Oval crowd was also a record at 22,000. Dewhurst and Ross scored in the first half and Sam Thomson, replacing Nick Ross (who had briefly joined Everton for a reputed £10 per month) in the only change from the previous year's final, added the third. There were six Scots in the side as well as genuine Prestonians in full-backs Bob Howarth and Bob Holmes and one amateur in skipper Dewhurst, a grammar school teacher.

FA Cup Final 1889: Preston North End 3 Wolves 0
Preston: Mills-Roberts; Howarth, Holmes, Drummond, Russell, Graham, Gordon, J Ross, Goodall, Dewhurst, Thompson.
Wolves: Baynton; Baugh, Mason, Fletcher, Allen, Lowder, Hunter, Wykes, Brodie, Wood, Knight.

Would North End ever be beaten? The answer was not long in coming. Stoke were the bottom club in both the league's first two years but after a narrow 1-0 victory over them in the opening game of 1889/90, North End's second game changed perceptions. On 21 September they lost an eventful match 5-3 at Villa Park after going 5-1 down. The *Daily News* called it an 'inexplicable result' which would nevertheless mean that 'other clubs will no doubt go on to the field against Preston with greater hope'. So it proved: at the end of October there were successive losses to Derby and Wolves, the latter game bringing a first home defeat.

North End had lost leading scorer Goodall to Derby, where the material benefits included taking over a pub with brother Archie, who had quickly moved on from Villa. So the supposed unbeatables had lost three of the first seven games and the Football League appeared to be turning into more of a contest. Yet they were defeated only once more in the remaining 15 matches, when Everton, eventual runners-up, won 2-1 at Deepdale in December.

The championship chase was much tighter than 12 months earlier but Preston prevailed again, securing the title by two points on the final day at the end of March, with a 1-0 win at Notts County. Nick Ross, back from Everton, this time outscored his brother Jimmy by 22 goals to 19. There was no double Double however. After seeing off Newton Heath 6-1 and Lincoln City 4-0, the holders surprisingly lost 3-2 at home to Bolton in the third round.

In his role as Football League treasurer, Sudell successfully proposed that from the following season the champions should receive a trophy, costing no more than 50 guineas (£52.50). Unimaginably, it proved too late for Preston, who have been trying to win it ever since, starting with three frustrating seasons as runners-up. The first of them, 1890/91, was notable for a decline in scoring to 44, when nobody managed more than six league goals and Everton took the title, albeit by only two points after Preston, having beaten them twice, lost two of their last three games including a costly 6-2 drubbing at Burnley.

In 1891/92 Sunderland's margin in the north-east's first title success was five points. North End never recovered from losing three of the first four games, the other one being a 3-1 win over the eventual champions. They did put six goals past Notts County in December, but only after five visiting players walked off, claiming the freezing conditions were unplayable.

It was a similar tale in 1892/93, with the Wearsiders finishing 11 points ahead over four extra games, as two other clubs (The

Wednesday and Newton Heath) joined the First Division and a Second Division began; Preston lost as many as ten of their 30 games and Sunderland beat them twice on the way to retaining the title. There was a better FA Cup run to the semi-final, ended by Everton at the third attempt. The Lancashire Cup was eventful too with Bootle beaten 6-4 in the semi-final as North End did their best to fritter away a 6-0 lead, before winning the trophy for the first time.

In the summer of 1893 the club became a limited company with Sudell losing the chairmanship. He had already given up his position as Football League treasurer and in 1895 was sensationally convicted of embezzling over £5,000 from the cotton mill at which he worked, in order to fund players' wages and expenses. After three years in prison, he emigrated to South Africa and became a sports journalist before dying in 1911, aged 61.

Despite the influx of a new group of players from Scotland, the 1893/94 season was effectively the end of a glorious era for Preston. Both Ross brothers played their last games for the club; Nick was diagnosed with tuberculosis and died the following August, aged only 31. North End dropped to 14th out of 16 and were forced to play a relegation test match, Jimmy Ross scoring in the 4-0 win over Notts County that secured First Division status.

Having also recorded a double hat-trick in the 18-0 FA Cup win over Reading during the team's otherwise barren run, he was lured to Liverpool for a £75 fee, continuing his prolific scoring there and later at Burnley. In the later stages of his career he played at Manchester City with Billy Meredith, becoming an important figure in the budding Players' Union.

Nobody was prolific enough to become an adequate replacement at Deepdale, though outside-left Adam Henderson did his best. A couple of fourth places in mid-decade and a second Lancashire Cup in 1895 were the highlights but there was no joy in the FA Cup and it would all end badly; the once unthinkable relegation, avoided by a single point in 1900, finally came to pass the following year.

* * * * *

Blackburn Rovers finished as second highest Lancashire club in the inaugural season, behind Aston Villa and Wolves as well as the champions. It was an uneven campaign, mixing performances like a first defeat in the fifth game, 6-1 at Villa, with the 6-2 win at home to FA Cup holders West Bromwich Albion and a deserved draw against The Invincibles.

Despite his five Lancashire Cup wins and three FA Cups, league football came too late for Fergie Suter. The celebrated Scot made only one appearance, in goal (!) just before Christmas 1888 in the 2-1 defeat away to West Brom.

While local rivals Olympic disappeared, Rovers carried on the town's reputation as FA Cup fighters, reaching the semi-final again and soon adding two more triumphs in the final, giving them five in the space of eight years.

The 1890 triumph was a record-breaker, a 6-1 win over Alliance side The Wednesday including the first hat-trick in a final, by England international Billy Townley. The semi-final against Wolves, only one place below Rovers in the league, was much tougher, Jack Southworth's goal being the only one.

FA Cup Final 1890: Blackburn Rovers 6 The Wednesday 1
Blackburn Rovers: Horne; James Southworth, Forbes, Barton, Dewar, Forrest, Lofthouse, Campbell, Jack Southworth, Walton, Townley.
The Wednesday: Smith; Morley, Brayshaw, Dungworth, Betts, Waller, Ingram, Woolhouse, Bennett, Mumford, Cawley.

Townley, a local man, later played for Darwen and Manchester City before becoming one of Britain's earliest continental coaches, his ten different teams including Bayern Munich and the Dutch national side at the 1924 Olympics.

He was still at Blackburn for the following year's final, and scored again in a 3-1 win over Notts County, as did Jack Southworth and George Dewar. In between times, the club moved from the Leamington Road ground to Ewood Park, but there would be no hat-trick of cup wins this time; in 1892, after Southworth scored all four in a win over Derby, West Bromwich knocked them out 3-1.

Frustratingly, two more successive semi-finals brought single-goal defeats by Wolves, then Notts County, both of whom went on to win the trophy.

League form, meanwhile, was slowly declining. In 1891 Blackburn only finished in the top six because Sunderland became the first club docked two points for fielding an unregistered player; they dropped to ninth in both 1892 and '93 and suffered from an early transfer sensation when Jack Southworth, top scorer in their first four league seasons, moved to Everton for £400 after 121 goals in 132 games.

Without him they were fourth, fifth and eighth, then slumped again to the bottom three in both 1897 and '98. In the second of those seasons five teams at the bottom all finished on the same number of points and having only Stoke below them on goal average (first introduced in 1894/95) Rovers were condemned to test match play-offs, losing three of the four games against Second Division sides Burnley and Newcastle.

Stoke and Burnley, knowing a goalless draw would suit both of them, then agreed a non-aggression pact in which hardly a shot was loosed off in a game described in the *Staffordshire Advertiser* as 'a complete fiasco'. Fortunately the time was right to accept Burnley's previous recommendation of an expansion to two divisions of 18, a happy compromise that saw all four test match teams playing in the top division. The Football League decided on automatic promotion and relegation from then on until play-offs were reintroduced in 1987.

In 1899/1900 Rovers were in the bottom five again; it would take the arrival of the next significant off-field figure to truly revive them.

* * * * *

With Olympic gone, Accrington, Bolton and **Burnley** became Rovers' main rivals until Darwen made it to the Football League in 1891. It was hard going however for the Turf Moor club, a mixture of Scots and local men, who had to apply for re-election in the very first Football League season and as well as surviving the Stoke City test match scandal were relegated twice before the turn of the century.

A porous defence was the problem initially as seven of the first nine games were lost, including successive defeats by 6-1 at Notts County and, embarrassingly for local pride, 7-1 at home to Blackburn when centre-forward Fred Poland played as an emergency goalkeeper. New keeper Walter Cox was brought in from Hibernian as one of three signings who oversaw a brief improvement that included leading Preston twice in December's 2-2 draw, but losing the final game 1-0 at Derby meant finishing fourth from bottom above the midlands trio of Derby, Notts County and Stoke.

In the re-election meeting nine new clubs including Bootle, Newton Heath and South Shore (Blackpool) applied and were given five minutes each to put their case, which did not prove convincing enough. The existing bottom four (all allowed to vote for themselves) got back in, Burnley receiving nine votes, and none of the new applicants more than five; Bootle got two and Newton Heath one.

One of the season's brighter moments was an England cap for winger Jack Yates, a Blackburn man who had played for Olympic and Accrington. He set an enduring record by scoring a hat-trick against Northern Ireland on what proved to be his first and only international appearance.

The second league season was worse, Burnley not winning a game until suddenly bursting into action on 1 March, beating Bolton 7-0 for the first of four successive wins. They revived sufficiently to finish above Stoke again and earn another re-election while Sunderland replaced the Potteries club, agreeing to compensate clubs for the extra costs in travelling so far north. Better was the Lancashire Cup with a 2-0 win over Blackburn in the final to take the trophy for the first time.

Rovers were the opposition for one of the most controversial of local derbies in December 1891 when the FA Cup holders, 3-0 down at half-time in deep snow, reappeared only reluctantly for the second half, then walked off when their captain Joe Lofthouse was dismissed for fighting. The 3-0 scoreline was allowed to stand.

The previous season Burnley had had their first five-figure gates for the visits of Aston Villa and Blackburn, but home crowds were aware that as well as conceding too many goals they lacked a regular scorer, nobody reaching double figures until the third season.

There was a regular improvement to finish eighth, seventh, sixth and fifth in successive years from 1891–94 as Arthur Sutcliffe effectively became the first manager, combining that role with secretarial duties. But leading players departed, including Peter Turnbull and goalkeeper Jack Hillman, who both left for Everton amid rumours that the Merseyside club had flouted the new maximum signing-on fee of £10, and then England international wing-half James Crabtree was sold to Aston Villa, for whom he played in the 1897 Double team.

From a high of fifth place, Burnley were often at the wrong end of the table and in some peril, as up to four teams could be involved in test matches. The 1894/95 campaign brought one point from the last eight games, causing a slump to ninth and two years later the worst materialised; under new manager Harry Bradshaw Burnley were bottom with only six wins from 30 games and forced into the mini-league of test matches, winning one, drawing one, but losing two of the four games, to be replaced by Second Division champions Notts County. Relegated for the first time, they proposed increasing both divisions to 18 clubs each but found insufficient support.

The Second Division title was won at the first attempt, losing only two games out of 30 and beating Loughborough Town 9-3 with five goals out of the 23 that season by Jimmy Ross, the former Preston 'Invincible' who had joined from Liverpool in March 1897. The season ended controversially with the Stoke City test match, after which both clubs were fortunate to retain their place in the top division.

The one downside for Burnley was that the first game with Stoke clashed with an FA Cup tie at home to Everton. They had finally progressed beyond the second round for the first time in 13 attempts by beating Woolwich Arsenal and Burslem but Everton ended the run 3-1 at Turf Moor.

Two seasons later they might have wished the old play-off system was still in place when suffering automatic relegation after finishing 17th of the 18 teams. In between times they achieved a best season yet with third place in the top division, but manager Bradshaw left to inspire Arsenal and the good work was undone within 12 months.

There was embarrassment at the end of the relegation season too when goalkeeper Jack Hillman, capped by England in 1899, was found guilty of offering Nottingham Forest players a bribe to throw the final game – and increasing the offer at half-time. Despite claiming after a 4-0 defeat that it had been a joke, he was banned for a year.

* * * * *

Bolton's trajectory in the first dozen years of league football was not dissimilar to Burnley's, though they were able to look down on them for much of the time until suffering relegation themselves in 1899. Recovering from those two extraordinary first games, both lost 4-3 at home after leading 3-0, they finished fifth in the first season and as high as third in 1891/92, only a point behind runners-up Preston after heading the table with eight wins from the first ten games.

Local lad Kenny Davenport, as already noted, found fame as the scorer of the first goal in Football League history and Welsh international full-back Dai Jones was an enduring hero, playing over 250 games in ten seasons. Jimmy Cassidy, signed from Glasgow Hibernians in October 1889, became an important goalscorer with 20 in 19 league and cup games, including five against Sheffield United in the club record FA Cup win of 13-0 the following February. That stood as an individual best until Tony Caldwell equalled it in 1983 against Walsall.

The oddity in that second campaign was that Wanderers finished in the bottom four with a fractionally worse goal average than Aston Villa and should have needed to apply for re-election, until claiming that the figures were wrong because they had lost to Notts County by only 3-0, not 4-0. The Football League let them off.

The season was also notable for reaching an FA Cup semi-final for the first time, recording double figures against Distillery of Belfast as well as Sheffield United and then knocking out Double winners Preston. The Wednesday salvaged Sheffield pride by winning the semi 2-1 in Birmingham.

Four years later in 1894 they would go a step further, to the final itself, one played nearer to home at Goodison Park rather than the Oval, which was now considered inadequate for such an occasion. After three wins against Second Division opposition, revenge was achieved over The Wednesday in the semi-final with two goals by the lyrically named Handel Bentley.

In the final, however, another Second Division side, Notts County, unexpectedly proved too strong, winning 4-1 with a hat-trick by Jimmy Logan. Bolton's goal by Cassidy was the merest of consolations, coming in the last few minutes when 4-0 down, and his team were 'woefully disappointing' according to the *Lancashire Evening Post* .

A new home was already being considered and in August 1895 Burnden Park, costing £130 rent per annum, was ready, a smart venue with a stand down each touchline that would soon be chosen to stage representative football. An estimated 15,000 to 20,000 turned up for the grand opening, an athletics event that incorporated cycling and a high diver, which was rather more than saw Everton beaten 3-1 in the first league match on 14 September. Settling in well that season, Wanderers finished fourth and lost another FA Cup semi-final to familiar Yorkshire foes The Wednesday in a replay.

The two clubs were to see plenty more of each other. In the spring of 1899 they were relegated together but the following season, after being drawn together once more in the FA Cup (Wednesday won again) both returned to the top division with Bolton Second Division runners-up, two points behind.

There had been ominous signs in what turned out to be Cassidy's last season, a low-scoring one after which a number of players left as the wages budget decreased. Once he departed for Newton Heath, Bolton made the drop just as Burnden was rewarded with its first FA Cup semi-final.

The Second Division proved much more enjoyable with only one game lost until mid-January, new man Laurie Bell, a Scot who had impressed while playing for Everton against Wanderers, scoring 23 goals. Throughout this time John Bentley was an increasingly important figure, becoming Football League president for 16 years from 1894, as well as chairman of Bolton and editor of *Athletic News,* ensuring that the Football League, if not Wanderers, had a good press.

* * * * *

By winning the final league match of the season in late April to finish seventh, **Accrington** did better than might have been expected from the critical comment that greeted their inclusion. A win in the final match, condemning Stoke to bottom spot on goal average, also meant they finished one place above Everton. They were the main beneficiaries of awarding one point for a draw, without which they would have been in the bottom three instead of seventh and have had to apply for re-election.

After another mid-table finish, that was their fate for two seasons in a row and in the next one, 1892/93, the worst came to the worst after promotion/relegation test matches were introduced. The Old Reds lost 1-0 to Sheffield United, the Second Division runners-up, on neutral ground at Trent Bridge and were relegated. As the worst-supported First Division club on gates of 4,000 they declined to play in the lower division with fixtures as far-flung as Newcastle and London, and joined the Lancashire League instead.

A respectable fourth place encouraged an application to rejoin the Football League, but while Ardwick and Bury received sufficient votes, Accrington were ten short. Dropping to 12th place out of 14 the next season, they switched to the Lancashire Combination but found financial problems increasing. On 14 January 1896, they suffered a 12-0 defeat by Darwen in the Lancashire Senior Cup – of which they had been proud winners three times – and disbanded.

Their plight, never easy when sandwiched between Blackburn and Burnley, had been exacerbated by the arrival of **Accrington Stanley**, a name adopted in 1893, two years after being founded as Stanley Villa. Admitted to the North East Lancashire Combination, Stanley became regular FA Cup contestants from 1896 and in the summer of 1900 joined the Lancashire Combination , where they would soon make a mark.

* * * * *

Overall then, the Blackburn-Bolton corridor, extended into a figure T by Preston to the west and Accrington and Burnley to the east was well represented in the world's first football league, mirroring the sport's roots in the county.

Lancashire, of course, had a sixth representative down on Merseyside, of whom more shortly, and gained a seventh in the fourth year of competition when **Darwen**, another of the great pioneering clubs, were elected for a decade that could reasonably be described as 'up and down'.

Following their great FA Cup exploits in the 1880s, the club outlasted their smaller rivals in the town like the Ramblers and Old Wanderers and played in the first two seasons of the Football Alliance from 1889–91. They finished only sixth of the 12 teams each time but benefited (with the returning Stoke) from their longstanding reputation in the sport to win election to the Football League when it was expanded to 14 clubs for the 1891/92 season.

It did not go well, when they finished bottom, conceding 112 goals, a record which would stand until they fared even worse seven eventful years later. The worst defeat, by 12-0 to West Bromwich Albion in March, has never been surpassed (and only once equalled) in the top division of English football.

Joining 11 former Alliance clubs in the new Football League Second Division in 1892, they finished third with a strong home record and won promotion back via the test matches, beating First Division Notts County 3-2 . The following season they were relegated again, with only Newton Heath below them, managing three mid-table seasons before featuring in the bottom two with Loughborough for two seasons running. In the second of them, the disastrous 1898/99 campaign, they were last, suffering 18 successive defeats and letting in 141 goals, both records that still stand.

The losing sequence lasted from 12 November to mid-March and included two separate runs of seven games without scoring. Champions Manchester City, Walsall and even Loughborough all beat them 10-0, contributing to an away record of one draw, 16 defeats and six goals scored against 109.

With gates down to three figures, they decided against applying for re-election, but at least the club kept going, and for no fewer than 110 more years, most of them at the new Anchor Ground. They were wound up in 2009, when a phoenix club AFC Darwen immediately emerged.

* * * * *

Liverpool had become a city in 1880, reflecting its huge increase in population from Ireland and Wales as well as the earlier slave trade, and the increasing importance of its docklands, notably in importing the raw material for the cotton industry. As noted in Chapter 1, **Everton** and Bootle soon emerged as its strongest football teams; now the former would split dramatically in two within four years of joining the Football League, their offspring Liverpool almost immediately replacing Bootle in more ways than one and helping to send them into oblivion.

The five-figure crowd turning up at Anfield for the first day of league football was twice as many as at any other game and a measure of Everton's potential, whatever Bootle might have felt. As Brian Tabner has pointed out in his exhaustive study of league attendances *Through the Turnstiles,* they had the highest average crowd for every one of the Football League's first ten seasons before being overtaken by Aston Villa. On that opening Saturday, winger George Fleming scored both goals in the 2-1 win over Accrington, although a 6-2 defeat at Bolton was an early indication that there were stronger sides around.

Third at the halfway stage, they fell away and seven defeats in the last ten games meant finishing eighth of the 12 sides. The weakness was in goalscoring; only bottom club Stoke City scored fewer than the total of 35 goals, with future England international Edgar Chadwick, signed from Blackburn Rovers, top scoring with only six.

Second to him was Nick Ross, signed from Preston's FA Cup-winning team and made captain, who arrived home after a fourth successive league defeat in March to find all his windows smashed by disgruntled supporters. Ross played at full-back, and had a notorious defensive partner in fellow Scot Alec Dick, who managed to antagonise most opposing supporters with his physical approach. After the 3-1 defeat at Notts County in October, having apparently struck a home player, he was hit on the head by an irate fan and became the first player to be officially reprimanded by the Football League.

Ross and Dick both departed before the second season of league football, when a dramatic improvement in all departments meant Everton should have been champions. Goalscoring improved notably to 65 and it was only losing two of the final four games at Accrington and West Bromwich that allowed Preston to finish two points ahead and retain their title.

Twelve months later they surrendered it to the Anfield side, who had found a real goalscorer in Fred Geary from Notts County. With left-wing pair Chadwick and Alf Milward, Geary made them into the most powerful attacking team in the country, adding 20 goals to his previous season's 21 at a rate of more than one per game. Burnley were beaten 7-3 and Derby twice humbled, 7-0 and 6-2, to add to the previous year's 11-2 FA Cup drubbing – still a record for both clubs. The achievement was marked a month later when Geary, Chadwick, Milward and vigorous little centre-half Johnny Holt all appeared for England in the 2-1 win over Scotland at Ewood Park (Anfield and Aigburth had already staged internationals against Ireland in 1889 and 1883 respectively).

Everton were the first club to be given the new championship trophy but with Geary missing much of the following season they slipped to fifth amid much drama off the field. Anfield's owner 'King John' Houlding, no doubt noting the club's profit of £1,700 in the title season, wanted another rent increase from £250 a year but was pushing his luck. A meeting of disgruntled members in January 1892 heard that local accountant George Mahon, the organist at St Domingo's and one of those who did not like the headquarters being on licensed premises, could secure a new ground close by in Goodison Road. It was bought for just over £8,000 and a limited company was formed.

Houlding briefly insisted on keeping the name Everton before founding Liverpool FC to play at Anfield in the Lancashire League. Thus was born one of the great football rivalries.

One of the great grounds too. Goodison Park, opened by FA president Lord Kinnaird on 24 August 1892, is described by Simon Inglis in his seminal work on British grounds as 'the first major football stadium in England'. It had stands on three sides, one of them covered, and a cinder bank on the fourth. Within 18 months it was the venue for the 1894 FA Cup Final between Notts County and Bolton and the following year a new stand was added and Goodison Road covered. The 'Toffees' nickname replaced the Black Watch because Mother Noblett's toffee shop was near the ground; to this day a woman in fancy dress parades around pre-match throwing sweets to the crowd.

It was an enjoyable first season at the new home in which the team finished third, just behind runners-up Preston, whose visit in February drew more than 30,000 to see them beaten 6-0. The following month came three closely fought FA Cup semi-finals against North End which put Everton in the final for the first time during a hectic spell of games.

On 16 March the Toffees drew the semi-final replay and in the league two days later won 4-2 away to potential cup final opponents Wolves, despite resting three of their England internationals with the second replay against North End in mind. In a third game in five days, Preston were finally knocked out 2-1 at Trent Bridge, and only five days later came the final against Wolves.

The venue, outside London for the first time, was Fallowfield, now the Manchester University sports ground, which proved inadequate to cope with all those who flocked there, naturally including thousands from Merseyside. The official attendance of 45,000 was twice capacity and probably an underestimate as well, after a stampede at the gates led to 'railings smashed like matchwood'. Frustration among spectators unable to see properly led to problems; the *Sporting Chronicle* reported that with 192 policemen present some of the fans 'went home with cracked heads'.

Even the pressmen had a poor view from the Pavilion, but the contemporary view was that strong favourites Everton had the better of the first half before in the 60th minute goalkeeper Dick Williams appeared to have the sun in his eyes as a lob from Wolves centre-half and captain Harry Allen went past him. 'Wolves played in a most plucky fashion,' added the *Chronicle*. 'Everton played a disappointing game in the second half.'

The 1894/95 season brought the first league derbies with Liverpool (see section below) and the runners-up position behind Sunderland, champions for the third time in four years. After reeling off eight straight wins at the start of the season Everton lost the services of striker Jack Southworth, an interesting character who had played for both Blackburn clubs and scored 36 times in 32 Everton games but was then forced into retirement aged 26 with a serious leg injury. After that he played only for the Hallé Orchestra, as an accomplished violinist.

In their new stadium, with a clutch of internationals, prominent in both domestic competitions and now donning the blue shirts and white shorts essentially unchanged ever since, Everton were clearly a major force. But honours were still elusive. In 1896 there was another third place in the First Division, then another FA Cup final and semi-final in successive seasons.

The 1897 final against league champions Aston Villa – who had beaten Liverpool in the last four to prevent a first Merseyside final – came on the back of six successive league defeats and brought another one, albeit only by 3-2 in a classic match widely described as the best final yet and attracting the biggest crowd of

65,891. All the goals came in a period of 25 minutes before half-time, Everton recovering from 1-0 down to lead with goals by Scottish international Jack Bell and Dick Boyle, only to concede twice more. Holding on to Jimmy Crabtree's headed goal enabled Villa to emulate Preston as winners of the Double.

The following season, Everton knocked out Blackburn (for the second year running), Stoke and Burnley, but Steve Bloomer's Derby County, their semi-final victims the previous year, took revenge by 3-1 at Molineux. Two successive fourth places in the league were followed by a slump to end the century; 11th place was the lowest yet and the FA Cup brought a 3-0 defeat by Southern League Southampton, inspired by the former Everton hero Milward.

* * * * *

By that time the rivalry with **Liverpool** was well and truly established. From setting up a new club as soon as Everton left Anfield in 1892 Houlding's men, playing in light blue and white halves, showed ambition and ability from the start. Failing to be elected to the Football League, they played for one season in the Lancashire League, and won it.

On 3 September Higher Walton were beaten 8-0 (half-time 5-0) in the club's first competitive game and by the end of the season they were champions on goal average ahead of Blackpool, the only team to win at Anfield. The newcomers also entered the FA Cup, beating Nantwich and Newtown before losing to Northwich Victoria in the third qualifying round.

April brought the first derby against an Everton XI in the Liverpool Senior Cup final, their neighbours playing a friendly against Scotland's Renton on the same day. Liverpool won it at Bootle in front of some 10,000 with a goal by Tom Wylie, one of their many Scots, and a player who had been at Everton but stayed at Anfield following their departure. The 'friendly derby'? After a rough game Everton made an official protest about the refereeing and the cup was not presented on the day. When it was, Liverpool had it stolen, along with the Lancashire League trophy, which together cost them £127 to replace.

All that was enough to win election to the the Second Division, extended from 12 to 15 clubs with Bootle dropping out, and Liverpool promptly won it in an unbeaten campaign of 22 wins and six draws. There was again a winning start, 2-0 away to fellow newcomers Middlesbrough Ironopolis on 2 September in which Malcolm McVean had the honour of scoring the first goal. By the end they had scored 77 goals in 28 games and although that was not the best in the division, the 18 conceded was easily the lowest total. Even then promotion was not assured but in a test match/play-off, Newton Heath, having finished bottom of the First Division, were beaten 2-0 and were relegated. Fielding nine players whose name began with 'Mc' and ten Scots in their opening match earned Liverpool the unoriginal nickname of 'team of all the Macs'.

Such recruitment did not come cheaply. J.J. Catton, the leading football journalist of the day, wrote that inducing players from Scotland to Merseyside 'seemed to require the wealth of Croesus and a Liverpool shipyard thrown in'.

To the south-east of Anfield, there is a very small street named after Houlding, linking Walton Breck Road and Oakfield Road. As his influence diminished soon after election to the League, however, Ulsterman 'Honest' John McKenna soon became the most influential figure. Later McKenna would become chairman from 1909 and Football League president from 1910 until he died in 1936.

W.E. Barclay was secretary-manager from 1892–96, an eventful period in winning successive Lancashire League and Second Division championships, then suffering relegation and immediately winning the title again to return to the top division for a longer (eight-year) spell. By 1896, when Tom Watson took over, Liverpool had also turned out for the first time in the municipal colours of red and white shirts, ending the odd (to modern eyes and sensibilities) four-year period of Everton playing in red and Liverpool in blue.

As Everton were First Division runners-up in 1894/95 and Liverpool bottom, it was hardly surprising that the Toffees had the better of the first two derby league games; or that they attracted what for the time were huge crowds. In a season when average attendances for the division were 7,500 there were reckoned to be up to 44,000, the highest-ever crowd for any Football League game, at Goodison on 13 October 1894 to see the home side win 3-0.

Gate receipts were also a league record of more than £1,026, and 'to the credit of the huge crowd, be it said, they behaved admirably', declared a front-page report in *Athletic News*. 'The players did not allow the excitement to get the upper hand of them, and bad cases of fouls were singularly few.'

The accompanying league table showed Everton on top with a 100 per cent record from eight games but their neighbours in the bottom three without a win.

Liverpool finally beat Stoke a week later for their only victory in the first 17 matches, including a 2-2 draw in the return derby thanks to a last-minute penalty by Jimmy Ross, watched by a best-of-season estimate of 27,000. Successive wins by 5-0 and 5-1 against Nottingham Forest and Derby offered hope of avoiding relegation but taking only one point from the last three matches meant finishing bottom in a tight finish, in which six other clubs were within three points of them.

This time a test match against Lancashire opposition brought a crucial defeat, Bury winning 1-0 despite having their goalkeeper sent off, to replace them in the top flight.

Liverpool's response was to send for more Scots, who helped take them to another play-off 12 months later, after storming to the Second Division title again with 106 goals in 30 games. It included the club's record league win, 10-1 against Rotherham, George Allan scoring four of them on his way to becoming the division's leading scorer with 25 in only 20 games.

He added three more goals in the four test matches required this time, after which Liverpool replaced Small Heath in the higher division and West Bromwich Albion stayed up in place of Manchester City.

At last the Anfield side managed to establish themselves in the top division, not as huge scorers but with a strong defence. They finished fifth, ahead of Everton for the first time, and reached a first FA Cup semi-final, losing 3-0 to Aston Villa.

Two years later they were in contention for the Double itself. An FA Cup semi-final against Sheffield United went to four games in March, the third of them abandoned with Liverpool ahead, only for the Blades to finish the sharper and go through to win the final. In the league the Reds, as they now were, achieved a first double over Everton, 2-1 and 2-0, and went into the final game needing to win away to Villa to pip the midlands club to the title. A 12th game in 43 days proved a catastrophic one, however; 5-0 down at half-time, the visitors were grateful just to suffer no further damage in the second half. Villa therefore pipped them by two points. Liverpool would not have to wait long for that first championship amid more ups and downs.

* * * * *

When Liverpool first joined the Football League in 1893 the club they replaced was neighbouring **Bootle**, who then disappeared altogether. Being passed over for Everton as the city's representatives for the initial Football League season was a body blow, and although they were among those admitted to the new Second Division in 1892, Everton establishing themselves even closer to home at Goodison that year as the best-supported club in the country proved fatal.

Like Blackburn Olympic, Newton Heath, South Shore and Witton (Blackburn), Bootle joined the new, badly organised Combination in the summer of 1888 and found more satisfaction from playing friendly matches in which they attempted to show themselves hard done by in missing out on the Football League.

What became a regular Boxing Day derby against Everton ended 0-0 at Anfield, and the return in March was a rough-house 3-3 draw. Stoke City, bottom of the First Division, were beaten 3-0 on Good Friday and Preston's newly crowned Invincibles were pushed hard in a 4-3 defeat.

In the Football Alliance the following season, with proper organisation and regular fixtures, Bootle made their case by finishing runners-up to The Wednesday, who they beat 4-1, as well as reaching the FA Cup quarter-final. Yet a gap to the very best had clearly developed. Everton, Division One runners-up who had taken one of Bootle's best players in future England centre-half Johnny Holt, beat them 3-0 on Boxing Day and 5-0 in the Liverpool Cup Final; Blackburn knocked them out of the FA Cup 7-0 and went on to win it.

From then on it was mostly downhill. Oddly, The Wednesday and Bootle went from being the top two in the Alliance one season to the bottom two the next. Everton knocked their neighbours out of the Lancashire Cup and beat them in the Liverpool Cup Final. The season after, 1891/92, saw Bootle in the bottom four after being bottom but one with two games to play. There were unfortunate scenes too after Darwen won an FA Cup tie that home supporters felt should have been postponed: referee John Lewis was pelted with snowballs and a Darwen player was attacked.

Bootle were nevertheless among those clubs who ascended from the Alliance to help make up the new 12-team Football League Second Division for 1892/93, along with new adversaries like Northwich Victoria, Burslem Port Vale and Sheffield United. It should have been their big chance, but Everton's dominance locally, together with the emergence of Liverpool at Anfield, took a further toll on what was becoming poor support .

Beginning with a 7-0 away defeat by Ardwick, they won the first home game 2-0 against Sheffield United but by the time of the return at Bramall Lane at the end of November, an 8-3 defeat, they were bottom of the table. Hopes of some money from an FA Cup run were ended with an early defeat by Liverpool Caledonians and despite an improvement in league form, crowds were down to 1,000. An even smaller one watched lowly Walsall Town Swifts beaten 7-1 at Hawthorne Road.

The last league game of the season did prove another small triumph: playing Lincoln City on 15 April with the losers in danger of having to apply for re-election as one of the bottom four. Bootle won 4-1, and Lincoln losing to Ardwick two days later confirmed they would finish below the Merseysiders, who ended up eighth out of 12 – but not knowing they would never play league football again. A Lancashire Cup semi-final meanwhile was lost 6-4 to Preston.

A fourth meeting against Liverpool in a friendly match on 29 April ended 2-2 in appropriately downbeat fashion, the *Liverpool Echo* recording, 'The last meeting for the season of the Bootle and Liverpool [teams] was but poorly patronised, Goodison Park proving too strong an attraction for the usual followers of the respective clubs.'

An end-of-season meeting of shareholders heard that the recent share issue had not been as successful as hoped and that Everton's move closer to them at Goodison had worsened the financial predicament. Expenditure for the season was £600 more than income and another £400 was owed. The club went into liquidation and followed Accrington as the first clubs ever to resign from the Football League.

* * * * *

The 1890s was the decade in which Merseyside and Manchester became simultaneously more closely linked and more bitter rivals, in both economic and sporting terms. On New Year's Day 1894, the £15m Manchester Ship Canal, 'the Big Ditch', was used for the first time after seven years of construction, leading to bitterly resented job losses in Liverpool as it bypassed their docks and tariffs. Four months later Queen Victoria officially opened it, on the same day that Ardwick were re-elected to the Football League as Manchester City; and in-between times, on 28 April, Liverpool met Manchester United's predecessors Newton Heath for the first time. No gentle friendly either; it was a crucial promotion/relegation test match.

Although not quite ready for the Football League in 1888, **Newton Heath** were a coming club, professionals for the past three years, with a group of patrons that included such members of the great and good as C.P. Scott, editor of the *Manchester Guardian*, and various local MPs whose ranks he would soon join. As previously mentioned, they recruited heavily in Wales and in 1888 had five members of the Welsh side that played Scotland in Edinburgh.

In the year before the Football League's foundation, the Heathens beat teams of the quality of Aston Villa and Nottingham Forest, then began the following season with wins in friendlies against League members Bolton and Blackburn. As frustrated as anyone by the failings of the Combination in 1888/89, they received a single vote when applying to join the Football League that summer and had to settle for the Football Alliance the following season as one of only three Lancashire clubs, with Darwen and Bootle.

Sunderland Albion were beaten 4-1 in the opening game in September in front of a modest 3,000 crowd at North Road, but Newton Heath finished only eighth of 12 clubs, and the following season were ninth, and second-lowest scorers.

The 1891/92 campaign brought a notable improvement that paved the way to the Football League, as Alliance runners-up to Nottingham Forest and top scorers. There were derbies too with the club who would soon beat them by eight years (1894 against 1902) in adopting the name of their city. For now, it was Newton Heath against Ardwick, the former confirming that they were a few steps ahead by taking three points from the Alliance encounters (3-1, 2-2) and winning an FA Cup first qualifying round tie 5-1.

Briefly linked, the pair parted ways again: having finished second, the Heathens accompanied Forest straight into the expanded Football League First Division, while Ardwick, who had been eighth, took part in the new Second Division.

The Heathens found it a big jump and were bottom of the heap for two successive seasons. The first game, away to the mighty Blackburn Rovers on 3 September 1892 brought a creditable 4-3 defeat, centre-forward Bob Donaldson scoring their first league goal when 3-0 down. Top scorer with 16, he was clearly made of sturdy stuff: in early October a training session included the unlikely exercise of hammer throwing and centre-half William Stewart, his sense of direction awry, hit Donaldson a fearful blow 'causing the unfortunate player to fall down insensible'.

He had recovered less than ten days later for the visit of Wolves, who were shocked not only by the state of the sodden pitch but by a 10-1 defeat (still a league record for both clubs), with hat-tricks for Donaldson and Stewart, which offered unrealised hope for the rest of the inaugural league season.

The North Road pitch was generally very poor, hard in some places, with thick mud in others. Nor were facilities quite Football League standard, with the local pub or hotel used for changing rooms, although a stand housing 1,000 spectators had been erected in 1891. The most attractive opposition would lead to five-figure crowds, a record being set when 15,000 turned up for a heavy defeat by the champions-elect Sunderland.

The Wolves result was all the more extraordinary for being the team's only win in the first ten games, leaving them bottom of the table, where they stayed until the finish, five points behind Accrington and condemned to the play-off test match on neutral ground. That brought a reprieve against Second Division winners Small Heath of Birmingham, 5-2 after a 1-1 draw. Notts County and Accrington, despite finishing well clear of the Manchester side, were relegated instead.

The first Football League season produced a tiny profit of £18 but a continuing debt of £314. It was not a promising position with which to vacate North Road for the neighbouring district of Clayton, formerly part of Droylsden, and not far from City's current Etihad Stadium. Downwind of the chemical works in Bank Street, Clayton had, it might be said, an atmosphere of its own. A disgruntled journalist once wrote that the reason for a goalless draw against Burnley was that the goalposts were 'so tainted with smoke as to be hardly discernible'.

Burnley it was who had provided the opposition on a more memorable occasion for the opening of the new ground at the start of the 1893/94 season. They went away beaten 3-2 in front of an estimated 10,000 crowd. But hopes of a new dawn proved unfounded.

Before Blackburn were beaten 5-1 in March (revenge for a 5-1 FA Cup defeat, all the goals coming in the first half) there was an alarming run of 14 defeats in 15 games which took the Heathens to the bottom of the table once more, with Darwen, Preston and Bolton just above them in an unhappy campaign for the north-west. This time there was no reprieve; in the test match, rivalry with Liverpool began in earnest with the first competitive meeting to see which of them would play in the top division the following season. The Merseyside club won 2-0 at Ewood Park, sealing Newton Heath's relegation along with Darwen. 'Liverpool deserved their victory, showing greater smartness all round and a far superior combination,' reported Scott's *Manchester Guardian* with no hint of bias.

An inglorious season, in which away form was shocking (one win and 14 defeats), also included first round defeats in both local cups by Everton (7-1) and Bolton.

There was an off-field sensation when the club sued journalist William Jephcott for libel. Writing as 'Observer' in the *Birmingham Daily Gazette,* the experienced midlands reporter had accused Newton Heath of 'brutality' and two of their players of deliberately kicking opponents in the 4-1 win at home to West Bromwich Albion on 14 October.

The Heathens secretary was able to present as evidence a letter from the referee, who said that in 14 years of officiating 'never have I had a pleasanter afternoon' and that the reporter was guilty of 'abominable scurrility' and 'gross partisanship'.

At the hearing in Manchester the judge found for Newton Heath but awarded damages of merely one farthing, swayed as he was by the defence solicitor's ingenious argument that far from affecting the club's business, 'the report was calculated not to keep spectators away but to attract them'. Heavy legal fees, however, contributed to a loss over the season of almost £600; and at the AGM the club president, echoing football directors down the years, lamented that they had 'lost large sums of money on players who had not been of the least use to them'.

Those players who remained, useless or not, found the Second Division easier to cope with. Walsall Town Swifts, beaten 14-0 in March, protested successfully about the state of a waterlogged pitch – and lost the rematch 9-0. Relegation also meant being reunited with the rivals now known as Manchester City, the first Football League derby taking place at City's Hyde Road ground on 3 November 1894.

There were 14,000 there to see a 5-2 win for Newton Heath, four of their goals being scored by inside-left Dick Smith, while the great Billy Meredith claimed both of City's on his home debut. The Heathens continued to have the better of derby meetings thereafter: of the ten league encounters before the end of the century, City won only two.

Further meetings with Liverpool were rarer, coming only in the Second Division season of 1895/96, when the Merseyside club won 7-1 at Anfield but lost the return in Manchester 5-2 with a hat-trick for Jack Peters.

For the rest of the decade Newton Heath struggled in vain to return to the top tier, despite often being in contention. Third, sixth and second, they twice lost out in test matches and were then fourth in three successive seasons from 1898–1900. Cup football was generally disappointing, but brought a run through five FA Cup rounds in 1897 before losing 2-0 to Derby County, and then a first success in the Lancashire Cup, beating Blackburn in the 1898 final.

Crowds, which could be as low as 4,000, peaked at 20,000 for a visit from City in what *The Umpire* newspaper called 'the Championship of Cottonopolis'. Scottish forward Joe Cassidy became the first Heathen to reach 100 goals for the club (in 174 games). But it was the enemy who beat them back into the top division.

* * * * *

If Newton Heath's ground left much to be desired, the Hyde Road enclosure **Ardwick** developed next to an engineering works in 1887 was equally unglamorous. 'When you went to the ground, you felt you were going along some subterranean passage to an enclosure that precluded enlargement and kept you under confinement willy-nilly,' recounted the LFA's official history.

Like their neighbours, however, they were a progressive club. A transfer spree in 1890 funded by benefactor John Allison extended to the England international Davie Weir as one of several recruits from Bolton, but went too far later that year when the club were found guilty of poaching a Burnley player and were briefly banned from meeting Football League teams they hoped to join.

That year too they entered the FA Cup for the first time, demolishing Liverpool Stanley 12-0 and then scratching from the tie against Halliwell to play a friendly with Higher Walton instead. As one news agency report pointed out, 'I suppose they know their own business but I may tell them that the best way for an unknown Club to gain prominence is to make a bold bid for the English Cup.' That word 'unknown' would have hurt; the season nevertheless brought a major landmark in winning the Manchester Cup, beating holders and neighbours Newton Heath 1-0 with a goal by the aforementioned Weir.

Fired by success and ambition, they applied for the first time to join the Football League, being increased from 12 clubs to 14, and missed out to Darwen and Stoke but secured the next-highest number of votes.

Having never belonged to any league was remedied with a place in the Alliance competition for 1891/92, where the only other Manchester team were Newton Heath. Averaging almost 7,000 crowds, Ardwick finished seventh of the 12 clubs and shaped up well against a number of Football League teams, defeating Bolton 4-1 to retain the Manchester Cup.

Come the expansion of the Football League from 14 clubs to 28 in 1892 by a merger with the Alliance, Ardwick joined the Heathens for a single season before the latter's promotion. Beginning with a 7-0 win over Bootle on 3 September 1892, they won five of the first six games but faltered in the second half of the season and finished fifth. The following season was dismal with 13th place out of 15 and a first-round exit from all three cup competitions; a 10-2 league defeat at Small Heath in March remains the club's worst (not the 9-1 loss at Everton in 1906 often quoted).

In 1894, with Manchester's prestige and prosperity greatly enhanced by the opening of the Ship Canal, Ardwick took advantage by adopting the city's name. Newton Heath, it seemed, had the same idea but Manchester FC (the rugby club) protested and the Heathens waited until the new century.

Their relegation that same year meant the two clubs were reunited, with the newly christened City, playing for the first time in plain light blue shirts, having the worst of things in finishing half a dozen places below them after the two derby defeats. 'Typical City' it might be said in retrospect; they were the division's highest scorers with 82 in 30 games, including a record win by 11-3 against Lincoln City, but conceded 72 and therefore finished in the bottom half of the table.

Billy Meredith, the 'Welsh Wizard', offered a hint of what was to come by scoring a dozen goals from the wing in the 18 league games of his first season since joining from Northwich Victoria. Born in Chirk, North Wales, to a family of strict Methodists, William Henry Meredith was working in the mines at 12 but was one of those lucky few who found a way out through football. Not the only one in his family either: older brother and fellow Welsh international Sam played for Stoke City.

With Chirk he appeared on the right wing in two Welsh Cup finals while having a dozen games for the struggling Northwich Victoria during their final season of league football 1893/94 when they finished bottom of the Second Division, two places behind the lowly Ardwick.

Bolton might have signed him but City did and threw him in for two eventful first matches; a 5-4 defeat at Newcastle where his crosses produced two goals and the 5-2 home defeat in the derby. It was evident that the club had acquired a character as well as a talent, noted for his slightly bandy legs and habit of sucking on a toothpick. Top scorer for three of the next four seasons, he never failed to reach double figures, always being prepared to come inside and shoot or meet a cross from the left. He mocked those wingers who 'require to shake hands with the corner flag before centring'.

In 1895, only a few months after signing professional with City, he won his first Welsh caps against Ireland and England

and inspired City to their best league performance to date as runners-up to Liverpool on goal average after 30,000 saw a 1-1 draw between them on Good Friday; but City missed out in the two-legged test matches, with heavy away defeats in the midlands by West Bromwich (6-1) and Small Heath again (8-0).

They had to wait until 1899 for promotion as champions, Meredith playing his full part in a season that he began with a hat-trick against Grimsby (7-2) and finished with a remarkable 29 in 33 games from outside-right. No frustration in test matches either; it was the first season of automatic promotion after Burnley contributed to the demise of play-offs with their bore war against Stoke. City, scoring 92 goals, were clearly the best team in the division even if Newton Heath in fourth place inflicted one of their five defeats. So it was City who would lead Manchester's challenge to Merseyside at the turn of the century.

* * * * *

For several years from 1894, both clubs nevertheless found themselves challenged, if not eclipsed, by an unexpected force from the north of their city. **Bury** were one of those who seemed to move almost effortlessly onward and upward from the start, in their case achieving league football within nine years and winning the FA Cup in 15.

After four years of friendlies they joined the new Lancashire League, finished runners-up to Higher Walton from Preston and were champions the following season.

Early winners of the Lancashire Junior Cup (1891), they graduated to the Senior Cup and in 1892 won that too, beating Newton Heath, Everton and Accrington, then Blackburn 2-0 in the final. It was during this cup run that the longstanding nickname began, when chairman J.T. Ingham said of the team's ability to beat another supposedly stronger opponent, 'We shall shake 'em, in fact, we are the Shakers.'

Cautiously deciding against applying to the Football League that year, when Ardwick and Newton Heath were accepted, they waited two more years. Weekly wages were a modest £12 in total but opponents were indeed shaken, and the Bury public stirred; in five years in the Lancashire League they were champions twice, runners-up twice and third once. Beating Southport and Stockport in the 1892/93 FA Cup by a combined aggregate of 17-1, they did, however, make a costly miscalculation in paying Rossendale £80 to switch the venue of their next tie to Gigg Lane – where they were shaken to lose 7-1.

The same season a record attendance of 14,700 came to the county cup tie against Bolton, leading to punishment by the LFA after the crowd encroached on to the pitch. The match had to be replayed at Bolton.

A year later they decided the time was right and were duly welcomed into the Football League Second Division with joint-top vote as one of four new sides, while Accrington (attempting to return), Blackpool and Rossendale failed to make it.

Results were stunning, right from the first game: on 1 Sept 1894 against the new Manchester City, captain Billy Barbour got the first league goal and Bury went on to win 4-2. Remaining unbeaten at home helped them become champions at the first attempt and in the test match at Blackburn they beat Liverpool 1-0 despite having goalkeeper Archie Montgomery sent off for retaliation quarter of an hour from the end.

In the top division they recovered from a bad start of four successive defeats to end up a comfortable 11th of 16, beating Blackburn home and away and the following season were ninth, only six points behind runners-up Sheffield United.

Bolton had become their fiercest local rivals and figured with them in the dramatic end to the 1897/98 season. Bottom with six games to play, Bury seemed doomed but they lost only one of those matches and on the final day beat Bolton 1-0 to avoid the last season of relegation test matches despite being one of five teams locked together on 24 points.

Wanderers had also knocked them out of the FA Cup in successive seasons, meaning the Shakers had never gone beyond the third round until the famous campaign of 1899/1900 that ended in the final at Crystal Palace. In the league they were a mere 12th with a single away win but cup victories over three First Division sides, Burnley, Notts County and Sheffield United, took them further than ever before.

The semi-finals paired the two Southern League sides, Southampton and Millwall, which left Bury to take on Nottingham Forest, who were just above them in mid-table. After a 1-1 draw at

Stoke's Victoria Ground, extra time was required at Bramall Lane before Bury edged through 3-2.

Southampton also needed a replay before being confirmed as the first southern club in the final since Old Etonians 17 years earlier. Although Woolwich Arsenal and Luton Town were the only southern clubs in the Football League, the Southern League was becoming a strong competition and many of its players were better paid than those in the League, who were shortly to be capped at £4 a week. The Saints, champions six times in eight seasons around this time, had further proved their worth by knocking out three First Division clubs, Everton, Newcastle (4-1) and West Bromwich, and had six internationals to Bury's two, left-wing pair Charlie Sagar and Jack Plant.

They had the majority of support too among the 68,945 crowd on a sweltering London day but started so badly with the sun in their eyes that Bury ran up a 3-0 lead in the first 23 minutes with goals by Jasper McLuckie (2) and Willie Wood. An expected Southampton revival did not materialise and ten minutes from the end Plant's goal completed a handsome victory. The following year Tottenham would win the Cup for the Southern League, but there was more to come from Bury.

1900 FA Cup Final: Bury 4 Southampton 0
Bury: Thompson; Darroch, Davidson, Pray, Leeming, Ross, Richards, W. Wood, McLuckie, Sagar, Plant.
Southampton: Robinson; Meechan, Durber, Meston, Chadwick, Petrie, Turner, Yates, Farrell, H. Wood, Milward.

* * * * *

Mirroring much of Bury's progress, albeit in less spectacular fashion, **Blackpool** were yet another club with a church background of sorts. They were formed in 1887 after a dispute among players who had joined together from Victoria FC and St John's to form Blackpool St John's. Those wishing to keep an affiliation with the church instead of playing for the new Blackpool FC initially stayed behind, though most joined later.

Playing at the Raikes Hall Gardens within the Pleasure Grounds complex, which benefited attendances, they won both the Fylde Cup and the Lancashire Junior Cup in their first season, the latter despite having protested that Deepdale, Preston was hardly a neutral venue for the final against Preston St Joseph's.

Like Bury, they played in the inaugural Lancashire League season of 1889/90, finishing fifth, and were runners-up to Bury (twice) and Liverpool in the following three years before taking the title themselves in 1894.

In 1891 they had entered the FA Cup and played a series of eventful ties that began with a 5-4 win away to Higher Walton in a qualifying round and continued against Fleetwood Rangers (4-2), Bury (3-3, 4-3) and Newton Heath (4-3). Sheffield United brought the run to an end in the first round proper (3-0) and knocked them out the following season too.

Older local rivals **South Shore** had been FA Cup entrants since 1882 and reached the quarter-final in 1885/86 but lost ground by declining to play league football until joining the Lancashire League in 1891. They were responsible in 1889/90 for a historic change in FA Cup rules after being drawn away to Chatham, who played in an open field, charging no gate money. The FA agreed with South Shore that in those circumstances home advantage should be given up.

Unlike Blackpool they were in the lower half every season and a merger seemed an increasingly sensible idea. Agreement was reached that the clubs would combine if Blackpool were successful with their application to the Football League in 1896 but although they duly topped the vote and joined the Second Division, South Shore unexpectedly had a change of heart and continued as a separate entity in the Lancashire League.

Blackpool made their Football League bow on 5 September 1896 after a long and fraught journey to play away to Lincoln City, where they lost 3-1 in dreadful conditions. A poor away record, winning only at Darwen and Small Heath, handicapped them but losing only once at home (also to Small Heath) meant finishing a respectable eighth.

In the second season they dropped to 11th and 12 months later not only ended in the bottom three but missed out on re-election by two votes. It may be that long railway trips to the Fylde coast counted against them, although clubs seemed happy to go as far as the north-east, with Newcastle having been Football League members since 1893 and Middlesbrough now joining them.

Back in the Lancashire League, the merger did now take place with struggling South Shore, many of whose players joined them, and exile lasted only one season. Loughborough, in the bottom four for all four of their Football League seasons, had a catastrophic campaign with one win and 100 goals conceded, Luton did not apply for re-election and Blackpool and Stockport County were voted in for the new century.

* * * * *

In New Brighton a local tower was built as an attraction to rival Blackpool's and although the football club founded in 1896 to help fill the huge Tower Athletic Ground in winter made the Football League in no time at all, they lasted only three seasons there.

New Brighton Tower won the Lancashire League almost immediately and on the back of an honourable 2-0 FA Cup defeat away to West Bromwich Albion in January 1898 they were elected to the expanded Second Division later that year.

Finishing fifth, only three points behind second-placed Glossop North End, was a fine effort. In the second season they dropped to tenth but despite fourth place in 1900/01, gates were poor and shortly before the next season it was decided they could not continue.

The record attendance was 10,000 for the visit of champions-elect Manchester City in that first Football League season but crowds of 2,000 for the first and last-ever fixtures better reflected the lack of support. It would be 1923 before league football returned to New Brighton, with a completely new club.

* * * * *

The game itself was slowly modernising, with such innovations as goal nets, penalty kicks, referees and linesmen instead of umpires, while the passing game superseded constant dribbling.

Attempts at financial rationalisation by officials worried about the cost of professional football led in 1891 to such measures as signing-on fees being limited to £10 in order to reduce the number of moves. Derby County soon proposed a maximum wage of £4 a week (£450 at present-day values), which was less than half what some of the best players were believed to be earning by the beginning of the new century when it was finally introduced. The first, short-lived players' trade union, the Association Footballers' Union, was founded in 1898 to fight it.

By that time average attendances in the top division of the Football League had risen from about 4,500 in the first season to 9,500. As we have seen, however, clubs like Accrington, Bootle and Darwen struggled financially even after achieving league status. Failure to get that far was a blow from which others like Birmingham St George's (denied membership of the new Second Division and wound up in 1892) and Halliwell never recovered.

Formed in 1877 a couple of miles north-west of Bolton, **Halliwell** entered the FA Cup for ten years from 1882/83, suffering a crushing 12-0 defeat by Sheffield Wednesday on the last occasion they reached the first round proper (January 1891). That year they were one of the clubs who started the Lancashire Combination when the Lancashire League refused to take the reserve teams of Football League clubs like Blackburn, Bolton and Preston (the two competitions would eventually make their peace and combine in 1903).

Hindley, Liverpool Stanley, North Meols, Royton and Skelmersdale United joined them but Halliwell, in their only attempt at senior league football, failed to finish the campaign, which was won (and retained in the following two seasons) by Blackburn's reserves.

The following season they lost an FA Cup qualifying round game 4-0 to Stockport County, successfully protested, but lost the replay 4-2 after extra time.

In early November, clearly in financial trouble, they played a friendly at Goodison Park against an Everton XI designed to provide some funds. Unfortunately, the *Manchester Courier* reported, 'There was only a small attendance of spectators.' A separate **Halliwell Rovers** club emerged in the 1894/95 season and played for four seasons in the Lancashire League but had disappeared within five years.

For the majority, however, the Football League had been a resounding success. If baseball in the United States led the way in professionalism (1869) and league competition (1876), McGregor's triumph encouraged the formation of leagues in, for instance, Scotland and Ireland within two years, as well as cricket's County Championship (organised on the same lines from 1890) and local leagues in Lancashire, plus the Lancashire and Yorkshire Rugby Leagues (1895).

From 12 clubs in 1888, the world's first football league had grown to 28 in only five years, with the advent of the Second Division. Stockport County and Oldham Athletic were next in line and 21 years into the new century the number of divisions would double, giving new opportunities to Accrington Stanley, Rochdale, Southport, Nelson, Tranmere Rovers and Wigan Borough as well as three dozen others from Ashington to Aberdare and Newport to Norwich.

As McGregor claimed in 1905, 'No principle ever formulated in connection with sport has caused so much really genuine, bona-fide competition as the league system.'

Chapter 3

Trophies and scandal (1901–19)

Lancashire to the fore; Liverpool down and up in Merseyside's first double; 'football's innocence destroyed' by the fix with Man United; players' union revived in Manchester; City's own scandal and Meredith's move across town; manager Mangnall's move the other way; Bob Crompton's defiant Blackburn champions at last; Bolton's yo-yoing; Burnley's FA Cup; greatest years of cup winners Bury and First Division runners-up Oldham; hard times and war time.

IN the first 15 years of the new century, until the Football League ceased operations for more important matters – belatedly many felt – Lancashire continued to exert a formidable influence both on and off the field. Liverpool (twice), Manchester United (twice), Blackburn Rovers (twice) and Everton all won the championship, and six times the FA Cup came back to the north-west; in the 1911/12 season the county had almost half of the top division's 20 clubs and in the final campaign three years later, with the First World War well under way, the top five in the First Division table were Everton, Oldham, Blackburn, Burnley and Manchester City.

Football League headquarters moved to the area in 1902 under a succession of Lancashire officials (and have remained there ever since), while Manchester was heavily involved in creating a revived players' union; as well as featuring in two of the era's principal scandals, caused in large part by the introduction of a maximum wage that remained unchanged from 1904 to 1920. Liverpool opposed it on the grounds that it would lead to illegal payments and they were proved quite correct.

Despite the occasional financial struggles of individual clubs, hardly unknown in any era, the Football League was considered to have been such a success that many more wanted a part of it. The original 12 from 1888 had grown to 40 in less than 20 years and would have been swollen further had existing members not voted against accepting the Southern League as a Third Division in 1909; a proposal understandably resented in the north of England. That would not come about until 1920 and a majority of aspiring northern clubs like Nelson, Rochdale, Southport, Tranmere Rovers and Wigan Borough would have to wait a further year, although Stockport County (1900) and Oldham Athletic (1907) were among those voted in earlier.

Meanwhile Manchester United secretary Ernest Mangnall helped organise the Central League, first won in 1911/12 by Lincoln City, then the reserve teams of United and Everton. Fortunately, United were less successful when they and Liverpool put forward a proposal that would have destroyed much of the colour of English football: that every home team should wear red shirts and every away team white.

* * * * *

The first full decade of **Everton-Liverpool** rivalry was one in which derby success tended to go to the former, who had a healthy record of finishing above their neighbours across the park. Yet the titles – in 1901 and 1906 – went to their rivals, despite the Blues taking three points out of four from them each time while finishing only seventh and 11th respectively. It was only in 1915, with the war begun but league football not over that they finally got their hands on the trophy again, 24 years from the previous triumph.

From September 1899 Liverpool did not win any of the 14 league derbies until October 1907. Yet in an extraordinary period they won two First Division championships in five years and suffered relegation in-between times.

In 1900/01 it all came down to the final game. Defeat at home to Everton in January was Liverpool's seventh already, yet in winning away to Sunderland, who would finish runners-up, the Reds began a run of nine victories and three draws in the remaining 12 games. Home crowds having risen to 20,000, there were only a fifth of that number to see them clinch the title with a 1-0 win at bottom club West Bromwich in April, inside-right John Walker getting the winner.

It was a time of modest goalscoring. Liverpool's 59 from the 34 matches was the First Division's best, centre-forward Sam Raybould's 16 leading their list. The following season brought the first FA Cup meeting between the Merseyside clubs, in which Liverpool, beaten 4-0 at Goodison a fortnight earlier, won 2-0 there in the first round replay, after a 2-2 draw at Anfield. The league defeat illustrated, however, what a poor fist they were making of defending their title. They lost 11 matches in all and finished only 11th while Everton came close to inheriting the title, finishing runners-up to Sunderland.

Liverpool had the edge in finishing fifth in 1903 on the back of 31 goals from Raybould but when he missed much of the following season and a number of players defected to the better-paid Southern League, catastrophe and relegation resulted, a 5-2 thumping at Goodison in April helping them on their way.

Once again the stay down below lasted only a single season, a triumphant one of 93 goals and a thrilling one on Merseyside as Everton came close to the Double. They knocked out Liverpool on the way to the FA Cup semi-final only to be edged out in a replay by eventual winners Aston Villa. Then, leading the league, they suffered successive Easter defeats by Manchester City and Woolwich Arsenal and lost out to champions Newcastle by two points.

In 1906 came a Merseyside double of a different sort; the league and FA Cup, but to different clubs. Liverpool, after previously winning the Second Division in 1894 had immediately been relegated; now they went to the other extreme, recovering from losing their first three games to storm to the title as Joe Hewitt provided the goalscoring support to Raybould and inside-forward Bob Robinson.

A Merseyside FA Cup final would have made it the most memorable of seasons but having both reached the last four the teams were drawn together at Villa Park. After a tight first half an unfortunate own goal by Liverpool's right-back Billy Dunlop, deflecting in a shot from distance, unlocked the game and within a minute little winger Harold Hardman scored the second. As the *Birmingham Daily Gazette* correctly pointed out, Liverpool, missing the injured Raybould, 'for some reason or other rarely do themselves justice when meeting their near neighbours'.

Hardman was a solicitor who played as an amateur, winning an Olympic gold medal in 1908, and later served as a Manchester United director and chairman for many years. Now he had the chance to become one of few amateurs in the 20th century to earn an FA Cup winner's medal. Standing in the way were Newcastle United, one of the era's great teams with their eventual record of three league titles and five cup finals from 1905–11.

Out of contention in the league, both clubs suffered a £50 fine for playing a weakened team in the run-up to the Crystal Palace final, where 75,609 saw a disappointing game between two of the country's most attractive sides.

Everton's Alex 'Sandy' Young, a Scot like his famous 1960s namesake, had a goal disallowed but then scored a legitimate winner from a pass by Jack Sharp, who with Harry Makepeace was one of two dual football-cricket internationals in the side.

FA Cup Final 1906: Everton 1 Newcastle United 0
Everton: Scott; Crelley, W. Balmer, Makepeace, Taylor, Abbott, Sharp, Bolton, Young, Settle, Hardman.
Newcastle: Lawrence; McCombie, Carr, Gardner, Aitken, McWilliam, Rutherford, Howie, Orr, Veith, Gosnell.

The following year Everton, third in the First Division, were up for the cup once more, against underdogs The Wednesday, with Bob Balmer joining brother Walter at full-back as their only change. Again the match was undistinguished – 'one of the poorest finals' said Football League founder McGregor – but this time Everton were on the wrong end of the result, the Yorkshire side running out 2-1 winners in the last minute after Sharp had equalised just before the interval.

Cup glory was of the reflected sort three years later, when Goodison Park, the best ground in the country with its two new stands and near-70,000 capacity, was chosen to stage the replay of the 1910 final in which Newcastle won at last, beating Barnsley. Everton, meanwhile, were taking the name of the club far afield, playing in eastern Europe in 1905 and South America in 1909, where one of Chile's most successful clubs was immediately founded and named after them.

Liverpool made an even worse fist of their title defence in 1906/07 than they had five years earlier, slipping to 15th and from then until the start of the war they were twice close to relegation. Brighter periods were an unexpected second place in 1910, when Jack Parkinson hit two of his 30 goals in an astonishing 6-5 win at home to champions Newcastle after being 5-2 down at half-time; and then a first FA Cup final four years later. A series of favourable ties with Second Division and Southern League opposition led to a more impressive semi-final victory over league runners-up Aston Villa at White Hart Lane, but there was a 1-0 defeat in the final, perhaps unluckily, by mid-table Burnley.

In that season Everton, who had been runners-up in 1909 (to Newcastle) and 1912 (to Blackburn), sank unusually low, only one place above their neighbours in 15th but for the final campaign before the Football League paused for war they revived spectacularly to take a first title since 1891.

Two months after war had been declared, 32,000 watched a 5-0 win at Anfield in early October (still their biggest derby success there) which got them going and included a hat-trick by the prolific Bobby Parker, signed a year earlier from Rangers. He went on to finish with 36 goals in 35 games as the title was secured by a point from Oldham Athletic, who were favourites until the penultimate week. It came a month after the Blues had lost the FA Cup semi-final to Chelsea.

As the championship was celebrated on one side of Stanley Park, however, a scandal was brewing on the other that would lead one Manchester newspaper to declare, 'Football's innocence is destroyed – perhaps forever.'

* * * * *

Even before the insecurities of war were added to maximum wage restrictions, **Liverpool** players had been subject to an investigation into match-fixing. Near the end of the 1912/13 season the controversial Arsenal chairman Henry Norris accused them of not trying in a 2-1 home defeat by Chelsea, Arsenal's relegation rivals. Although Norris later apologised, the episode was embarrassing for 'Honest' John McKenna, his friend and the Football League president.

The evidence in 1915 was much more serious. Towards the end of the season, Liverpool were comfortable but **Manchester United** were struggling, sitting only just above the London pair Tottenham and Chelsea, who occupied the bottom two places. United knew they faced three away games in a week after the Good Friday visit of Liverpool, in which two goals by George Anderson gave them a surprisingly easy 2-0 victory, in the latter stages of which both sides appeared content with just that result.

Relief at the win did not prevent jeers from a suspicious home crowd of 18,000 as United's Patrick O'Connell – not the regular penalty taker – put a spot-kick well wide and Liverpool's Jackie Sheldon, formerly of United, did the same. Reports soon began surfacing that large amounts had been wagered on just that scoreline. On 24 April, three weeks after the match, as Old Trafford prepared to stage the FA Cup final, a bookmaking firm announced in the press, 'We have solid grounds for believing that a certain First League match played in Manchester during Easter weekend was squared ... Further, we have information that several of the players of both teams invested substantial sums on having the correct score.'

A long inquiry by the Football League and then the FA confirmed it. Eight months later, the FA finally published a damning verdict: not only had several players of each club profited by betting on a 2-0 home win but some had 'persistently refused to tell the truth' about the matter.

Although the committee suspected other players of involvement they found sufficient proof against only seven, not all of whom actually played in the game.

Sheldon, Bob Purcell, Tommy Miller and Tom Fairfoul had all been in the Liverpool side but although Enoch 'Knocker' West was in the United team the clubmates found guilty with him, Sandy Turnbull and Arthur Whalley, had not played. All were banned for life but the two clubs were deemed to be unaware of the fix and escaped any punishment.

As the FA's deliberations were held in private, little detail came out publicly until West unwisely decided to sue for libel. That case was finally heard in July 1917, where his protestations of innocence were ruined by the testimony of Sheldon, who admitted to being the ringleader and agreeing with his old team-mates West, Turnbull and Whalley at a meeting in the Dog and Partridge pub in Manchester that the result would be 2-0, with United scoring once in each half – hence the wild penalty miss before half-time.

Even United's Anderson gave evidence against West, who he said had boasted of winning £70 (14 times his weekly wage) for a bet at odds of 7/1. Liverpool's Fred Pagnam said he had been approached but wanted nothing to do with it and almost ruined the whole plan with a shot that hit the bar to the fury of his team-mates. United's Billy Meredith, knowing nothing of the plot, said he had been suspicious because team-mates kept passing to West instead of him.

West appealed in vain against the verdict and never played again; nor did Turnbull, tragically killed on the western front in 1916. But the other players were given a pardon as part of the Armistice and three of the Liverpool trio plus Whalley played in the next Football League meeting of the clubs on Boxing Day 1919.

There was more dirty linen to be publicly washed. In March 1918, Anderson was sentenced to eight months in prison for conspiracy to defraud by attempting to fix other games. Players from Everton and Oldham said he had offered them money to throw games against Blackpool and Blackburn respectively that year, both of which they won.

Without the two points against Liverpool, it transpired, United would have gone down. They were thus fortunate to keep their First Division place when the Football League resumed in August 1919. Of the bottom two, Chelsea, considered to be main victims of the conspiracy, were reprieved but despite the top division being extended from 20 to 22 clubs, Tottenham were relegated, furious for evermore that greatest rivals Arsenal, having finished only fifth in the Second Division, beat them on a vote for the final place.

* * * * *

It was an unhappy episode for **United**, who had established themselves with two First Division titles and an FA Cup win between 1908–11, and increased the prestige of Manchester football by staging the FA Cup finals of 1911 (a replay) and 1915, when Crystal Palace was requisitioned for war work.

Such prestige and status had seemed a long way off at the start of the century when Newton Heath were a middling Second Division club, who at the end of the 1901/02 season had gates of 2,000, avoided a re-election vote only on goal average and had to be saved from bankruptcy.

At a crucial meeting in April, full-back Harry Stafford, a great early stalwart who had signed from Crewe in 1896, said he not only knew four men who would contribute £500 each but he would do the same. One of them, local brewer John Davies, put in £3,000 to cover debts of £2,670 and pay for new players. A name change was proposed, suggestions including Manchester Central and Manchester Celtic; one of the benefactors, James Brown, successfully put forward Manchester United.

From that day fortunes improved. The first game under the new name and with red shirts replacing the white ones worn since 1896, was a 1-0 win at Gainsborough Trinity on 6 September 1902 and a week later an estimated 15,000 turned out for the first home game to see Burton United beaten by the same score.

New secretary-manager Ernest Mangnall, arriving from Burnley, built on fifth place that season and during his nine years in charge was able to bring the club their first national trophies, before defecting to City. Important new signings with Davies's money included the incomparable centre-half Charlie Roberts, costing £400 from Grimsby Town in April 1904 as a 20-year-old. Forming a formidable half-back line with Dick Duckworth and Sandy Bell, he was a significant reason for the further improvement in successive third-place finishes behind Second Division champions Preston (1904) and Liverpool (1905), followed by promotion at last in 1906.

Runners-up to Bristol City after losing only four games, United were joint-top scorers with 90 goals, 54 of them shared between the inside-forward trio of Scots John Peddie and John Picken on either side of former England centre-forward Charlie Sagar.

Promotion meant being reunited with Manchester City, who had been relegated in 1902 but immediately went back up despite taking only one point from the two derby games. United, however, were able to take massive advantage of the payments scandal involving 17 City players banned from June 1906 to 1 January 1907 (see next section).

Mangnall signed up five of them including, sensationally, the great Billy Meredith himself, whose feelings of injustice encouraged him to become a leading light, along with Roberts and United goalkeeper Herbert Broomfield, of the revived Association Football Players' Union. The original Association Footballers' Union had lasted from only 1898–1901, failing to prevent implementation of the £4 maximum wage, but Manchester now became an important centre for the new organisation, whose first meeting was held at the Imperial Hotel in December 1907.

When the union decided to join the General Federation of Trade Unions, a worried FA ordered members to resign or face the consequences. United players were prominent among those who refused and deadlock in the run-up to the 1909/10 season was only broken at the 11th hour when suspensions were lifted, the union was recognised and bonus payments allowed in addition to the £4 wage.

The more immediate upshot of the City scandal was that on New Year's Day 1907 United gave a debut to four of their former rivals and one of them, Meredith, made the only goal for another, Sandy Turnbull, to beat visiting Aston Villa in front of a crowd of 40,000 – quadrupled from the previous home game.

Thus strengthened, they finished eighth in the top division (City were in the bottom four) and a year later were champions of England for the first time. A stunning start brought 13 wins and 48 goals from the first 14 games and despite oddities like a 7-4 defeat at Liverpool in March, United had effectively sealed the title before easing off and still finishing nine points clear. Turnbull was top scorer with 25 as well as achieving dubious fame as the first player sent off in a Manchester derby after punching City's George Dorsett.

A summer tour to central Europe followed and included a riot at the game against Hungary's Ferencvaros (who would inflict a bitterly disappointing European Fairs Cup semi-final defeat on them almost 60 years later), then a win in the new FA Charity Shield, defeating Southern League champions QPR 4-0 in a replay.

As often happened in that era, defending the league title proved problematical. United started well again but fell away, the derby win over City in January being the only one in 14 league games. The FA Cup proved more successful, although there was an element of good fortune in the quarter-final victory over Burnley, who had led 1-0 when the original game was abandoned amid heavy snow 18 minutes from time.

At the second attempt United won through 3-2, then defeated champions-elect Newcastle in the semi-final at Bramall Lane with a goal by Londoner Harold Halse. From then until the final a month later they played seven league games with conspicuous lack of success, including a 1-0 defeat and goalless draw against cup-final opponents Bristol City.

Turnbull was an injury doubt, having been out for some time, but skipper Charlie Roberts, aware of the team's lack of goals, advised playing him and was rewarded midway through the first half; Halse shot against the bar and Turnbull, unmarked, knocked in the rebound. It proved to be the only goal. Meredith, a cup winner with both Manchester teams in the space of five years, received rave reviews for his performance on the right wing, although, oddly, he would finish the season without a single goal to his name from 38 games.

FA Cup Final 1909: Manchester United 1 Bristol City 0

Manchester United: Moger; Stacey, Hayes, Duckworth, Roberts, Bell, Meredith, Halse, J. Turnbull, S. Turnbull, Wall.
Bristol City: Clay; Annan, Cottle, Hanlin, Wedlock, Spear, Staniforth, Hardy, Gilligan, Burton, Hilton.

Triumphs prompting renewed ambition, the club had already begun to talk again of a move from Clayton and discussed a venue as far away as Trafford Park, Stretford, six miles to the west. Suggestions of a 100,000 capacity had been scaled down to 80,000 and John Davies gave £60,000 towards the fine new stadium, while Manchester Corporation paid one-twelfth of that for the Bank Street ground (now the car park of the Manchester Velodrome).

Old Trafford was ready just over halfway through the following season. On 22 January a mere 7,000 turned up to see Tottenham beaten 5-0 in the final game at Clayton. Four weeks later 45,000 were at the new home, where Liverpool spoilt the celebrations by winning 4-3 after trailing 2-0 and 3-1.

The club had moved from 'the quagmires of Clayton to the springy lawns of Old Trafford', the *Manchester Guardian* said, predicting it would take time to get used to. Any talk of a curse was quickly quashed, however, when they stayed unbeaten there not only for the rest of the season, finishing fifth, but throughout the whole of the following campaign to take a second title in four years – thanks in no small part to Liverpool.

Early on 60,000 came to see City beaten 2-1 with a winning goal by the prolific 'Knocker' West, who had been signed from Nottingham Forest, and when Aston Villa were beaten in the FA Cup in February a new record of 65,101 was set. It looked as if the Villa would have their revenge by taking the title after defeating United 4-2 and sitting top going into the final day. But while third-placed Sunderland were thrashed 5-1 at Old Trafford, Liverpool of all people did United the hugest of favours by beating Villa 3-1.

Mangnall's team then added the Charity Shield in remarkable fashion by beating Southern League champions Swindon Town 8-4, Halse scoring six times. It was the manager's last principal trophy before unexpectedly departing for City after the derby match in September 1912, and the title would be United's last for 41 years.

* * * * *

In the meantime **Manchester City** had been engulfed in a prolonged scandal of their own. Second Division champions in 1899, they were a satisfactory seventh in their first season back in the top division, only to suffer relegation two seasons later as bottom dogs before returning as champions the following year.

Financial problems had been resolved with significant help from the Hulton family of Manchester newspaper proprietors, founders of the *Sporting Chronicle* and *Athletic News*, who made money available for some important signings.

Meredith, of course, had arrived from Northwich Victoria as long ago as 1894 and was now joined by forwards like Sandy Turnbull and Billy Gillespie, who took some of the goalscoring burden. He still scored 22 himself in the Second Division championship season of 1902/03 and a year later was heavily involved in not only the club's greatest season to date but the subsequent disgrace.

An impressive First Division campaign ended as runners-up, three points behind The Wednesday, who City beat in the FA Cup semi-final at Goodison as Turnbull continued his run of scoring in every round.

Second Division Bolton Wanderers were the opponents for the first all-Lancashire final and favourites City were deserved winners by all accounts without being at their best, even if there were strong suspicions of offside against skipper Meredith before he dribbled from the halfway line to score the only goal.

One of Manchester's *Athletic News* correspondents was unable to offer much of an opinion either way; situated imaginatively above the Crystal Palace ground in a balloon that sailed far away, his supposed bird's eye view offered no view at all.

The match was also a unique triumph for the family of secretary-manager Tom Maley, whose brother Willie was in charge of Celtic, Scottish Cup winners a week earlier. But Tom's pride came before a humiliating fall.

FA Cup Final 1904: Manchester City 1 Bolton Wanderers 0
Manchester City: Hillman; McMahon, Burgess, Frost, Hynds, Ashworth, Meredith, Livingstone, Gillespie, Turnbull, Booth.
Bolton Wanderers: Davies; Brown, Struthers, Clifford, Greenhalgh, Freebairn, Stokes, Marsh, Yenson, White, Taylor.

Serious matters off the field became apparent within a few weeks of the cup win. The FA, keen to enforce the new maximum wage and the maximum signing-on fee of £10, had been investigating the ambitious Derbyshire club Glossop, who played in the Football League from 1898–1915, including one season in the top division.

Irregularities in the transfers of two Glossop players to City led to the latter being fined £250 in October, with one of the players suspended for the rest of the season, three City directors banned and one suspended for life.

Worse was to come. Following a crucial away game with Villa on the final day of the 1904/05 season. City, needing a win to have any chance of the title, lost 3-2 (to end up third) in a game that degenerated into violence with Turnbull attacked on the pitch and then in the Villa dressing room.

Another FA investigation followed and came to the most unexpected and sensational conclusion, 'W. Meredith, having offered a sum of money to a player of Aston Villa to let Manchester City win the match ... is suspended from football from 4th August until April 1906.'

After initially denying everything, the Welshman, increasingly upset that City could not and would not pay him during the season-long ban, turned whistle-blower and said he had offered a bribe at the suggestion of manager Maley and with his team-mates' knowledge; additionally he handed the FA details of illegal payments which included his own wage of £6 being 50 per cent more than was permitted.

The club's argument, like Preston's at the time of admitting professionalism, that everyone was doing it, was never likely to appease the governing body, who came down hard. Seventeen players were suspended from June 1906 until the following January, Maley and a former chairman were banned for life, and fines were imposed on City again as well as all 17 players.

Four of those had already joined other clubs. As mentioned in the previous section, five more moved to United including Meredith, who enjoyed a new lease of life in helping them finish above their neighbours for the next seven seasons.

Amid all the uncertainty of the FA's ongoing investigations City did well to finish fifth in the 1905/06 campaign but for the next season Maley's successor Harry Newbould from Derby County had to find half a new team, who lost their second game 9-1 at Everton and finished four from the bottom. They revived remarkably in United's championship season of 1908 and with one extra point would have been runners-up in a Manchester one-two, but another 12 months on slumped to 19th and a cruel relegation on goal average after losing five of the last six games. Dark looks were cast in the direction of Leicester, whose 12-0 defeat at Nottingham Forest after they had been out celebrating a wedding saved their hosts, and Manchester United, whose defeat at Bradford City spared the Yorkshire club, also at City's expense.

As in 1903 they returned at the first time of asking as champions, a crowd of 40,000 watching the derby against runners-up Oldham, but apart from holding their own in a series of low-scoring games with United there was no more success until winning both parts of the first wartime Lancashire Section leagues in 1916. They were helped from early March onwards by the return of Meredith as a guest player, sowing the seeds of a permanent move later.

* * * * *

Despite their defiance in winning the league championship in 1912 and 1914, **Blackburn Rovers**, five times FA Cup winners between 1884 and 1891, risked being eclipsed by Manchester and Merseyside from early in the new century.

In 1902/03 relegation was avoided by four points only after an FA inquiry into a suspicious 3-0 Rovers win at Everton in the penultimate game. Grimsby Town, who finished just beneath them, protested and Rovers secretary Joseph Walmsley was banned for life, although it was accepted that Everton players had not accepted any inducements to lose.

The *Blackburn Times* considered that the club 'have signed plenty of useless men and few good ones'. Wing-half Kelly Houlker, an England international, was sold to the Southern League champions Portsmouth but fortunately the great Bob Crompton would remain with the club for the whole of his playing career from 1896 to 1920. He was captain of Rovers at 21 and of England three years later, winning 41 caps, of which 22 were as captain.

With Crompton at full-back the defence could be steady enough but lack of goals was generally a problem. For the next two seasons from 1903–05 the margins of safety were only two points and then three and it took the promotion to chairman in 1905 of Lawrence Cotton, an appropriately named textiles man, to improve fortunes, rebuild the ground and put up the money for better players.

A director since 1891, and future mayor of Blackburn, he financed the signing of men like Welsh international striker Billy Davies from Wrexham, while Houlker returned from the south coast.

A priority was improving Ewood Park, which soon had a capacity of 40,000. The Darwen End was covered in 1905 and the main stand, designed by Archibald Leitch, was opened on New Year's Day 1907, having cost almost £25,000.

That season they finished only three points off relegation but by the end of the decade under long-serving manager Robert Middleton the team were back nearer the top, in fourth and then third place, and in 1911 there was a first FA Cup semi-final for 17 years. Southend, Spurs, Middlesbrough and West Ham were beaten but the run ended at the hands of Bradford City, a top-six team at the time.

In 1911/12 Rovers made the last four again, losing this time to West Bromwich Albion in a replay, but by then they were experiencing the unexpected excitement of a title challenge. A mid-season run of 11 games unbeaten pushed them up the table, and beating Everton away 3-1 (with no suspicions this time) made them favourites. Even losing 5-1 to mid-table Woolwich Arsenal could not derail the challenge and a 4-1 win at home to West Bromwich not only made up for the FA Cup defeat three weeks earlier but clinched the title.

The 60 goals were spread around, Scottish international Walter Aitkenhead leading the way with 15 of them. In an era of bigger attendances and at the much-improved Ewood, the average of under 18,000 was perhaps disappointing, being only the tenth highest in the country and emphasising how much greater was the potential of the big-city clubs. Cotton's financial support, however, enabled them to break the British transfer record for players like Danny Shea at £2,000 from West Ham, then Hearts centre-forward Percy Dawson for £2,500. The reward was a second Football League championship in three seasons.

Winning seven of the first eight games of 1913/14 set them up and a Christmas double of 5-0 and 5-1 against Preston in successive days kept the momentum going. Unbeaten from 17 January to 28 March, Rovers secured the title by drawing 0-0 at Newcastle over Easter. Average crowds crept above 20,000 for the first time and Shea's 28 goals broke the club record. It was at least a riposte to Manchester and Merseyside, even if Everton took the title away in 1915, when having the top five in the First Division emphasised Lancashire's remarkable dominance.

* * * * *

Bolton, like Manchester United, spent that final season at the wrong end of the table, but were at least back in the First Division (and FA Cup semi-finalists) after relegation in 1899, 1903, 1908 and 1910. Regularly they proved themselves too good for the lower division but struggled in the higher one.

Back in the top division, November 1900 brought a first 20,000 crowd to Burnden for Manchester City's visit amid a couple of seasons of consolidation but in 1902/03 Wanderers did not manage a single win until as late as the 23rd game, at home to Notts County in January. Five successive wins led to a modicum of optimism but they still finished bottom, ten points from safety, as well as being beaten 5-0 at home by Second Division Bristol City in the FA Cup.

It took two seasons to return, the first of them most notable for reaching the FA Cup final and that controversial 1-0 defeat by City after Bob Taylor's semi-final winner against Derby.

Promotion came in 1904/05 with champions Liverpool on the back of 11 straight wins from the start of November. Centre-forward Sam Marsh and Walter White, a Scottish international who later moved to Everton, scored 50 of the 87 league goals between them, Marsh being the country's top scorer.

Albert Shepherd, an England international and the other principal scorer, became more prolific than Marsh and had racked up 90 in 123 games when he left in 1908 for Newcastle, where he was regularly top scorer and got two in the successful 1910 FA Cup Final.

For Bolton, these were the yo-yo years; up in 1905 and sixth twice in succession, then down again by a single point in 1908 as Notts County saved themselves by winning at Burnden then drawing controversially at Chelsea amid raised eyebrows. The following season they were back as champions but straight back down for just one more season, returning in 1911 with Joe Smith and Ted Vizard formidable partners on the left.

At last came a period of not just consolidation but challenge with finishes of fourth (only six points behind champions Blackburn), eighth and sixth as well as a losing FA Cup semi-final appearance against Sheffield United in 1915.

Bolton were one of those clubs who would come back stronger after the war; and with Smith at his peak would soon feature in one of the most famous FA Cup finals of all.

* * * * *

For almost 60 years from 1902 the town of **Preston** was the home of the Football League, though never again of its champions. Tom Charnley became Football League secretary and moved the organisation's headquarters to his modest house close to Deepdale before finding an office in Winkley Street.

North End, after living for a dozen years on the reputation of The Invincibles, had succumbed to relegation in 1901, returning three years later with runners-up Woolwich Arsenal, who finally gave London and the south a First Division club to stand alongside Lancashire's five.

Centre-forward Percy Smith contributed 26 goals and within two years at the higher level Preston were runners-up to Liverpool under William Sudell's successor as manager, E.H. Barr. He was able to call on a particularly strong defence and although only one team in the whole division scored fewer, Dickie Bond on the right wing supported Smith well and outscored him, as well as becoming the club's first England international for ten years.

Third in the newly extended division were Sheffield Wednesday, whose home game with North End in January, a feisty 1-1 draw, led to the ground being closed for 14 days and Preston's players fined £1 each for alleged gestures to the crowd through the visitors' dressing room window.

Second place, however, proved the highest point for almost half a century as Charlie Parker took over for a succession of mid-table seasons and then some to-ing and fro-ing to succeed Bolton as the area's yo-yo club. They were relegated in 1912 with Bury, although only a point behind Liverpool and Oldham, made an immediate return as champions with Burnley, then went straight down and straight back up before the pause for war. Among the comings and goings, Peter McBride lost his place in goal after 14 seasons, and Alf Common, once the first £1,000 footballer, joined in the 1913 Second Division championship season, lasting less than a year.

On 24 April 1915 Preston played away to Derby with the winners taking the Second Division championship: Derby did it 2-0 in what proved to be the last Football League game for four years. Amid the misery of the next few years the town had the prospect of First Division football again to sustain it.

* * * * *

The greatest years in **Bury's** history came early. From 1895 until 1912 they were a First Division club, believed to have the smallest population of any reaching that level, and twice in four seasons they descended on London and walked off with the FA Cup by the remarkable aggregate margin of 10-0.

As recounted in Chapter 2, Southampton were 4-0 victims in 1900. The following season the Shakers achieved fifth place in the top division, six points short of champions Liverpool after losing three games late on. In the top eight for the following two campaigns they were also able, in 1902/03, to achieve a successful treble in the FA Cup, Lancashire Senior Cup and (jointly with Manchester City) the Manchester Senior Cup.

A modest crowd of 5,000 for the start of the FA Cup run at home to Wolves (1-0) grew to four times as many after victory away to holders Sheffield United by the same score brought a home tie with Notts County. Another 1-0 win meant a semi-final against title challengers Aston Villa in front of a 50,000 crowd at Goodison Park, where goals by Jack Plant, Charlie Sagar and Billy Richards shocked the favourites and earned Bury's team of mostly local men another final.

The game against mid-table rivals Derby County, with whom they had shared the points in two league meetings, should have been close but turned into the biggest victory in a final before or since.

Taking advantage of an injury to opposition goalkeeper Jack Fryer, the Shakers scored four times in 11 minutes of the second half to add to the opening goal from skipper George Ross. Sagar, Joe Leeming, Willie Wood and Plant scored the four and when Leeming claimed his second the 6-0 scoreline was a new record that has stood ever since. Furthermore Bury had won the trophy without conceding a goal.

The one-sided nature of the game did not impress neutrals, however. The *Daily Chronicle* complained, 'Briefly and candidly the cup final was a fiasco. Bury defeated Derby County by six goals to none, and it might have been twenty. That it was not is testimony to the mercy exercised by the victors rather than to the defence of the losers.'

Those FA Cup triumphs were followed by four seasons in the lower reaches, surviving in 1904/05 only because the First Division was extended to 20 clubs. But there was another relegation campaign in 1910/11 before going down the following season, 12 points clear at the bottom with only six wins. Down they stayed until 1924, but the name of Bury was well and truly in the history books.

* * * * *

Relegated in 1900 after causing play-offs to be abolished with their non-aggression pact against Stoke, **Burnley** took 13 years to return to the top division. It was a generally miserable time, leavened only by third place in 1901, just missing out on an immediate return. Only two years later they were bottom of the Second Division and had to go cap-in-hand to retain their Football League status. Ernest Mangnall departed as manager to Manchester United, where he had sustained success.

It was a new decade before things picked up, under the management of John Haworth. An Accrington man, he joined in 1910, changed the club's colours from 'unlucky' green to the claret and blue of champions Aston Villa, and pulled off important signings in Bert Freeman from Everton, who would score 115 goals over the next ten years, and centre-half Tommy Boyle from Barnsley. In 1911/12 Haworth's improving team finished third and built on that to win promotion and an FA Cup semi-final place the following season, and then the trophy itself.

Previously there had been barely one decent FA Cup run, in 1909, ended in the fourth round by Manchester United in front of an unusually large Turf Moor crowd of 16,850. Now a quarter-final win at Blackburn, watched by a packed house of almost 43,000, earned a place in the last four for the first time. There, Burnley held First Division leaders Sunderland 0-0 at Bramall Lane before losing the replay 3-2 at St Andrew's, Birmingham.

Freeman rattled in 31 league goals to follow his 32 the previous season and ensure promotion. He was top scorer again in the First Division campaign that brought 12th place but best of all, ended up scoring the goal that won the FA Cup.

Revenge was taken over Sunderland in a quarter-final replay and then Sheffield United were beaten by 1-0 in a replayed semi-final at Goodison Park, Boyle claiming the only goal.

105

So on 25 April 1914 Burnley met Liverpool at Crystal Palace with the chance to win their first major trophy. There were 72,778 present, including for the first time the reigning monarch, King George V. Jerry Dawson, goalkeeper for the past six seasons, but injured in the semi-final, nobly admitted he was not fully fit and recommended that Ronnie Sewell play in his place, the understudy keeping a clean sheet as the Clarets completed a fifth victory over a First Division club.

It was Burnley's skipper Boyle who received the trophy from King George after Freeman scored the only goal. His dad had reportedly travelled from Australia to watch, although given the sailing time he must have known something before the semi-final a month earlier.

FA Cup Final 1914: Burnley 1 Liverpool 0

Burnley: Sewell; Bamforth, Taylor, Halley, Boyle, Watson, Nesbit, Lindley, Freeman, Hodgson, Mosscrop.
Liverpool: Campbell; Longworth, Pursell, Fairfoul, Ferguson, McKinley, Sheldon, Metcalfe, Miller, Lacey, Nicholl.

Bolton eliminated the holders the following season in the third round before Burnley completed a league double over them in finishing fourth in the First Division, ending the era on a high that was to go even higher.

* * * * *

Voted out of the Football League in 1899 but back in after a single year in the Lancashire League, **Blackpool** struggled in the bottom half of the Second Division for nine successive seasons. In 1909 and again in 1913 they were bottom of the heap and faced a re-election vote but this time found other clubs in more forgiving mood and were reprieved – a fate that eluded Chesterfield Town, who had finished above them, and only returned 12 years later.

Harold Hardman, later a star at Everton and a director then chairman of Manchester United, became a regular on the wing in that first season back, when a fine start of 11 games without defeat was followed by deterioration and 12th place, with crowds if anything smaller than before, rarely rising above 2,000 and dropping for Barnsley's visit to an estimated 500.

A 10-1 defeat at Small Heath in March remains the joint worst in the club's history.

Bloomfield Road, home from the turn of the century, saw an improvement for the first local derby with Preston in November 1901, a reported 6,000 turning out, increased to 7,500 for Manchester United's visit in September 1905 and 9,500 to see Burnley three years later.

It was still worth switching the attractive FA Cup tie of 1905/06 against First Division Sheffield United to Bramall Lane, where the Seasiders managed to have the best of both worlds by earning £300 and gaining a surprise 2-1 victory with two goals by inside-right Harry Hancock. A further £650 from the next round at Newcastle was more welcome than the 5-0 defeat.

Ceding ground advantage in the next few years brought badly needed revenue from defeats at West Ham, Newcastle again and Manchester United but no more giant-killing. Not until 1910/11 was there much improvement in league form, when seventh place was the best yet and Burnley's visit late in the campaign attracted a new record gate of 14,500, which the same popular visitors improved by a further 500 the following year.

The next uplift in the league only came in 1914/15, with a final position of 10th on the back of finding a notable goalscorer at last in Joe Lane from Sunderland, who hit 28 in 38 games.

* * * * *

The number of Football League clubs around Manchester was growing, with Stockport County and Oldham Athletic added in the first decade of the 1900s. **Stockport**, founded as Heaton Norris Rovers in 1883, were yet another church team, Congregational in their case, who changed names in 1890 to Stockport County to reflect the new county borough status.

Winning the Lancashire League in 1900, helped them into the Football League alongside Blackpool, where away games at Leicester Fosse on 1 September and Burslem Port Vale two days later brought three points and, perhaps, over-optimistic expectations, immediately tempered when the first home game brought a 5-0 thrashing by New Brighton Tower.

County ended up losing 20 of their 34 games and having only Burton Swifts below them in the table, a second ballot being required to keep them in the League after tying in the first one with Doncaster Rovers. In 1902, they moved south to the local rugby league club's home of Edgeley Park but four successive seasons in the bottom three caused their fellow clubs to run out of patience. In 1904 they were banished for a year, having lost 75 games in those four seasons, only to be returned – at Doncaster's expense – for the 1905/06 campaign and a healthy mid-table finish for three years running.

Surviving after that until the war years was something of a struggle, often in tandem with Blackpool. They were the bottom pair in 1912/13, although comfortably re-elected. Remaining a Football League team was an achievement and on the resumption after the war the new Third Division North would offer a safety net. In the FA Cup, although they had entered since 1892, County only ever made the first round proper once until 1905/06 and the only win of note was 4-1 against Bolton in 1910, spoilt with defeat in the next round three weeks later at home to Southern League Leyton.

* * * * *

Oldham Athletic, in contrast, made great strides from their first Football League season of 1907/08, when they were only two points from shooting straight into the top division.

Originally named a fragrant Pine Villa AFC, they were founded in November 1895 by the Goddard family, father John being mine host at the Featherstall & Junction Inn. An older club, Oldham County, joined the Lancashire League and agreed to share their ground on Garforth Street, Chadderton with the newcomers, then formed a reserve side, which made such an arrangement impractical.

In 1897/98 Pine Villa joined the Oldham Junior Association Second Division, won the title and were runners-up in the First Division a year later. Oldham County having been liquidated, it was suggested they take over the County ground on Sheepfoot Lane. That was done in the summer of 1899 with a name change, reflecting the wider district but keeping the red and white shirts and blue shorts. Joining the Manchester Alliance, they finished third, then runners-up.

Progress in the new century was equally swift, taking in the semi-professional Manchester League at another new ground, Hudson Fold, for four seasons and then in 1904 the Lancashire Combination, leading to first discussions about the Football League.

That was almost achieved in the summer of 1905/06 when Londoners Clapton Orient were forced to apply for re-election after finishing bottom in their first season in the Second Division. The Latics missed out by one vote, the League being reluctant to lose one of only three London clubs at that stage.

That year they had returned to the old Athletic Grounds at Boundary Park as well as entering the FA Cup for the first time, losing to Hull. Gaining wider reputation by taking part in the competition, they were ready for another application to the Football League in the summer of 1907, which became a protracted and slightly dubious one involving payment to a club dropping out.

Having failed again despite a proper campaign and driven by a combination of frustration and desperation, Oldham made a bizarre application to join the Southern League after Fulham moved up. Fellow northerners Bradford Park Avenue applied as well and secured the vacancy. Oldham then learnt that Football League club Burslem Port Vale had financial problems and offered them £1,000 and two players if they resigned and the Latics were elected in their place. That was precisely what happened.

If the methods were unusual, the aim had been achieved and Oldham justified it with a fine first season that began on 7 September 1907 with a 3-1 win at Stoke and finished in third place, only two points behind promoted runners-up Leicester. It was a campaign marred only by a £10 fine for the stoning of the Fulham bus.

Sixth place the season after was followed in 1910 by being runners-up to Manchester City, winning none of the first five games, then 14 of the last 16. Nearly 30,000 watched the decisive 3-0 success against Hull at the end of a close race, in which Hull and Derby both had the same number of points but inferior goal averages. Inside-right James Fay, a future players' union chairman, scored 26 goals and soon wing-half Hugh Moffat and inside-forward George Woodger won England caps.

A crowd of 34,000 came to the first home game in the top division, a 2-0 defeat by Newcastle, and seventh place, with neighbours City and Bury a long way behind, was an excellent effort in the top division; gates also benefiting from the presence of seven other Lancashire clubs in the top flight. After one narrow escape from relegation, two further seasons of remarkable progress followed.

In 1913 there was a run all the way to an FA Cup semi-final against league runners-up Aston Villa, lost only 1-0 at Ewood Park; and in 1914/15 came the greatest season in the club's history. Fourth the previous year with former United skipper Charlie Roberts in the side, Oldham missed becoming champions of England by one win, allowing Everton to pip them by a point and a better goal average when the Latics, needing just two more points, lost their final two games at home to Burnley and Liverpool.

They had lost another important match in highly unusual circumstances at Middlesbrough when right-back William Cook, a respected Lancashire cricketer, was sent off with Boro 4-1 ahead; he refused to go, causing the game to be abandoned. The FA suspended him for 12 months and the result stood.

What the team lacked was a 20-goal-a-season man, as became apparent when scoring only once in the crucial last three games of the campaign.

Oldham had achieved much in a short time on half the crowds of the main Manchester and Merseyside clubs, but they would never reach quite such heights again.

* * * * *

Even if Bolton and Everton lost the two FA Cup semi-finals of 1915 (Sheffield United winning the 'Khaki Cup Final' against Chelsea), league football came to a halt with Lancashire in a dominant position, winning four of the last five championships, and having the top five clubs in that final season, separated by only three points.

Now, however, thoughts had to turn from regional rivalries to the national interest. As Sir Arthur Conan Doyle put it, 'There is only time for one thing now, and that thing is war.' He had tried to make that point earlier on, as one of those prominent public figures who had objected to professional sport continuing long after Britain declared war on Germany on 4 August 1914.

Two days later at Clayton Green near Preston, a Football League management committee meeting decided to carry on much as usual, arguing in a statement signed by president John McKenna on the eve of the new season that 'our great winter game should pursue its usual course'. The FA, in a letter on 4 September, requested all clubs to make their grounds available on non-matchdays for drill and to have a special appeal at games encouraging 'players and spectators who are physically fit' to join the armed forces.

At the end of March 1915 following a special general meeting of the Football League, the intention was still to keep going for 1915/16, despite no summer wages and the maximum in season being decreased from £4 to £3 – just the sort of financial uncertainty that prompted the Manchester United-Liverpool fix that very week. Not until 3 July was the Football League formally suspended at a meeting at Blackpool Winter Gardens. Gates had dropped by 50 per cent overall, even if 20–30,000 still turned up for the Merseyside and Manchester derbies; players took wage cuts and clubs like Blackpool applied for money from a relief fund set up by the Football League.

Before conscription was introduced early in 1916, many Lancashire players and officials had already enlisted in the Army or Navy. Many served in the 17th and 23rd Middlesex infantry battalions, which became known as the Footballers' Battalions, the first of them having been set up in December 1914.

Differing opinions about the 1915/16 season were shown by Blackburn Rovers declining to compete in the regional leagues which had been organised, while Stoke played in the north-west competition as well as **Southport Central** (founded 1881 as forerunners of Southport FC) and **Rochdale** (founded 1907), co-opted as temporary members and receiving a boost that would serve them well later on. Southport were even allowed a name change to Southport Vulcan, the first example of a sponsor's name appearing in a club's title.

The format for four war-time seasons was for a so-called Principal competition of all clubs, then a Subsidiary one in much smaller groups of four. For the last two campaigns the Principal champions then met the midlands winners over two legs.

Manchester City emerged as winners in that first season from Burnley. In the second year Blackburn joined in, Stoke and Port Vale made up the numbers and Liverpool became champions from Stockport. Stoke finished ahead of Liverpool in the Principal section of 1917/18 before losing the play-off against Leeds City, the 'Midlands' (sic) winners.

In 1918/19, the Armistice having been signed on 11 November, Everton finished top losing only one game, but were then beaten 1-0 by midlands champions Nottingham Forest over two matches.

Rather more important than defeats on the pitch were the heavy losses suffered by the two Middlesex battalions, running to more than 1,000 men, in battles like those of the Somme (1916) and Arras (1917). Among those lost in the latter were Sandy Turnbull, the Manchester City and United FA Cup winner. Blackburn's England international Edwin Latheron (East Surrey Regiment) died at Passchendaele in October 1917 and overall more than two dozen listed as professional footballers with north-western clubs failed to return.

Chapter 4

Cold winds of change (1920–39)

Keeping pace with Huddersfield and Arsenal in years of economic struggle; missed pools opportunity; goals galore for Liverpool's Hodgson and Everton's Dean; Bolton's chaotic Wembley debut and 1920s FA Cup treble before north-west's worst-ever season; Blackburn take Villa down with them; City at Maine Road – the champions relegated; United's grim '30s; Blackpool's Jimmy Hampson tragedy; slow decline of Oldham; Third Division North for Rochdale, Tranmere and others; but only briefly for Nelson, Stalybridge and Wigan Borough; from South Liverpool, a new New Brighton.

CELEBRATING its silver jubilee in 1928, the LFA felt able to claim, 'The Lancashire Clubs have kept pace with the growth of the game in a way that few counties can boast. All the First and Second Division grounds have been rebuilt with the result that most of them have found favour for representative games.' The author could point to 14 First Division titles, 12 Second Division championships and 16 FA Cup wins. Appropriately that year, Everton and Manchester City won the top two divisions and Blackburn took the FA Cup, allowing proud county FA officials to pose with all three trophies.

Nevertheless, Huddersfield Town had superseded Liverpool as the team of the 1920s, and for all Everton and City's efforts, Arsenal would hold that title in the '30s. In 1932/33, for the first and last time to date, there was not a single Lancashire team in the First Division's top ten; and the period between the wars was a particularly grim one for Manchester United, relegated three times from 1922–37 and once within a single defeat of dropping into the third tier.

From 1921 the Third Division North increased the area's representation but it was a struggle for many clubs, and the nationwide economic malaise, which naturally hit industrial towns and cities hardest, soon saw the demise as Football League teams of Nelson, Wigan Borough and Stalybridge; Rochdale almost followed. These were hard times. In 1922 football's maximum wage was reduced by £1 to £8 per week (£6 in summer) and by 1933 unemployment was at record levels of 25 per cent.

One badly missed opportunity for new revenue concerned the weekly football pools founded in 1923 by John Moores, who initially had coupons handed out at Old Trafford. Many politicians and preachers were against the idea and in 1936 the Football League finally declared war; whether this was out of conviction (many of their leaders being in the Methodist tradition) or because they wanted a share of the money is not clear. The key question was whether fixtures were copyright and should therefore be paid for by the pools firms.

A proposal by Will Cuff, a predecessor of Moores as Everton chairman, to keep fixtures secret each week until it was too late for printers, was carried; newspapers didn't like it and many clubs feared an adverse effect on gates if supporters didn't know until Friday evening who or where their team were playing.

So it proved. On the first Saturday of this peculiar arrangement, 29 February 1936, bad weather including snow also affected games but gates were down from 318,000 the previous year to only 193,000.

The following week the Football League persisted, but the press found out the matches in time for Friday morning's papers, and clubs voted to scrap the plan. A Parliamentary Bill to make the pools illegal was thrown out 287–27; but still there was no benefit for football's ailing finances.

* * * * *

If **Liverpool's** reputation was tarnished by the 1915 fix with Manchester United, there was little effect on the playing side; apart from Tom Fairfoul, three of the four players banned 'for life' appeared briefly again after the war, although all had left by the time the team won consecutive championships in 1922 and 1923.

Two fourth places had offered encouragement for new manager David Ashworth, a former referee who took over after Tom Watson died in 1915. With Elisha Scott in goal Liverpool conceded fewest goals in three of those four seasons and only a lack of scoring kept them from finishing as at least runners-up in the first two years. In neither championship season did they score most goals, but had by far the best defence each time.

The inside-forwards Harry 'Smiler' Chambers and Dick Forshaw led the way in each of the title-winning seasons, in which there was a comfortable six-point margin both times, easing up towards the end. Foundations for the first one were laid by a long unbeaten run from the start of December 1921 until mid-March as newly promoted Tottenham surprisingly led the challengers.

Chambers scored 19 goals, Forshaw 17 and for the following campaign they had a more effective centre-forward in-between them in the returning Dick Johnson. Those three contributed 55 of the team's 70 goals as Sunderland finished runners-up with Herbert Chapman's emerging Huddersfield Town third (and destined to be champions for the next three seasons).

Almost as pleasing was not losing a single one of the eight games over that period against Everton. From 1921–25 matches were played back to back against the same opponents and when the Reds lost both derbies in autumn 1923 hopes of a championship treble were already disappearing; they finished no higher than 12th, with the Blues seventh.

Ashworth had surprisingly left in February before the second title win for what appeared to be a much less attractive position at Oldham, and Scot Matt McQueen, who had played in the original Football League team of 1893 took over for the next five years – four of them after having a leg amputated following a road accident.

There was no further championship challenge in that time and in the season he stood down, 1927/28, Liverpool became caught up in the most congested relegation struggle in First Division history. The bottom nine clubs were separated by just two points, but crucially the Reds beat Spurs 2-0 in their penultimate game and it was the London side who went down with Middlesbrough. Fortunately McQueen had signed one of the club's great goalscorers in Gordon Hodgson. Recruited after starring for a South African touring team, he would score 241 goals in almost ten years, a total exceeded only by Ian Rush and Roger Hunt in Liverpool history.

Impressing too as a Lancashire cricketer, he might have had a formidable partner in Bill 'Demon' Devlin, surprisingly sold to Hearts in 1927 soon after scoring four against both Bury and Portsmouth (the latter losing 8-2 at Anfield after being 6-0 down at half-time). Hodgson later became a respected manager of Port Vale but only six months after being unsuccessfully interviewed for the Liverpool job in 1951 he died of throat cancer.

By the time he left for Aston Villa in January 1936 the Reds had still made no further challenge in either the First Division or the FA Cup. Afterwards, in 1936 and 1937, when Matt Busby had joined from Manchester City to become part of an all-Scottish half-back line, they were only three points off relegation, and only once in the 1930s did they reach the quarter-final of the FA Cup, going out to Chelsea in 1932.

That run included a 2-1 win at Goodison in the third round, a success to put alongside the Anfield triumphs of 7-4 in February 1933 (without Hodgson) and 6-0 two years later.

After the war Busby would make the fateful decision to move on to Manchester United. But Liverpool had the nucleus of a side to regain the championship.

* * * * *

Occasional embarrassing Anfield defeats or not, **Everton** became the more successful Merseyside club between the wars, above all in the 1930s, when they took two First Division titles and an FA Cup. And if Liverpool had Hodgson, the Blues had Bill 'Dixie' Dean matching him goal for goal.

Even allowing for the ravages of wartime on playing staff, to drop to 16th place after resuming as the reigning league champions from 1914/15 (and champions of the Lancashire Principal in 1919) was a huge disappointment, as was 20th place in 1922 and a stunning 6-0 home defeat by Second Division Crystal Palace in the FA Cup while Liverpool became champions. Wild fluctuations continued even after Dean's arrival amid praise for the quality of Everton's football.

Born in Birkenhead in January 1907 and growing up as an Evertonian, Dean signed for his local club Tranmere Rovers at the age of 16, allowing him to leave his job on the railways. A haul of 27 goals in as many games in the 1924/25 season earned him a move across the Mersey towards the end of that campaign for a fee of £3,000.

On debut in a 3-1 defeat at Arsenal, 'Dean played fairly well but there was a sad lack of support accorded him', according to one report. The obvious question for the next two years was how poor the Blues might have been without him. Big but fast, with a fierce shot in either foot and superb in the air, he thrived on the service of wingers like Sam Chedgzoy and the little Scot Alec Troup. Like many other forwards he benefited too from a relaxation of the offside rule by which only two players instead of three needed to be goal-side. In the last season under the old rule, 1924/25, Huddersfield were champions with 69 goals; from then on the total required would be nearer 100, peaking with Arsenal's 127 and Aston Villa's 128 in 1930/31.

In the first season of the change, Dixie hit 32 in 38 games including four hat-tricks, but as well as losing 5-1 at Anfield Everton were only 11th. A motorbike crash in May 1926 caused a fractured skull to threaten his career, if not his life, but physical strength saw him through to return to a struggling side next autumn and score in five successive games. Without his 21 goals in 27 league games the team would surely have gone down, conceding as they did 90 times and as in 1922 landing only one place and four points off relegation.

That made the *annus mirabilis* of 1927/28 all the more remarkable, even with a crop of new signings including former England goalkeeper Ted Taylor and future captain Warney Cresswell. Dean was unstoppable, starting with 17 goals in his first nine games, including all five in the win over Manchester United. When he missed a match at home to West Ham through playing for England in Belfast, the Blues won 7-0; he returned to score eight in the next three fixtures.

The new Bullens Road double-decker stand allowed almost 66,000 to see the derby, a 1-1 draw in which Dean for once did not score. That was a rarity. Going into the final match at home to Arsenal (who had beaten them in two thrilling league and cup games at Highbury) the Blues were already champions and most interest was on whether Dixie could register his seventh hat-trick of the season to beat the 59 league goals scored by Middlesbrough's George Camsell the season before in the Second Division. He did it with a header eight minutes from time to total 60 in just 39 games, out of a grand total for the season including England internationals and other representative games of 82 in 49.

Who could have forecast relegation within two years? Dean continuing to score at almost a goal per game (49 in 54) made the collapse all the more shocking. But the defence conceded 75 and 92 respectively and from 18th in 1929 the Blues lost out in the tight relegation struggle of 1929/30. Rallying too late with four wins and a draw, they finished bottom, with the eight teams above them no more than four points better off. Forty-two years after joining the Football League, Everton were a Second Division side, leaving only Blackburn and Aston Villa of the original members not to have suffered that fate.

Fortunes improved dramatically. Exile lasted a single season and the championship of the Second Division by seven clear points with 121 goals was followed 12 months later by the First Division title; a feat to match Liverpool's of 1906.

Dean naturally played a major role: 39 Second Division goals, including 23 in 12 games (scoring in each one) either side of New Year, and nine in a long FA Cup run. That ended through a goalkeeping error in the semi-final against West Bromwich at Old Trafford, where 300 people among the 20,000 locked out were reported injured. Then Dean hit 45 in 38 games (five each against Sheffield Wednesday and Chelsea) as the Blues became champions of England again. At the other end of the pitch Ted Sagar was now in goal for the first of his 463 league games in 23 years.

Arsenal, runners-up in 1932, soon began to dominate the decade with manager Chapman having invented the third-back game, and Lancashire suffered its worst league season of all in 1932/33, when 11th-placed Everton were the county's highest club. Liverpool, Blackburn, Manchester City, Bolton and Blackpool all lay beneath them, the latter pair going down to leave the north-west's thinnest representation for many years.

The Blues compensated in the FA Cup, going all the way to Wembley, albeit with a fortunate 2-1 semi-final victory over West Ham, a struggling Second Division side. The final against Manchester City was the first in which numbers were worn, from 1-22, and skipper Dean, with the number nine on his back, proved a significant figure. He unsettled the City defence from the start and scored the second goal after left-winger Jimmy Stein had tapped in; Jimmy Dunn headed a third.

FA Cup Final 1933: Everton 3 Manchester City 0
Everton: Sagar; Cook, Cresswell, Britton, White, Thomson, Geldard, Dunn, Dean, Johnson, Stein.
Manchester City: Langford; Cann, Dale, Busby, Cowan, Bray, Toseland, Marshall, Herd, McMullan, Brook.

Cliff Britton from Bristol Rovers, a future Everton manager, was outstanding then and for much of the next five moderate seasons that preceded another surprise title win, in 1938/39.

Joe Mercer had displaced Britton for club and country, and Tommy Jones of Wales was an outstanding centre-half. In attack, the 17 year-old Tommy Lawton was signed from Burnley at the start of 1937 and quickly replaced the ageing Dean, who eventually became a publican in Chester, there to reflect on 377 goals from 431 games. In his second full season Lawton, regarded by many as the better all-round player, scored 28 league goals for a team no higher than 14th, then increased that to 34 in the 1938/39 title-winning season.

Everton won their first six games to lead early on and did the double over Liverpool; at the Goodison game in September the national anthem was played to 'celebrate' Neville Chamberlain's return from Munich promising peace in our time. The Blues finished four points ahead of Wolves, who had inflicted an extraordinary 7-0 defeat on them in February as well as knocking them out of the FA Cup.

In April Lawton's goal gave England a rare win at Hampden Park, the first there since 1927, and a week later the title was sealed. But less than a year after Chamberlain's promise, the league programme was halted after three games and so, as in 1914, Everton went through the war years as reigning champions.

* * * * *

Everton's gain from Lawton was **Burnley's** loss, even if the £6,500 fee for a teenager was more than welcome for a club that made historic strides immediately after the First World War before sliding into the Second Division in 1930 – and with gates dropping to 8,000 not looking like returning.

Within two years of the resumption of league football, the Turf Moor club had been runners-up for the first time and followed it with a first title. In the first post-war season a modest 65 goals were sufficient to earn second place and had it not been for a winless run from Boxing Day to mid-February (plus a 6-2 home defeat by Bradford) things would have been even better. That gave them the confidence to get over three successive defeats to start the 1920/21 campaign, after which they didn't lose in 30 matches from 4 September to 26 March.

Oldham and Aston Villa were hit for seven and Sheffield United for six with two main goalscorers to the fore: centre-forward Joe Anderson claimed five in Villa's visit and four against the Blades towards his 25 for the season and inside-right Bob Kelly hit four against the Latics. Manchester City ended the run over Easter but were beaten in the return and without winning any of their last six games Burnley were champions.

A strong start the following season faded out to leave them third but there would be little more to enthuse over. In February 1924 a record crowd that still stands today of 54,775 saw victory in the FA Cup over Huddersfield, who were on their way to the first of three successive championships; Burnley eventually lost the semi-final 3-0 to Villa.

A big increase in crowds to over 30,000 in the championship season had halved within three years and the club were reported to have earned less than £2,000 in a whole season in 1923 while Bolton took four times as much from an FA Cup semi-final and final alone.

The Clarets took longer than most to get to grips with the new offside rule of 1925/26, losing the first game 10-0 at Villa and conceding eight to both struggling Manchester City and high-flying Bury before Christmas. By the end they had let in 108, the worst in the division, but unlike City they survived by a point after winning the last two games. Yet in the same high-scoring season they won 7-1 at Birmingham with a double hat-trick by winger Louis Page.

Perhaps unsurprisingly in view of the goals conceded, it was the last season as first-choice of keeper Jerry Dawson, who finally left two years later after a club record 569 games. That season Burnley stayed up by a single point again, thanks to midlander George Beel's 35 goals and after a further season in the bottom four (Beel with 30 goals) not even the centre-forward could save them from the drop with Everton in 1929/30.

In both 1931/32, with the average crowd well below five figures, and the season after, there was serious danger of dropping into the Third Division North, ending up two points above the relegated pair with a late flourish each time.

Reaching the FA Cup semi-final in 1935 – losing 3-0 to eventual winners Sheffield Wednesday – was a rare ray of sunlight in a dark period of six successive seasons in the wrong half of the Second Division. Another was the arrival that year of Boltonian Lawton on amateur forms. He became Burnley's youngest ever player at 16 in March but 16 goals in 25 games meant he was unlikely to stay for long. By the time the Germans marched into Poland there was still no sign of the Clarets' revival, which would come unexpectedly soon after the war.

* * * * *

'What a name, what a club and what a team' raved the *History of the Lancashire Football Association* about **Bolton Wanderers** in 1928 during the most successful decade in their history, which brought three FA Cup wins and a regular place in the top six of the First Division.

Captain Joe Smith was the catalyst with a run of goalscoring seasons that included a club record 38 in 1920/21 and third place behind Burnley and Manchester City. Another Bolton record was established in the same season with the transfer for £3,500 of inside-forward David Jack from Plymouth, who would become a key figure, and in January 1922 a crowd of 66,442 turned out for City's visit.

A third successive season in the top six, in 1921/22, was followed by a famous FA Cup campaign concluding in the first Wembley final. It began at Norwich in January, Jack scoring in five successive ties as Leeds, Huddersfield in a replay, Charlton at the Valley and Sheffield United in an Old Trafford semi-final were all beaten. And so to Wembley.

The Empire Stadium was built ahead of the proposed British Empire Exhibition of 1924/25 at a cost of £750,000 just as the FA were considering a new home for their cup final; Stamford Bridge held 76,000 and was the venue from 1920–22 but would have caused a problem if Chelsea reached the final, as they almost did in 1920. The FA agreed to stage the final for 21 years even before the builders moved in and were so delighted with the new 127,000 capacity stadium that secretary Frederick Wall fatefully declared, 'At last we have a ground for everyone who wants to see the cup final.'

Not quite. With a London side, Second Division promotion contenders West Ham United, playing the biggest game in their history, the already keen interest was intensified. Although six-figure crowds had attended the final three times before the war, the FA failed to make the occasion all-ticket and by the time King George V arrived, so many people had spilled on to the pitch from overflowing terraces, with thousands more still outside and many simply climbing in after the gates were closed, that an embarrassed Wall told the monarch, 'I fear, Sir, that the match may not be played. The playing ground is covered with people.'

Those who surged forward for a close-up of the King in the royal box were somehow persuaded to leave via a tunnel to the exhibition grounds and much credit was also given to a horse called Billy ridden by PC George Scorey, one of many extra police officers told to get himself to Wembley as soon as possible. Having gone along with the story of the 'white horse final' for many years, Scorey cast some doubt on it in 1957 when he told a friend that Billy was more of a light grey and that photographs and newsreels at the time had largely been overexposed.

As those on the pitch realised there would be no game unless they moved back, some sort of order was slowly restored, and almost an hour late play began, with the King having been unable to greet the players as planned and many spectators still uncomfortably close to the touchlines. More than once they spilled on to the pitch and play had to be stopped, while at a truncated half-time interval it made good sense for the teams simply to stay where they were.

By that time Bolton were ahead, David Jack having scored Wembley's first goal in only the third minute. Jack Smith added a second early in the second half and his namesake Joe was able to collect the cup from the royal box once police officers had shepherded white-shirted Wanderers players through the throng.

FA Cup Final 1923: Bolton Wanderers 2 West Ham United 0
Bolton: Pym; Haworth, Finney, Nuttall, Seddon, Jennings, Butler, Jack, Jack Smith, Joe Smith, Vizard.
West Ham: Hufton; Henderson, Young, Bishop, Kay, Tresadern, Richards, Brown, Watson, Moore, Ruffel.

It was a deserved victory, as West Ham's manager Syd King was the first to concede, but the aftermath was naturally concerned with what the *Sunday Pictorial* called 'Cup final chaos that was nearly a disaster'. The paper claimed that nearly 1,000 people were treated for injuries and added, 'It was a deplorable opening of the "finest sports arena in the world". It could not cope with the biggest football crowd ever assembled.'

When Bolton returned in 1926 for a Lancashire derby against Manchester City, the principle of all-ticket finals was belatedly established. It had taken Wanderers eight games to get there, not one of them against another First Division team and there was only one change from three years earlier, Harry Greenhalgh coming in at full-back for the injured Alex Finney.

Several Bolton players took calming 'nerve powder' before the game and it seemed to work in an exciting final in which their goalkeeper Dick Pym distinguished himself before David Jack scored the only goal. 'Not a great deal between the teams ... the quality of the football being a credit and worthy of two of the outstanding teams from the County, which has the strong claim to be regarded as the hub of Soccer football,' wrote a proud *Bolton Evening News* reporter.

Three more years and the Trotters were back again but without either Joe Smith, who left for Stockport having scored 277 league and cup goals, or David Jack, sold to Arsenal for football's first five-figure fee, which disgruntled fans believed was to fund a new stand. Despite for once being in the lower half of the table, Bolton maintained their 100 per cent Wembley record by defeating relegation-threatened Portsmouth with goals by Billy Butler and Harold Blackmore in the last dozen minutes.

League form meanwhile had been consistently good since the war with finishes of sixth, sixth, thirteenth, fourth, third, eighth, fourth and seventh. Third place in the 1924/25 campaign, only three points behind champions Huddersfield, followed a run of 17 successive home wins. From seventh place in 1928, however, they spent five seasons outside the top 12, the last of them bringing relegation by two points in 1933. Jack Milsom, signed from Rochdale, was a useful goalscorer but despite his first-half hat-trick in the final game against Leeds, won 5-0, rivals won as well to send Wanderers down with Blackpool in a close finish.

In February there was a classic example of how attendances could fluctuate in hard times. Another FA Cup tie at home to City attracted a record 69,912 but for Portsmouth's visit four days later just 3,101 turned up.

An immediate return to the top division was thwarted by a draw at Lincoln on the final day of 1933/34, allowing Preston to pip them, but a year later they returned ahead of West Ham on goal average and embarked on another good FA Cup run. Over 70,000 watched a draw at Tottenham and then more than over 67,000 saw the quarter-final at Goodison, where Everton were beaten 2-1. The semi-final against West Bromwich Albion was drawn 1-1 but the First Division side won the replay 2-0 at Stoke after two mistakes by the normally reliable Finney.

Fred Swift had become the regular goalkeeper, suffering a bad day on Bolton's return to the top division in a 7-0 defeat away to City with his brother Frank between the posts for the home side. Avoiding relegation by two points the following season, they survived comfortably until the war.

* * * * *

Third in the last season before the war, **Blackburn** were soon overshadowed after it by greatest rivals Burnley and then Bolton's FA Cup exploits. Only one point off relegation in 1919/20, they were frequently in the bottom half of the table in a period brightened only by winning the 1928 FA Cup, and in 1936 they finally went down for three years before returning as champions.

In that first post-war season the great Bob Crompton played only two games before concentrating on business interests and then joining the club's board. His final match was a 5-2 defeat at Bradford in February during the middle of a long run without a win, but Rovers saved themselves in the last four games, scoring 14 goals in three unlikely home wins over Aston Villa, Manchester United and Sheffield United, plus a draw at Old Trafford. They were still a point behind even then but United did them another favour by beating Notts County, who went down.

The first full-time manager, Jack Carr, an England international and successful player with Newcastle, was appointed in February 1922, a season also notable for a Boxing Day crowd at home to Preston of 52,656 that remains an Ewood Park record for a league game. Carr reverted to secretary-manager after three and a half years, having been unable to lift them above mid-table.

Cup semi-finalists in 1925 (losing 3-1 to Cardiff City), they benefited under the new offside law from the scoring exploits of centre-forward Ted Harper from Kent, whose 43 league goals in 37 games was the highest in the country and set a club record. It included no fewer than five in the away game at Newcastle in September when Rovers triumphed 7-1, finally destroying the Geordies' famed offside trap. Remarkably Harper later became Preston's record scorer in a single season (1932/33) and then did the same at Tottenham, so until Jimmy Greaves surpassed him by one in 1963 he held the seasonal record at three different clubs.

In December 1926, midway through another difficult season, the hugely popular Crompton was given the position of 'honorary manager', in effect the equivalent of general manager. The appointment had the desired effect in a run to the 1928 FA Cup Final.

League form was again moderate, as a 6-1 home defeat by Bolton early in January confirmed, but a week later the FA Cup campaign began with a 4-1 thumping of Newcastle, continuing with wins over Exeter City after a replay, Port Vale and Manchester United in front of big crowds and then a semi-final at Leicester against Arsenal. Jack Roscamp's goal beat the Londoners.

The task at Wembley was to prevent Huddersfield achieving the first league and cup Double since 1897. Roscamp set Rovers on their way after less than a minute, barging goalkeeper Billy Mercer and the ball into the net. Tommy McLean scored a second and although noted Scottish international Alec Jackson retrieved one goal, Roscamp scored his second near the end for a 3-1 win.

'A grand finale for Lancashire and Huddersfield could not complain,' said the *Sunday Times*. Some 100,000 celebrated as the trophy arrived back in Blackburn after Rovers's sixth success in seven finals. The following season brought a record 62,522 to see a 1-1 draw in the quarter-final at home to Bolton, who won the replay 2-1 in front of even bigger crowd and went on to keep the cup in Lancashire.

By the early 1930s Rovers were in the bottom half again, the town suffering from unemployment in the cotton mills, crowds falling and Bob Crompton resigning after complaints about his autocratic style. 'One is naturally a little disappointed,' he said. In 1936 the threat of relegation finally came true, Rovers taking fellow founding members Aston Villa with them by winning the penultimate game 4-2 at Villa Park.

The Second Division offered little respite. Accrington Stanley recorded a famous FA Cup victory over their neighbours (January 1937) and there was even danger of falling into the Third Division North in the spring of 1938, when Crompton was summoned back from his position as manager of Bournemouth. He was again a general manager but exerted enough influence for the team to survive by two points.

For the following season Crompton took full charge and transformed a young side into Second Division title winners with an uncomplicated style that brought 17 home wins and 95 goals in all. A draw at Bramall Lane on the final day gave them the title ahead of runners-up Sheffield United.

First Division football returned to Ewood with a 2-2 draw against Everton on 2 September but the next day war was declared and everything changed.

* * * * *

Starting the interwar years as a top eight team with good FA Cup prospects, **Manchester City** finished as only City could; a unique achievement in becoming English champions for the first time and then going down only 12 months later.

Manager Ernest Mangnall managed to keep almost all the pre-war side together including two good scorers in Tom Browell from Everton and Horace Barnes from Derby County and for the second full season he took them to the runners-up position behind Burnley with 31 goals from Browell. The most dramatic event of the campaign, however, was the fire that raged through the main stand and dressing rooms of the Hyde Road ground the evening after Bonfire Night. Fortunately the ground was empty at the time.

United offered the use of Old Trafford but City soldiered on, staging a home game with Huddersfield only seven days later. The board had already been considering a new home like the Belle Vue pleasure gardens and the incident concentrated minds, resulting in the acquisition of a new site on Maine Road, Moss Side, two miles to the west, which would have a handsome main stand but no other cover.

On 25 August 1923 an impressive crowd of 56,993 gathered there to see Sheffield United beaten 2-1. As Manchester United had been relegated, there was no derby game so it remained the highest league gate of the season but in March no fewer than 76,166 turned up for the FA Cup quarter-final against championship contenders Cardiff City. The Welsh side held out for a goalless draw but a Browell goal in extra time won City the replay, earning a semi-final against Newcastle at St Andrew's, which they lost 2-0.

That defeat was notable for being the final game played by Billy Meredith, at the age of 49 and eight months. He had rejoined City permanently for the start of the 1921/22 season, aggrieved with United over a delayed testimonial payment, and he played 25 games as the team finished tenth, but appeared in only three league games over the following two seasons, the last of them the week before the Newcastle semi-final. His final record was 151 goals in 394 Football League and FA Cup games for City, 35 in 332 for United and ten in 39 for Wales.

The regular centre-half and captain in the early 1920s was one of the great all-round sportsmen, Max Woosnam, who had represented Cambridge University at football, cricket, tennis and golf, won a tennis gold medal at the 1920 Olympics and missed the start of City's 1921/22 season to play for Great Britain in the Davis Cup.

He had left by 1925/26 and so had manager Mangnall, his contract not renewed, when the club achieved what might be regarded as a typical City double: an FA Cup final and relegation. The new manager was David Ashworth, the man who had led Liverpool to the 1922 title and then mysteriously walked out for Oldham.

City's inconsistency was perfectly illustrated in the space of three days in October; an 8-3 win against Burnley in which Browell scored five was followed by a defeat by exactly the same score at Sheffield United.

Goalscoring prowess was evident too in the run to the semi-final with wins over Corinthians, Huddersfield, Crystal Palace (11-4) and Clapton Orient yielding 27 goals. The draw for the last four caused great excitement by throwing together the two Manchester sides for the first time in the competition since Newton Heath had beaten Ardwick in 1891. Bottom of the table or not, City went into the tie knowing they had drubbed United 6-1 at Old Trafford two months earlier, the biggest victory margin in the derby.

At Bramall Lane, they had the better of their neighbours again and comfortably so, by 3-0 with Browell scoring twice. 'Grim Manchester Semi-Final' was one headline, which did not bother the winners one bit.

Bolton having beaten Swansea by the same score, it was to be an all-Lancashire final. King George V, who had made a rare appearance at a league ground to watch City beat Liverpool in March 1920, was present again and was introduced to a new captain in wing-half Jimmy McMullan from Partick, but this time he saw them beaten by the only goal.

They were managerless too, Ashworth having been sacked in November and no successor appointed until Leicester's Peter Hodge took over just in time for the crucial final First Division game. Seven days after the final, City went to Newcastle with three teams below them, but while Leeds and Burnley both won to save themselves, Hughie Gallacher's hat-trick inflicted a 3-2 defeat on the Citizens, who went down knowing that they would have stayed up if Billy Austin had not had his penalty saved. They had scored 89 goals, which was more than most teams, including runners-up Arsenal.

Browell left for Blackpool but with Tom Johnson still scoring prolifically, City should have bounced straight back, only to be denied promotion by just about the thinnest margin ever. Middlesbrough, who won 5-3 at Maine Road on Christmas Day with George Camsell scoring all five, were always likely champions with City and Portsmouth chasing second place.

On the final day a crowd of over 49,000 spilled on to the pitch to celebrate City's 8-0 win over Bradford City, only to discover that Pompey, kicking off 15 minutes later, had scored exactly the number of goals they needed by beating Preston 5-1. Despite ending up with 21 goals fewer than City's 108, Portsmouth had a fractionally better goal average of 1.775 to 1.770 and went up. 'Never has there been such a cruel blow in the history of the League,' lamented Manchester's *Athletic News*.

Promotion was only delayed 12 months and achieved as clear champions in 1927/28 with exactly 100 goals as well as the highest average crowd in the country of 37,468, twice reaching 60,000 plus. Left-wing pair Eric Brook and Freddie Tilson were signed from Barnsley in time for the run-in, going on to become important players throughout the 1930s. Johnson added 19 to his 25 the previous year and then a club record 38 in 39 games back in the First Division (five of them in a 6-2 win at Everton) for an eighth-place finish.

Another significant signing for the new decade was teenage inside-forward Matt Busby from Scotland, who would overcome serious homesickness, be converted to wing-half, and go on to become a significant figure in Manchester (and Merseyside) football.

Busby made his debut wearing the number ten shirt in November 1929, when City finished an impressive third, after Johnson was surprisingly sold to Everton with 158 league goals to his name. Tommy Tait took on the scoring mantle with 28 but the following autumn was also sold, to Bolton, and for a few seasons most joy came from Manchester United's relegation (they stayed down for four seasons) and the FA Cup. In three years from 1932–34 City reached the semi-final every time and twice went on to Wembley.

A high-scoring run to the last four in 1932, with Busby now established at right-half, was ended by Arsenal, the team of the decade, who won 1-0. The last-minute goal was credited to Cliff

'Boy' Bastin, though these days it would probably be regarded as own goal by City's keeper Len Langford, who punched it into the air and in off bar and post.

Manager Hodge left immediately, returning to Leicester, but a year later after wins at Bolton and Burnley, City came through their semi-final, hanging on to beat Derby County 3-2 at Huddersfield before their 3-0 defeat by Everton (see above).

Langford gave an uncertain performance in goal and lost his place at Christmas with a knee injury, being replaced by a young Frank Swift from Fleetwood, who was regular from the time he took over. It was nevertheless an inauspicious start, with a 4-1 defeat followed a week later by conceding seven at home to West Bromwich.

Yet 'Big Swifty' missed just one game in more than five years before the war. So he was between the posts as City reached a third successive semi-final in 1934, a remarkable crowd of 84,569 having watched the narrow quarter-final win over Stoke City and Stanley Matthews. The semi-final, back at Huddersfield, was far easier as Aston Villa were thrashed 6-1 with four goals by Tilson.

City had finished three points in front of their Wembley opponents Portsmouth in the First Division, and beat them 2-1 at home three weeks before the final. They repeated the dose after being behind at half-time, with two more goals by Tilson, giving him 15 in two FA Cup campaigns.

Another record attendance was set in February 1935 when 79,491 – the highest for a Football League game at that point – saw a 1-1 draw with the leaders Arsenal, who were on their way to completing a hat-trick of titles, with City fourth this time.

A year later the club paid Blackpool a near record fee of £10,000 for inside-forward Peter Doherty who in his first full season, 1936/37, earned a championship medal in dramatic fashion. Such an outcome hardly seemed possible at Christmas, with 20 points from 20 games, having just conceded five goals in successive matches at Sheffield Wednesday and Grimsby. From there City went on a long unbeaten run, ended only by a shock FA Cup quarter-final defeat away to giant-killers Millwall of the Third Division South.

In the league, however, there was no stopping Doherty's team, the Irishman having emerged as leading scorer too. Liverpool were hit for ten goals in two games over Easter, followed by a 6-2 romp at Brentford which put City second behind Arsenal. The latter's visit on 10 April had all the makings of a title decider and it went City's way, 2-0. Top of the table and with a game in hand they needed only to avoid a classic calamity, and for once managed to do so for the first Football League championship in the club's history. A 2-2 draw at Birmingham on the final day ensured they remained unbeaten in the league since Christmas Day, Doherty admitting he punched in the equalising goal for his 30th of the season; left-wing partner Brook had weighed in with 20.

After the championship trophy came the cup for cock-ups. Top scorers in the whole division the following season, including two sevens and two sixes, City somehow contrived to be relegated. As the pressure built towards the end they beat West Brom 7-1 and Leeds 6-2 but on the last day lost 1-0 to fellow strugglers Huddersfield and returned to the dressing room to hear that every other result had gone against them. Big Swifty and his defence had been beaten 77 times and City were down by two points, with United of all clubs taking their place. Ouch.

* * * * *

Despite that greatly enjoyed finale, three spells in the Second Division and very nearly one in the Third, plus one FA Cup semi-final lost heavily to City meant it was hardly a golden period for **Manchester United**.

Surviving in the top tier only after the players arranged their Liverpool match-fix, United stayed there in mid-table for two more seasons before collapsing in 1921/22, winning only eight games and scoring 41 goals in a season that began with a 5-0 defeat at Everton.

England international Frank Barson, a robust centre-half, came from Aston Villa for £5,000 and was influential in promotion three years later, edging out rivals Derby County, who attracted almost 60,000 to Old Trafford as results and crowds improved again. Conceding only 23 goals was far and away the best in the country, ever-present Mancunian goalkeeper Alf Steward having been given his chance after four years on the books.

He had a some bad days back in the First Division the following season, conceding seven at Blackburn, five at Liverpool and six at home to City, who then put three past him in the FA Cup semi-final. The consolation was that at the end of the campaign United were staring down from a satisfactory ninth place at their relegated neighbours.

The club's prestige was enhanced by staging a first international, between England and Scotland, at Old Trafford, which they then bought outright for just over £10,000 but in the epic relegation struggle of 1927/28 United only just survived as one of the seven teams a point above relegated Tottenham. Only a 6-1 win over Liverpool on the final day, with no questions asked this time, spared them.

Next they played second fiddle in Manchester for eight long seasons, enduring in 1930/31 a dreadful one after beginning with 12 successive losses – the worst start in any major European league until Italian club Benevento in 2017; it ended in relegation by ten points, the final nail having been knocked in the coffin at Anfield in April. Conceding 115 goals, a defence with Steward still in goal had gone from the country's best to worst in five years.

As early as October, after losing the derby 4-1, fans passed a vote of no confidence in the board and although a threatened boycott of Woolwich Arsenal's visit didn't materialise, some shocking home attendances later in season reached a low point at 3,679 against Leicester; the average was below 12,000. Herbert Bamlett resigned before the bitter end, having proved one of the least successful managers in the club's history.

Financial problems came to a head later that year when the bank refused any further credit and James Gibson, owner of a local clothing firm, rode to the rescue with £2,000 and an offer of more for players. The matchday band were only saved when reducing their price to two guineas (£2.10p). Optimism as 33,000 came to see a Christmas Day win over Wolves was tempered by the return game the next day – a 7-0 defeat at Molineux.

Things would get worse and in 1934 United were the closest they have ever been to the Third Division. An injury-hit season in which 38 players were used drew to a close a week after City had won the FA Cup with United going to Millwall in 21st place, one point behind the Lions, who had an excellent record at their feared south London Den. After being denied an early penalty, the home side froze, however, conceding a goal to outside-left Tommy

Manley midway through the first half and after Laurie Fishlock, the Surrey and England cricketer, missed a good chance for them, right-winger Jack Cape got a second and United stayed up by a point. 'More Like Mice Than Lions' was the *Daily Herald* verdict on the home side.

It was a historic low point for United. In two more seasons they were promoted as champions with Charlton Athletic, sealing promotion with two wins over Bury in a run of 19 games unbeaten. At Gigg Lane thousands of their own fans, 'oily, begrimed and jubilant Manchester workmen', poured on to the pitch to celebrate. But while the Londoners went on to finish runners-up to City, United went down once more, bottom but one.

Next, as champions City managed to get relegated in 1938, United replaced them to conclude an extraordinary couple of years for Manchester football. They needed a win at home to Bury on the final day and got it 2-0 in front of 53,604 to go up with Villa, who thus ended their first exile from the top division.

Three important acquisitions that season were Stan Pearson, spotted by the chairman spending one of his occasional weekends in Bournemouth, Johnny Carey, the versatile Dubliner, and Jack Rowley from Wolves. Each was starting a period of more than 15 years with the club, and exciting years they would become.

✳ ✳ ✳ ✳ ✳

Having returned to the top division at the first attempt in 1914/15, **Preston** stayed up by two points in the first post-war campaign, but went down again in 1925 for nine seasons. Highlights from that period were almost entirely in the FA Cup with a losing 1921 semi-final (2-1 to Spurs) and the following year's final controversially lost to Huddersfield.

Survival in the first post-war season was largely due to new signing Tommy Roberts from Leicester for a bargain £500, scoring 26 of the 57 league goals. It was one of his that won the crucial final game at Everton after home captain Dickie Downs missed a penalty. Sixteenth for three consecutive seasons, they achieved a rare consistency, as did Roberts with goal tallies of 18, 18, 28 and 26. When he was sold to Burnley early in 1924/25, however, North End paid a heavy price and went down, seven points from safety with nobody reaching double figures.

Roberts's return from Turf Moor for two seasons brought some joy and goals until he suffered a broken leg in a road accident. Promotion, missed by five points then four, was finally achieved as runners-up to Grimsby in 1934.

A feisty new Scottish wing-half named Bill Shankly was instrumental in the success, with Jimmy Milne as his partner. Six wins in the final seven games secured the return, a point ahead of Bolton and Brentford, and a record 40,177 turned out for the FA Cup victory against Northampton Town.

Seventh place in the second season back was a good effort, let down by a poor away record and was followed by losing the FA Cup Final, 3-1 to Sunderland after taking the lead, and then an outstanding 1937/38 with third place, a record gate and another cup final appearance.

They did all that without a manager. Scotsman Tommy Muirhead unexpectedly resigned in the summer, but a 5-3 win at Everton early on received widespread praise and suggested great things. Too many draws eventually cost them the title, which went to Arsenal, only three points ahead. The Londoners beat them twice in the league and were watched by the current Deepdale record of 42,684 in a critical April game but North End humbled them 1-0 at Highbury in the fifth round of the FA Cup when George Mutch, signed from Manchester United, continued his run of scoring in every round. He netted again in the comfortable quarter-final win at Brentford, then in the semi-final against Villa.

Against Huddersfield at Wembley Mutch was the central figure once more as revenge was taken in the sweetest manner. In the 1922 final the Yorkshire side had prevailed with a penalty following a foul shown to have been outside the area. This time, with the extra half-hour almost up and no score, Town's captain Alf Young tackled Mutch a fraction outside but a penalty was again awarded and a dazed Mutch ('I don't remember aiming at goal') smacked in the winner off the underside of the crossbar.

FA Cup Final 1938: Preston North End 1 Huddersfield Town 0 (aet)
Preston: Holdcroft; Gallimore, A. Beattie, Shankly, Smith, Batey, Watmough, Mutch, Maxwell, R. Beattie, H. O'Donnell.
Huddersfield: Hesford; Craig, Mountford, Willingham, Young, Boot, Hulme, Isaac, MacFadyen, Barclay, Beasley.

* * * * *

Blackpool, strugglers before the war, resumed in encouraging fashion, although it took until 1930 and several different managers to finally get out of the Second Division. Major Frank Buckley (1923–27), later to achieve greater fame with Wolves, was one of them, but it was under Harry Evans, who was only granted the title of 'honorary manager' that they made the big step.

Centre-forward Joe Lane was sold to Birmingham in March 1920 for a record fee after he had scored 67 goals in 99 games and pushed the club towards an eventual fourth place in the Second Division that season. Without him they were top of the table for a long spell the following year but missed out on promotion because of a poor finish with only one win in the last eight games.

Buckley took over in 1923 to achieve another fourth place, with tangerine shirts introduced for the first time. Former miner Harry Bedford was now the main scorer with 88 in three seasons, which earned him two England caps and then a £3,000 move to Derby County in 1925.

Successors proved surprisingly easy to find. First came Billy Tremelin with 31 in a season, then the even more prolific Jimmy Hampson, picked up from Nelson for only £1,000. In 1927/28 he contributed 31 at almost a goal a game, then pushed his team back up to eighth with 40 in 41 games and finally beat even that club record with 45 in what proved to be the championship season of 1929/30.

Winning 12 of the first 14 games established the Seasiders as contenders from the start, with Chelsea and fellow Lancastrians Oldham as strong rivals. By a quirk of the fixture list Blackpool played Chelsea twice in successive days at Christmas, and Oldham twice over Easter, taking three points out of four from the Londoners and all four from the Latics. In-between times successive five-goal defeats by Tottenham and Bradford City were shrugged off. A huge crowd of 45,304 at Boundary Park saw a 2-1 away win on Easter Monday to seal promotion, Hampson missing a penalty but still securing his 45th goal to finish as the country's top scorer.

Predictably the First Division proved hard work. In three seasons Hampson hit another 73 league goals but Blackpool conceded no fewer than 312 in that time and after two successful relegation struggles, won by a single point each time, they finished bottom in 1932/33.

Hampson stayed on, suffering from injuries, and under Joe Smith, beginning a managerial reign of 23 years, promotion back to the top division was achieved in 1937 as runners-up to Leicester, despite the gifted Irish inside-forward Peter Doherty having been sold to Manchester City for £10,000.

The return to the top was marred by one of the great tragedies in the club's history. On 10 January 1938, two days after playing in the FA Cup win at Birmingham, Hampson drowned on a fishing trip when his yacht collided with a trawler. Aged only 31, his record was 252 goals in 373 games in just over ten years; not bad for £1,000. The Seasiders finished 12th and then 15th before the war, spending heavily on players like George Eastham Snr and Jock Dodds.

After five years in their chairman's racing colours of light and light dark blue stripes, the famous tangerine (not orange, please) reappeared from 1938. In 1939/40 Blackpool won their first three games, so they were sitting on top of the First Division when a halt was declared for more important matters.

* * * * *

The war treated **Oldham** harshly. First Division runners-up in 1919, they were left short by injuries and transfers and were never far from relegation before suffering the drop in 1923, bottom of the table with nobody scoring more than six goals.

For most of that time they earned the least gate money and in the relegation season had smaller crowds, at under 14,000, than three Third Division South sides. A dismal 4,000 watched what would be their final First Division home game for almost 70 years.

A record low of 35 goals was repeated two years later when they almost dropped further, surviving at the expense of Crystal Palace by beating them 1-0 away on the final day – the joint-top scorers had five each.

Managers like Charlie Roberts, having played centre-half for two seasons after signing from Manchester United, and David Ashworth, in his second period, had only a year each in charge, although Bob Mellor had three spells, starting in 1924, and would remain as secretary until 1953.

There was one better campaign, finishing third in 1929/30 after a rare promotion chance was lost because of two defeats by Blackpool over Easter and then one to Barnsley on the last day, leaving them two points short. Finally they went down again in 1935 with three draws and no wins from 21 away games. The previous year just 2,986 had watched the 7-0 win over Hull.

First experiences of the Third Division North were better than might have been expected, with the exception of a notorious 13-4 defeat at Tranmere on Boxing Day 1935; Oldham's players apparently having celebrated the previous day's 4-1 win rather too enthusiastically.

* * * * *

For a while **Bury** seemed likely to carry on after the war as they had performed before it, the definition of a mid-table Second Division side. But after a couple of years in the top six they eventually returned to the top tier as runners-up in 1924, pipping Derby County, who had scored a dozen goals more, by the tiniest of margins on goal average.

Close call or not, once back at the highest level, the Shakers twice finished fifth and in 1926 were fourth behind such contemporary giants as Huddersfield, Arsenal and Sunderland, the highest placing in their history.

During that period, centre-forward Norman Bullock was clocking up a goodly number of his record 539 appearances, which produced 127 goals and earned him three England caps (two goals). Signed as an amateur in 1920, he played until 1935 and was manager for four years, returning for a second spell from 1945–49.

Tragedy struck the club in April 1927 when full-back Sam Wynne collapsed and died from a brain haemorrhage during a match away to Sheffield United. He was in his first season with them, having joined from Oldham, where he went into the record books as the first player to score twice for each team, at home to Manchester United in October 1923.

By 1929 Bury were back in the Second Division and often in contention for promotion again, no more so than in 1936/37, missing out to Blackpool by three points. On New Year's Day 1937, when it was already clear that the Lancashire pair were promotion rivals, a crowd of 34,386 turned up at Gigg Lane for the Seasiders' 3-2 victory, setting the ground record.

By 1939, however, they had reverted once more to middle-of-the-table status.

* * * * *

A 20-team Third Division North finally came into being in 1921, a year after what was effectively a southern version. With Grimsby Town moved from the southern section to a more obvious northern berth, and Stockport County relegated from the Second Division, there were 18 places to fill. The Football League management committee recommended 14 clubs including Accrington Stanley (from the Lancashire Combination), plus Nelson, Rochdale and Tranmere Rovers from the Central League. That left four places for 14 clubs, which went to the Central League's Southport and Stalybridge, Wigan Borough from the Lancashire Combination and the Midland League's Halifax Town. Merseyside pair South Liverpool and West Stanley missed out.

Stockport, although reluctant joiners as the relegated side, proved to be the first champions of the new division and its best supported team, a year after a match that has often been wrongly described as having the smallest Football League attendance of all time.

On 7 May 1921, County's Second Division game against Leicester was moved to Old Trafford because Edgeley Park had been closed by the FA after previous crowd trouble. The match was played immediately after Manchester United's First Division game with Derby, which attracted at least 10,000 and it is highly improbable that all of them immediately left before the second game. What has been officially recorded is that only 13 extra people paid to watch the Stockport match rather than the double-header, whereas the *Athletic News* report mentions around 2,000 staying on.

Even in that relegation campaign, County averaged crowds of almost 9,000 and the loyalists were rewarded the following season. After winning five of their first six matches and then going unbeaten from New Year's Day 1922 until Easter, they sealed the title by beating Darlington in front of an impressive attendance of 18,500.

Surviving by a single point in the Second Division, they finished above Manchester United the following year, when goalkeeper Harry Hardy became the club's only England international in a 4-0 win over Belgium at West Bromwich Albion.

Relegation followed in 1926, well clear at the bottom with 97 goals against. Stoke City, who accompanied them, returned immediately, but Stockport became Stuckport in a frustrating spell, finishing sixth, third, second, second and seventh, then after one mid-table season in 1931/32, third, third, seventh and fifth before a deserved championship title in 1936/37, losing only five games with the tightest defence in the land.

Joe Smith, the former Bolton FA Cup winner, and Frank 'Bonzo' Newton, were among the principal goalscorers, followed a little later by Alf Lythgoe, whose record 46 out of the team's 115 in 1933/34 included a couple in the 13-0 demolition of Halifax Town.

The Hatters had become the Lilywhites, red and white stripes of the early days having given way to blue shirts, then white with black shorts. Unfortunately their new status lasted only one season, that defence now being pierced 70 times and leaving them bottom by five points.

* * * * *

A Third Division North allowed Accrington to have a Football League club for the first time since the inaugural members named after the town dropped out in 1893 (disbanding three years later, as recorded in Chapter 2). Their collapse naturally helped the unconnected **Accrington Stanley** gain greater prominence, although they would have dramas of their own down the years.

The first of those was being found guilty of retaining almost £6 in gate money from a Lancashire Junior Cup tie and receiving a suspension only lifted when four of those involved were banned. Moving up from the Lancashire Combination, however, they attracted some of the best gates at the new level, around 8,000 regularly turning out at the new Peel Park, home since 1919.

Fifth place in the inaugural season, as second highest scorers, was followed by a slow falling away down the table until bottoming out in 19th place five years later. In the constant battle for support with First Division Blackburn and Burnley, there was not surprisingly a decline in crowds at that time to about 4,000, and then 3,000 in the '30s, an economically depressed period in which the club maintained mid-table status until the last two seasons before the war.

Neighbouring Blackburn had briefly dropped into the Second Division when they were humbled 3-1 by the Reds in a 1937 FA Cup replay, which led in turn to a lucrative if unsuccessful trip to Manchester City for a fourth-round tie watched by 39,000.

In both those last two campaigns they were bottom and forced to apply for re-election, the second time after winning only seven games out of 42 and finishing 11 points behind the field. They had sufficient friends to maintain Football League status comfortably each time, receiving 41 votes to 15 for Shrewsbury Town (who would have to wait until 1950) and then 29 compared to the aspiring South Liverpool's five.

* * * * *

Bottom of the Third Division North in its first season were **Rochdale**, whose history was described by one chronicler in 1928 as one of 'struggle against difficulties' and has remained so ever since.

Rochdale Town, disappearing in 1903, were quickly replaced by the current club at the same ground, known as St Clements playing field, or Spotland, where they bravely turned professional in the Manchester League. Tenth out of 16, the Dale ambitiously went for the Lancashire Combination and were voted into the Second Division for the 1908/09 season, finishing tenth once more. A good crowd of 5,000 turned up for the derby against Heywood, rather less – 150 – for the visit of Turton in heavy snow.

Basking in promotion to the Combination's First Division as well as winning the Lancashire Junior Cup, the directors were emboldened to make a first application to the Football League, but attracted only one vote. Pressure was growing from both north and south for a Third Division, however, with Rochdale pushing hard and able to pull in almost 10,000 for a big FA Cup tie like the one against Luton Town in 1911, drawn 1-1 before losing the replay.

Combination champions in 1912, they moved to the new Central League and after faring well as temporary members of the regional war-time league were obvious candidates for the Third Division North afterwards.

Their first Football League game was an eventful 6-3 win over Accrington on 27 August 1921 with a hat-trick by inside-forward Reg Owens, but although he scored another in the 7-0 win over Walsall in December, a month when heavy winds brought down the roof of the main stand, both results proved illusory. Like that gale, conceding 77 goals was costly and necessitated a first application for re-election.

From bottom spot, however, the prolific Potteries record-breaker Bert Whitehurst was able to inspire four top-six finishes in succession from 1924–27 as well as earning himself a transfer to Liverpool (where he was less successful). Twice Rochdale were runners-up, a point short of promotion behind Wolves in 1924, and top scorers with 105 goals in 1927, when Whitehurst set the current club record of 44.

He claimed five that season in their record league win, 8-1 over Chesterfield, and four in a record 8-2 FA Cup win against Crook Town which, dispiritingly, was the club's only success in the competition in 13 years.

Decline was swift, with only one top-ten finish before the war and financial problems looming. In 1930/31, with only Nelson below them, the club were threatened with closure despite the town's most famous daughter, Gracie Fields, offering support. Then after Wigan Borough resigned during the following season, the Dale were left bottom with one of worst records in Football League history; 17 successive defeats, 11 points from 40 games and 135 goals conceded.

To come through it, and the rest of a troubled decade, was an achievement in itself.

* * * * *

Being the width of the Mersey away enabled **Tranmere Rovers** to grow and survive in Birkenhead when Bootle had failed in Liverpool itself. Never anything like rivals to the city's established big two, they became something akin to popular little cousins occasionally offered a helping hand in the form of a player, a manager or a lucrative friendly, and maintaining Football League status from 1921–2015 before regaining it three years later.

New research has shown that a team known as Tranmere Rovers, who dropped the Rovers tag after only a year, existed from

1881 but disbanded seven years later and had no connection with the present club, although this did not prevent the present-day Rovers erroneously celebrating their centenary in 1981.

Being recommended by the Football League management committee for a place in the new Third Division North was nevertheless a reward for almost 35 years of competition, begun by entering the Liverpool and District Challenge Cup in 1886 and then various leagues in Liverpool and Lancashire, between which they moved around with confusing irregularity.

The club's reputation was clearly enhanced by winning the reorganised Combination in 1907/08 then switching to the Lancashire Combination, winning promotion in 1912 at the current Prenton Park ground and taking the First Division title two years later.

Only then did the FA Cup bring any joy after 14 largely barren years, with a club record 13-0 win over Oswestry United, including five goals for Phil Smith, before a home defeat by Wrexham.

After the war years, winning the championship again in 1919 led to a couple of seasons in the Central League as replacement for the defunct Leeds City reserves, paving the way for the Football League itself.

Results there were initially modest, though a mid-table campaign in 1923/24 brought a ground record crowd of some 15,000 to see the champions-elect Wolves, as well as the debut of Dixie Dean, ten days before his 17th birthday. For once he failed to score, but rattling in 27 in 30 games the following season for a struggling team led to the move he had always desired to his beloved Everton as Rovers sank to the bottom two.

From that low point they were regularly in the top half of the table and often the first six, including two successive fourth places from 1930–32 and then a serious promotion challenge in 1935/36, fuelled by one extraordinary result. Top of the table on Christmas Day, Rovers would have been upset by a 4-1 defeat away to Oldham, who by all accounts took the festive spirit rather too literally before the return game at Prenton Park next day.

By the time the Latics staggered back to the dressing room at half-time, they were 8-1 down, Robert 'Bunny' Bell having scored five times despite the heavy mud. Rovers were in double figures before Oldham got their second and at 11-4 there were fully 20 minutes left. Not until the last couple of minutes did Bell strike twice more, giving him a new individual record of nine, which would have been ten had he not put a penalty wide. Yet the record lasted only four months until Luton Town's Joe Payne, switching from wing-half to play his first senior match as a centre-forward, scored ten in a 12-0 win over Bristol Rovers.

By then Bell had followed the path to Goodison Park taken by Dean 11 years earlier but even after his predecessor left he was given only a handful of games each season, ending up with nine goals in 14 appearances. Without him Tranmere faded badly and missed out on promotion by five points, only to go up as champions two seasons later following the return of another noted striker.

Tom 'Pongo' Waring, Birkenhead-born, had made his name with Rovers by scoring a goal a game from 1926–28 and moving to Aston Villa for a hefty £4,700. At his Villa Park peak in 1930–32, having set a club record of 49 league goals in a season, he played five times for England (four goals), alternating with a certain W. Dean. He then returned to Merseyside via Barnsley and Wolves, and saw Tranmere into the Second Division for the first time, two points clear of Doncaster.

The stay was for a mere 12 months as they finished bottom, badly outclassed and suffering 31 defeats; but after 50 years they had touched new heights.

* * * * *

Southport had to rely on a ballot to secure one of the four remaining Third Division North places but received seven more votes than nearest challengers Castleford, whose town was destined to remain a rugby stronghold.

Like Tranmere and Rochdale, the Sandgrounders came out of the Central League, having in their case first applied to the Football League fully 20 years earlier. That reflected the ambitious nature of the senior team in a popular Victorian seaside town, evolved from a local rugby club and first playing football in November 1881 against a Bootle reserve team. They were competing in the FA Cup as early as 1882, meeting the famous Blackburn Rovers in the first round (and losing 7-0) the following season.

In 1888 the name Southport Central was adopted as part of bold new plans including professionalism and an end to using only local talent, and after joining the new Lancashire League in 1889 they were well placed almost every season; runners-up in 1899, 1901 and 1902 and the last champions when it folded in 1903, moving into the Lancashire Combination and drawing crowds of up to 6,000 at the Scarisbrick New Road ground.

Lancashire Senior Cup winners in 1905, when moving to Ash Lane (renamed Haig Avenue in 1921), they left for the Central League with Rochdale in 1911 and like them enjoyed a boost as temporary members of the regional wartime league, as well as being allowed to adopt the sponsored name of Southport Vulcan (after a local factory) for one season.

Having been placed only 19th out of 22 in the Central League of 1920/21, Southport were not expected to pull up any trees in the Third Division North, but snapped a few branches in finishing ninth. A crowd of 7,000 saw the opening game, a draw against Durham City, and in the 7-1 win over Grimsby early on, Billy Glover scored six. He was also the marksman in the remarkable 1-1 FA Cup draw away to First Division Blackburn in January 1922, which led to over 12,000 watching the replay (a 2-0 defeat).

There were some notable later FA Cup runs around the turn of the decade, with regular financial problems making the receipts all the more welcome; for instance the £2,000 made from the 1926/27 run to the fourth round. Blackburn, still in the top division, were beaten 2-0 this time before a 3-1 defeat at Liverpool in front of more than 51,000 and in 1928 it was the fourth round again, knocking out Fulham before losing at home to Middlesbrough.

Then came a significant arrival in centre-forward Archie Waterston, surprisingly released by Tranmere in the summer of 1930. Turning up for a trial at Haig Avenue he was gratefully welcomed and by the end of the season was heavily involved in three club records by scoring 31 goals in 29 games, five of them in the record 8-1 win over Nelson on New Year's Day, and the club's only FA Cup quarter-final. Successive giant-killings at home to Millwall, Blackpool (with two Waterston goals) and Bradford PA brought a lucrative trip to Everton for a 9-1 defeat.

The following season there was an even heavier cup loss, 9-0 by eventual winners Newcastle, but only at the third attempt, after a heroic draw at St James' Park and a record crowd of 20,010 for the replay.

League form meanwhile fluctuated between comfortable mid-table, the bottom four (1923, 1926, 1935, 1936) and the top four in 1925 and 1939 to finish on an upbeat note as Joe 'Hat-Trick' Patrick succeeded Waterston.

* * * * *

The most immediately successful club of the new 1921 intake, **Nelson**, just a few miles north of Burnley, were unable to sustain their initial momentum and within ten years had been cast out of the Football League to begin a long struggle for survival that has continued for much of the time since.

Founder members of the Lancashire League in 1891, they were champions within five years, scoring 105 goals in 30 games and soon made a first unsuccessful application to the Football League. Before joining it they would be briefly expelled by the Lancashire FA, then close down for much of the First World War, yet emerge strong enough to move up from the Central League in 1921.

A crowd of 9,000 turned up at the Seedhill ground to greet league football with a 2-1 defeat by Wigan Borough on 27 August before a 4-1 win away to the same opposition propelled them towards a brief spell as league leaders. That did not last and they finished 16th of the 20 clubs but the following year Scottish player-manager David Wilson led a charge to the championship title, four points clear of Bradford Park Avenue, who had beaten them 6-2 in the opening game.

Second Division football began with 12,000 present for Clapton Orient's visit in August 1923, a figure that was never surpassed in a disappointing campaign that ended bottom but one, two points short of safety. Highlights were beating Manchester United at Old Trafford in March and then champions Leeds United in the final game with two goals from centre-forward Joe Eddleston, leading scorer for the third successive season.

With only one club promoted from each of the Third Division sections, a valiant effort to return to the higher level within 12 months failed by five points and was never on the cards again. Suffering like many others from the economic climate – they once had to ask Accrington for an advance of £25 on gate money – Nelson were ominously bottom in 1927/28, when Durham City were voted out. After three more unsuccessful seasons, Nelson suffered the same fate. Bottom in 1931 with only six wins, half as many as any other team, they tied on the initial re-election vote with Chester but lost the second ballot 28-20.

So a sixth defeat in succession, 4-0 at Hull on 2 May 1931, turned out to be the club's last game in the Football League. In 1936, back in the Lancashire Combination, they folded before the start of the new season and were replaced by a new club, Nelson Town, but reformed after the Second World War in the Combination. Refusing to give up hope of a return to the Football League, they applied every year until 1957, but only received any significant support once, when the Third Divisions were extended in 1950. Nelson were given 11 votes, still too few to match successful Midland League clubs Shrewsbury Town (30) and Scunthorpe United (17).

* * * * *

Only a few months after Nelson left the Football League, **Wigan Borough** did the same, and in mid-season, causing at least one newspaper to ask, 'Was the Third Division North a mistake?'

Every club trying to establish football in an acknowledged rugby league town had known difficult times. In November 1920 the club took over the Lancashire Combination fixtures of Wigan United, who had lost all nine games and been expelled for illegal payments; despite finishing bottom-but-one they were elected to the Third Division North. There they finished in the bottom four, above Tranmere, Halifax and Rochdale, before rising to fifth the next season and fourth by 1929.

In that year they set a ground record for Springfield Park when 30,443 came to see The Wednesday win 3-1 in the FA Cup third round – no disgrace as the Yorkshire side went on to become Football League champions three months later.

Gates were initially among the top half-dozen in the new section at over 7,500 and averaged five figures in that second season but fell away badly. By 1931 they were down to barely 3,000 and the club were threatened with expulsion from the Football League for having fallen so far behind with wages. Despite not paying players during the summer and selling two of the better ones to Sunderland and Tottenham, debts were over £30,000 by September, with gates insufficient to support a £100 weekly wage bill.

Borough began the new season with two wins, the first of them 4-0 away on Chester's debut as a league club, but the financial problems continued seemingly regardless of results. Two days after a 5-0 defeat at Wrexham on 24 October, Borough resigned, the first club to do so voluntarily in mid-season.

Local solicitor Frank Platt, who had been working on a reconstruction plan, said, 'The association football public of Wigan have shown once again that they have no desire to maintain league football in Wigan. Every opportunity has been afforded them of trying to save the club from resigning from the league.'

Manchester Central (see Non-league chapter) and Prescot Cables wanted to take over their fixtures but instead Borough's results were expunged, the table that season comprising only 21 teams playing 40 games each. Wigan had played 12 times, winning three and losing eight, but did not have a single local derby to help with gate revenue. The last home match, against Carlisle on 17 October, was watched by 2,667.

At the end of the season a new club, **Wigan Athletic**, were founded but did not receive a single vote when applying for a Football League place; that would have to wait 46 years. Instead the new Latics joined the Cheshire County League, which they won for three seasons running from 1934–36.

* * * * *

Down in their new league, Wigan found the third of the unfortunate local trio to drop out of the Football League in the interwar years. **Stalybridge Celtic** lasted the shortest time of all, managing only the first two seasons of the Third Division North before opting out for a less expensive life in the Cheshire County League.

Officially founded in 1909 with possible links dating back to the much earlier Rovers and Town clubs, Celtic had a keen benefactor in Herbert Rhodes, who played for the team and based their colours on those of his racehorses.

They turned professional in 1911 and immediately became champions of the Lancashire Combination Second Division, then made a bold move to the Southern League Second Division in 1914, incurring considerable travel costs to take on opposition comprising mostly Welsh clubs plus Coventry, Stoke and Brentford, but furthering their ambition.

Joining the Central League after the war cut down on travelling and led to a place in the newly expanded Football League. A 6-0 win over Chesterfield to start life there suggested Celtic could be among the stronger members and they finished seventh, slipping four places the following season.

Average gates, however, were less impressive than finishing positions, and dropped from over 5,000 in the first season to under 3,500 in the next, which was worse than anyone except struggling Durham City.

Unwilling to lose any more money, the club resigned their place and reverted to the Cheshire County League, making way for **New Brighton**, who would remain a Football League side for almost 30 years. Their history is intimately bound up with that of **South Liverpool** (see Non-league chapter), whose earliest ambition, as their name implies, was to become a force in the south of the city, rivalling Everton and Liverpool further north.

Failing, however, to make any impression when applying for Football League membership in 1914 and 1921, and having difficulty finding a new ground, the club moved several miles north-west, crossing the Mersey in June 1921 to Sandheys Park in Rake Lane, Wallasey and changing their name to New Brighton, where Second Division football, it will be remembered, had been played from 1898 to 1901 (Chapter 2).

Pushing to bring back league football to the town, the new club attracted only seven votes in the summer of 1922, when Rochdale were comfortably re-elected with 31, but were in luck 12 months later when the Third Division North was expanded by two clubs to give the four divisions 22 each.

New Brighton, having finished third in the Lancashire Combination for two successive seasons, were unanimously elected along with Doncaster Rovers and justified their place, finishing ten points clear of the re-election places with crowds of 6,500 and then in only their second season ending up third, level on points with the runners-up Nelson.

That would, however, be their high point, both in terms of league position and attendances. After three more seasons in mid-table they dropped into the bottom half and stayed there, twice finishing bottom but one and then underneath everyone in 1935/36 with gates down to 3,000.

The penultimate campaign before the war in new maroon and white stripes did have its moments, most memorably in holding Tottenham to a goalless draw in the FA Cup fourth round before succumbing 5-2 in a replay watched by 36,004 at White Hart Lane.

Interlude I

War

The three-match season of 1939/40; ban on organised sport quickly lifted but with restrictions; goalscorers cash in; emergence of Liddell, Finney and Mortensen; Stanley Matthews a most welcome guest for powerful Blackpool, who join Preston and Bolton as War Cup winners; prisoners of war at Deepdale; United bombed out for eight years.

AT the start of the two great wars of the 20th century, government and sporting authorities alike were unsure how to react, partly because the public were divided. Was it right that fit young men should continue playing football, cricket and rugby while contemporaries were risking their lives for king and country? Or was some sort of entertainment desirable to offer relief from the strains of war and help maintain morale, not least among the 1.5 million troops who spent their time in Britain?

As we have seen in Chapter 3, professional football carried on regardless for a full season after the declaration of war in July 1914, allowing Everton to win a second league championship and Preston to claim promotion back to the First Division. In 1939 the authorities reacted decisively in suspending organised competition, but then had second thoughts.

The growing threat of fascism in Germany and Italy had affected sport long before then. In 1935 there were 14 arrests for disturbances after Tottenham, with a large Jewish population nearby, was the insensitive choice of venue for England's international against Germany. For the return game in Berlin three years later and England's 1939 friendly in Milan players were obliged to give the fascist salute.

At a home game with Sunderland on Easter Saturday 1939 Bolton's captain Harry Goslin (who would be killed on active service in Italy five years later) made a speech urging spectators to sign up with the Territorial Army, after which the club's first team joined the 53rd Field Regiment, Royal Artillery. Liverpool were another club who enlisted en masse.

The 1939/40 season began with the threat of war growing ever stronger. On the first Saturday, 26 August, there was a full programme attended by much lower gates than normal of about 600,000, a pattern repeated at the subsequent midweek games and then what turned out to be the final matches on the second Saturday. On that day, 2 September, Germany invaded Poland and the following morning the Prime Minister, Neville Chamberlain, went on the radio to announce that Britain was at war.

After three games Blackpool were the First Division's only 100 per cent club and Everton were also unbeaten, Tommy Lawton having already scored four times; Preston and Blackburn were without a win. In the Second Division Burnley had failed to win a game, while in the Third Division North, Accrington and Blackpool were the only teams with three wins. Stockport were without a point.

The Government, concerned that sporting events would be obvious targets for air raids by the feared Luftwaffe, quickly banned all sporting events, only to think again as the so-called phoney war of several months' duration began. As early as 8 September, Football Association and Football League representatives met as the sport's War Emergency Committee and the blanket ban was repealed.

Payment was restricted to no more than 30 shillings (£1.50) per player per match with no bonuses and there were drastic regulations around the size of crowd and distance teams could travel. Early friendlies included a Manchester derby that attracted only 7,000 to Old Trafford to see City win 3-2, while Everton won the Merseyside derby 4-1 at Anfield.

Ten regional leagues were set up, although six of the 88 Football League teams initially declined to play; Accrington (from 1940–44) and New Brighton (1942–46), missed four seasons each; Blackpool and Bolton played only the second half of the 1940/41 season.

Team selection naturally depended on who was available, or even in the country at the time, and all clubs used guest players – Matt Busby turned out for six other clubs in all as well as Liverpool. The quality could be variable and renowned goalscorers cashed in. Lawton was naturally prolific wherever he played (on Christmas Day 1940 he turned out for both Everton and Tranmere); Manchester United's Jack Rowley once scored eight in a game for Wolves and seven for his own club (in the 13-1 win over New Brighton); in January 1941 James Currier scored five for City in successive games against Rochdale in aggregate wins of 15-2; Billy Liddell began to make his mark and his name at Liverpool while Tom Finney was doing so at Preston and Stan Mortensen at Blackpool.

After a bad winter in 1939/40 the season was extended into June to allow a League Cup to be played. With crowds as low as 250 for Bolton v Burnley, Bury won the league and Blackburn went through to the first Football League War Cup Final at Wembley against West Ham. Although national morale was hardly high after the retreat from Dunkirk, 42,399 turned out to see Hammers' Sam Small score the only goal.

For the 1940/41 season the format changed in the north-west to two divisions, North and South (the latter including several midlands clubs). Teams played as many games as they could manage but were ranked bizarrely according to goal average rather than their points-per-game averages. Oldham fitted in as many as 37 games, Blackpool only 20. Finney's Preston, playing most home games at the Leyland Motors ground while Deepdale housed prisoners of war, won the northern division and the national cup, drawing the final 1-1 with Arsenal in front of 60,000 at Wembley, then winning the replay 2-1 at Blackburn. Bobby Beattie scored the crucial goal and instead of medals Preston's players received wartime savings vouchers worth 15 shillings (75p) each.

Blackpool, with RAF man Stanley Matthews based on the Fylde coast and an invaluable regular guest, were particularly strong. In 1941/42 Jock Dodds took advantage of the great man's service from the wing by scoring 65 of the season's 183 goals, topping the first northern section, before Manchester United just pipped them to the second. The following year Blackpool and Liverpool won the two league sections, Blackpool taking the League North Cup and beating Arsenal 4-2 in the national final in front of 55,000.

In 1943/44 Blackpool won another league, Bath oddly taking the second section, and the Seasiders lost a two-legged northern final to Aston Villa. For the last wartime season Lancashire's main success came from Bolton. They took the northern cup on a 3-2 aggregate over Manchester United and by the time they defeated Chelsea, the London winners, at Stamford Bridge on 2 June, war had been over for almost a month.

Matthews and Lawton were regularly in demand for the wartime internationals that began in November 1939 and could attract huge crowds, most notably at Hampden Park for Scotland against England. Although the FA spread home games round the country, surprisingly few were played in the north-west. When a rare one was, against Scotland at Maine Road in October 1943, a crowd of 60,000 were rewarded with an 8-0 England win which skipper Stan Cullis called the finest football he had ever seen; City's Frank Swift was in goal, Everton's Cliff Britton and Joe Mercer at wing-half and Matthews supplied four-goal Lawton in attack.

The previous month Blackpool's Mortensen, an England reserve at Wembley, achieved an unusual distinction when he was summoned on as a substitute for Wales after Ivor Powell was injured.

Bolton skipper Goslin, who had played in four of the earlier England games, was one of an estimated 80 professional footballers past and present who did not live to see peacetime. Others from Lancashire clubs included his team-mate Walter Sidebottom, whose ship was torpedoed in the English Channel; Blackburn pair Albert Clarke and Frank Chivers; Bury's William Poole; William Summer of Everton; Liverpool and England defender Tom Cooper; Hubert Redwood, a right-back who played almost 100 games for Manchester United and Ben Carpenter, who had just joined the club; Jack Owen of Preston; the much travelled Sam Jennings, who was manager of Rochdale in 1937/38; and a long list from Tranmere including Ernie Davies, Stanley Docking, Stanley Duff, Stanley Gooding, Kenneth Haimes, Jack Kearns, Gerald Roberts, Gordon Rosenthal and Jack Watson.

Grounds also suffered. In March 1941, during the period that Winston Churchill referred to as the country's darkest hour, there was serious damage to the main stand at Old Trafford, which had to be demolished and led to United spending eight long years at Maine Road; from 8 March 1941 until 24 August 1949 they did not play at their real home.

Goodison Park was also hit, which led to both clubs being among ten in the First Division who claimed money for repairs from the War Damage Commission. United were eventually given by far the largest amount of £22,278, Everton's £5,000 being the next highest.

Chapter 5

That's entertainment: Stan and Tom and Nat – and Matt (1946–60)

Matt Busby revives United before the tragedy of Munich;
Matthews and Finney build the Blackpool-Preston
rivalry – but only one of them wins any medals;
Burnden Park disaster and the Lion of Vienna;
Merseyside pair swap fortunes and First Division place
pre-Shankly; City's familiar ups-and-downs; Burnley
unfashionable champions; Blackburn's ten years below
stairs; plenty of Third North and Fourth Division
strugglers; New Brighton voted out of the league.

ALTHOUGH the Football League wanted the 1945/46 season to be a return to full normality, clubs opted for one more year of regionalised games. In the north, Sheffield United won the main section from Everton, Bolton and homeless Manchester United, while a split lower section was won by Accrington in the north-west part of the region and then Rotherham from Rochdale in what was effectively a Third Division North.

With clubs being keen to maximise gate receipts as well as minimise travelling costs, the FA Cup was played for the only time on a two-legged basis as far as the semi-final, where Bolton went out 2-0 to Charlton, having come through the trauma in the previous round of English football's greatest disaster to date, at Burnden Park.

It would be the first of two tragedies to strike the region in a dozen years, with the devastation of Matt Busby's Manchester United 'Babes' to follow in 1958. Each carried a terrible irony; Bolton's blackest day and 33 deaths were caused by the very enthusiasm for public entertainment of any sort that followed six years of war and in particular the desire to see sporting heroes like Stanley Matthews, who was playing for visiting Stoke that day, while the horror of Munich came about through United's admirable defiance of the insular Football League, who wanted nothing to do with European competitions.

Right from the resumption of peacetime football, attendances boomed, peaking in 1948/49, with more than 41 million watching league games at an average of 22,333 across all four divisions. Eleven clubs, including the two Manchester sides (both playing at Maine Road), Liverpool and Everton, averaged over 40,000 per home game.

There was a huge thirst for football and apart from a few clips on Pathé News in a local cinema, just about the only way to watch stars like Matthews and Stan Mortensen, Tom Finney and Nat Lofthouse was in person. Live football on television – for those fortunate enough to have one – was rare, although the north-western teams featured heavily in its timeline.

For technical reasons coverage of the first televised international match, between England and Scotland in April 1938, and the FA Cup Final between Huddersfield and Preston the same year were confined to the London area. Blackburn's fifth-round defeat at Charlton in 1947 was the first FA Cup tie other than a final to be shown and 1950s games against foreign opposition under the floodlights that First Division clubs were slowly installing proved popular.

From 1955 the BBC began paying around £5,000 a year for short highlights shown on Saturday nights. The fledgling ITV, born that year and reaching the north-west as Granada in May 1956, wanted to show 26 league games on Friday or Saturday evenings, but found the clubs lukewarm because of fears about the effect on attendances – already falling away from the 1949 peak.

The short-lived experiment began with a First Division game between Blackpool and Bolton on 9 September 1960, unfortunately missing star attraction Matthews, who might have been expected to add even more to the television ratings than he could always be relied upon to put on the gate. ITV showed the second half of Blackpool's uninspiring 1-0 victory while the Beeb were reckoned to have had the better of things later the same night with the Olympic football final from Rome (Yugoslavia 3 Denmark 1) and highlights from Tottenham's 3-2 win at Arsenal, the seventh successive victory of Spurs's famous Double season. Tottenham then refused permission for their home game against Aston Villa to be shown a fortnight later and the experiment was dead almost as soon as it had begun.

Not that there was any great incentive for the clubs. Blackpool and Bolton received a modest £557 while the Football League took four times as much. *Match of the Day* was still four years away, but television's enthusiasm for the sport was understandable; and what highlights and personalities they might have found in Lancashire once football resumed on a national basis in the late summer of 1946.

* * * * *

Team game or not, the story of **Manchester United**, Blackpool, Bolton and Preston in this period was in many ways the tale in each case of one local hero. For United that man was Matt Busby, who had of course already served their two greatest rivals with distinction.

Overcoming early difficulties at City in the late 1920s, he had found his best position as a constructive wing-half and, as we have seen, featured in their FA Cup finals of 1933 and '34 before moving two years later to Liverpool and therefore missing out on City's extraordinary championship-relegation sequence.

While rising to the rank of sergeant major in the war, he continued playing where and when he could, appearing for half a dozen clubs, making friends and contacts and being offered the managership of Ayr United. Had Liverpool offered an equivalent promotion, football history would have been changed; instead they wanted only an assistant to manager George Kay, who would stay in charge until 1951.

So when Busby received a letter from United's chief scout and fixer Luigi 'Louis' Rocca in December 1944 about 'a great job for you' he was immediately interested. United had Walter Crickmer, loyal and devoted, working in the outmoded role of secretary-manager and wanted something more up to date.

A board meeting in February 1945 heard the glad tidings that Busby was looking for a manager's job and preferred the Manchester area for 'family reasons'. Chairman James Gibson was impressed by his 'honesty of purpose', respected his desire to be manager in fact as well as name, and trusted him sufficiently to agree a five-year contract starting at £15 per week, rather than the three years originally proposed. The board were happy too for Busby to make what proved an inspired appointment of Jimmy Murphy, a former West Bromwich and Wales international, as his assistant.

Frustratingly, the 1945/46 season had to begin without them and when Matt was finally demobbed in October, he took over a team that had performed modestly the previous season and was still sorting itself out, having started badly in the Football League North with only one win in the first 11 games.

Of the team that played in his first match, a 2-1 win at home to Bolton, only five were still in place for the last one of the season, including Jack Rowley, centre-half Allenby Chilton and goalkeeper Jack Crompton. More importantly, they had been joined later in the season by Johnny Carey, Jimmy Delaney, Stan Pearson, John Aston Snr and Charlie Mitten, all playing a part in the rise from 16th to fourth place.

All of them would be stalwarts too of a first full Football League season that began with five straight wins, the last of them in front of a 65,000 crowd; four games from the finish United were potential champions but they lost the most important of them 1-0 at Anfield to finish a point behind Liverpool as runners-up. Rowley scored 26 of the 95 goals and another 23 the following season when they were second again, albeit further behind Arsenal. The two derbies with returning mid-table City, both of course at Maine Road, attracted over 70,000 each, and for Arsenal's visit the crowd was a Football League record of 83,260 (officially increased from the figure of 81,962 published at the time); but the campaign highlight was Busby's first trophy, the 1948 FA Cup.

Unusually he had predicted they would be champions but had to make do with the not inconsiderable consolation of the cup after one of its most memorable finals.

An exciting campaign brought First Division opposition at every stage, beginning with one of the most thrilling of ties, a 6-4 win away to Villa, who scored in the first minute, then found themselves 5-1 down at half-time (what the BBC would have given to show that one live). Pearson and Johnny Morris finished with two apiece. The fourth-round tie against champions Liverpool was unusual in that United were drawn at home but so were City; no moving games to Sunday in those days, so it was played at Goodison Park, where Busby's team put on a superb display to beat the champions 3-0. Charlton and Preston were beaten comfortably and in the semi-final at Hillsborough Pearson's hat-trick saw off Derby County to earn a final against Stanley Matthews and Blackpool.

It was another classic in which United, playing in blue, conceded a goal from an unlucky penalty early on and were 2-1 behind at the interval, but effectively won the tie with three goals in 14 minutes from Rowley, Pearson and right-half John Anderson.

'This was Wembley's finest final' was the *News of the World* headline. 'A match of overflowing talent, glorious and dramatic,' said *The Times*. Aston at left-back coped well with Matthews, and skipper Carey, who had been converted from ordinary inside-left to wing-half then outstanding right-back, was as calmly composed as ever.

FA Cup Final 1948: Manchester United 4 Blackpool 2
Manchester United: Crompton; Carey, Aston, Anderson, Chilton, Cockburn, Delaney, Morris, Rowley, Pearson, Mitten
Blackpool: Robinson; Shimwell, Crosland, Johnston, Hayward, Kelly, Matthews, Munro, Mortensen, Dick, Rickett.

Another indication of the respect in which Busby was already held was that just before the start of the following season he was back at Wembley, not for the FA Charity Shield (played at Highbury in October), but as manager of the Great Britain team which finished fourth in the London Olympics.

Turning back to the day job with a championship title in mind, he oversaw a third successive second place, this one five points behind Portsmouth. The two derbies with City were again drawn and defence of the FA Cup looked promising with a series of easier draws bringing big wins over Bournemouth (6-0), Bradford (5-0) and Yeovil (8-0) but a semi-final defeat in a replay by Wolves, who under Stan Cullis would become great rivals for the next ten years.

In August 1949 United finally went back to Old Trafford for the first time in eight years, staging a pre-season practice game and then beating Bolton 3-0 in a midweek match watched by 41,748. They subsequently dropped a surprising number of home points and finished fourth.

There were two notable departures over the next couple of years from the FA Cup-winning forward line. Johnny Morris became Britain's most expensive player when joining Derby for £24,000 and Charlie Mitten, who scored a hat-trick of penalties in the 7-0 win at home to Aston Villa, started an ill-fated but richly rewarded jaunt to the outlawed Colombian League after 113 consecutive games.

His wing partner Delaney was phased out too in 1950/51 as United finished second once more, this time to Tottenham, but the following season they were champions at last. They managed only one extra point but added an extra 21 goals, chalking up 19 in the final four home games against Liverpool, Burnley, Chelsea and Arsenal, with old faithfuls Rowley (30) and Pearson (22) again leading the way. 'M. Busby has shown himself as great a coach as he was a player,' said an editorial in the proud *Manchester Guardian*.

The post-war team was packed with local lads and there were more to come, as products of a youth system originally instigated by Walter Crickmer before the war continued to arrive. After the champions dropped to bottom place in an autumn slump in 1952, youngsters and new signings appeared. Roger Byrne was moved from left-wing to left-back, Johnny Berry, signed from Birmingham, made the outside-right berth his own; powerful Tommy Taylor arrived in the spring from Barnsley and there were opportunities for kids like David Pegg (outside-left), Eddie Lewis (centre-forward) and John Doherty (inside-forward).

Then, right at the end of a season finishing no higher than eighth, Jackie Blanchflower, the brother of Tottenham's Danny, and City fan Dennis Viollet came in and a teenage giant from Dudley called Duncan Edwards became a debutant at 16.

That season the FA Youth Cup was instigated. Like Real Madrid in the European Cup soon afterwards, United would win it for the first five seasons, starting with a 7-1 demolition of Wolves in the first leg of the inaugural final; more than 20,000 came to watch a team including Eddie Colman, Liam 'Billy' Whelan, Edwards, Pegg and Albert Scanlon.

Not for the first or last time Wolves could only curse their luck at missing out on local boy Edwards. He had been recommended to Busby by of all people Joe Mercer, the future City manager who helped out with coaching the England schoolboys team in which the young wing-half starred.

It was a changing of the guard with a last full season for Carey, who retired and became Blackburn manager, Aston, who scouted for United and Pearson, who signed for Bury. Slowly the youngsters forced their way into Busby's confidence and team, which finished fourth (1954) and fifth (1955); then in 1955/56 were such dominant champions that the 11-point margin was the best since Blackburn in 1914 and remained so until three points for a win were introduced in the 1980s. Beating City 2-1 on New Year's Eve sparked a run of one defeat, at Preston, in the last 17 games.

The 1956/57 season was the one in which United should have made history as Double winners. Retaining the title was never in doubt, the first defeat – 5-2 at home to Everton – not being suffered until the unlucky 13th match. Two games earlier on 6 October came a momentous debut when the 17-year-old Bobby Charlton played for the first time, at home to the club bearing his surname; the young Bobby dazzler scored twice in a 4-2 win and although used sparingly had 11 goals in 16 league and cup games by the end of the season.

The great new adventure that season was European Cup football, after the club defied a Football League management committee terrified of the impact of European competition. A craven Chelsea had given in and declined to compete in the first year but United were adamant and in September made a dramatic impact by winning 2-0 away to Anderlecht in Brussels with goals by Viollet and Taylor, then crushing the Belgians 10-0 at Maine Road. The Old Trafford floodlights were not ready for another six months so City's ground also hosted the victories over Borussia Dortmund and, memorably, Athletic Bilbao (from 5-2 down on aggregate at one stage) to ensure a hugely glamorous semi-final against holders Real Madrid.

On 11 April Busby's team, in all red, suffered a 3-1 away defeat in front of 130,000 and in the return, with Charlton playing his first European game for the injured Viollet, they went 2-0 down before salvaging some pride and a draw with goals by Taylor and Charlton.

Although the league title was secure, talk of a unique Treble was over, and the first Double of the century was controversially denied them by mid-table Aston Villa after Peter McParland, the Northern Ireland winger, battered goalkeeper Wood in only the sixth minute with a shoulder charge that fractured his jaw. Eight years before substitutes were belatedly allowed, Blanchflower went in goal and was beaten twice by McParland in the second half before Taylor headed in an Edwards corner.

'The odds were stacked too high and a rugged Villa side stepped in to snatch the cup from as gallant a set of losers as ever Wembley has seen,' wrote Frank Swift, City goalkeeper turned journalist. It was a bitter disappointment, though anyone who used the word 'tragedy' was reminded of the truer meaning nine months later in Munich. Meanwhile the quality of the team was universally acknowledged. 'Manchester United have been the most effective combination since the war,' read the 1957/58 *FA Year Book*.

A feature of Busby's teams was how consistently he stuck with the same XI. That applied particularly in the 1956/57 championship season and for the first half of the following one, when the team barely changed until Christmas: Wood, ex Darlington, in goal with Bill Foulkes and Byrne at full-back and Blanchflower in-between them; Eddie 'snake hips' Colman at right-half and Edwards on the left; Berry and Pegg on the wings, with Viollet and the shy Dubliner Whelan backing up Taylor as inside-forwards.

But a third of those first 21 games were lost, allowing Wolves to build a lead at the top of the table. When Busby shook things up with the introduction of Ulsterman Harry Gregg from Doncaster Rovers in goal (the first major signing for four and a half years), Mark Jones back in defence, Charlton at inside-forward and Kenny Morgans and Albert Scanlon on the wings, there was an unbeaten run including two FA Cup wins, a 2-1 first-leg lead in the European Cup over Red Star Belgrade and a pair of devastating First Division performances in demolishing Bolton 7-2 (including a Charlton hat-trick) and then Arsenal 5-4 in one of the finest games Highbury had ever seen.

If Real Madrid had not yet peaked, United fancied they were closing the gap on the European champions, qualifying for a second semi-final after another dramatic game, the 3-3 draw in Belgrade in which they had led 3-0 with Charlton scoring twice.

The story of what happened on the journey home on 6 February 1958 is all too well known; a stop for refuelling at snowy Munich, two unsuccessful take-offs and, as good humour on board turned to something darker, a fateful third attempt. The dreadful death toll included eight players, three of them England internationals in Duncan Edwards (after a two-week fight), Roger Byrne and Tommy Taylor; former secretary-manager Walter Crickmer, 38 years at the club; coach Bert Whalley and trainer Tom Curry; and eight newspaper men including Frank Swift.

Berry and Blanchflower were so badly injured they never played again. Busby had the last rites read twice but battled on. Charlton lay in a hospital bed and had names of the dead read to him from a German newspaper.

No directors were on the trip as one of their number had collapsed and died in London on the Saturday. Nor were Wilf McGuinness, who had almost 20 first-team games behind him but was injured, or Jimmy Murphy, who was on duty with the Wales team playing Israel in a World Cup tie at Cardiff; Whalley had taken his place and probably his seat.

So it fell to Murphy to hold things together back at home, recalling Jack Crompton from a coaching job at Luton to assist him. The scheduled, eagerly awaited Wolves league match on the Saturday was postponed but United chairman Harold Hardman requested that the FA Cup fifth-round tie at home to Sheffield Wednesday be put back just four days from 15 February to the following midweek.

United were allowed to sign two cup-tied players in Aston Villa's volatile wing-half Stan Crowther and the clever little Blackpool inside-forward Ernie Taylor (though Burnley's dictatorial chairman Bob Lord criticised the notion of clubs being asked to help United). By the time of the printer's deadline for the match programme it was still impossible to know who would play for the home team, so the 11 spaces were left blank. The side that eventually turned out comprised grieving crash survivors Gregg and Foulkes (captain), seven players from the reserves and third team plus Crowther (signed only an hour before kick-off) and Taylor.

Irishman Shay Brennan, a defender playing on the left wing, scored twice and Alex Dawson once as Wednesday were swept aside 3-0 for the most emotional victory in the club's history to that point. In the sixth round West Bromwich Albion, a top-four First Division side, were held at the Hawthorns, then beaten by Colin Webster's goal, made by the returning Charlton. In the semi-final, United benefited from errors by Fulham's goalkeeper Tony Macedo to win a replay 5-3 at Highbury with a hat-trick by Dawson.

At Wembley, however, Bolton disappointed everyone outside their own town (except possibly Bob Lord) by winning 2-0, the second goal coming when Nat Lofthouse barged Gregg and the ball over the line. Busby, struggling on a walking stick and allowing Murphy to lead the team out, was on the touchline, having returned to England on 19 April, the day that Bobby Charlton scored on his England debut at Hampden Park and a third great Manchester football man, Billy Meredith, died aged 83.

League form collapsed with only one win in 14 games after Munich, meaning United finished ninth, but there was one more hurrah in the European Cup semi-final. They beat AC Milan 2-1 at Old Trafford without Charlton before an eight-day trip by train to and from Italy, where the return leg was lost 4-0.

Invited by UEFA to compete again the following season along with champions Wolves, United were denied permission by the authorities, the FA suddenly changing their mind after the first-round draw had been made. The snub left a sour taste but may have been ultimately helpful to the exceptional achievement of finishing as runners-up to Wolves with only one new signing; the disappointing inside-forward Albert Quixall cost a British record £45,000 from relegated Sheffield Wednesday.

Charlton and Viollet scored 50 of the 109 league goals and the next season Viollet broke Jack Rowley's seasonal scoring record with 32. But there would be no more trophies until Busby built another new team.

* * * * *

It was an era of some great entertainers playing for comparatively unfashionable clubs, which under the retain-and-transfer system could simply refuse to let them move anywhere else for the same maximum wage. In Lancashire alone, Bolton had Lofthouse, Preston had Tom Finney (in both cases for all of their career) and **Blackpoo**l had Stanley Matthews.

Stan was the exception among that exalted trio in having been transferred from Stoke City in May 1947, after falling out with manager Bob McGrory and having enjoyed his wartime football stationed just outside Blackpool. He was 32 when he joined, convinced he had at least five more years in him – which proved too modest by far.

Joe Smith, the former Bolton stalwart who became Blackpool manager in 1935, believed in him far more than McGrory at that stage and knew he could build a formidable forward line round the combination of Matthews and 'Morty'.

Centre-forward Stan Mortensen, whose name came from his Norwegian sailor grandfather, joined the club in May 1938 but did not play a league game until after the war. His potential was evident much earlier, notably during the Football League North campaign of 1945/46, scoring all four goals in the opening game and totalling 38 in as many league and cup matches. When First Division football resumed he scored in the first three games and was easily Blackpool's top scorer with 28.

Matthews joined a team that had finished fifth in the top division and in his first season the partnership with Mortensen took them to the first of three FA Cup finals in five years. The Seasiders had a sound defence too, which did not concede a goal until the semi-final in the 1948 run. In that Villa Park game Second Division Tottenham were beaten 3-1 after extra time with a Mortensen hat-trick giving him nine of their 18 goals in five ties. Before the final Matthews was named as the first Footballer of the Year with Morty runner-up, but United proved too strong (see section above).

The following season Matthews even contemplated moving on, hoping for a change of luck after missing several months through injury. He settled for a self-imposed one-six diet, eating nothing on a Monday but extra fruit and vegetables for the rest of the week; and after a quarter-final defeat by Liverpool in 1950, the following year brought another chance. Allan Brown's penalty won the sixth-round tie at home to Fulham and Birmingham were beaten in a semi-final replay with goals by Mortensen and winger Bill Perry.

The final, however, belonged to another of the great individual forwards of the era, Newcastle's Jackie Milburn, who scored both goals in a 2-0 win as the *Sunday Express* bemoaned Blackpool's 'stupid offside tactics … clear evidence of weakness'.

Newcastle retained the cup the next year but finally relinquished it in 1953 to a giant-killing by Rotherham United as the path opened up for Blackpool once more after beating champions-elect Arsenal in the sixth round at Highbury.

Oddly Mortensen did not score at all before Wembley, Scottish inside-forward Jackie Mudie getting the semi-final winner against Spurs after intercepting Alf Ramsey's back-pass.

If the 1948 final produced classic football, 1953's had the drama plus all the excitement of Coronation year and a widespread feeling it would be Matthews's last chance. Stan shared that belief and was uncomfortably conscious of a promise made to his dying father in 1945 and kept to himself ever since – that he would one day win the FA Cup.

Saturday, 2 May 1953 was that day, making Matthews, according to the *Sunday Pictorial* headline 'The happiest man in the land'. But how close he came to a third disappointment. Lofthouse scored after only two minutes and although Mortensen equalised via a deflection, Scottish international Willie Moir had Wanderers ahead by the interval. In the dressing room skipper Harry Johnston as usual had more to say than manager Smith, but both wanted Matthews to push up more and Ernie Taylor to get him the ball.

Before they could do so, Bolton's injured left-half Eric Bell, playing on the wing with his thigh heavily strapped, made the score 3-1 and although Mortensen retrieved one goal from the third goalkeeping error of the game, his team were just a few minutes away from losing another final when he smashed a free-kick in for his hat-trick.

Extra time would surely have favoured Blackpool with 11 fit men, but they did not need it. In one of the great sequences of English football history, Taylor beat his man and found Matthews on the right with only left-back Ralph Banks in front of him. Banks fell for the old routine of a feint to the left and swerve towards the byline, though even then Matthews fell as he cut the ball back. To his surprise it was not Mortensen, who had moved wider to make the space, but Perry, switched inside from the left wing, who arrived to drive in the dramatic winning goal.

'What an end to a great career,' said the BBC commentator Kenneth Wolstenholme as the camera homed in on Matthews at the final whistle. He was not the first or last to underestimate the great man's endurance.

FA Cup Final 1953: Blackpool 4 Bolton Wanderers 3
Blackpool: Farm; Shimwell, Garrett, Fenton, Johnston, Robinson, Matthews, Taylor, Mortensen, Mudie, Perry.
Bolton: Hanson; Ball, Banks, Wheeler, Barass, Bell, Holden, Moir, Lofthouse, Hassall, Langton.

Matthews had his medal (plus a cigarette lighter which the club generously gave to each of the players) but it was Blackpool's last cup of cheer before losing in successive seasons to a pair of Third Division North giant-killers Port Vale and York City, both of whom reached the semi-final and were unlucky not to make Wembley itself.

In the First Division the Seasiders were in the top half for ten out of 11 seasons from 1949/50, although the exception in 1954/55 brought a narrow escape from relegation, Matthews, Morty and all, surviving thanks to another heroic effort from Perry with a hat-trick in a 6-1 away win at Manchester City.

Mortensen then left for Hull City, having been top scorer nine times in ten seasons and joint top with Brown in the other one. He missed out on a First Division runners-up place in 1955/56, albeit way behind Manchester United. It began with a 3-1 win at Arsenal that many felt was Matthews's best-ever club game – among them Arsenal manager Tom Whittaker, who had unsuccessfully tapped him up the previous year, offering promotional work which would have doubled his maximum £15 football wage.

That season there was a record crowd of more than 38,000 for the visit of Wolves and the team scored 86 goals. The lowlight was an embarrassing 6-2 home defeat by deadly rivals Preston, with injured goalkeeper George Farm at centre-forward scoring one of the Blackpool goals. Matthews, despite playing only two of

England's nine games that season, was named the first European Footballer of the Year. Behind him, local lad Jimmy Armfield, another England star who would stay with an unfashionable club, had come into the side at right-back and would ride to training on a second-hand bike which he parked under the main stand. On matchdays he would walk, mingling with the crowd.

The 1956/57 season was another good one, in fourth place with 93 goals, Mudie scoring 32 of them. The season ended with the last of Matthews's 54 England games, 23 years after his first, before he made way for Blackburn's Bryan Douglas. From 1958–60, after Joe Smith was succeeded as manager by Ron Suart, he was often left out although there could still have been a fourth FA Cup final for him in 1959; he played in all six ties but the Seasiders were knocked out 1-0 by Luton in a quarter-final replay.

By then centre-forward Ray Charnley had become the main scorer but a 6-0 home defeat by reviving Manchester United in February 1960, with Blackpool down to 11th place, was a sign of things to come for both clubs.

* * * * *

For **Preston** these were the Finney years. Relegated in 1949, when Tom played barely half the games, they came back in two seasons and were First Division runners-up on goal average in 1953 and 1958, third in 1957 and FA Cup finalists in 1954 before a 1960s decline.

Thomas Finney, born in a road next to Deepdale in April 1922, was sensibly made to continue his plumbing apprenticeship before signing professional forms for his local club the year after their 1938 FA Cup Final. Small and slight at that time, he was in the team for both matches in the War-time Cup win of 1941 over Arsenal, but would have to wait for an official league debut until August 1946, playing in front of an admiring Bill Shankly and making one and scoring in the 3-2 win over Leeds.

Losing 7-0 at home to Blackpool in the last game of the 1947/48 season, North End finished seventh for the second successive season, which meant that relegation 12 months later came as a shock. Despite signing Bobby Langton from Blackburn for a record fee of almost £15,000 they suffered through Finney missing 18 league games because of various injuries and Shankly departing for management with Carlisle, believing Preston cheated him out of a lucrative benefit match. Poor away from home again, they also suffered a 6-1 home defeat by rampant FA Cup holders Manchester United, and beating Liverpool on the final day failed to lift them above Huddersfield, who they had defeated twice, or Middlesbrough, who had lost 6-1 at Deepdale.

Finney stayed loyal despite plenty of interest and they were promoted back within two years. With Will Scott taking over as manager from the club committee and inside-forward Eddie Quigley signed for a club record fee, as well as Tommy Docherty brought in as a forceful young wing-half, the title was earned by five points from Manchester City. From Christmas Day until Easter Monday they won 14 successive games, virtually ensuring the title. Charlie Wayman from Southampton also proved a fine signing and top scored with 27.

The team looked strong enough to make an impression in the First Division and duly finished seventh with 24 more goals from Wayman, while Finney could now be relied on to chip in with double figures from the wing. Doing the double over Blackpool was a welcome bonus.

Only a year later they were desperately close to becoming champions for the first time since 1890. They missed out in the end because of a poor start – three wins from the first dozen games – and some heavy defeats by United (twice) and Chelsea also proved costly when goal average sums were done at the end. In the penultimate game championship rivals Arsenal were beaten 2-0 at Deepdale before almost 40,000; Finney's calm penalty then beat Derby 1-0 to put his side top. Arsenal, two points behind with a better goal average, had to beat Burnley, a top-six team, at Highbury and trailed 1-0 but came through 3-2. So Burnley's goalkeeper Des Thompson, younger brother of the Preston keeper George, was unable to win his sibling a championship medal.

The disappointment of failure was put into context by a shocking accident which resulted in the Sheffield Wednesday forward Derek Dooley having his broken leg amputated after a collision earlier in the year with Preston's Thompson when gangrene set in.

The following year's dip to mid-table was compensated for by a run to Wembley and an exciting final. Derby, Lincoln and Ipswich

(6-1) were beaten, then Leicester at the third attempt. The semi-final at Maine Road was won 2-0 against Wednesday with a prolific Wayman on the scoresheet again.

Finney received the Footballer of the Year trophy on the eve of the final but modestly reckoned that the next day at Wembley against West Bromwich Albion was just about his worst performance in a Preston shirt. Although Albion were runners-up in the league, ten points ahead of their mid-table opponents, the nation seemed convinced Finney would get his winner's medal like Matthews a year earlier. Preston led 2-1 with Wayman's disputed goal ('The referee has given offside,' said commentator Wolstenholme, but he hadn't). Albion's soft winner spoilt the script.

'Just a reminder to our supporters that there's always another year,' Finney told reporters. But they went out at Sunderland in the fourth round. In the meantime Finney went to the 1954 World Cup, which proved no more enjoyable than four years earlier, when he was in the side sensationally beaten by the USA.

The 1955/56 season brought a narrow relegation squeak despite scoring 73 goals. North End sank into trouble near the end and losing the last three left them a single point ahead of relegated Huddersfield. Four straight defeats to start the following season suggested another struggle but a transformation followed and led to two glorious years.

Finney, moved to centre-forward by acting manager Jimmy Milne, scored 23 goals, followed by a career-best 26 the year after, and with 26 and then 34 from little Tommy Thompson, North End were third and then runners-up; and the pair were picked together to play for England. Only Spurs, scoring 104 goals, prevented them being second in 1957 on goal average and 12 months later champions Wolves were the only side ahead of them.

Preston had peaked. Docherty left for Arsenal and in 1959/60, a second successive mid-table season, Finney decided enough was enough. Long-standing groin and back problems meant he was never going to outlast fitness fanatic Matthews. He bowed out at the end of that season with his most league appearances (37) and as top scorer for the only time at the club. The team finished ninth and his final game was at home to Luton on 30 April, almost 30,000 turning out with schoolboys sitting all along the touchline. Almost symbolically, relegation was only a year away.

Never one to bemoan his fate, the philosophical Preston plumber had been denied a league championship and an FA Cup by the narrowest margins; as well as a lucrative move to Italian club Palermo, which his club refused to sanction. Despite scoring 210 goals in 474 league and cup games, he never recorded a hat-trick, the closest thing being a game at Leicester in March 1958 when he scored twice but managed to miss two penalties. He became club president, was knighted in 1998 and died in 2014.

* * * * *

Stanley Matthews, Tom Finney and **Bolton's** Nat Lofthouse won 163 caps between them in the same era, yet astonishingly only played together for England three times, two of them at the 1954 World Cup. When Lofthouse made his name as the Lion of Vienna on England's 1952 summer tour, for instance, Finney was at outside-right but Matthews was having two full seasons out of favour with the notoriously erratic selectors, and the lesser-known Billy Elliott of Burnley was dancing down the other wing.

Lofthouse went to the same Castle Hill school in Bolton as Tommy Lawton, who was six years his senior. On the ground staff from September 1939 just after his 14th birthday, he worked in a coal mine as a Bevan Boy and made his Wanderers debut as a 16-year-old in March 1941 with two goals in a 5-1 win over Bury. Conscripted in 1943, he continued to play whenever he could. Quickly forging a reputation as a powerful centre-forward, he appeared in the Wartime Cup final win at Chelsea in 1945 and made a full league debut against the same opposition at Stamford Bridge on 31 August 1946, scoring twice in a 4–3 defeat as Lawton hit two for the home side. That was five months after the worst day in the club's history, when 33 people died at the second leg of the FA Cup quarter-final at home to Matthews's Stoke.

The local paper had already warned about one entrance to Burnden Park, on the railway embankment side, being 'tragically inadequate' – a tragically appropriate description.

With Bolton confident of earning a semi-final place after a 2-0 win in the away leg, and the added attraction of seeing Matthews, an estimated 85,000 tried to attend the game. The eventual Home Office report found that because a frightened youngster wanted to leave the crush, his father picked the lock of an exit gate, enabling a 'rush of people' to gain access. Two barriers collapsed in the north-western corner.

The report criticised a delay in closing some turnstiles and too many people being admitted, but concluded the disaster was 'inflicted by a crowd upon itself'. Police unaccountably urged the referee to resume the game, which players of both teams were reluctant to do; at one point Matthews was sickened to see body bags on the touchline. Perhaps unsurprisingly it finished goalless, after which Bolton lost the semi-final 2-0 to Charlton.

In the league their record was poor, with Lofthouse lacking goalscoring support, as final positions of 18th, 17th, 14th and 16th showed. They only picked up in the new decade, reaching eighth place in 1950/51 and fifth the season after, when inside-forward Ray Parry became the youngest player in the top flight of English football, aged 15 and eight months.

Bill Ridding, once (1932/33) top scorer for Manchester United, became manager in October 1950 having previously been in charge at Tranmere and would remain so for 18 years including two FA Cup finals.

Lofthouse scored on his England debut the following month and earned his nickname in May 1952 with two goals away to Austria after being incensed by newspaper criticism when he had been kicked from pillar to goalpost in the previous game against Italy.

Bolton were in the bottom half of the First Division again for the 1953 cup run, when the Lion roared and scored in each round, including the final. Given the luck of the draw, Wanderers did not play any First Division teams; even semi-final opponents Everton were in the bottom half of the Second Division, though they fought hard in an exciting game at Maine Road before going down 4-3 with Lofthouse scoring twice.

At Wembley (see Blackpool section above) they led 3-1 after 55 minutes, only to be undone by Matthews and Mortensen. One consolation for Lofthouse was to be named Footballer of the Year; another was to pip Blackpool to fifth place the following year before both sank into the bottom six within 12 months.

In April 1954 Fiorentina wanted Lofthouse, offering £40 a week at a time when the maximum wage in England was £15, but like Preston with Finney, the club held on to him.

He was still going strong in 1958 when they reached Wembley again. After a fine 3-0 win at high-flying Preston, Bolton needed a replay following a goalless draw in the mud against renowned cup fighters York City of the Third Division North. Lofthouse did not score in the sixth round win over champions-elect Wolves, watched by over 60,000 at Burnden Park, and was injured for the semi-final derby against Blackburn at Maine Road, where his stand-in Ralph Gubbins scored both in a 2-1 victory.

As Manchester United's opponents three months after Munich, Bolton might just have been the least popular FA Cup finalists ever. They were a physical side composed mainly of Lancashire lads, in which Roy Hartle was apt to shout to his full-back partner Tommy Banks in the hearing of some battered winger, 'When tha's finished wi' him, chip him over t' me.' Unsurprisingly there was no sentiment on the day, Lofthouse scoring as early as he had done in the 1953 final and then knocking goalkeeper Gregg and the ball into the net for an extraordinary second goal.

FA Cup Final 1958: Bolton Wanderers 2 Manchester United 0
Bolton: Hopkinson; Hartle, Banks, Henin, Higgins, Edwards, Birch, Stevens, Lofthouse, Parry, Holden.
Manchester United: Gregg; Foulkes, Greaves, Goodwin, Cope, Crowther, Dawson, Taylor, Charlton, Viollet, Webster.

In the autumn of 1958 Lofthouse was recalled by England after an absence of 17 months at the age of 33 and scored in a 5-0 rout of Russia. Wales the following month was the last of his 33 internationals (in which he scored 30 goals) but in a high-scoring First Division season Bolton finished fourth, their best performance since 1927, beating United 6-3 and finishing as one of six Lancashire sides in the top half of the table.

Suffering from an ongoing ankle injury, Nat announced his retirement in January, only to turn out for the reserves the following season; and with the first team struggling after one win in the opening ten games he returned for a 1-1 draw at home to United. Just before Christmas he was injured again in a draw at Birmingham and finally admitted defeat, but without him the team survived in 18th place, safe by three points. He had played six games, scoring three goals to give him a grand total of 255 in

452 league games, 285 in all. A nine-foot statue of him was erected at the club's new stadium in 2013.

* * * * *

On Merseyside, **Everton** resumed after the war as league champions yet not only failed dismally to live up to that billing or come anywhere close in the ensuing 15 years, but found Liverpool succeeding them.

Theoretically it was the summer of 1939, just after the title win, before Theo Kelly was promoted from secretary to become the first official manager long after most clubs. Like everyone else Kelly had only three games (a win and two draws) before the league was abandoned and after tenth and 14th places and a poor start to the 1948/49 season he went back to the secretary's office and was succeeded by former Blues FA Cup winner Cliff Britton from Burnley.

The new man's low-scoring side (Tommy Lawton had been sold to Chelsea in 1945) struggled for three seasons and went down in the last of them, 1950/51, the main excitement having come from the 1950 FA Cup semi-final against Liverpool, who won it 2-0 at Maine Road before losing the final to Arsenal. Reading in the *Daily Post* that they would 'never lose with greater credit' was little consolation to the Blues.

Despite spending a club record £20,000 on future Burnley manager Harry Potts, they went six games without scoring in March and were left needing a point from the final game to stay up; it was humiliatingly lost 6-0 to bottom club Sheffield Wednesday, who went down with them.

The return from the Second Division took three seasons, the second of them bringing the lowest finish in the club's history (16th in the second tier) with only a notable FA Cup run to redeem it, beating Manchester United before losing the semi-final 4-3 to Bolton from 4-0 down.

Fortunately Britton had found a goalscorer in Dave Hickson, signed from Ellesmere Port, who scored 25 the following season out of 92, including successive wins over Derby (6-2 away), Brentford (6-1) and Plymouth (8-4). Passing Liverpool, who were on their way down, was a bonus but another run of lower-mid-table finishes meant the end of Britton in 1956 and there was no further improvement under the former Scottish amateur international Ian Buchan.

Moving on up came about only after a record 10-4 defeat at Tottenham in October 1958 and the subsequent appointment of Johnny Carey, who since captaining Manchester United with such distinction had made a reputation as a gentlemanly but successful manager with Blackburn and the Republic of Ireland.

By the end of the decade the Blues had not been in the First Division's top ten since 1947. Under new chairman John Moores, Carey was about to change that for the better, though not to reap the full benefit.

* * * * *

If **Liverpool** had a figure in the immediate post-war period to rival Matthews, Finney and Lofthouse, in local popularity at least, it was Billy Liddell. The ruggedly handsome Scot made his debut for them in 1940/41, playing for a long time as a left-winger before converting to centre-forward after the team's poor start to the 1954/55 season.

In the Football League North campaign of 1945/46 he scored 18 times in 26 appearances on the wing, second only to centre-forward Willie Fagan. The official resumption of league football featured an abundance of goals at both ends in Liverpool games as in successive September matches there was a 7-4 win over Chelsea then a 5-0 defeat away to Manchester United.

The defence then stabilised with Bob Paisley settling at left-half after a difficult start. Manager George Kay beat Everton to the signature of Newcastle forward Albert Stubbins, who would later be immortalised on the front of the Beatles' *Sgt. Pepper's Lonely Hearts Club Band* album (because John Lennon was amused by his name). He rattled in 24 goals, as did Jack Balmer, setting a record with three successive hat-tricks in November as Liverpool went top of the table.

Recovering from a 5-1 home defeat by Wolves (4-0 at half-time), and then four successive defeats over the new year, they came again in a storming finish, losing only one of the last 16 games (at Blackpool) and winning the last one away to fellow contenders Wolves. Still there was a fortnight to wait in the extended season, knowing that Stoke City could overhaul them;

but the Potters lost their final match to Sheffield United, giving Liverpool the title.

It could have been the century's first Double but in the FA Cup semi-final there was a surprise 1-0 defeat by Second Division Burnley with their iron-clad defence.

Champions or not, the Reds would lose First Division status for the first time since 1905 before challenging for another title. In defence of it in 1947/48 they dropped to 11th despite almost 50 goals from Balmer, Stubbins and Liddell, and a handsome double over Everton by 3-0 and 4-0. As attendances boomed everywhere there were almost 79,000 to see the derby at Goodison the following season, a 1-1 draw, Liverpool finishing only 12th.

In the Merseyside FA Cup semi-final of March 1950, Paisley and Liddell were the goalscorers as Liverpool won through to meet Arsenal. Paisley was then unlucky to be left out as an Arsenal team with Denis Compton playing four days before his retirement won 2-0. 'Liverpool ... were outmatched by a better all-round team,' according to the *Sunday Times* reporter, who picked out a Merseysider, albeit an Arsenal player, as man of the match, 'Joseph Mercer was the master tactician.' The former Evertonian and future Manchester City manager still lived on the Wirral and often trained at Anfield.

George Kay had not been well and in 1951 was replaced by the Brighton manager and Charlton Athletic FA Cup-winning captain Don Welsh, who had guested with some success for Liverpool in the war. After two more mid-table seasons under him, however, Liverpool began to sink. In 1952/53 they needed to beat Chelsea in the last match to avoid going down, and the following year finished rock-bottom. There was not a single win from early December to April and three different goalkeepers conceded almost 100 goals between them as the Reds exchanged places with the Blues across the park.

In the Second Division campaign of 1954/55 the defence was almost as bad, conceding 96 – the worst in the division – including nine in a record defeat at Birmingham in December. Liddell, now at centre-forward, scored there for the fifth successive game and must have despaired at what was happening behind him; his 30 goals helped the team total 92 but earned nothing better than 11th place.

The highlight of the season was the FA Cup-fourth round tie at Goodison where Everton, readjusting comfortably to the First

Division after promotion were obvious favourites but ended up drubbed 4-0 after Liddell opened the scoring against the run of play. In 1955/56 he reached 400 league games but it was a deeply frustrating period of six near-misses at regaining First Division status.

Liddell played his last FA Cup game in the 1958 quarter-final defeat at Blackburn, missing the following season's humiliation away to Worcester City, when the non-league side won 2-1. Phil Taylor, a member of the 1947 championship team, had been promoted to replace Welsh as manager but resigned in November 1959, making way for the man who would make Liverpool a power in the land once more.

Since leaving Preston in 1949 to manage Carlisle United, Bill Shankly had progressed via tough jobs at Grimsby Town and Workington to Second Division Huddersfield Town. He was interviewed by the Liverpool board when Kay left in 1951, making a good impression, and although Welsh was appointed the directors did not forget him.

At Huddersfield he had a promising side with future World Cup winner Ray Wilson at left-back and a young Denis Law breaking through, but Shankly became frustrated by lack of funds, notably when he wanted to bring Ron Yeats and Ian St John south from Scotland. Despite usually being a little behind Liverpool in the table, the Terriers tended to have good results against them, like a 5-0 romp at Leeds Road in October 1958.

By the time Liverpool lost there again a year later Taylor had already decided to leave, his last significant act being to lure Dave Hickson from Everton in a rare switch between the clubs. The board were convinced Shankly was their man. Initially held to a month's notice by Huddersfield, he left before Christmas and took charge for the first time for an anti-climatic game at home to promotion contenders Cardiff City watched by a modest 27,291; the Welshmen won 4-0 and finished the season as runners-up to Aston Villa, but Liverpool, eight points behind in third, had already shown signs of improvement under the new manager.

They were doing so as early as January, when they lost at home to Manchester United in the FA Cup fourth round after Bobby Charlton scored an early goal.

Although unimpressed by facilities at either Anfield or the Melwood training ground, Shankly knew he had the makings of a good squad. Hickson quickly formed an effective partnership with a young Roger Hunt and by the end of the season each had 21 league goals. Liddell was still around as back-up, Jimmy Melia was a clever little playmaker, Alan A'Court was an England outside-left, and outside-right Ian Callaghan was given four games in April just after his 18th birthday.

Shankly made a new goalkeeper and centre-half his priorities and tried to sign Jack Charlton from Leeds United, about to be relegated from the First Division. Don Revie hung on to him and before too long there would be battles galore between the two managers. Shankly had plenty to work on but much to do.

* * * * *

As Manchester United prospered under Matt Busby, **Manchester City** played second fiddle in a difficult period leavened only by successive FA Cup finals and victory in the second of them in 1956.

Apart from Peter Doherty's acrimonious departure for Derby County, the cup provided the first big headline after the war in its two-leg season of 1945/46 with another City-esque effort. Who else could win an away leg 3-1 (at fellow Second Division side Bradford Park Avenue) then contrive to lose the home match by as extravagant a margin as 8-2. And this against a team they had beaten 6-0 the previous month.

Under secretary-manager Wilf Wild, who soon gave way to former captain Sam Cowan, City recovered sufficiently to take revenge over Bradford by 7-2 in a strong start to the first full league season, which was maintained throughout to make them champions with an unbeaten run of 22 games interrupted only by a 5-0 FA Cup defeat by another Second Division side, Birmingham. The campaign finished (in mid-June) with inside-forward George Smith scoring all five goals in the defeat of bottom club Newport County to finish with 23.

Back in the top division a respectable tenth place was achieved mainly on the back of a tight defence in which Frank Swift was still goalkeeper and future manager Les McDowall shared centre-half duties with the versatile Joe Fagan. Hostilities with United were resumed as landlord and tenant, the four league games under that arrangement all being drawn, although Busby's team were runners-up each season.

Swift retired in the summer of 1949, only to be called back for four more games until City unearthed a controversial successor in Bernhard 'Bert' Trautmann from St Helens Town, attracting unfavourable comment and threatened boycotts on the grounds of being a German. Club captain Eric Westwood attempted to defuse the opposition by declaring 'there's no war in this dressing room'. Others needed convincing about the blond native of Bremen after he conceded seven goals in the Derby mud in his third league game, but it was lack of a potent attack (nobody reaching double figures) that sent City to relegation by three points when they failed to win from Christmas 1949 until April.

Once in the side Trautmann slowly won over City fans and missed only half a dozen games in almost seven years until his most famous match, the 1956 FA Cup Final. During that period McDowall returned from Wrexham as manager and stayed for 13 years, the longest peacetime reign at the club. He signed wing-half Roy Paul from Swansea, and oversaw promotion straight back to the top division with Dennis Westcott and Smith a powerful attacking force. They were backed up in the First Division by Ivor Broadis from Sunderland and Don Revie from Hull, both costing £25,000 yet City survived in 1952/53 only by a point after victory over Blackpool, who fortunately were far more interested in the following Saturday's FA Cup final against Bolton and submitted 5-0 at Maine Road.

Revie, however, was to be the central figure in a tactical plan – and even give his name to it – that carried City to three much-improved league seasons and two cup finals before the rest of the First Division rumbled it.

Given how utterly England had been humbled by Hungary in 1953/54, losing 6-3 and 7-1, it was perhaps surprising that only City copied the notion of using a withdrawn centre-forward like Nándor Hidegkuti, who had so bemused the England defence. City did not have a Ferenc Puskás to take advantage – who did? – but at least they saw the possibilities.

Initially the plan was tried in the reserves towards the end of that season by trainer Fred Tilson (an old number nine himself), with great success. Losing the first game of 1954/55 5-0 at Preston might have deterred many coaches but McDowall was persuaded to persevere. Ken Barnes was brought in at right-half to link up with Revie and in their next seven games City won five and drew two.

Revie, wearing the number nine shirt, played as a modern midfielder setting up attacks as well as scoring goals himself and laying on others for attacking inside-forwards Johnny Hart and Billy McAdams.

The team were briefly top of the table after beating Busby's emerging United 3-2 and in the return in February pulled off a stunning 5-0 victory at Old Trafford. 'Revie plan still has them baffled' was one headline. In between times, City knocked their neighbours out of the FA Cup as well, almost 75,000 watching the 2-0 victory with goals by Revie and Joe Hayes.

Away wins at Luton and Birmingham in the next two rounds brought a semi-final against big-spending Sunderland, an ultimately unsuccessful Bank of England club. Welsh left-winger Roy Clarke's goal won it at Villa Park but in City's first final since 1934 the other major north-eastern club Newcastle, winners in 1951 and 1952, did the hat-trick for Jackie Milburn.

City set a trend by walking out in tracksuits but had barely got them off before Milburn headed the opening goal in 45 seconds. Recent signing Bobby Johnstone, in for the injured Hart, equalised but City had fallen victim to the almost traditional Cup final injury, Jimmy Meadows tearing knee ligaments when his studs caught in the lush turf, and Newcastle added two further goals.

Ten times previously beaten Wembley finalists returned to win the following year and in 1956 City did so, as well as having their most successful First Division season between the title-winning years of 1937 and 1968. With Johnstone often taking on the role of Revie as the deep-lying centre-forward they ended up fourth despite an inevitable falling away between the FA Cup semi-final and Wembley.

Two of the earlier ties required a second game, against Blackpool and Liverpool (with a 2-1 win at Anfield), then Everton were beaten in the sixth round with goals by Hayes and Johnstone. Johnstone's header won the semi-final against Tottenham before he missed the last four league games through injury to give McDowall a selection conundrum.

He solved it by allowing Revie to keep the number nine shirt and role while Johnstone played on the wing in place of the absent Bill Spurdle. City, in their smart maroon shirts with the white pinstripe, took an early lead through Hayes, from Revie's clever flick; were pegged back by Noel Kinsey; but won with two second-half goals, by football-cricketer Jack Dyson and Johnstone.

'A titanic struggle that had almost everything,' said the *News of the World*.

It included the usual FA Cup final injury, but in an unusual fashion. In the last 20 minutes Trautmann threw himself at Peter Murphy's feet and was knocked out. Insisting on staying on, he blacked out in another collision but again carried on and was sufficiently well protected by his defence to preserve the 3-1 scoreline.

It proved to have been a dangerous strategy when he visited hospital four days later in some pain and was discovered to have broken a bone in his neck.

FA Cup Final 1956: Manchester City 3 Birmingham City 1
Manchester City: Trautmann; Leivers, Little, Barnes, Ewing, Paul, Johnstone, Hayes, Revie, Dyson, Clarke.
Birmingham City: Merrick; Hall, Green, Newman, Smith, Boyd, Astall, Kinsey, Brown, Murphy, Govan.

Trautmann succeeded Revie as Footballer of the Year but did not play again until December in a disappointing campaign that City finished in 18th place. Two more characteristically unpredictable seasons followed as they reached fifth in 1957/58, top scoring with 104 goals yet conceding 100 including defeats of 9-2 at West Bromwich and 8-4 at Leicester, then survived in 1958/59 only by winning the final game at home to Leicester while Aston Villa conceded an 88th-minute goal to neighbouring West Bromwich Albion and went down instead.

* * * * *

From unpromising pre-war years and 16th place in the Football League North in 1946, **Burnley** surprised even their own supporters by securing immediate promotion back to the First Division. Back in their traditional claret and blue after a period of white and black and with a new manager in Cliff Britton, they followed Manchester City to promotion on the back of two long unbeaten runs and the country's best defence, conceding a miserly 29 goals.

Almost as exciting was the run to the FA Cup final, beating First Division champions-elect Liverpool in the semi-final replay with Ray Harrison's goal. Charlton won the final after extra time as the ball burst for the second year running, Burnley's missed chances including Harry Potts's shot against the bar.

Without an outstanding goalscorer the worry was how they would fare at the higher level but the defence was again excellent, second only to champions Arsenal and enabling third place to be achieved, level on points with runners-up Manchester United.

The early 1950s were notable for the emergence of one of the Turf Moor greats, Northern Irishman Jimmy McIlroy. Signed from Glentoran, he stayed in the side from the day of his debut at Sunderland in October 1950 when he replaced Potts (transferred to Everton) at inside- left. It was the first of almost 500 games over the next 13 years which would include a league title and European Cup appearances.

Slowly the seeds of that team were coming together; Tommy Cummings was already established at centre-half and wing-half Jimmy Adamson first appeared like McIlroy in 1950/51. In the spring of 1953 the Clarets sat on top of the First Division, having found a goalscorer in Bill Holden to finish off McIlroy's creativity. But they lost half a dozen games to end no higher than sixth.

Towards the end of the '50s they were regularly up there again in a fine period for Lancashire, normally along with some combination of the two Manchester clubs, Bolton, Blackpool and Preston

Then came the glorious campaign of 1959/60. Harry Potts had returned to Turf Moor as manager in January 1958 and brought together the championship team, with Ray Pointer and Jimmy Robson as the joint spearhead ahead of McIlroy, and a goalscoring right-winger in John Connelly. Scottish international Adam Blacklaw was in goal, John Angus and Northern Ireland's Alex Elder at full-back with the solid Cummings between them; Bobby Seith, Adamson and Brian Miller shared the wing-half roles and left-winger Brian Pilkington completed the forward line.

The more fashionable Spurs and Wolves were favourites for most of the season, which included Robson scoring five in the 8-0 drubbing of Nottingham Forest. Losing 6-1 at Molineux on 30 March put doubts in many minds and with games in hand Burnley needed a win at Maine Road in the final match to top the table for the first time all season – the time it mattered most. In front of almost 66,000 including the anxious Wolves manager Stan Cullis, Pilkington scored early on and after Denis Law set up an equaliser for City, reserve winger Trevor Meredith, in for the injured Connelly, scored the goal that won the title.

'Champion Burnley: Thanks to £20 winger' read the front page of the next morning's *Daily Mail,* referencing what Meredith had cost from Kidderminster three years earlier. 'This £11,000 team fought off a tenacious second-half challenge by City to end Wolves's dream of the Cup and League double,' said the match report. 'Adamson revealed himself as not only a great wing-half but a great captain.'

He was one of the best never to receive an England cap, certainly, though he became Walter Winterbottom's assistant at the 1962 World Cup and turned down the chance to succeed him before the job was offered to Alf Ramsey.

Despite having scored 21 goals fewer than Wolves, Burnley were champions by a point, which meant inclusion in the sixth season of the European Cup (see next chapter).

* * * * *

Having spent the war years looking forward to First Division football again, **Blackburn** lasted only two seasons, losing a manager before the end of the first one, which the team finished in the bottom six. Eddie Hapgood, the distinguished former Arsenal and England captain, resigned his first managerial post in February 1947, claiming interference by directors. Will Scott took over but lasted only eight months as Rovers lost 7-1 at home to lowly Middlesbrough on their way to relegation with Grimsby Town.

Younger players were finally drafted in, as Hapgood had wished, but aside from a 1952 FA Cup semi-final (lost 2-1 in a replay with Newcastle) the club made no impression until after Johnny Carey's arrival as manager in the summer of 1953.

The genial pipe-smoking Irishman had inherited Matt Busby's mantra 'keep playing football' and added one or two of his own such as 'fizz it about'. In his first season Tommy Briggs and inside-forward Eddie Quigley contributed 54 goals of the 86 that took Rovers to within a point of promoted Leicester City and Everton, crucially losing the penultimate game 4-0 at Filbert Street.

Future England captain Ronnie Clayton was now in the side at wing-half, having made a debut aged 16, after being released by Preston as too small. In 1954/55 the team rattled in 114 goals, the highest in the country, yet finished only sixth after conceding 79; the 5-4 home defeat by Notts County was a typical result. Briggs hit 33, an astonishing seven of them in the 8-3 win at home to Bristol Rovers. Yet he didn't score at all when Middlesbrough were beaten 9-0 in November, Frank Mooney and Quigley grabbing hat-tricks.

Carey had them fourth again in both 1956 and 1957 and finally achieved promotion in dramatic style in 1957/58. Going into the final day London pair West Ham and Charlton both had 55 points and Rovers 54 with their final game to come at The Valley. West Ham duly clinched the title by winning at Middlesbrough while a 56,000 crowd saw Rovers go 4-1 up at Charlton and hang on to win 4-3 and secure second place.

A fine team included winger Bryan Douglas, who had joined Clayton in the England side, plus future Scotland World Cup manager Ally MacLeod on the left wing, with Roy Vernon and clever little Peter Dobing at inside-forward.

Carey was lured away to Everton and Aberdonian Dally Duncan was brought in from Luton Town to establish Rovers in mid-table and take them to the 1960 FA Cup Final.

In the promotion year of 1958, Rovers had reached the last four, knocking out both Everton and Liverpool before losing narrowly to Bolton at Maine Road. The Lancastrian drama this time took in a replay win at Blackpool and then a famous quarter-final at Turf Moor, where bitter rivals Burnley took a three-goal lead before Douglas, Dobing and in the last few minutes Mick McGrath denied them; 'one of the greatest comebacks in the club's history' according to Rovers' official website. A 2-0 win in the replay led to a semi-final with Sheffield Wednesday, who were beaten by two goals from extrovert Northern Ireland centre-forward Derek Dougan.

Dougan then chose the day before the final against firm favourites Wolves to hand in a transfer request and had a poor game at Wembley in one of the most disappointing and one-sided of all finals, won 3-0 by Wolves after Rovers full-back Dave Whelan broke a leg. 'The Dustbin Final' was what the *Daily Sketch* called it.

More encouraging was winning the 1958/59 FA Youth Cup with future internationals Mike England, Keith Newton and Fred Pickering in a team that beat Manchester United in the semi-final and then Bobby Moore's West Ham.

* * * * *

Resuming after the war in the Second Division, **Bury** lasted for 11 years until 1957 but were never once in the top ten. They started slowly under manager Norman Bullock in the bottom six despite the presence of local man Eddie Quigley, mentioned above with both Preston and Blackburn. Originally a full-back, he scored all five goals when moved to centre-forward against Millwall in February 1947 and never looked back. In October that year he joined Sheffield Wednesday for £12,000 and the Shakers sank into the bottom three at the end of the campaign.

After scaling the heights of 11th place in 1948/49 they were involved in a relegation struggle just about every season until finally making the drop; even in 1951/52 when recording a record 8-2 win over Southampton, which was further improved on in September 1958, when Tranmere were demolished 8-1 at Gigg Lane.

Conceding 90 goals in 1955/56 was a warning, even though 86 were scored, which was more than runners-up Leeds United, with Walter Kelly and former United hero Stan Pearson to the fore. In the following campaign the goals against increased to an ominous 96 and those scored dropped to 60. Only Port Vale let in more and they were the only side below the Shakers. That meant one season, 1957/58, in the Third Division North for the first time before the split into Third and Fourth Divisions, where they regrouped and would soon be elevated again.

In all that time the FA Cup brought no longer a run than the fourth round. But it did attract Gigg Lane's record attendance of 35,000 for Bolton's visit in January 1960, and five years earlier Bury had taken part in the most prolonged tie between two

Football League teams in FA Cup history, which took five attempts to resolve.

The original match at home to Stoke City, placed a little higher than Bury in the Second Division, was drawn 1-1 with a goal by Tommy Daniel in front of more than 20,000 and after the same player forced extra time in the replay four days later, the game had to be abandoned with eight minutes left because of a violent snowstorm. The following Monday they tried again on neutral ground at Goodison Park, and played an exciting 3-3 draw, followed two days later at Anfield by a 2-2 stalemate. At Old Trafford the following week the matter was finally resolved 3-2 in Stoke's favour with a second goal by Tim Coleman, once again in extra time. All that had taken nine hours 22 minutes. Having just met twice at Christmas as well (3-2 to Stoke and 1-1) it is fair to say the two well-matched sides had seen more than enough of each other for one season.

* * * * *

These were hard times too for **Oldham**, lasting for only one season with Bury when ascending to the Second Division in 1953, struggling and always likely to be in the Fourth Division when the south and north split, after which they could have gone out of the Football League altogether.

In the first season after the war they were a bottom-four team along with Accrington and Southport. Even at that lowly level, however, there was benefit to be had from the national thirst for entertainment; from a little over 7,500 attending the first home game of the 1946/47 season 19,000 saw the start of the next campaign and 35,200 came to see Hull towards end of 1948/49 when promotion seemed possible.

Hull went up with the Latics finishing sixth, and two years later after former England captain George Hardwick came from Middlesbrough as player-manager they were fourth in a season notable for an 11-2 win over Chester; 16 year-old Eddie Hopkinson, the future Bolton and England goalkeeper, was between the posts for that game and Eric Gemmell, top scorer in four seasons out of five, scored a record seven.

In 1952/53 came further improvement and promotion: the decisive game was a goalless draw at Bradford City after 27,681 saw the final home match against Stockport, lifting the season's average to over 16,000. An elderly team struggled in the Second Division, however, and lasted only 12 months, finishing bottom with eight wins and losing 17 of 21 away games.

Hardwick resigned in 1955, crowds having dropped by over 10,000 in one season, and Oldham, regularly at the wrong end, unsurprisingly dropped into the newly created fourth tier, which dramatically reduced the number of local derbies, causing a further fall-off in crowds; the average dropped below 5,000 in 1959/60, when bottom but one and requiring re-election.

Fortunately new signings like Bert Lister and Bobby Johnstone would bring about happier days.

* * * * *

Having done little more than survive in the 1930s, **Rochdale** fared even worse than Bury and Oldham after the war, spending every season until 1960 (and well beyond) at the lowest level.

There was a deceptively encouraging start and in the fourth season they were third, four points behind champions Doncaster with a solid defence that conceded under a goal a game and an attack that scored 68. Gates were over 8,000 for the third successive season but had already peaked. From there it was downhill to the bottom four in 1951/52 as the lowest scorers (47) in the whole Football League.

In-between a couple of glamorous FA Cup visits from Chelsea (1951) and Charlton (1955) the Dale went out in the first round six times in seven seasons. It was a minor achievement to scrape into the top half of the table in 1958, and with it the new Third Division, only for Harry Catterick, manager since 1953, to move on to Sheffield Wednesday, and grim reality to return. In one of the highest scoring of all Football League seasons they were bottom dogs with only 37 goals, again the worst in the country; five clubs hit 100 or more.

Settling in the middle of the Fourth Division, Rochdale would take a while to get out of it.

* * * * *

Bottom of the Third Division North in the two seasons immediately before the war, **Accrington** rose to the heights of 20th immediately afterwards, albeit once again with the lowest gates in the country of under 4,000. Safely re-elected in 1951 and 1953, fortunes improved dramatically under Walter Galbraith, who made them runners-up in 1955, when they once fielded an all-Scottish team against Rochdale and crowds averaged almost 10,000.

Third in 1956 and '57, second again in '58 without ever being close to promotion, they were prolific scorers with 96, 92 and 95 in successive seasons. One of the many Scots on the staff, George Stewart, signed from St Mirren for only £1,500, scored five against Gateshead in November 1954, set a club record with 35 the season afterwards and had totalled 136, another club record, when he was sold to Coventry City in 1958.

The club felt emboldened to acquire an expensive new Burnley Road stand from the Aldershot tattoo ground at a cost of almost £20,000, but selling Stewart began a decline that would have catastrophic consequences: relegation to the Fourth Division followed as bottom club in 1960, conceding 123 goals, and far worse was to come.

* * * * *

While also stuck in the Third Division North, **Stockport County** could often be found in the upper reaches. Fourth in the first season back, third in 1952 with the best defence under manager Andy Beattie, and fifth five years later, they were a respectable mid-table side who easily qualified for the Third Division, only to drop out of it immediately along with Rochdale. They would race them back, just as the 1960s wore on.

County could also claim a world record in March 1946, when a single match, the Third Division North Cup replay against Doncaster, lasted for a startling three hours and 23 minutes. Scores were level at 2-2 after 90 minutes plus extra time, which in that competition necessitated a golden goal winner. It proved hard to find. Stockport had one effort disallowed in the 173rd (!) minute, forcing 22 weary players to continue. Shortly before 7pm the referee reluctantly called a halt because it was too dark to carry on. The second replay a week later brought no such problems: Doncaster won 4-0.

Stockport possessed a notable father and son team in Alex and David Herd, who on the last day of the 1950/51 season turned out together as inside-forwards against Hartlepool. Alex signed in March 1948 from Manchester City, where he won league and cup honours, and scored 35 goals in four seasons for County. David came through the juniors but after fewer than 20 league games was lured away by Arsenal in August 1954, going on to become a Scottish international and later joining Manchester United.

In 1950 Edgeley Park had its record attendance of 27,833 for the FA Cup fifth-round tie against First Division Liverpool, which was lost only 2-1 after equalling the previous best run from 1935. This one involved beating Second Division clubs Barnsley and Hull City.

Eighteen months later striker Jack Connor arrived from Bradford City to become the club's record league scorer over the next five years with 132 goals, including fives against Workington (November 1952) and Carlisle (April 1956) and FA Cup hat-tricks in successive years against North Shields (1952) and Chester (1953). He had left by the 1957/58 FA Cup run in which First Division Luton Town lost 3-0 at Edgeley and West Ham were given a good game at Upton Park before coming through 3-2, former Burnley centre-forward Bill Holden scoring for County in both games. Relegation followed in the inaugural Third Division season of 1958/59.

* * * * *

Tranmere, although fifth and fourth in successive seasons in the early 1950s, were unable to benefit further from the relegations suffered by Everton and Liverpool.

They had a long-serving manager in Ernie Blackburn, previously with Wrexham and Hull, who lasted from 1946–55. So did stalwart defender Harold Bell, who astonishingly played in every league game for nine years to set a Football League record. Scoring a hat-trick on his wartime debut as a 16-year-old in 1941, he might have been expected to flourish in attack but was soon moved to defence and from the start of the 1946/47 season was ever-present for 375 games until August 1955.

Fourth place in 1950/51 on crowds of almost 10,000 was the highest finish in that time, and the FA Cup provided interest and welcome revenue for the next couple of seasons. In 1951/52 Rovers's run took them as far as the fourth round after a long drawn-out second-round tie against Blyth Spartans that went to four games and ended up at (supposedly) neutral Goodison Park with a 5-1 win.

Then a stunning 2-1 victory away to First Division Huddersfield was followed by defeat at Chelsea in front of nearly 60,000.

The following year's run began with an 8-1 demolition of Ashington, Harry Atkinson scoring six times, and led to a glamour tie in the third round at home to Tottenham. A crowd of 21,537 saw Rovers take the lead with a goal by Lloyd Iceton before conceding an equaliser and going down to a record 9-1 defeat two days later at White Hart Lane.

By 1956/57 they had dropped to 23rd before Irish international and Evertonian Peter Farrell took over as manager. His team did well to make the new Third Division by finishing 11th the following season, justifying their status there with seventh place in 1959 and crowds averaging almost 12,000. But a fall was not long in coming.

* * * * *

Southport, with the loyal Gordon Hunt secretary-manager from 1937–58, were often in the doldrums and required re-election twice in the first three post-war seasons. Haig Avenue therefore missed out on the national attendance boom, which was beginning to wane before their top-six finishes in 1953 and 1956.

Regular changes of colours did not greatly improve fortunes. Having swapped red shirts for black and white stripes before the war, they tried green and white hoops for two unsuccessful years immediately after it, reverted to the stripes and then from 1954 changed from Newcastle to Wolves in old-gold and black.

Alan Ball Snr, who would be manager in the 1970s, had two spells in the post-war sides that finished in the bottom two twice in those first three seasons. It might have been all three; in the middle one, a much revamped side was struggling at Christmas until Ball returned from Birmingham with Arthur Turner. An improvement led to 15th place but in autumn 1948 Turner left for Crewe.

The following season was comfortable and on 27 December a record league crowd of 14,766 saw the 3-2 win over Rochdale. Sustained improvement came at last with a top-six place in 1953, although they lacked firepower with experienced winger Jack Billingham's 16 goals making him leading scorer.

In 1955/56 there was a run of 19 games without defeat and a record 57 points, though once again they were lowest scorers in the top half. From there came a depressingly swift decline to the bottom three for the next two years, condemning the Sandgrounders to the new Fourth Division, where they finished bottom of all 92 clubs for the first time in history. With Trevor Hitchen as manager following a successful spell with Wigan, they had begun reasonably, especially at home, but were hopeless on the road, losing 19 of 23 games and drawing the other four.

Hitchen made way for Everton's Wally Fielding as player-manager, who oversaw a rise of only three places and a much less comfortable re-election vote in 1960. There was strong support for Peterborough United from the Midland League to be brought into the fold and to the relief of Oldham and Southport it was Gateshead who were made the fall guys. The voting for the four places was: Oldham 39, Peterborough 35, Hartlepool 34, Southport 29, Gateshead 18.

Like Oldham, Stockport, Tranmere and Rochdale, Southport would escape the bottom division in the sixties but in their case not for long.

* * * * *

At least the aforementioned north-western quintet survived as Football League clubs to see in the swinging 1960s, by which time **New Brighton** had long gone. Struggling badly for support before the war (see Chapter 4), they moved to the Tower Grounds, as previously used by New Brighton Tower (1898–1901) and pulled in a record league attendance of 14,291 for the local derby with Tranmere in September 1946. They did, however, have the lowest crowds in the Football League for three of the five seasons they managed post-war. Worse, they finished bottom of the pile in two of those, with a high of 14th place (1949/50) in-between.

History was made in March 1947 when 51-year-old manager Neil McBain, once a wing-half and Scottish international with Manchester United, Everton and Liverpool, answered an emergency of the type more common during the war years and played in goal away to Hartlepool. He kept the score down to three but was sacked in February 1948 during the first of the two seasons at the bottom of the league. McBain later managed Leyton Orient, Watford, Ayr United and, more exotically, Estudiantes de la Plata of Argentina, who would cross United's path in a momentous collision some 20 years later.

It was unfortunate to finish bottom in 1951 just as Workington were launching a strong bid for Football League membership. Like Wigan Athletic, they had only narrowly failed the previous summer and although Accrington, the other Third Division North supplicants, received 46 votes (only two below the maximum) New Brighton polled just 18 to Workington's 28 for the final place.

Determined to carry on, they merely took the place of their own reserve team in the Lancashire Combination. Moving to Leasowe in 1954, they had one recorded attendance of 19 but did enjoy a fine FA Cup run in 1956/57. Stockport (3-3, 3-2), Derby (3-1 away) and Torquay (2-1) were added to the list of league clubs they had beaten as a non-league team before comeuppance arrived at Turf Moor in the fourth round. Burnley won 9-0 despite New Brighton's penalty-specialist goalkeeper Stan Hurst saving one as usual.

Invincibles: Preston North End, Football League champions and FA Cup winners 1888/89. Manager/chairman William Sudell, later sent to prison, is third from right, back row. In the front row are main goalscorers Jimmy Ross (in cap) and Johnny Goodall (centre).

Shakers: Bury's 1903 FA Cup winners, who beat Derby County by a record 6-0 in the final. Five of them also played in the Cup win three years earlier.

Merseyside celebrates a triumphant 1905/06 season: Liverpool league champions and Everton FA Cup winners (after beating their near-neighbours in the semi-final).

When they won their first league title in 1908, Manchester United were still playing at Bank Street, Clayton, barely half a mile from Manchester City's current Etihad complex.

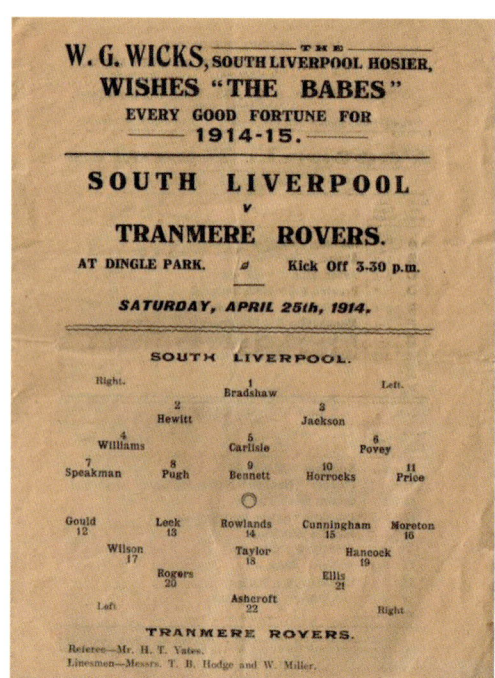

Derby day: South Liverpool's Lancashire Combination game with champions-elect Tranmere Rovers in 1914 attracted a crowd of 18,130.

Football League Division 1 1914/15

	P	W	D	L	F	A	Pts
Everton	38	19	8	11	76	47	46
Oldham	38	17	11	10	70	56	45
Blackburn	38	18	7	13	83	61	43
Burnley	38	18	7	13	61	47	43
Manchester C	38	15	13	10	49	39	43

High five: Lancashire lead the way with the top five in a tight finish, Oldham wasting their best-ever chance to become champions.

The day Bolton Wanderers became the first winners of a Wembley FA Cup final amid chaotic scenes.

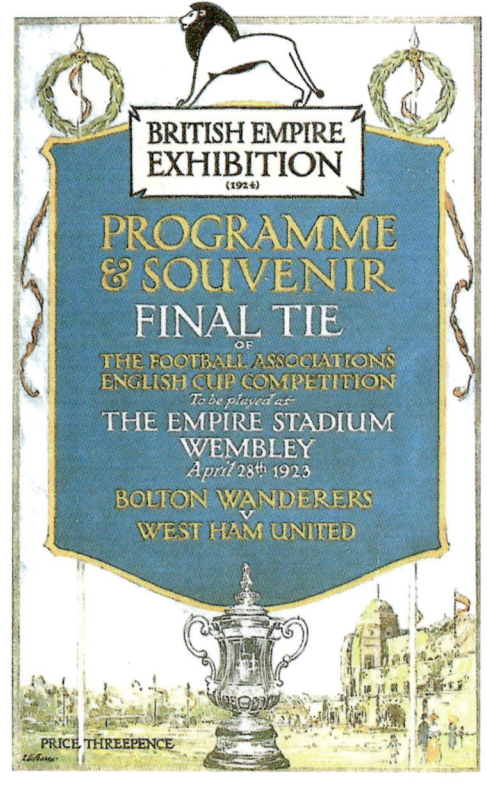

English music-hall star George Robey kicks off as Preston Ladies, representing England, take on France in London, May 1925. (Getty Images)

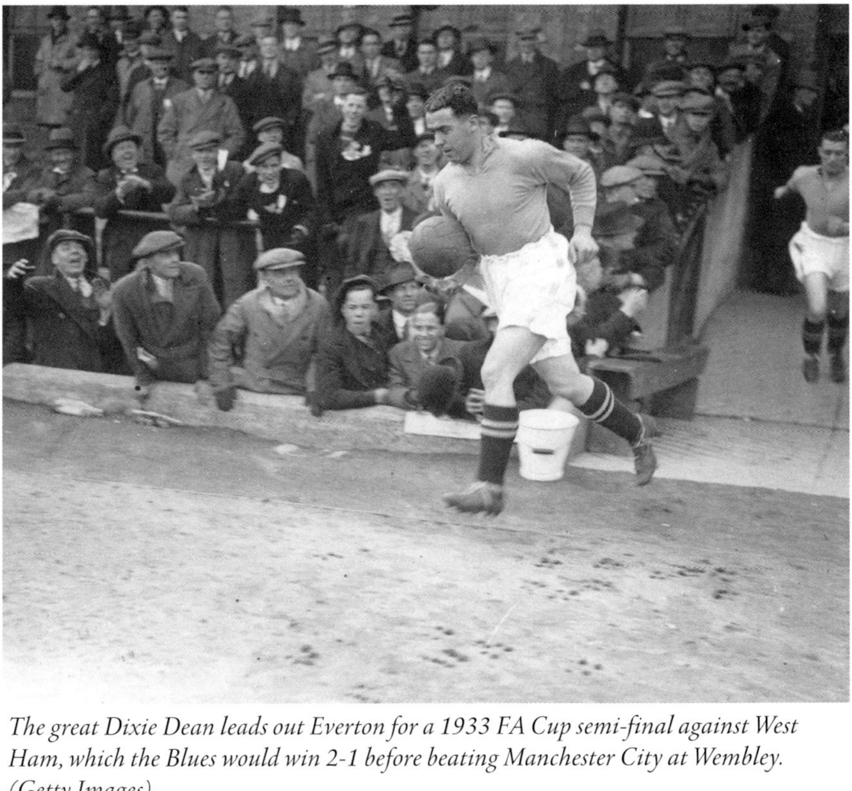

The great Dixie Dean leads out Everton for a 1933 FA Cup semi-final against West Ham, which the Blues would win 2-1 before beating Manchester City at Wembley. (Getty Images)

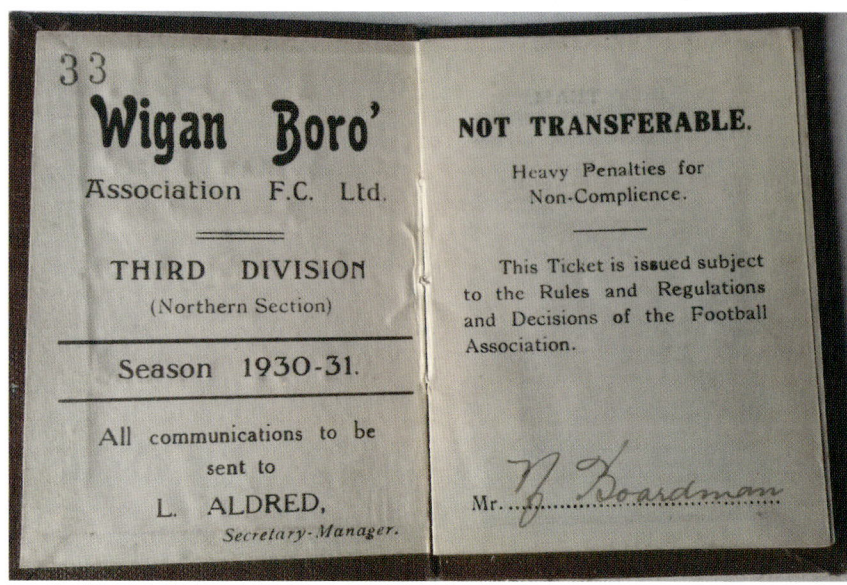

A boys' season-ticket costing five shillings (25p). The following season's would have been poor value: Wigan resigned from the league in October.

Women and children are passed to safety at the 1946 FA Cup game between Bolton and Stoke City, at which 33 supporters died. (Getty Images)

1948 – Stanley Matthews (Blackpool)
1949 – Johnny Carey (Man United)
1950 – Joe Mercer (Arsenal)
1951 – Harry Johnston (Blackpool)
1952 – Billy Wright (Wolves)
1953 – Nat Lofthouse (Bolton)
1954 – Tom Finney (Preston)
1955 – Don Revie (Man City)
1956 – Bert Trautmann (Man City)
1957 – Tom Finney (Preston)

Eight of the first ten players voted Footballer of the Year were from Lancashire clubs. (And one of the others, Joe Mercer, was a Merseysider.)

It was known as the 'Matthews final', although Stan Mortensen scored the hat-trick.

THE FOOTBALL ASSOCIATION CHALLENGE CUP COMPETITION

FINAL TIE
BLACKPOOL v BOLTON WANDERERS

SATURDAY, MAY 2nd, 1953   KICK-OFF 3 pm

EMPIRE STADIUM

WEMBLEY

Chairman and Managing Director :   SIR ARTHUR J. ELVIN, M.B.E.

OFFICIAL PROGRAMME · ONE SHILLING

Wigan Athletic set out on another successful Lancashire Combination season (they finished champions), but were still 25 years away from the Football League.

Matt Busby in a Munich hospital after the 1958 crash, slowly coming to grips with the size of his task in rebuilding Manchester United.
(Getty Images).

Burnley's 1960 Football League champions and European Cup contestants. Skipper Jimmy Adamson with the trophy and Jimmy McIlroy, appropriately, at his right hand. (Getty Images)

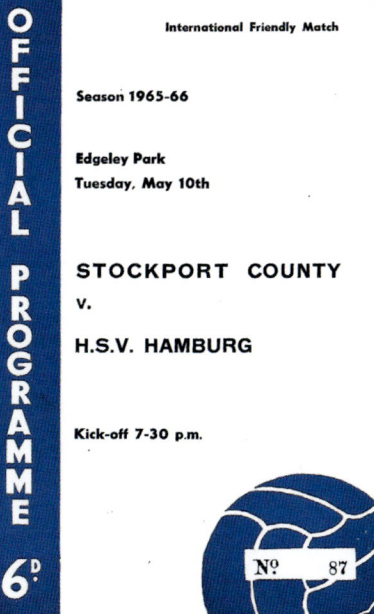

In May 1966 Uwe Seeler and Willi Schulz turned out at Edgeley Park for Hamburg. Two months later they were in West Germany's team that lost the World Cup Final to England.

Bury beat local rivals Bolton 2-1 in March 1969, but still went down from the Second Division; and down from the Third two years later (Got, Not Got).

Manchester City prepare for a title-winning 1967/68 campaign, with Francis Lee still to join them. Back: Book, Horne, Heslop, Ogley, Dowd, Oakes, Pardoe, Doyle. Front: Summerbee, Connor, Bell, Crossan, Jones, Young, Coleman.

Roy McFarland (third from right, back row), had only a couple of games left at Tranmere before moving to Brian Clough's Derby when this picture was taken in the summer of 1967. But George Yardley (second from right, front) scored 27 goals to keep them in the Third Division.

The front cover photograph looks a little older than 1972 as Southport take on Reading at Haig Avenue, a year before winning the Fourth Division. (Got, Not Got)

George Best has three Stoke City players off balance, including goalkeeper Gordon Banks, as he prepares to score in Manchester United's 2-1 win at the Victoria Ground, March 1971. (Getty Images)

Bill Shankly explains his stunning and premature decision to retire, July 1974.

The Holy Trinity, immortalised outside Old Trafford. Left to right: Best, Law, Charlton.

One in, one out: July 1978 and Wigan replace Southport in the Football League.

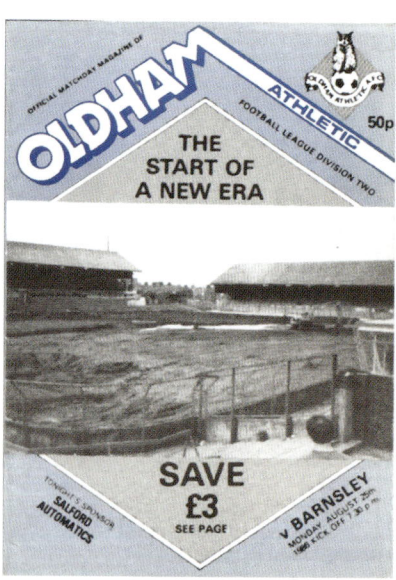

An artificial pitch means a successful new era at Boundary Park from August 1986.

The Friendly Final of 1986, to be repeated three years later under a Hillsborough cloud.

Blackburn's man of steel, Jack Walker, lifts the Premier League trophy his money had helped to bring to Ewood Park. (Getty Images)

The corks are popping after Ole Gunnar Solskjaer's goal wins the 1999 Champions League final for Alex Ferguson and Manchester United. (Getty Images)

It really did happen. From 3-0 down to a superior Milan in the 2005 Final, Liverpool equalise in the space of six minutes. (Getty Images)

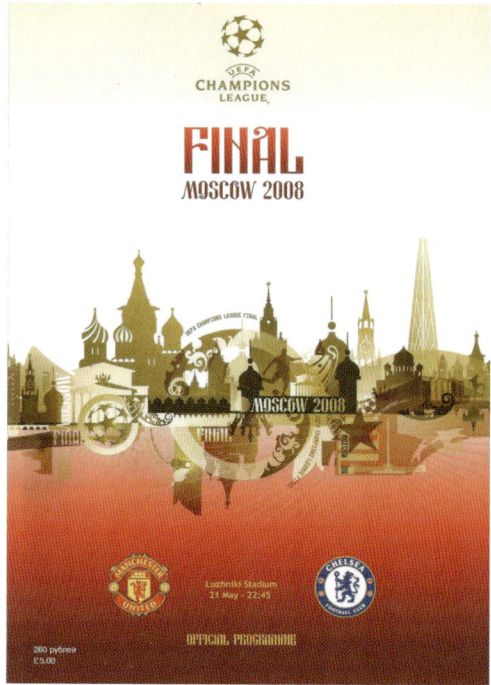

Midnight in Moscow (and later than that) as United sink Chelsea on penalties.

'Agueroooo!' One touch takes the ball, just, past QPR defender Taye Taiwo before the most famous goal in Premier League history wins the 2012 title. (Getty Images)

Chapter 6
Swinging (1961–70)

Goals and wages up, crowds down and reform rejected;
divide begins between big cities and the rest as Preston,
Bolton, Blackburn, Blackpool are all relegated; Everton
and Liverpool lay down a powerful Mersey beat; Allison
boasts he'll overtake United, who win the European
Cup after City's league title; Burnley runners-up
and European competitors before slow decline; Bury's
eventful decade; Ken Bates's great plans for Oldham;
Tranmere, Southport, Stockport turn to 'pay-night
football'; Rochdale reach a League Cup final; but
Accrington collapse in mid-season.

T HE Swinging Sixties, exciting as they turned out to be in the north-west's major football and music venues, began with attendances in 1960/61 falling by almost four million in a single season, despite a record number of goals in the Football League.

Everton, second only to Tottenham with over 43,000 per game at Goodison, and the two Manchester clubs were healthy enough, as were Liverpool in their last unsuccessful promotion push at almost 30,000, but four of the five lowest average gates in the First Division were in Lancashire: at Bolton (21,669); Blackburn (19,300); Blackpool (18,528) and relegated Finney-less Preston (16,894).

The latter pair drew fewer people than Fourth Division runners-up Crystal Palace. And lowest of all 92 clubs' crowds were Accrington Stanley (3,293), who in March 1962 played their last Football League game, becoming the first to collapse in mid-season since Wigan Borough exactly 30 years earlier.

Outside Manchester and Merseyside, north-west football was suffering not so much from an economic downturn as from prosperity; cars proliferated and motorways were opening, starting with the Preston Bypass in December 1958 and M1 the following year.

Bypass Preston was what many people did, heading for the big cities, including Sheffield and Leeds across the Pennines; in 1962 both Sheffield clubs were in the top six of the First Division while Leeds were beginning their journey under Don Revie from deep in the Second Division to First Division contention; their average crowds increased from 13,500 to 30,000 in four years.

For others it was the dismaying cycle of losing players, matches and supporters in that order. After 1950s local heroes like Tom Finney, Nat Lofthouse and Stanley Matthews departed, Preston, Bolton and Blackpool were all relegated by 1967 (as were Blackburn a year earlier and Burnley in 1971). Once the maximum wage was abolished in 1961, new stars like Peter Thompson and Howard Kendall of Preston, Alan Ball and Emlyn Hughes (Blackpool), Fred Pickering (Blackburn) and Francis Lee (Bolton) would end up with the big four clubs of Manchester and Merseyside.

Concerned by declining crowds and increased costs, the Football League's secretary Alan Hardaker and president Joe Richards drew up a radical 'Pattern for Football', recommending that there should be five divisions of 20 clubs each, with the lower two regionalised into north and south, and four up and down throughout. Any club seeking re-election two years running would lose their place, and the season, after starting with the new Football League Cup, would run from October to June.

The media liked it but when voted on in June 1963 it proved too far-reaching to achieve the required three-quarters majority, falling eight votes short.

'It was defeated by selfishness and shallow thinking,' Hardaker said later. 'Too many clubs could see no farther than their own little worlds.' That might also have been said of the Football League, the organisation that tried to prevent English clubs having anything to do with European football.

Too many First Division clubs did not want to risk one bad season in which they finished 19th or 20th and got relegated; similarly the smallest ones were frightened of losing their league status after two bad years.

In an otherwise celebratory article about the Football League's 75th anniversary that year, journalist Ivan Sharpe, who wrote the organisation's official history, felt compelled to remark, 'Reorganisation has become essential. There are more clubs than the country can adequately equip and support.' In retrospect, it was remarkable that Accrington proved not the first of many but the last for a long time.

* * * * *

As the Mersey beat began to resound through the country, **Everton** initially made most noise. In 1960 chairman John Moores gave his manager Johnny Carey money to spend on players like goalscoring inside-forward Roy Vernon from his old club Blackburn (£27,000), wing-half Jimmy Gabriel from Dundee (£30,000) and Northern Ireland international winger Billy Bingham from Luton, before a £55,000 swoop on Hearts in November for full-back George Thomson and centre-forward Alex Young, the Golden Vision himself.

From the bottom half of the First Division in 1959/60, they moved up to fifth a year later, their highest post-war finish, but Moores was impatient. At that summer's Football League AGM, Carey confronted him over rumours about his future and was famously sacked in the back of a black cab. What the Everton hierarchy had been looking for was what Harry Catterick, once manager of Rochdale, had achieved at Sheffield Wednesday, runners-up that season and the only team remotely close to the Tottenham Double winners of 1961.

Satisfied with nothing but the best, as the club's motto had it. And within two years of Catterick taking over, the Blues were champions. In 1962 they rose just one place to fourth but added goalkeeper Gordon West, Sheffield Wednesday's combative little captain Tony Kay for £60,000, plus forwards Dennis Stevens from Bolton and Johnny Morrissey in a rare deal with Liverpool, while trading playmaker Bobby Collins to Leeds (where he would become 1965 Footballer of the Year).

In the championship season of 1962/63 there was a thunderous return to Merseyside derbies with a 2-2 draw at home to promoted Liverpool watched by no fewer than 72,488, and winning six of the last seven games (after a second derby draw) ensured they finished six points ahead of the field with 20-plus goals from both Vernon and Young. The season's main disappointment was a tame European debut against Jock Stein's Dunfermline, who ousted them from the Fairs Cup 2-1 on aggregate.

As champions Everton were of course entitled to enter the European Cup, where another immediate exit occurred, caused this time by the formidable Inter Milan, who progressed in classic Italian style with a 1-0 win following a goalless draw, and went on to win the final. Catterick reacted by bringing in centre-forward Fred Pickering from Blackburn and left-back Ray Wilson from Huddersfield.

The 1964/65 season included one of Goodison's most notorious games when after 38 violent minutes of the First Division match against Leeds, the referee took both teams off the field 'like an exasperated teacher walking out on a class of unruly boys', *The Guardian* reported. Don Revie's newly promoted side were unashamedly physical and the Blues decided to meet fire with fire. Remarkably, the home team's Sandy Brown was the only player sent off, albeit as early as the fourth minute, for a retaliatory punch at Johnny Giles.

Further notoriety followed two months later when Kay was sensationally sent to prison with two former Sheffield Wednesday team-mates who like him had bet against their side in a game away to champions Ipswich. Arguing that they were merely taking out insurance against missing out on a win bonus was regarded as no defence and together with Peter Swan and David 'Bronco' Layne, he was banned for life; the punishment was later lifted but Kay, who never played professionally again, could reasonably have expected to have been in England's 1966 World Cup squad with club-mates Wilson and Pickering.

The Blues managed fourth place and the following season were FA Cup winners, 12 months after Liverpool. Having seen off the pride of Manchester, beating City after three games and then

United in the semi-final with Colin Harvey's goal, they created headlines before the final, firstly when Catterick made ten changes against Leeds to avoid injuries (incurring a £2,000 fine for the club) and then dropped Pickering for the final, bringing in the little-known Mike Trebilcock, a £20,000 signing from Plymouth Argyle.

At 2-0 down after half an hour fans were questioning his judgment, just as they had done when he dropped golden-boy Young in January for 16-year-old Joe Royle. But the Cornishman dramatically scored twice in five minutes before Derek Temple took advantage of a defensive slip to burst though for the winner. The Everton fan racing on to the pitch joining the celebration and losing his jacket to a chasing policeman became a symbol of more innocent times.

Catterick believed in building on success and in August he added World Cup-winner Alan Ball from Blackpool, who was able to pose for photos before the opening game at Fulham with England team-mates and full-back partners Wilson and George Cohen. With Pickering suffering from injury, Ball even became top scorer in a season notable for another expensive acquisition in Howard Kendall from Preston, to complete the most famous midfield in the club's history with Ball and Harvey.

Sixth that season, the Blues moved up to fifth a year later but suffered the setback of an FA Cup final defeat despite being firm favourites against mid-table West Bromwich Albion, who won 1-0 with Jeff Astle's goal.

The 1968/69 season brought further improvement to third (as well as a semi-final defeat by City after again knocking out United) and a year later Everton were champions again. In an explosive start 15 of the first 18 games were won before Leeds reeled them back in, only to fall foul of fixture congestion. The Blues stayed unbeaten from mid-January and Catterick was able to celebrate a second title, built he said on 'pure football ... with no destroyers' – a rebuke to the more physical approach of Leeds, Arsenal and Liverpool.

That trio, however, would define the style of the early 1970s and win the trophies to prove it, while Everton's decline was to be swift.

* * * * *

When television highlights as we came to know them began on a new BBC2 programme called *Match of the Day* on 22 August 1964, the venue was Anfield, home of the new Football League champions **Liverpool**, with commentator Ken Wolstenholme standing on the pitch in what he called 'Beatleville' to introduce an exciting game against Arsenal that was won 3-2 in the last few minutes. With BBC2 available to so few people at that time, the programme was watched by an audience of 20,000 – less than half the number in the ground – but it proved popular enough to earn a BBC1 slot from the following season and become a national institution.

Part of Merseyside's appeal for the media at the time was the emergence of pop culture. The Beatles had their first hit 'Love Me Do' in October 1962 when Liverpool had been playing for two months back in the top division. A year later the Kop, already adapting chart hits for their own purposes, adopted 'You'll Never Walk Alone', the Gerry and the Pacemakers version of a *Carousel* song, which chimed in perfectly with Bill Shankly's version of collective football and a one-for-all mentality.

Liverpool had not only finally made it back to the First Division under the ebullient Shankly but succeeded Everton as champions in their second season there. When they won the Second Division at last in 1962 after so many near-misses, the focus outside Merseyside was nevertheless on the more romantic triumphs of Ipswich Town, the shock First Division winners under Alf Ramsey, and equally unfashionable Leyton Orient, whom Everton outcast Johnny Carey transformed into runners-up to Liverpool.

The Reds' promotion season was largely a cakewalk with only one point dropped in the first ten games and 99 goals scored, 41 of them in as many games by Roger Hunt, setting a new club record. Before the season began Shankly had got the two men Huddersfield refused to buy for him, towering centre-half Ron Yeats from Dundee United and Hunt's new partner Ian St John (Motherwell).

Once in the top division the squad was further strengthened after a slow start by two more Scots, wing-half Willie Stevenson and goalkeeper Tommy Lawrence, then winger Peter Thompson from Preston to play on the opposite flank to Ian Callaghan, the regular outside-right. The championship season also had a sluggish beginning with the first three home games all lost, but took off after defeating defending champions Everton 2-1 at Anfield at the end of September. After three wins in four days at Easter the title was sealed by beating Manchester United 3-0, Burnley 3-0 and Arsenal 5-0.

The following year's win over Arsenal on *Match of the Day* was one of only four in the first 16 games and Shankly's men were soon concentrating on two exciting cup runs. In the FA Cup, they had been losing semi-finalists in 1963 to bogey team Leicester, but laid the bogey two years later in a sixth-round replay, then defeated Tommy Docherty's young Chelsea 2-0 in the semi-final to qualify for one of many high-profile meetings with Revie's Leeds.

It passed more peacefully than the latter's encounters with Everton and was actually quite dull for 90 minutes, followed by a livelier period of extra time. Hunt headed them in front from a cross by Gerry Byrne, who had broken his collarbone early on; Billy Bremner equalised but St John headed the winner.

The thousands of Liverpool followers, chanting 'Ee-aye addio, we're going to see the Queen', contributed to what *Sunday Express* veteran Alan Hoby called 'the most delirious and emotional scenes I can ever recall in a Cup Final'.

FA Cup Final 1965: Liverpool 2 Leeds United 1 (aet)
Liverpool: Lawrence; Lawler, Byrne, Strong, Yeats, Stevenson, Callaghan, Hunt, St John, Smith, Thompson.
Leeds United: Sprake; Reaney, Bell, Bremner, Charlton, Hunter, Giles, Storrie, Peacock, Collins, Johanneson.

Three days after Wembley Liverpool were ready for the next challenge – a semi-final in their first European Cup campaign. 'If we win [the FA Cup] we'll win the European Cup as well,' Shankly had said the day before the final.

At home to Inter, the holders and conquerors of Everton, Kop turnstiles were closed more than two hours before kick-off, the FA Cup was paraded round the ground, and the Italians wilted in an intimidating atmosphere, losing 3-1 to a team playing in their special all-red European strip.

It was 'the greatest show they have ever given', the *Daily Post* believed.

In Milan, however, it was Liverpool's turn to feel the force of a fanatical home crowd and a referee who did them no favours in a 3-0 defeat. Inter went on to retain their trophy.

In 1965/66 Shankly's team were champions again, effectively using just 12 players; only two others even got on the pitch, making just four starts between them. A strong first half of the season set up the triumph, and included a glorious performance in beating Everton 5-0. Going out at home to Chelsea in the FA Cup third round probably helped, but after knocking out Celtic in the European Cup Winners' Cup semi-final, Liverpool returned to Glasgow for the final and contrived to lose it 2-1 to Borussia Dortmund in driving rain.

Fog rather than rain was the problem in Amsterdam the following season when any hope of a European Cup challenge was derailed by Johan Cruyff's emerging Ajax, leading 4-0 at half-time and winning 5-1. Calling them 'defensive' was outrageous even by Shankly's standards of hyperbole and far from overcoming the deficit at Anfield as he had promised, the Reds were held 2-2. Losing to Everton in the FA Cup fifth round three months later led to a miserable end to the league season and fifth place.

Blackpool teenager Emlyn Hughes and Chelsea centre-forward Tony Hateley (for a club record £96,000) were recruited but while the former lived up to Shankly's prediction as a future England captain, Hateley lasted only a season, in which Liverpool managed third place behind the two Manchester clubs.

A year later they were runners-up to Leeds, conceding a miserly 24 goals but being seen to be lacking a first-class centre-forward to support Hunt and the deeper-lying St John. In 1969/70 they dropped to fifth, Hunt left for Bolton after a club record 285 goals, and an FA Cup defeat to Second Division strugglers Watford convinced Shankly and Bob Paisley that it was time for changes.

* * * * *

Winning the First Division seven times in eight seasons from 1963–70, as well as a European Cup, Cup Winners' Cup, three FA Cups and a League Cup established Lancashire as the dominant force in English football to a degree never seen before. **Manchester United** would contribute to that list but, understandably slow to escape from the shadow of Munich, began the decade inconsistently before the holy trinity of George Best, Denis Law and Bobby Charlton came together.

In 1959/60 they had scored 102 goals, 32 of them from Dennis Viollet, but conceded 80. In successive games the following season they beat Chelsea 6-0, Manchester City 5-1 and Tottenham's Double winners 2-0, then went down 6-0 at Leicester and 7-2 at home to Sheffield Wednesday in an FA Cup fourth round replay. Four different goalkeepers were tried that season and Matt Busby attempted but failed to sign a clutch of new defenders, including Ron Yeats and Ray Wilson, who both ended up on Merseyside, and Blackpool's Jimmy Armfield.

For two years things were no better with seventh place twice and then 15th, before a genuine relegation struggle the very year that Law was rescued from a stay at Torino that he hated almost from the off. He cost £115,000 in the summer of 1962 and even after wing-half Pat Crerand arrived from Celtic the following February four more successive defeats put them in serious trouble at the bottom.

Drawing a crucial derby 1-1 away to City, who were also struggling badly a point behind, helped United more than their neighbours but not until beating bottom club Orient in the penultimate game after trailing at half-time were they safe.

That meant being able to concentrate on the following week's FA Cup final against Leicester. Because of the snow and ice they had not even been able to play their third-round match against Huddersfield until the first week of March, a month in which they won four ties to progress to a semi-final against Second Division Southampton. A scrambled goal by Law won a poor game to earn a final against a top-four Leicester team who had beaten United 4-3 the previous month.

At last the clouds of a dark season were blown away at Wembley in an exhilarating game. Gordon Banks kept them at bay until Law beat him after half an hour and David Herd doubled the lead when Banks could not hold Charlton's shot. With ten minutes left Ken Keyworth headed Leicester back into contention but Banks dropped a cross by Johnny Giles, playing because Nobby Stiles was injured, and Herd scored his second to secure victory. It was Giles's last competitive game before joining Leeds, a Second Division club who doubled his modest United wages and made him determined to prove United wrong.

A first trophy for six years, along with Law's 29 league and cup goals, offered hope of greater things. The following September, a slim 17-year-old from Belfast called George Best made his debut on the wing at home to West Bromwich Albion.

He did not play again until after Christmas, following a 6-1 Boxing Day defeat at Burnley, which was reversed 5-1 with his first United goal, and thereafter he stayed in for the rest of a season that finished in second place behind Liverpool and with an FA Cup semi-final surprisingly lost 3-1 to West Ham in the heavy mud of Hillsborough. Four days later, still feeling the effects, United crashed out of their first European Cup Winners' Cup venture by going down 5-0 away to Sporting Lisbon.

Law had scored 30 league goals and almost matched that the following season when they became champions. Promoted Leeds, to Giles's delight, were the only team to beat them at Old Trafford and then knocked them out of the FA Cup in a semi-final replay violent even by the wild west standards of the time. United responded with six straight league wins, the crucial one being 1-0 at Elland Road, where winger John Connelly scored. It ultimately meant United won the title on goal average – from Leeds, who also lost the FA Cup Final.

Another new European experience was playing in the Inter-Cities Fairs Cup, beating Everton 3-2 on aggregate but losing a semi-final play-off to Ferencvaros of Hungary in the middle of June.

Everton had their revenge in the 1966 FA Cup semi-final after United's title defence had been undermined by a poor start. Just like two years earlier there was a double disappointment in a matter of days, the Everton defeat having been preceded by going out of the European Cup semi-final to Partizan Belgrade. So the season's outstanding memory was the previous European round, beating Benfica 5-1 in their own Lisbon back yard with one of teenager Best's greatest performances earning him the title 'El Beatle'. 'George just went out and destroyed them,' said an admiring Busby.

The next meeting with Benfica would be an even more famous one, brought about by United winning the 1967 championship to qualify for another attempt at the European Cup Busby coveted so much. Unbeaten in the league from Boxing Day on, they had the triumvirate of Best, Law and Charlton at its peak, scoring 45 league goals, and with more than useful back-up from Herd.

With Alex Stepney now in goal and David Sadler a regular in different positions, the title was clinched in the grand manner, a 6-1 win at West Ham marred only by the crowd trouble that was beginning to afflict British football. 'Twenty Injured As Soccer Crowd Starts Riot' (*Sunday Express*) was the sort of headline that would become increasingly common. 'They do not need such thugs among their following,' wrote Brian James in the *Daily Mail*.

This time the title defence was more impressive and came down to a thrilling climax with, of all people, Manchester City. When City, now under the potent partnership of Joe Mercer and Malcolm Allison won 3-1 at Old Trafford in late March it left both teams and Leeds all on the same number of points. Leeds would miss out, as they so often did at the time, the Manchester pair going into the final day level on points, with City clearly ahead on goal average. They appeared to be facing the harder game at Newcastle but came through it 4-3 while a nervous United, missing the injured Law, fell behind at home to lowly Sunderland and were beaten 2-1.

Four days later Busby's team played their European Cup semi-final away to Real Madrid with only a narrow 1-0 lead earned by Best's goal from the first leg. Trailing 3-1 after a traumatic first half, the players backed Busby's decision to 'go right at them' and were rewarded with goals from two defensive players, Sadler, and a most unlikely goalscoring hero in centre-half and Munich survivor Bill Foulkes.

Having known all season that the final would be played at Wembley, United must have felt this might be their best chance and, after Madrid, that everything was at last falling their way in Busby's great quest.

'I have always had the conviction that one day Manchester United would win the European Cup,' he told reporters. 'The thing that disturbs me most is that everybody seems to think we're just going along to Wembley to pick up the cup. We are playing one of the best teams in the world.'

Benfica, finalists for the fifth time in eight years, fully deserved that accolade. They fell behind to Charlton's rare headed goal from Sadler's cross after 55 minutes but Jaime Graca equalised from a knockdown by the towering centre-forward José Torres. With a few minutes left the great Eusébio finally escaped from Stiles's vigorous clutches and was clean through, only for Stepney to bring off a save so good that the Benfica man applauded him.

It was a turning point. From being, as Charlton and Stiles admitted, on their knees, United came again in extra time. Best wriggled through the defence to restore the lead, Kidd celebrated his 19th birthday with a goal and Charlton, symbolically, swept in the fourth goal to give Busby his cup.

At the after-match party an emotional manager took the microphone and sang 'What A Wonderful World'. Charlton, in tears at the final whistle, was too exhausted even to attend.

European Cup Final 1968: Manchester United 4 Benfica 1 (aet)
Manchester United: Stepney; Brennan, Dunne, Crerand, Foulkes, Stiles, Best, Kidd, Charlton, Sadler, Aston.
Benfica: Henrique; Adolfo, Humberto, Jacinto, Cruz, Graça, Coluna, Augusto, Eusébio, Torres, Simões.

After the achievement of 29 May 1968 and the knighthood immediately conferred on Busby, there was little more joy to be had for him or anyone else at Old Trafford. In the next two years United finished 11th and 8th with nobody reaching 20 league goals either time. Defeat by an aggregate 2-1 in the Inter Continental Cup against Estudiantes of Argentina only confirmed that the Anglo-Argentine wounds of 1966 had not healed; Stiles was sent off in an away leg of 53 fouls, as was Best at home.

After defeat by new enemy Leeds in January 1969, at which point United had scored six goals in their previous nine games, Busby announced he would relinquish team affairs at the end of the season and become general manager. 'United is no longer just a football club,' he said, 'it is an institution. I feel the demands are beyond one human being.'

Unfortunately even limited demands proved beyond the younger, track-suited team manager the club wanted. Wilf McGuinness, a promising wing-half whose career was ended at 22 by a broken leg, was appointed chief coach before Milan ended United's European Cup defence with a 2-1 aggregate win in the semi-final.

Keen to make a mark, McGuinness unwisely dropped Charlton and Law for one game after a bad start to the new season that brought an eighth-place finish and losing semi-finals against major rivals City (in the Football League Cup) and Leeds (FA Cup).

It was hardly disastrous even if the crowd dropped below 27,000 for one game (ironically won 7-0); but losing another League Cup semi-final the following season to Third Division Aston Villa, then dropping into the bottom five with a 4-4 draw at Derby on Boxing Day 1970 spelt the end for McGuinness. 'Too young, too close to us,' was Law's verdict.

* * * * *

Denis Law was a key figure at **Manchester City** earlier in the decade and would be so again. Having escaped relegation by the skin of their teeth in 1959, the club broke the British transfer record in March 1960 by paying Huddersfield £55,000 for him. Law, who had been wanted by a long list of clubs including Arsenal and Everton, admitted he might have done better for himself and did so within two years, financially at least, by moving on to Italy before United rescued him.

In his last FA Cup tie with City he set an unwanted record by scoring six times away to Luton before the game was abandoned; City, not untypically, lost the rerun four days later.

In the meantime they finished 15th, 13th and 12th without him and in 1962/63 suffered the ignominy of relegation after the controversial 1-1 draw at home to fellow strugglers United (who equalised from a dubious penalty) and a 6-1 thrashing at West Ham.

It took three seasons and a significant change of manager to return. In 1964/65 there were twice crowds of below 10,000 and to supporters' horror one City director even broached the possibility of merging with United, or at the very least, ground-sharing at Old Trafford.

For the next season Joe Mercer replaced manager George Poyser, making inspired signings in his assistant Malcolm Allison, recently sacked by Plymouth Argyle, and winger Mike Summerbee from Swindon Town. The flamboyant Allison, schooled at West Ham, was among the new breed of British coaches heavily influenced by continental football, and claimed that at Plymouth he had been the first English manager to use a sweeper; that player was Tony Book, who he persuaded Mercer to recruit as a 32-year-old in the summer of 1966.

City had just won the Second Division, losing only five games, securing the magisterial Colin Bell from Bury and making a wider mark by knocking First Division sides Blackpool and Leicester out of the FA Cup and taking eventual winners Everton to three games in the quarter-final. Lacking a prolific centre-forward, they struggled for one season in the First Division, finishing 15th, then Allison insisted on moving Summerbee there and on the back of five successive wins a title challenge was launched. Bell and Neil Young were already goalscoring forwards; now there was the powerful Summerbee and in the autumn when Francis Lee was added from Bolton the mix was complete.

Allison had developed an early dislike of United's air of superiority and, outspoken as ever, promised to overhaul them within three years; this from a Second Division club. Now, in the third year, they ended up duelling with their crosstown rivals for the championship of England.

Losing at home to United in September was an early setback but Lee's arrival sparked off another unbeaten run, including a 4-1 December defeat of Tottenham that became known as the 'ballet on ice'. The crucial 3-1 win at Old Trafford in March after George Best had scored in the first minute was worth as much psychologically as the two points and after taking only one point from two games in mid-April City won three on the trot to leave the title in their hands, as long as they could win away to mid-table Newcastle.

Their supporters made up almost half the crowd of 46,300 who saw the home team twice equalise goals by Summerbee and Young. Young and Lee appeared to have secured the title before Newcastle reduced the deficit to 4-3 but with United losing at home to Sunderland even a draw would have been good enough. The team was: Mulhearn, Book, Pardoe, Doyle, Heslop, Oakes, Lee, Bell, Summerbee, Young, Coleman.

Lee, Bell, Summerbee and Young all scored between 14 and 19 goals as City earned respect for an approach to football every bit as exciting as United's. 'This team with so many friends,' the *Sunday Express* called them.

If the average attendance was still 20,000 below that of their neighbours, who were about to become European Cup winners, Allison had technically achieved his bold boast about overtaking them in three years. He was less successful in predicting City would 'terrify Europe to death'. Before the 1968/69 European Cup began with two Manchester clubs competing, City had won only one league game out of nine. Fenerbahçe of Turkey then knocked them out in the first round.

Apart from isolated performances like a 7-0 thrashing of Burnley, league form was so poor that they finished in the bottom half of the table in a season redeemed by the FA Cup. Single-goal victories did the trick against Tottenham in the sixth round, then Everton at Villa Park thanks to centre-half Tommy Booth's goal and at Wembley, once again in their smart red and black stripes and with Allison banned from the touchline. Young thrashed in the only goal to beat relegated Leicester. Skipper Book did not play until January because of injury but remarkably was still named joint Footballer of the Year with Derby's Dave Mackay, and Allison was promised the world by Juventus on a ten-day trip to Italy before deciding to stay put.

One year on with Joe Corrigan the new goalkeeper and Book still going strong in front of him at 35, two more major trophies were captured. First came the Football League Cup, a more prestigious bauble at last after the introduction of a Wembley final three years earlier. It was a tough journey there, with wins over both Liverpool and Everton then an epic two-leg semi-final against United watched by almost 120,000 fans. City won the home leg 2-1 but were losing by the same score at Old Trafford until Summerbee scrambled a winner. At Wembley City came from behind to beat West Bromwich Albion with goals by Mike Doyle and Glyn Pardoe.

League form was flagging again but in the European Cup Winners' Cup semi-final, Germans Schalke were beaten 5-1 at Maine Road and then goals by Lee and Young won the final against Górnik in Vienna, where pouring rain kept the crowd down to only 10,000. That made four major trophies in three seasons. But Allison, believing Mercer had promised him the manager's job by 1967, was growing restless.

* * * * *

As defending champions in 1960/61 **Burnley** went through an exhausting season of 63 games, including a first European venture, and still achieved fourth place. European Cup football came to Turf Moor on 16 November 1960 when 36,742 saw Stade de Reims, the runners-up in 1956 and 1959, beaten 2-0 with goals by Jimmy McIlroy and Jimmy Robson. Losing 3-2 in France took the Clarets through to a quarter-final against Hamburg, who were beaten 3-1 in Lancashire. There was then a wait of two months for the second leg, when the Germans came through 4-1 with two goals by local hero Uwe Seeler in front of more than 71,000.

Eight times in the league that season Burnley scored five goals or more, totalling 102, plus 35 more in the cups. They beat the Tottenham Double team 4-2 and drew 4-4 at White Hart Lane after being 4-0 down, but three days after the Hamburg defeat Spurs overcame a tired Clarets side by a flattering 3-0 in the FA Cup semi-final. Burnley might reasonably have been spared the new Football League Cup but whereas other top teams ducked out, they went as far as another semi-final, playing 11 competitive games in April and eventually losing a third match to Aston Villa 2-1.

Another memorable season followed in 1961/62, scoring 101 First Division goals and leading the table but faltering so badly that only one of the last ten games was won, allowing Alf Ramsey's unfashionable Ipswich to steal the title by three points. Having reached the FA Cup final against Tottenham was a complication and although Robson equalised at Wembley, the London side retained the trophy 3-1. Wing-half and captain Jimmy Adamson was named Footballer of the Year, then went off to the 1962 World Cup as England coach.

The following season was notable for the departure of McIlroy to Stoke City, a home for ageing but still talented footballers having their careers elongated by a sympathetic manager in Tony Waddington. Knocked out of the FA Cup early by Liverpool, Burnley performed better late on even without McIlroy, to finish third. Andy Lochhead had taken over as new spearhead to lead the scorers, soon to be joined by Ulsterman Willie Irvine as Ray Pointer left for Bury. There was one more fine league season in 1966, another third place, level on points with runners-up Leeds as Irvine scored 29; and as a result, one Fairs Cup season, winning three ties and surviving a wild night in Naples before a narrow quarter-final defeat by Eintracht Frankfurt.

The slow decline was at the very least consistent as they finished 14th for no fewer than four successive seasons from 1967–70. Winning the FA Youth Cup in 1968 showed that the club's junior set-up was still finding and honing talent, but players like Dave Thomas, Ralph Coates, Steve Kindon and Martin Dobson would all prove too good to keep for as long as the Clarets would have wanted, just like Glaswegian winger Willie Morgan who left for Manchester United. A crowd of below 10,000 for one of his last games in the spring of 1968, repeated the following year, illustrated the fundamental problem.

* * * * *

Preston were the first of the suffering Lancashire First Division clubs to go down, significantly in the season after Tom Finney's retirement. By the end of the decade they would even drop one division lower.

As the rest of the Football League contributed to the highest-scoring season in history, 1960/61, North End managed a mere 43, exactly half as many as Newcastle, the other relegated club. Manager Cliff Britton resigned and Jimmy Milne took over for seven years in which they were only once close to promotion but did reach the FA Cup final in the same season.

That was the 1963/64 campaign, in which the burly Alex Dawson, once of Manchester United, scored 30 goals in a settled Second Division side not far behind Leeds United and Sunderland, and then added six more in an FA Cup run that began with victories in replays at Deepdale over First Division sides Nottingham Forest and Bolton.

The luck of the draw then helped in producing two Fourth Division opponents, Carlisle United and Oxford United, both beaten only by a single goal, and while Manchester United and West Ham were thrown together in one semi-final, Preston drew Second Division relegation strugglers Swansea, who took the lead at sodden Villa Park but were beaten by Tony Singleton's long-range effort.

Wing-half Howard Kendall, aged 17, had scored the winner against Forest but only played in the final because regular wing-half Ian Davidson was disciplined for claiming he had to attend a funeral in his native Scotland – which proved not to be the case. Kendall did well enough and his team led twice through Doug Holden and Dawson before Ronnie Boyce's late header decided an exciting final. 'Preston shocked the Londoners and surprised the whole world of football with the quality and splendour of their play,' the *Sunday Express* reported.

Any hopes of a promotion challenge the following season quickly disappeared, however, even though Dawson and Brian Godfrey scored 51 goals between them. The defence conceded 81, almost the worst in the division, and 12th place was followed by a further drop to 17th, only four points off relegation, in 1966.

Another mid-table season saw Kendall sold to Everton and after finishing four points from the drop in 1968, the worst came to the worst two years later, defeat by Blackpool confirming relegation with Aston Villa as two of the founding fathers of league football dropped into the third tier for the first time. Scottish midfielder Archie Gemmill, destined for Derby County, was top scorer with a mere six goals.

* * * * *

Bolton followed Preston down in 1964 and after one near-miss at returning, were grateful not to sink into the Third Division with them.

Nat Lofthouse, as previously mentioned, was forced to retire at the end of 1960 and a generational shift came in one of his last games, when 16-year-old Francis Lee joined him in the attack and scored on debut. The team finished no higher than 18th, only three points clear of relegation, were in the same position two years later, and in 1963/64 made the drop. Needing to win the last game at home to Wolves they crashed 4-0. There were nearly 28,000 to see them go but earlier gates, like Burnley's, had dropped to four figures.

Lee, still a teenager, was leading scorer in the relegation season and again in the Second Division, with good support from powerful Welsh centre-forward Wyn Davies. Their goals, contributing to a total of 80, suggested promotion straight back was likely but a poor finish allowed surprise package Northampton Town to take the runners-up spot six points ahead.

Inevitably both men moved on, Davies to Newcastle and Lee to Manchester City, and although a good proportion of the £140,000 fees was spent, Wanderers became a mid-table Second Division team and then something worse.

After Bill Ridding ended 17 years as manager in 1968, his replacement Lofthouse and new signing Roger Hunt from Liverpool could do little better than keep them out of the Third Division's clutches. They finished 17th, a point above famous names in Villa and Blackburn and in 1970 just avoided the bottom six as Villa and Preston suffered the big drop.

* * * * *

As with Preston and Bolton, so, eventually with **Blackburn**. Having won the FA Youth Cup in 1959, they had a group of younger players to carry them through the early 1960s, before decline and relegation. England internationals Ronnie Clayton and Bryan Douglas were still going strong in the first half of the decade, winger Douglas starting all four games at the 1962 World Cup in Chile, although Rovers had dropped from 8th to 16th.

In an eventful 1963/64 season they finished in the top seven with 89 goals, 32 of them from Andy McEvoy and 23 from Fred Pickering. Both were on target in the 7-2 drubbing of Tottenham and on Boxing Day each scored a hat-trick in the memorable 8-2 win away to West Ham which put Rovers top of the league, yet the following day at Ewood Park McEvoy's goal was answered by three from the Londoners after Ron Greenwood made only one change to his team, by dropping Martin Peters.

Following that with tenth place in 1964/65 and another 83 goals (McEvoy 29, John Byrom 25) gave no sign of what was to come. In August 1965 a polio outbreak that began in Little Harwood made national headlines, costing the life of a teenage girl and affecting more than 100 other people. Rovers players were immunised before leaving for a pre-season tour of Germany but two matches had to be postponed early on, Douglas was injured in a friendly and the prolific Byrom and McEvoy lost their goalscoring touch.

Seven of the first eight games were lost and Rovers never caught up. By the final whistle, having lost 12 of the last 13, they were fully 13 points behind at the bottom. Losing 30 games was the joint-worst record of any First Division team in history and

211

three of the last four home matches were watched by fewer than 8,000 fans.

Byrom and Mike England were sold and although John Connelly arrived from Manchester United after falling out with Matt Busby, and finished top scorer back in the Second Division with a modest 11, Rovers were seven points off promotion in fourth place, manager 'Jolly' Jack Marshall resigning after six and a half years.

In January 1967 newspapers reported there were 4,000 holes in Blackburn roads, giving John Lennon a line for a song and making the town world famous when the Beatles released *Sgt. Pepper's Lonely Hearts Club Band* that summer. Days in the life of local football fans, however, remained disappointing; Rovers were not turning anyone on in finishing 8th and then 19th, the final home game against Crystal Palace in April 1969 attracting a crowd of 4,777. The same month Douglas and Clayton both retired, having played over 1,150 games between them.

* * * * *

Blackpool found the decade a struggle even before relegation in 1967, the year after Blackburn.

From a mid-table position they dropped to 20th in 1960/61, requiring a late rally with Stanley Matthews back in the side to avoid relegation. Newcastle, beaten 2-1 at Bloomfield Road in April with Ray Charnley's goal, went down instead, a point adrift despite having scored almost 20 goals more than the Seasiders. Losing 6-2 to Second Division Scunthorpe was a reminder of how long gone was FA Cup glory, and just like Blackburn, Bolton and Burnley crowds of below 10,000 were recorded.

Matthews's departure for Stoke in the autumn of 1961 after 428 games (plus 87 as a wartime guest) was truly the end of an era, although two comfortable mid-table seasons followed, thanks largely to Charnley's goals, which won him an England cap. In 1961/62 his 36 included half a dozen in the League Cup, where Blackpool reached the semi-final but lost to Second Division Norwich.

Alan Ball, a bundle of ginger-haired teenage energy who made a reputation early on by bawling out Matthews in training, was top scorer in a poor 1963/64 campaign that ended in 18th place, followed by 17th. In 1966 he won the World Cup as a Blackpool player but soon afterwards joined Everton.

Charnley soldiered on, top scorer in all competitions for a ninth successive year, but that last one ended in relegation. Not until mid-October was a league game won and Newcastle were the only team to lose at Bloomfield Road (6-0). Knocking Manchester United out of the League Cup 5-1 and winning away to both Everton and Liverpool were among the few other highlights.

Stan Mortensen was a hugely popular choice to replace Ron Suart as manager and should have achieved instant promotion back to the top division. The Seasiders won their last seven games in pursuit of Queens Park Rangers only for the London side to pip them on the finest of goal averages, benefiting from a last-minute own goal at Villa Park.

A year later Mortensen was sacked for finishing only eighth, an unpopular decision that the board felt was justified when successor Les Shannon from Bury led a successful promotion campaign, finishing runners-up to Huddersfield despite scoring only 56 goals. Pleasingly, promotion was secured with a 3-0 away win at Preston that condemned the old rivals to the Third Division.

* * * * *

Bury had their most eventful decade since dropping out of the First Division in the 1920s, encompassing a championship title, a major semi-final, two relegations and one further promotion. After all that they ended up where they had started in the Third Division.

In the triumphant championship season of 1960/61 under Dave Russell they won 30 games and scored 108 goals; no fewer than five players scored 15 times or more. Up in the Second Division, however, they had only one good season, finishing eighth in 1962/63, five points behind promoted Chelsea, and reaching the semi-final of the League Cup. An away win against First Division Leyton Orient took them there and against Birmingham City they were only narrowly beaten 4-3 on aggregate.

Otherwise they were never far above the relegation places: three points away in 1964 and two points clear two years later, before making the drop in bottom place a year later with Northampton Town.

Another prestigious semi-final was reached in 1966, losing to Sunderland in the FA Youth Cup, which appeared to offer hope for the future. Colin Bell, just too old for that team, made his debut in 1963/64 and was finally lured away by Manchester City to boost their Second Division championship win in the spring of 1966.

A little surprisingly after such a poor 1966/67 season, the Shakers bounced straight back as runners-up to Oxford United, as the country's top scorers with 91 goals; Bobby Collins, late of Everton and Leeds, provided much of the ammunition. Bobby Owen scored 25 times before leaving for City after relegation the following season, while local lad Alec Lindsay departed for Liverpool for £67,000 just before the transfer deadline.

The Shakers had gone down, up and down again in successive seasons, all under Les Shannon, who then left for Blackpool. Successor Jack Marshall lasted three months. It had been an interesting decade but supporters were tiring of the lack of consistency, and crowds, having dropped below five figures in 1963/64, were around 4,500 by the end of the decade.

* * * * *

When local businessman and Burnley season-ticket holder Ken Bates decided in 1965 to buy into football, he wanted an under-achieving club that had been successful in the past and had a large catchment area. Of the few that were available Third Division **Oldham Athletic** best fitted the bill.

Bates bought 19,000 of the 40,000 shares issued and despite being taken aback by the ramshackle state of Boundary Park, he lost no time announcing that they would be a First Division club 'by 1970'. Within a couple of years that had been upgraded to 'working towards European football'. Meanwhile his appointee as manager Jimmy McIlroy was going to be 'held in the same awe as Matt Busby'.

In fact the former Burnley maestro departed halfway through his five-year contract in September 1968 and by the end of that season Bates had also left to concentrate on business rather than his 'expensive hobby'; and Oldham were bottom of the Third Division. The dawn of 1970 found them in the Fourth Division's bottom six, with Europe looking some way off, though to be fair, Bates did introduce such exotic ideas as a newspaper-sized programme, hospitality boxes and orange shirts with blue shorts. Football had not heard the last of him, by a long way.

Earlier in the decade Oldham had climbed out of the Fourth Division as runners-up to Brentford in 1963, having defeated Southport 11-0 on Boxing Day with centre-forward Bert Lister scoring six – all with his right foot. Lister joined in 1960, having failed to tie down a place at Manchester City and went on to score 97 league goals for the Latics, which would have been 100 had his hat-trick against Accrington in 1961 not been chalked off when Stanley withdrew in mid-season.

Future manager Jimmy Frizzell was another stalwart of the 1960s side, which had a comfortable first season up in the Third Division but was close to relegation on a couple of other occasions before finishing bottom in 1969.

* * * * *

Rochdale had their glory early, as nothing less than finalists of the Football League Cup in its second season. In the first, 1960/61, Rotherham United of the Second Division reached the final, by beating Third Division Shrewsbury Town. Now, with half a dozen leading teams still excusing themselves, the Dale progressed past Southampton (after a replay), Doncaster Rovers, Charlton Athletic and York City to the two-leg semi-final, where the draw brought them Blackburn Rovers.

Unfashionable competition or not, there were almost 10,000 at Spotland to see Joe Richardson score twice for the home side and former Rovers forward Ron Cairns add a crucial late third after Bryan Douglas pulled one back. 'Fourth Division Rochdale held Blackburn in the first half and then surprised the First Division club after the interval with a fiery, spirited display,' one local paper reported.

Fred Pickering put Rovers ahead in the second leg but Yorkshireman Stan Hepton equalised with a 30-yarder and although Douglas got another, the Dale held on for a stunning 4-3 aggregate victory.

A fortnight later the other First Division semi-finalists, Blackpool, went out to Norwich, who spoilt Rochdale's big day in the final by winning the first leg in Lancashire 3-0 and followed up with a 1-0 success at home.

It was still a fine achievement by a team who then spent the rest of the Sixties oscillating between the top seven (1963 and 1965) and the bottom six (1964, 1966, 1967, 1968). Tony Collins was manager for more than 350 games from 1960–67, Bob Stokoe taking over for a year and forging the promotion team of 1968/69 before Len Richley finished the job.

Goalkeeper Les Green left the previous summer for Brian Clough's Derby, where he would win a Second Division championship medal, but Chris Harker came in from Bury via Grimsby and conceded only 35 goals in 46 games as the side finished third, returning to the third tier for the first time since 1959.

* * * * *

Stockport and **Southport** mirrored each other's fortunes with almost uncanny consistency throughout the '60s.

Locked together in the lower reaches of the Fourth Division, they each had to apply once for re-election, the Sandgrounders in 1964 and County, after finishing rock bottom, a year later. Perversely, it was that season that County pulled off their most famous FA Cup result, holding First Division champions Liverpool 1-1 at Anfield with a first-half goal by Len White before losing the replay 2-0 to the eventual winners, Roger Hunt scoring both.

Southport also set a couple of FA Cup records early in the decade: beating Macclesfield Town 7-2 in 1960 and achieving highest receipts for their inaugural floodlit match, the third-round tie at home to Shrewsbury in January 1962; half the lights were switched off during half-time to save money, until it was pointed out that it cost more when switching them back on for the second half.

By 1965/66 both clubs improved sufficiently to achieve mid-table respectability and then in 1967 they were promoted together. Stockport, having forsaken their white shirts for royal blue, were champions under Eddie Quigley, who brought together a highly experienced side.

Future Manchester City man Ken Mulhearn was in goal, with a renowned defensive pairing in Matt Woods, once an FA Cup finalist with Blackburn, and Eddie Stuart, who won three First Division titles with Wolves and joined from Tranmere. The attack at various times featured old internationals Derek Kevan and Albert Quixall (England) and Len Allchurch (Wales); Bert Lister from Oldham and Rochdale, and Frank Lord, also winding down his career.

Southport, with Scottish international Alex Parker at full-back, had promoted another Evertonian, Billy Bingham, from coach to manager, and were five points behind as runners-up. Bingham left to become a successful manager of Northern Ireland as the two clubs then finished together in the middle of the Third Division for two seasons running, only a point apart each time, and come 1970 both were relegated. Stockport had a dreadful season, winning only half a dozen of their 46 games and scoring 27 goals while Southport collapsed late on, taking only seven points from the last 11 games but still ending up only a couple of points short of saving themselves.

Even in the 1970s their paths would only briefly diverge.

* * * * *

'Friday night and the gates are low,' sang Birkenhead band and **Tranmere Rovers** fans Half Man Half Biscuit. For Tranmere, like Stockport and Southport, Friday football, or 'pay-night soccer' was nevertheless perceived as one way of attracting crowds amid heavy competition from more illustrious neighbours.

In Rovers case it began in 1963/64, the first of three successive seasons in which they launched a promotion bid before finally succeeding with the fourth. The initial 'pay-night' game was in August 1963, when Carlisle United were beaten 6-1, though the visitors went on to gain promotion with Rovers seventh. Fridays, and better results, brought a 66 per cent increase in crowds for the 1964/65 season, up to 11,400. It was one of two frustrating campaigns in which Tranmere finished fifth. They were a point behind Oxford United and then in 1966 were pipped on goal average by fourth-placed Colchester despite scoring 23 times more. Barry Dyson got 30 before leaving for Crystal Palace early the next season.

Dave Russell, manager since leaving Bury in 1961, finally got Rovers up in 1967, along with Stockport and Southport, whose visit to Prenton Park in late-April attracted 15,555; a 2-1 away win meant they and not Tranmere were runners-up. Football-cricketer Jim Cumbes was in goal, with Roy McFarland enjoying one season in front of him at centre-half, clearly destined for greater things; Brian Clough and Peter Taylor soon stole him from under Liverpool's noses for Derby.

Scot George Yardley led the scorers after returning from emigration to Australia and placing a newspaper advert requesting a trial with anyone. It was the first of his two spells with the club. He missed the glamorous FA Cup fifth-round tie at Everton in 1968 (lost 2-0) with a serious kidney injury but still scored enough goals in his second spell to finish with almost 70 for the club in 122 league games.

Yardley contributed to an excellent Third Division season in 1968/69 which had Rovers in the top six and among the highest scorers with 70 goals. Russell left in December 1969, making way for Jackie Wright, a Blackpool full- back in the 1950s.

Just like Southport, useful links continued with Everton and, especially, Liverpool, who would soon supply key figures in goalkeeper Tommy Lawrence and Ron Yeats.

* * * * *

A 1980s advert for the Milk Marketing Board had a young Liverpool fan asking his pal, '**Accrington Stanley**, who are they?' Had they still been a Football League club at the time he would reasonably have been expected to know. Instead they had become a byword for anonymity as only the second club ever to drop out of the competition during the season.

From the late-19th century, the town, sandwiched between Blackburn and Burnley, has faced a struggle to sustain league football. For three of the first four Football League seasons, the original Accrington club had the lowest crowds and attracting an average of no more than 4,000 in the next one lay behind their decision in 1893 to drop into the Lancashire League rather than the Second Division.

From the historical high recounted in the last chapter, finishing second, third, third and second in successive Third Division North seasons in the mid-1950s, when average gates briefly approached 10,000, Stanley were not only on their way down but heading towards oblivion.

Relegated in 1960, the year Burnley were champions and Blackburn FA Cup finalists, they stayed just clear of the bottom six, though still only two points away from having to beg for re-election. Gates, already down by 50 per cent to barely 4,000 in the Third Division, dropped another 500 in the bottom tier, and financial problems became more serious than ever.

Results in 1961/62 were poor from the start, especially away from Peel Park, and from October onwards the only victory was in the FA Cup at Stockport. Yet any hope of a lucrative third-round tie against one of the big teams was ended by defeat to Hartlepool.

Striker George Hudson, who had scored 35 goals the previous season, was sold to Peterborough, the club were banned from buying any new players because of existing debts, and by the start of February, there had been no win in 11 league games with only two goals scored. On the 11th, the Football League asked for details of the club's financial standing and next day the chairman resigned, citing debts of almost £10,000, which proved to be a long way below the true figure of £62,000 (the equivalent today would be £895,000).

Burnley's chairman Bob Lord, not normally a man to bother about the misfortunes of other clubs, unexpectedly intervened, promising to buy shares. Six further games were played in the meantime without any victories, which meant the record from 33 games was five wins, eight draws and only 19 goals scored. Not surprisingly Stanley were bottom of the table, yet only two points behind Hartlepool and Chester.

Lord now told a creditors' meeting that the game was up and a letter of resignation was sent to the Football League. The players turned up next day for training and were stunned to be met by the PFA secretary Cliff Lloyd, who told them the club was finished.

Belatedly, the town rallied round, with one man donating £10,000. Club president Sir William Cocker claimed they could carry on until the end of the season but an attempt to rescind the resignation letter failed when the Football League insisted that on legal advice they had to accept it.

The last home game, on 26 February, had been a 2-0 defeat by Rochdale, in front of an improved attendance of 2,650 and after a further midweek defeat at Doncaster, the final game was a 4-0 loss at Crewe on Friday 2 March 1962.

Although many believe the club went into liquidation, they actually joined the Lancashire Combination Second Division for the following season and won promotion a year later. That lasted only one season and in 1966 Stanley did disband, before starting up again two years later, finding a ground at The Crown, and eventually fighting their way back into the Football League.

'The club that wouldn't die' is the slogan on the official website. Whether or not Cocker was right that the end of regionalised lower divisions in 1958 was a mistake, the surprise has to be that more clubs did not follow them out of the league.

Interlude II

Women

Scottish (male) ruffians; England games in Blackburn, Manchester and Liverpool; 'Nettie Honeyball' and the British Ladies' FC; Dick, Kerr's Ladies, self-styled world champions; FA's draconian ban; new beginnings and St Helens' cup finals; Everton, Liverpool and City; but no United for almost 100 years.

THE most famous women's team in the country was established in Lancashire; and it was not Manchester City. Women had played the game formally at least as early as the series of 'internationals' beginning in May 1881 when representatives of Scotland and England met at Easter Road, Edinburgh (already the home of Hibernian), and then in Glasgow, where (male) ruffians invaded the pitch, forcing players to flee and causing cancellation of the next scheduled game at Kilmarnock.

Down south less than a week later, Blackburn Olympic staged the next match in the series, which 'England' won 1-0 to avenge defeat in Edinburgh, but the following month two games at the Cheetham ground in Manchester were both abandoned after further crowd invasions as 'the wildest confusion prevailed'.

Drink may well have been involved, but whether the spoilsports were objecting to the very idea of women playing football or just indulging in some sport of their own at the expense of public order and the attendant police remained unclear. Undaunted, the

221

teams then set off for Liverpool and the Cattle Market Grounds in Stanley, where the locals proved more sympathetic and three closely contested matches were played.

One of the English players, Nettie Honeyball – almost certainly a pseudonym – set up the British Ladies' Football Club in 1895, describing football as 'a manly game that could be womanly as well'.

* * * * *

The Dick, Kerr's Ladies team was formed in 1917 by workers at a Preston factory who enjoyed kickabouts in their lunch break. The odd-looking comma in their name stemmed from the fact that the firm Dick, Kerr & Co was the product of a merger between two companies; John Kerr, owner of the latter, became MP for Preston in 1903. Originally a locomotive and electrical firm, the company was converted at the outbreak of the First World War, like many others, to manufacture munitions.

The team's exploits over the next 50 years and some 800 games (losing only two dozen) have been chronicled by Patrick Brennan (www.donmouth.co.uk) and club historian Gail Newsham in her book *In a League of Their Own*.

They were by no means the first in their field, teams like the Lancashire United Transport Company from Atherton and the Preston Army Pay Corps existing earlier, but a manager with a flair for publicity and public relations, Alfred Frankland, ensured they became the best known. Smartly turned out, they looked surprisingly modern in black-and-white striped shirts, black shorts and socks, as well as matching woollen hats.

Frankland, having failed to establish a proposed Lancashire Ladies' competition, was apt to dub Kerr's 'world champions', although defeats by teams like the Lancaster Ladies and Whitehaven were not unknown (the north-east was something of a hotbed of the women's game, one of its first competitions being based around munitions factories, who sent an 'England' team to play Northern Ireland in Belfast on Boxing Day 1917).

The day before that, Kerr's played their first game, at Preston North End's Deepdale ground against another local factory, attracting a crowd of 10,000 which raised almost £500 for the nearby Moor Park hospital.

Although the firm became part of English Electric in 1919, the Kerr's team continued to play under their original name. As well as games in Lancashire and further north, they ventured to Chelsea's ground for one of four matches against a visiting French international side in April and May 1920, the other venues closer to home being Deepdale, Stockport and Hyde Road, Manchester. Although this appears to have been a genuinely representative French side, drawn from teams all over the country, it is odd that the FA regards them as the first international matches, as it was clearly a Kerr's team, who in October that year reciprocated by visiting France for four matches, drawing equally good crowds and remaining unbeaten.

At Christmas a game at Goodison Park attracted a huge crowd – some 10,000 more than Everton's Football League average – to see them play St Helens. '£3,000 gate at ladies football match' headlined one local newspaper report. It continued, 'Over 45,000 witnessed the ladies football match at Everton's ground on Monday, between Dick Kerr's Preston team and St Helens on behalf of disabled soldiers, when the receipts amounted to over £3,000. Dick Kerr's team won by four goals to nil.' Many subsequent reports have upped the crowd to 53,000 and claimed anything from 10–14,000 being locked out.

Not everybody was happy, however. Whether or not Football League clubs feared this new attraction, and the further possibility of professionalism for women, a number of critical newspaper letters, articles and editorials began appearing the following year. Questions were raised about the level of expenses charged by teams like Kerr's, doctors and football figures as prominent as the managers of Arsenal and Tottenham spoke of the 'injurious effects' women could suffer, and a political element was introduced when a number of games were played in support of striking miners, whose industry had just been returned to private ownership, prompting drastic wage cuts amid wild talk of a Bolshevik revolution.

On 5 December 1921 the FA Council discussed the matter and issued the following statement, 'The council feel impelled to express their strong opinion that the game of football is quite unsuitable for females and ought not to be encouraged. Complaints have also been made as to the conditions under which some of these matches have been arranged and played, and the appropriation of receipts to other than charitable objects. The council are further of the opinion that an excessive proportion of the receipts are absorbed in expenses and an inadequate percentage devoted to charitable objects. For these reasons the council request clubs belonging to the association to refuse the use of their grounds for such matches.'

The decision was front-page news, the *Daily Herald* headlining 'Check to girl footballers' and reporting, 'Women's football received a setback yesterday when the Football Association Council unanimously passed a resolution condemning it.'

It was clearly a serious blow to the development of the women's game, confined from then on to clubs and grounds outside the national governing body's jurisdiction, and with no prospect of official support or funding. Kerr's were therefore unable to use Deepdale but continued to play at Ashton Park in Preston.

A short-lived Ladies' Football Association was formed in response that same month after meetings in Liverpool and Blackburn with almost 60 clubs present. 'Lancashire and Yorkshire are swarming with clubs,' one of the vice-presidents told the press. Few of them would survive for long.

Kerr's were not among the 23 clubs who took part in the first and only Ladies' FA Cup of 1922, although Fleetwood, 'Manchester United', Mersey Amazons and Rochdale did and were drawn together to save travelling costs. Like the male equivalent in earliest days it was a rather haphazard competition, eventually won by Stoke Ladies against Doncaster.

Kerr's, meanwhile, took off for an ambitious tour of North America, learning on arrival that the Canadian FA had refused them permission, and playing instead against nine USA men's teams with creditable results.

From then on as the FA ban began to bite painfully they played far fewer games. In 1937, now known as Preston Ladies, they received a challenge from Edinburgh City Girls to play a match that was extravagantly billed 'the Championship of Great Britain and the World'.

Frankland had no doubt about success, claiming, 'I believe our present Preston forward line is the best ever seen in women's football. I am certain we shall win.' At Squires Gate, South Shore, Blackpool on 8 September, the team fully justified his faith, winning 5-1 after scoring all their goals in the first half, three of them by centre-forward Edith 'Ginger' Hutton.

Regular visits by French teams continued after the Second World War, including two matches played in the early fifties at Manchester's Belle Vue speedway stadium, but the number of clubs in England had severely diminished.

Arthur Frankland died in 1957, having already ceded some of his duties to Kath Latham, who then took over running the club, finally and reluctantly disbanding it in 1965 because of a lack of players. The irony was that within a few years, amid a new mood of feminism comparable to that of the suffragette days, women's football would be officially recognised again. A Women's FA was formed in 1969 and after a world cup was held in the following two years, FIFA and UEFA began to urge national governing bodies to offer official recognition. In 1971, exactly half a century after imposing their ban, the FA decided that perhaps women might be tolerated after all.

The FA Cup was revived that year, and Southampton were easily the most successful club, reaching the first nine finals until an all-Lancashire affair in 1980 when St Helens beat Preston North End 1-0.

St Helens then lost two of the next three finals, their 1983 conquerors, Doncaster Belles, becoming the dominant club with 11 finals in 12 years. In the 1990s the more established men's clubs began to take an interest, as Arsenal Ladies, formed in 1987 with the backing of their parent club, became the major trophy winners, including the first Women's Super League of 2011 with Everton (previously Leasowe Pacific) third and Liverpool bottom.

Arsenal helped push attendances for the cup final into five figures, which grew to almost 25,000 and then beyond 30,000 when the final was moved to Wembley in 2015.

The club formed as Manchester City Ladies in 1988 was relaunched in 2014 with full backing from the men's club as Manchester City Women, and making almost as many marquee signings. Controversially given a Super League place in 2014 at the expense of the much more established Doncaster Belles, they won the title in 2016 with an unbeaten record, and followed with their first FA Cup in 2017, beating Birmingham City 4-1. That year and the following one they reached the semi-final of the Champions League, losing to eventual winners Lyon each time.

City had therefore joined Liverpool, the 2013 and 2014 league champions, and Everton as the north-west's representatives, the Merseyside pair both playing at the Widnes rugby league ground. But Manchester United dropped their senior women's team in 2005 and were only persuaded back into the fold for the 2018/19 season, fully professional for the first time and confident that the big four of men's football in the north-west would soon have an exact female equivalent.

Chapter 7
Mersey beats all (1971–90)

Liverpool's successful succession; Shankly-Paisley-Fagan-Dalglish and trophies galore amid the horrors of Heysel and Hillsborough; two Merseyside FA Cup finals and two Everton titles under Kendall for the 'soccer capital of the world'; United down with the Doc but back in style before Fergie's uncertain beginnings; City's one trophy, downs and ups; narrow escape for Burnley; Blackpool's sad decline is even quicker; Lofthouse out and back at Bolton; Blackburn lose managers to top division but gain a benefactor; Wigan in for Southport on second ballot; Oldham's success story.

T HE early-1970s were a time of footballing austerity. In 1970/71 goalscoring dipped to a post-war low only ten years after the record high. Much of the football became a dour, over-physical spectacle and with hooliganism proliferating, attendances gradually fell away from 30 million in 1967/68 to below 25 million six years later, sinking to the low point of 16.5 million after the horrors of the 1985 Bradford fire and the riots at Luton and Heysel. Bill Shankly or not, **Liverpool** found themselves characterised with Arsenal and Leeds United at the pragmatic end of the spectrum, ruthlessly efficient teams built on miserly defences; yet, one Derby County title aside, they were the trio most likely to win the major trophies.

At the start of the new decade, Shankly was ready for a shake-up. Goalkeeper Ray Clemence, a steal at £15,000 from Fourth Division Scunthorpe, had come into the side at the back end of 1969/70 and stayed there. Left-back Alec Lindsay arrived from Bury, big Larry Lloyd came from Bristol Rovers and became an England international, effectively replacing Ron Yeats at club level. Further forward were Brian Hall and Steve Heighway, footballers with degrees inevitably known as Little Bamber and Big Bamber after the presenter of *University Challenge,* Bamber Gascoigne. Roger Hunt had gone, Ian St John too was dropped by Shankly, who brought in John Toshack from Cardiff City.

The defence was outstanding, conceding just 24 goals in 42 games during 1970/71, but the attack was feeble, averaging exactly one per game, which meant nothing better than fifth place for the second year running.

Apart from beating Everton from 2-0 down, such excitement as there was came in Europe and the FA Cup. In the Fairs Cup, the Reds beat Bayern Munich 3-0 at Anfield with an Alun Evans hat-trick but Leeds knocked them out in all-English semi-final, 1-0 on aggregate after two typically grim games.

In the domestic competition there was a Merseyside semi-final in which Everton were beaten 2-1 at Old Trafford as goals by Evans and Hall turned round a half-time deficit. At Wembley the task was to prevent Arsenal performing the second Double of the century, ten years after Spurs; in extra time Heighway beat Bob Wilson at his near post but after a scrambled equaliser Charlie George thumped in the winner and was so exhausted he just lay down in celebration.

In the press box Charlton Athletic goalkeeper turned journalist Sam Bartram announced that at last there had been a worse cup final than his old club's against Burnley in 1947. 'Sorry, lads – you're bores' headlined the *Sunday People,* applying the insult to both sides equally.

Liverpool, Shankly insisted, were 'a team of boys ... that will last for ten years.' He knew he needed more; and the best addition was sitting in the stand at Wembley that day, signature secured. Kevin Keegan was another steal from Scunthorpe, who cost only £35,000, and signed for £50 a week after boldly asking the manager for a £5 increase. Impressive in pre-season, he was picked for the first game of 1971/72 at home to Nottingham Forest, turned up nearly half an hour late because of the unaccustomed crowds and scored after 12 minutes.

Darting everywhere in crowd-pleasing fashion and with no little skill, Keegan immediately became the perfect foil for the taller, stronger Toshack. Winning 12 out of 13 games in the spring should have earned him a championship medal in his first season but right at the death the Reds faltered. Losing 1-0 at Derby and drawing 0-0 at Arsenal, they ended up a point behind champions Derby in third place. It was symbolic that the failure to score in those two games cost them. Toshack was leading scorer with only 13.

Shankly wanted Frank Worthington to liven up the attack but the hard-living Huddersfield maverick found that high blood pressure in two different medicals a week apart cost him a move. Celtic's Lou Macari was another who got away, stolen by Manchester United.

In 1972/73, however, Keegan matched Toshack with 13 goals apiece, raising the total to 72 and bringing a first championship since 1966. The title was tied up at Anfield against Leicester (who had signed Worthington with no ill-effects) after which there was still a two-legged final to play in the newly named UEFA Cup.

After Liverpool had knocked out Spurs, the holders, in the semi-final, the home leg of the final against Borussia Mönchengladbach was abandoned with less than half an hour played because of a waterlogged pitch. Toshack, dropped for that game, returned the next night to terrorise the Germans with some good old British centre-forward play and Clemence saved a penalty in a 3-0 win. That proved crucial when the German side scored two early goals in the second leg. They were unable to manage a third and Liverpool had their first European trophy.

The following year they added the FA Cup but the sensation of 1974 was that two months after an easy 3-0 victory over Newcastle at Wembley, with Keegan scoring twice, Shankly stunned everyone by announcing his retirement. He had made his decision immediately after the final, influenced perhaps by the fact that his wife Nessie had mentioned the possibility when she was ill the previous year, 'and was quite hostile when I said no'.

Aged 60, he was tired at the time after another gruelling season of 62 games, but it was clearly a premature decision for one whose whole life centred around football – as underlined by his infamous quote about the sport being much more important than a mere matter of life and death.

Furthermore he was clearly expecting to have continued involvement with the club, whether as a director, ambassador or just a sounding board. Liverpool, however, wanted a clean break, not a repeat of Manchester United's experience with Sir Matt Busby in the background haunting successive managers. Shankly, although never close to the taciturn club chairman, John Smith, was understood to have swallowed his considerable pride after only a few weeks and asked for his job back. It was too late, for his assistant Bob Paisley had already been crowned as an admittedly reluctant successor.

For a while Shanks continued to turn up at the Melwood training ground, then more frequently at Everton's, which backed on to his house in West Derby. Everton, he said sadly in his autobiography, had made him more welcome. So did Tranmere Rovers, where he became a consultant within a few months of the new season beginning, recommending a young winger called Steve Coppell to Liverpool and then, when nothing was done, to his friend Tommy Docherty at Manchester United– who once called the bright young economics student 'my greatest signing'.

Apart from a testimonial, Shankly's last act after 748 games in 15 years at the club was to lead out the team one last time for the Charity Shield game against Leeds, the first at Wembley, where Keegan, sent off with Billy Bremner, threw his shirt down and was banned for a draconian 11 games.

Liverpool had finished well behind champions Leeds in the First Division, suffering from the same old goalscoring problem as Keegan with 12 was their top scorer out of a modest 52. What no one could reasonably have expected was that Paisley would not merely emulate but supersede his boss, winning among his 20-odd trophies no fewer than three European Cups; the trophy Shankly most coveted and the absence of which he counted as his greatest regret.

On the backroom staff for 20 years after retiring as a Liverpool wing-half in 1954, the new man lacked his predecessor's gift of the gab and never built quite the same relationship with supporters, yet presided over a staggeringly successful team.

From the start he was his own man, converting Ray Kennedy, the Arsenal striker who was Shankly's last signing, into an international midfielder. Buying Phil Neal (Northampton Town) and Terry McDermott (Newcastle), two more future England internationals, helped make Liverpool runners-up to Derby in his first season, 1974/75, then champions and UEFA Cup winners in his second.

Beating Queens Park Rangers 2-0 just before Christmas 1975 turned out to be unexpectedly important, as by Easter the unfashionable London side under Dave Sexton were heading for their first title. They were top after finishing their programme but Liverpool had one game to come, needing a win or low-scoring draw away to relegation-threatened Wolves. Quarter of an hour from time the home side led 1-0 but a flurry of goals by Keegan, Toshack and Kennedy secured Paisley's first championship. 'This was the night when the Liverpool fans finally took Paisley to their hearts,' reported the *Liverpool Echo*.

The European final, earned with a narrow victory over Barcelona, was equally dramatic, as Bruges took a 2-0 half-time lead at Anfield in the first leg. Three second-half goals again decided the game and Keegan's strike in Belgium forced a draw to win the trophy.

At the start of the 1976/77 Keegan announced with characteristic independent mindedness that he wanted to try his luck abroad. It could have made for a difficult last season, and did to some extent impair his relationship with supporters, but Paisley's Liverpool, proving no less formidable than Shankly's, had nothing less than a Treble in their sights.

Although beaten five times by Christmas, including a 5-1 loss at Aston Villa, they kept going even as the cup games mounted up. In April Everton were left furious at being denied victory in Merseyside's FA Cup semi-final when a hairline offside decision ruled out what would have been a winning goal. Champions after a draw with West Ham on 14 May – becoming the first team to retain the title since Wolves in 1959 – Liverpool headed for a Wembley date with Manchester United a week later knowing there was also a first European Cup final to come in Rome.

United denied them a first domestic Double by winning 2-1 with a deflected goal but four days later an estimated 25,000

Scousers were in the Eternal City to see Mönchengladbach beaten 3-1. Danish international Allan Simonsen equalised McDermott's first-half goal but BBC commentator Barry Davies conveyed the universal astonishment that it was hard-man Tommy Smith who stole forward to head in Heighway's corner. Neal's penalty wrapped up victory.

European Cup Final 1977: Liverpool 3 Borussia Möenchengladbach 1

Liverpool: Clemence; Neal, Jones, Smith, Kennedy, Hughes, Keegan, Case, Heighway, Callaghan, McDermott.
Borussia: Kneib; Vogts, Klinkhammer, Wittkamp, Bonhof, Wohlers (Hannes 79), Simonsen, Wimmer (Kulik 24), Stielike, Schaeffer, Heynckes.

Keegan, who had been brought down for the penalty, was playing his last game before joining the new European Cup Winners' Cup holders Hamburg for four times his Liverpool salary. Much as he admired Paisley, he admitted that the club was never quite the same for him once Shankly left, believing 'something should have been done to keep him in the family'.

But just as with the managerial succession, so the club came up trumps with Keegan's replacement. Kenny Dalglish from Celtic was the 20-goal-a-season man they had lacked since Roger Hunt, and so much more besides. When Hamburg visited Anfield in December for the European Super Cup the Germans' new superstar suffered the double humiliation of a 6-0 defeat and the Kop singing 'We all agree, Dalglish is better than Keegan'. Few of those present would have known that he had appeared for the Liverpool B team in 1966, when his father said he was too young at 15 to move south.

The club's stock could hardly have been higher, as the new England manager Ron Greenwood emphasised by picking six Liverpool players plus the departed Keegan to start his first match in September, having recalled Ian Callaghan after 11 years.

Unexpected new rivals were on the horizon, however. As Liverpool were winning the European Cup, Brian Clough's Nottingham Forest squeezed out of the Second Division in the third promotion place, then signed Peter Shilton and stormed to the First Division title by losing only three games, seven points ahead of Paisley's team, who now fielded Dalglish's Scotland team-mate Graeme Souness in midfield.

Matches between the two were invariably dominated by defences, 15 meetings in four seasons producing only 15 goals, with six goalless draws. In the 1978 League Cup Final Forest beat their fellow Reds in a replay with the only goal in three and a half hours – a disputed penalty. Liverpool's considerable consolations were to retain the European Cup, Dalglish's goal beating Bruges at the favourable venue of Wembley, then to win their domestic title back in 1979, conceding just four goals at home, but only after Forest eliminated them from the European Cup in the first round and matched them by going on to become champions of Europe for two seasons running.

By 1979/80 Paisley had a fourth league title in five seasons and his team were playing the sort of entertaining football they had been urged to rediscover, centre-forward David Johnson from Ipswich Town exactly matching Dalglish's 37 league goals over two seasons.

The following season they were only fifth in the league as Johnson lost his way and young Ian Rush was not quite ready to take over; yet it was three European Cups in five seasons (and five in a row for English clubs). The unlikely hero was left-back Alan Kennedy, whose fine individual effort in the Paris final beat a Real Madrid team including England winger Laurie Cunningham. Kennedy had already scored at Wembley to save the League Cup Final against West Ham before a rare goal from Alan Hansen (originally rejected by Liverpool as a 15-year-old) won the replay.

The 1982 championship was won after a classic second half of the season, confirming that all the boot room wisdom and habits accumulated down the years tended to give Liverpool greater endurance than the rest. Twelfth at the turn of the year and unwisely written off, Paisley's team lost two games out of 25 from Boxing Day, including a run of 11 wins in a row. Rush was top scorer for the first time, Mark Lawrenson from Preston was in defence and Dublin midfielder Ronnie Whelan was a Wembley scorer in the League Cup Final win over Spurs.

Paisley, piling up the trophies for fans he called 'my type of people', decided one more season would do him and signed off with one of his most comfortable title wins plus the inevitable League

Cup – that one enjoyably won against United with another Whelan goal in extra time. In the league a run of 18 games without defeat from December to April saw off all-comers; Rush, again outscoring Dalglish, got four of the five at Goodison in a 5-0 romp.

Veteran Joe Fagan continued the boot room succession and to the despair of any challengers won a Treble in his first season. In the league Rush scored 32, including five at home to Luton; the League Cup was won in 1984 for a fourth successive year, beating Everton 1-0 in a replay with a goal by Souness. Most strikingly, the European Cup was won again, on the home ground of final opponents Roma. Neal's goal was equalised but Kennedy's unerring left foot was yet again decisive in the penalty shoot-out after goalkeeper Bruce Grobbelaar, urged by Fagan to 'try and put them off' did his wobbly legs act.

Souness decided to accept the riches on offer from Sampdoria and in 1984/85 the three trophies won in Fagan's first season were all surrendered, but the figure that mattered most was 39 – the number of Juventus fans killed when Liverpool supporters stormed a supposedly neutral section at the European Cup Final. The decaying Heysel Stadium in Brussels may have been a foolish choice for the continent's most prestigious match, which came nowhere near excusing the behaviour that dragged the reputation of English fans even lower.

There had already been serious trouble before, during and after the drawn FA Cup semi-final against United at Goodison Park, before the battle switched to Maine Road, where Liverpool were beaten 2-1. Mindful of having also lost their league title to Everton, and finally given up the League Cup, the red hordes went to Brussels believing they had all sorts to prove and the worst of them were indulging in drunken skirmishes and shoplifting long before kick-off.

Once fatalities had occurred and a crumbling wall collapsed, the principal question was whether the final should go ahead. For better or worse, the authorities decided it should, fearing further mayhem if thousands of supporters were released into the city, with Italian *ultras* intent on revenge. Understandably it was a low-key match that the players mostly hated, Liverpool barely raising a protest when a disputed penalty allowed Michel Platini to win the cup for Juventus.

Twenty-six Liverpool fans were eventually charged with manslaughter, of whom 14 were found guilty. The FA feebly banned the club from European competition for 12 months but UEFA trumped that with five years for all English clubs, costing Everton an immediate European Cup shot, and ten years for Liverpool, who eventually served six.

It was an appalling way for Fagan, whose retirement had previously been announced, to end his two years in charge and a hugely testing situation for Dalglish to take on in the already daunting role of player-manager. Yet the appointment, which ensured he did not follow Keegan and Souness abroad, kept the job in-house again and once more proved astonishingly successful.

Dalglish picked himself to start in only 17 league games in 1985/86, but turned out for the title run-in as United and then Everton both lost their place at the top. Although Liverpool were beaten at home by their neighbours in February it was their last defeat and on the final Saturday at Chelsea they became champions with an 11th win in 12 games, leaving them two points ahead of the Blues. Appropriately Dalglish himself scored the only goal.

Seven days later the Reds were back in London for Merseyside's first FA Cup final, won 3-1 from behind with two goals by Rush and one from South African-Australian Craig Johnston for a team not fielding a single England-qualified player (Lawrenson, born near Preston, had opted for the Republic of Ireland).

In contrast to the horrors of 12 months earlier the whole mood of the day was good-humoured, supporters of both sides uniting in chants of 'Merseyside' before their teams undertook a joint homecoming parade drawing an estimated quarter of a million. 'A gesture badly needed by a game and a city bruised in the last year,' said the *Daily Post*. 'Merseyside reminded the millions watching on TV that the area is still very much the soccer capital of the world.'

FA Cup Final 1986: Liverpool 3 Everton 1
Liverpool: Grobbelaar; Lawrenson, Beglin, Nicol, Whelan, Hansen, Dalglish, Johnston, Rush, Molby, MacDonald.
Everton: Mimms; Stevens (Heath 72), Van den Hauwe, Ratcliffe, Mountfield, Reid, Steven, Lineker, Sharp, Bracewell, Sheedy.

Liverpool thus joined Tottenham and Arsenal as the 20th century's only Double winners to date. If there was a smallest of consolations for the European ban, it was to concentrate emphatically on domestic football with such success that they could have won both trophies four times in five years.

Two seasons of big spending started with Irish internationals John Aldridge and Ray Houghton arriving for the 1986/87 campaign, then John Barnes and Peter Beardsley after Rush left for an unsuccessful year with Juventus.

In the first of them Liverpool were ahead of Everton in March after 12 unbeaten games, only to slump uncharacteristically, losing four out of five and finishing nine points behind their rivals. The League Cup final was lost to George Graham's reviving Arsenal, after Fulham had been beaten 10-0 at Anfield in an earlier round. In the penultimate game of the season Dalglish made his last appearance until one ceremonial cameo as a substitute in 1990.

In 1987/88 they were top from autumn onwards en route to one of the easier title triumphs, in which a 5-0 demolition of Nottingham Forest was one of the great performances of the era, and only two games were lost. Having been knocked out of the League Cup by Everton but beaten them in the FA Cup, Dalglish's team were made the hottest cup final favourites in memory by those observers who underrated opponents Wimbledon. The belligerent south London side were seventh in the First Division, had only narrowly lost at Anfield six weeks earlier and won there the previous season.

Vinnie Jones's outrageous challenge on Steve McMahon in the first minute set the tone, and Dave Beasant saved Aldridge's second-half penalty after Lawrie Sanchez had headed the only goal eight minutes before half-time.

Rush hurried back from Italy for the following campaign, when the greatest climax to an English season followed the worst tragedy. Lying fifth at New Year, Liverpool were on a run of 11 successive wins going into the FA Cup semi-final against Forest on 15 April, an occasion which cost 96 supporters their lives and led to a 27-year campaign to achieve justice for them.

In the aftermath players and the manager were attending up to four funerals a day, taking an emotional toll on Dalglish that only became evident two years later. They resumed training two weeks later, after what looked a key game against new rivals Arsenal at Anfield, due on 22 April, had been postponed, restarting with a goalless draw at Everton amid waves of mutual appreciation.

It would be the Blues in the FA Cup final too once Forest were beaten 3-1. Another emotional Merseyside occasion brought a similar result to three years earlier, 3-2 this time, with Aldridge scoring early and substitute Rush grabbing two in the 30 minutes of extra time forced by Stuart McCall's late equaliser.

Two league games remained. Three days after Wembley, West Ham were demolished 5-1, the scoreline being hugely significant as it meant goal difference was now four better than opponents Arsenal, who had scored more but would need to win 2-0 at Anfield to take the title by virtue of their tally. Not since Everton in February 1986 had any team achieved such a result yet George Graham's side, playing with David O'Leary as a sweeper, brought off his plan to the letter, scoring early in the second half and snatching the most dramatic of winning goals from Michael Thomas in the final minute.

The game was shown live on television, ITV having secured an exclusive four-year contract for £11m, and proved such a momentous occasion that the principle of live coverage of league games – a failure when Blackpool played Bolton all the way back in 1960 – was established forever. It would become a crucial part of football finances and fuel the sport's inflationary tendencies to the benefit of players, managers and agents; though not supporters and subscribers.

For downcast Liverpool it should have been another Double, and a further one went begging the following year. Having beaten Crystal Palace 9-0 on the way to regaining their championship, they somehow managed to lose a chaotic FA Cup semi-final to the same lowly opposition 4-3. Dalglish considered stepping down that summer. The toll was telling and it would not be long until it broke him.

* * * * *

Manchester may have regarded its teams as among the most colourful in the largely grey 1970s but the decade yielded only one major trophy each for City and United.

At Old Trafford, Frank O'Farrell, a genial Irishman in the mould of Johnny Carey, who had made Leicester City Second Division champions, was the chosen man to right **Manchester United's** ship after Wilf McGuinness. He found it no easier to escape the long shadow cast by Sir Matt Busby.

For half a season O'Farrell was everything the club desired. Despite being forced to play the first two home games of 1971/72 elsewhere (Anfield and Stoke's Victoria Ground) because of crowd disturbances the previous season, United won both and until Christmas they were outstanding, sitting top of the pile after losing only two of the first 20 matches. Best, Law and Charlton were still among the goals, Brian Kidd weighed in and young midfielder Sammy McIlroy was coming through. From there it all went wrong, with seven successive defeats including a 5-1 thrashing at Leeds to finish no higher than eighth for a third successive season.

The 1972/73 season saw the break-up of the holy trinity and an alarming slump to the bottom six. The elegant Martin Buchan came into central defence from Aberdeen but forwards Ian Storey-Moore and Ted MacDougall were less successful and a disenchanted Best was playing up, missing training and then announcing his retirement aged 26. 'I kept packing it in, just to find havens to disappear to,' he once said.

Knocked out of the League Cup at home to Bristol Rovers and 21st in the First Division, United were humiliated 5-0 at Crystal Palace nine days before Christmas and Scotland manager Tommy Docherty was offered the job. He accepted only after much thought and by the end of the season had lifted them only three places to 18th despite increasing the Scottish contingent with signings like Lou Macari, George Graham, Alex Forsyth and Jim Holton.

The top scorer was Charlton, with just six goals – two of them penalties. A disillusioned man, he announced his retirement and played his 754th and last game at Chelsea on the final weekend before joining Preston for an unsuccessful spell as manager.

Law, who started only nine league games in an injury-ridden campaign, was upset to be given a free transfer but delighted when at the end-of-season Footballer of the Year dinner City's new manager Johnny Hart offered him a move back to Maine Road.

He would haunt United at the end of the following season, which was even worse than what had gone before. Just as Docherty should have been moulding his own team, Second Division football for the first time since 1938 became a serious possibility; then probability. Best came back from mid-October to January but the holiday had done him no good. On 3 January he played his last game in a 3-0 defeat at QPR, leaving United 20th in the table. At the start of April they were bottom, and a minor recovery with four wins in five games came too late.

In the penultimate game, Law of all people back-heeled the only goal at Old Trafford, then invading fans caused the game to be abandoned (though City's 1-0 win stood) and because Birmingham had beaten Norwich, United were down. Once again the leading scorer (McIlroy) had just six goals to his name; goalkeeper Alex Stepney, with two penalties, scored as many as striker Kidd, another former European Cup hero, who played 21 games.

The crowds had never deserted them and stayed loyal in the Second Division. There were nearly 45,000 to see Millwall rolled over 4-0 in the first home game and almost 59,000 at the last one, when Blackpool were beaten by the same score to seal the title by three points. Docherty's attacking signings had now come off – Stuart Pearson from Hull City at centre-forward, then Steve Coppell from Tranmere and, back in the First Division, Gordon Hill, a cocky young winger from Millwall.

Even in the Second Division United reached a League Cup semi-final, which they narrowly lost to Norwich, who were promoted back with them, and the promise was maintained in an impressive return to the higher level with third place behind Liverpool and QPR. There should have been a trophy to end the campaign after deservedly beating Derby in the FA Cup semi-final. But Second Division Southampton, who had also gone down with United two years earlier, sprang a surprise at Wembley and won with a goal by Bobby Stokes.

Sixth the following year but second-highest scorers once again, United returned to the national stadium and this time won the cup, denying Liverpool the Double with goals by Pearson and Jimmy Greenhoff, signed from Stoke to join younger brother Brian in the side.

Just as things seemed to be going so well again, there was a traumatic 1977 close-season after Docherty confirmed that he was in love with the wife of the club physiotherapist, Laurie Brown.

Directors initially backed him, only to change their mind. In July he was sacked and the board went for Dave Sexton, who had earlier replaced the Doc at Chelsea, then taken unfashionable QPR to within a point of the championship.

Quietly spoken and wary of the press, Sexton was the absolute antithesis of his predecessor and supporters never took to him in the same way. Losing a dramatic 1979 FA Cup Final 3-2 to Arsenal in the last minute and finishing runners-up to Liverpool a year later were insufficient to win over either fans or the board.

Times were changing. Paid chairmen were now permitted and in February 1980 Martin Edwards replaced his father Louis, who died a month after Granada TV's *World In Action* exposé of him. Busby was made president. In 1980/81 Sexton's team won their last seven games to finish eighth but the football was not what United expected and Edwards had already decided on a change. The lack of goals was summed up by major signing Garry Birtles from Nottingham Forest at £1.25m labouring through 32 matches before scoring.

Ron Atkinson from West Bromwich Albion, as flamboyant as the Doc, was third choice at best behind Lawrie McMenemy and Bobby Robson but that pair chose to stay loyal to smaller but successful provincial clubs in Southampton and Ipswich Town. Albion's thrilling 5-3 win at Old Trafford in December 1978 had stuck in the mind of directors and supporters, and it was a popular enough appointment to follow the very different Sexton.

After failing to win any of his first four games, Atkinson poached Remi Moses and then Bryan Robson from his former club to good effect. If the underwhelming total of 51 goals the previous season was increased by only eight, he did get Birtles into double figures, along with Frank Stapleton from Arsenal. Third place was a bit more like it, and the defence with Gary Bailey established in goal was the best in the division for the second year running.

League positions of third, then fourth three times were consistent enough without threatening Merseyside's eighties domination, and after losing the 1983 League Cup final to Liverpool there were two FA Cup finals as well: a 4-0 win over Brighton in a 1983 replay after almost throwing away the first game ('he finds Smith, and Smith must score, and he hasn't, and Bailey has saved it'); and two years later a win against the odds with Norman Whiteside's goal to deny Everton the Double after Kevin Moran was sent off. In-between times there was an exciting European Cup Winners' Cup run, featuring a 3-0 home win over Barcelona which led to a semi-final, narrowly lost to Juventus.

With Dutchman Arnold Muhren a classy replacement for Ray Wilkins, who went to Milan, something of the old United style had returned, and goalscoring picked up with the introduction of young Welshman Mark Hughes. Fourth place was nevertheless as good as it got for Atkinson and a bad start to the 1986/87 season cost his job. United were 19th in the table with crowds dropping below 40,000 when a heavy League Cup defeat at Southampton saw the end of him.

Alex Ferguson, who had an influential supporter in board member Bobby Charlton, had done great things for Aberdeen in breaking Scotland's Old Firm monopoly and stayed with them despite at one time agreeing to join Tottenham. As he realised the scale of the task at Old Trafford, things actually got worse, a defeat at Oxford on 8 November in his opening game and a 2-0 loss at Norwich a week later dropping United to bottom but one.

Wins over Manchester City in both the league and FA Cup put him in credit, as did a revival to finish 11th. A moribund youth system, poor scouting and a drinking culture all had to be addressed. In the meantime signing Viv Anderson (Arsenal), Brian McClair (Celtic) and Steve Bruce (Norwich) helped the new United reach the runners-up spot behind Liverpool in Ferguson's first full season, McClair becoming their first player to reach 20 league goals since Best two decades earlier.

McClair could not keep it up and for two seasons United's goals tally dropped to a dismal 45 and then 46, leading not surprisingly to a place in the bottom half each time. The second of them, 1989/90, could have dramatically changed the future of Manchester United, beginning as it did with the supposed new owner of the club, one Michael Knighton, out on the pitch in full United kit, ball juggling in front of the Stretford End. Martin Edwards, who wanted out, had told Ferguson nothing would change under the new owner; yet Knighton, it subsequently emerged, had promised the manager's job to Graeme Souness, who was tiring of life at Rangers, once the takeover was complete.

That day never arrived. Knighton failed to come up with the bargain £10m asking price, and Edwards stayed on, destined to make an awful lot more than that when he finally sold.

The day before an FA Cup third-round tie at Nottingham Forest in January 1990 he told Ferguson his job was safe even if United, lying 15th in the table, were beaten. Mark Robins's goal won the game anyway and following three more away ties the same player was the hero in a thrilling replayed semi-final against Second Division Oldham after a 3-3 draw. On 17 May, though still only 13th in the league, United had the first of Fergie's trophies. Following another dramatic 3-3 draw, with Steve Coppell's Crystal Palace, the manager reluctantly dropped goalkeeper Jim Leighton, replacement Les Sealey kept a clean sheet and the replay was won with left-back Lee Martin's goal.

FA Cup Final 1990: Manchester United 1 C. Palace 0 (after 3-3 draw)

Manchester United: Leighton; Ince, Martin (Blackmore 88), Bruce, Phelan, Pallister (Robins 93), Robson, Webb, McClair, Hughes, Wallace.
Replay: Sealey for Leighton. No subs.
Crystal Palace: Martyn; Pemberton, Shaw, Gray (Madden 117), O'Reilly, Thorn, Barber (Wright 69), Thomas, Bright, Salako, Pardew.
Replay subs: Barber (Wright 64); Salako (Madden 79).

Ferguson's United were on the up and going to stay there.

* * * * *

After having the upper hand over United in the first half of the 1970s, **Manchester City** were second best again by the end of it and their one trophy did not come until 1976, by which time the Mercer-Allison combination was long gone.

As European Cup Winners' Cup holders they lost both legs of 1970/71 semi-final to English opposition in Chelsea and the following year missed out on the First Division title, when Allison, team manager at last, insisted against Mercer's advice on playing new signing Rodney Marsh for the run-in. Marsh, a maverick striker, was not fully fit and his tendency to hold the ball disrupted the fast tempo of a team that failed to win five of its last eight games and finished a point behind the champions Derby despite being top scorers with 77; 33 of them to Francis Lee.

In summer 1972 Mercer, feeling unwanted, went to Coventry City as general manager but Allison, though it pained him to admit it, was not the same without him, as his subsequent career emphasised. Even at City his one season in sole charge, 1972/73, ended prematurely when he left for Crystal Palace, announcing, 'My relationship with the players has soured. I couldn't motivate them.'

On the last day of the season he returned to win 3-2 at Maine Road, which left City tenth but did not prevent Palace going down (as they did again the following season into the Third Division). Mike Summerbee made a pertinent observation about him, 'The best coach this country has ever produced but not a good manager of a football club.'

Under Johnny Hart, a natural number two, then disciplinarian Ron Saunders and initially Tony Book, City did nothing more than lose the 1974 League Cup Final 2-1 to Wolves and enjoy Manchester United's relegation. The popular Book, however, soon improved them.

Winning the 1976 League Cup by beating Newcastle with Dennis Tueart's overhead kick earned that one trophy and the year after – despite Colin Bell missing the whole season after a bad injury in a 4-0 League Cup win over United the previous November – they were only a point shy of champions Liverpool. United, doing the double over them, could be said to have deprived their neighbours of the title. All the old attacking stalwarts, plus Marsh, had now departed, Joe Royle from Everton featuring up front, although Brian Kidd and Tueart outscored him.

Fourth place in 1978, with Mick Channon replacing a fading Royle, was the last time they would finish above United for a good many years. Since the Cup Winners' Cup days, European adventures had been a disappointment too with three defeats in the first round of the UEFA Cup and only a 5-2 aggregate success over AC Milan in a better run during 1978/79 to remember with pride.

In the summer of 1979, after finishing 15th, chairman Peter Swales pushed for Allison to come back as team manager with

Book moved upstairs but it was not a happy return. After an embarrassing FA Cup defeat by Halifax Town, 17th place in the table and then a dozen games without a win to start the 1980/81 season, Big Mal was gone again, the club having spent wildly on players like Steve Daley (£1.45m) and Preston's Michael Robinson (£756,000).

John Bond, once a team-mate of Allison's at the West Ham 'academy' that produced so many coaches, lifted City from bottom to finish 12th, as well as reaching the League Cup semi-final (losing 2-1 on aggregate to Liverpool) and then the FA Cup final. Everton were knocked out in the sixth round, Ipswich 1-0 in the semi-final with Paul Power's goal, and at Wembley it took Tottenham two bites, including a lucky equaliser and then Ricky Villa's wonderful individual goal, to win the trophy.

Making a statement they could not really afford by signing Trevor Francis for £1.2m that September, City were top at the turn of the year, only to finish tenth, and the following year they slumped even more dramatically in mid-season and went down. It hardly seemed a likely outcome even for the most unpredictable of clubs when Bond suddenly resigned in January following a 4-0 FA Cup defeat at Brighton with the team in the top half of the table. Under caretaker John Benson they won only three of the remaining 17 games and lost the final one at home to Luton, who therefore saved themselves and sent David Pleat skipping across the Maine Road turf in celebration.

Fourth and then third in the Second Division under former Celtic captain and manager Billy McNeill, City scrambled back up by beating Charlton 5-1 in front of a 47,000 crowd but after two more years they were back down again, victims of a goalscoring famine and a dreadful away record. A total of 36 was the joint worst in the club's history.

Again it took two seasons in this up-and-down decade to return. Mel Machin was the manager as City finished runners-up to Chelsea in 1988/89 – the days of supporters carrying inflatable bananas – despite having lost the previous season's top scorer Paul Stewart to Tottenham. Throwing away a 3-0 lead at home to Bournemouth in the penultimate game was typical but Trevor Morley's goal at Bradford got them the second automatic promotion place.

They finished the 1989/90 season level on points with United but under Ferguson the big beast across town was belatedly stirring.

* * * * *

Unlike the Manchester clubs, **Everton** did not even manage one trophy in the 1970s. League Cup runners-up in 1977 was as close as they came until their 1980s revival. Not until then could they hold heads as high as the team across the park; when they beat Liverpool 1-0 in October 1978 it was a first derby victory since November 1971, a run of 16 games in all competitions.

The championship team of 1970 disintegrated with unexpected suddenness. 'The start of five great years,' Alan Ball had predicted, but the first three of them brought finishes of 14th, 15th and 17th. By 1972 Ball solved his financial problems by joining Arsenal and in the spring of 1973 with another lowly finish imminent, manager Harry Catterick was moved upstairs after 12 eventful years.

The jovial Ulsterman Billy Bingham, a member of Everton's 1963 championship team, brought about an improvement to seventh place in 1974 and then a genuine championship challenge the following season with record signing Bob Latchford from Birmingham City among the goals and the elegant Martin Dobson from Burnley replacing Howard Kendall in midfield. The Blues lost fewer games than anyone but ended up a close fourth, three points short of champions Derby.

Bingham brought in one of the great characters in Duncan McKenzie, whose detractors felt his greatest attribute was an ability to jump over a Mini. But he had played only a handful of games before Bingham was sacked in January 1977 with Everton languishing too far down the table. Two days earlier they had beaten Stoke in the FA Cup and the new man Gordon Lee, hired from Newcastle, was able to take them all the way to controversial semi-final defeat by Liverpool as well as a prolonged League Cup final that only came to life at the third meeting when Aston Villa won 3-2.

In his first full season, 1977/78, Lee's team finished third behind Nottingham Forest and (inevitably) Liverpool but they were the division's highest scorers with 76, a remarkable 30 of them from Latchford. The feat earned him the £10,000 prize offered by a national newspaper to anyone in the top two divisions reaching that figure and his fine form led to a dozen England caps.

Latchford's five goals against Wimbledon in the League Cup early the following season (an 8-0 win) and an unbeaten start that lasted until 23 December raised false hopes; the Blues were top for one week in February but fell away badly and ended up only fourth, a full 17 points behind you know who. The first win over Liverpool for seven years, with a goal by the popular midfielder Andy King, was a small consolation for the title going back to Anfield.

Lee survived a dreadful 1979/80 season, four points above relegation with an FA Cup semi-final defeat by West Ham and a couple of crowds only just over 20,000; another poor campaign saw him gone a year later.

Kendall, having made a success of his first managerial position at Blackburn, was a natural appointment, turning his old club into a top eight team, then FA Cup winners, and twice champions.

Yet in that third season of two Wembley visits he was considered to be on the brink of dismissal in January 1984, lying 18th in the table. Adrian Heath's late equaliser in the League Cup at Oxford was as notable a turning point as Mark Robins's Manchester United goal at Forest a few years later. Everton went on to the final and only lost to Liverpool in a replay (1-0 after a 0-0 draw) but went one better in the FA Cup. High-flying Southampton were beaten in the Highbury semi-final by another Heath goal and at Wembley the Watford chairman Elton John was left in tears as Andy Gray, signed from Wolves earlier that season, barged his way past goalkeeper Steve Sherwood for the first goal and Graeme Sharp added the second.

From the confidence of a first trophy, two followed in 1984/85 and dominance was finally wrested from Liverpool, who finished the season shamed at Heysel.

Losing the first two league games turned out not to matter, nor did losing three of the last four. A 5-0 victory over Manchester United in October a week after winning at Anfield illustrated the potential of a team in which Paul Bracewell now partnered Peter Reid in central midfield with regular goalscorers Trevor Steven and Kevin Sheedy on either side of them.

Liverpool for once trailed 13 points behind in second place at the finish and were beaten twice, as well as in the Charity Shield.

Five different players reached double figures even though Gray, injured early on, was not one of them. There could have been a Treble too but three days after winning the Cup Winners' Cup Kendall's tired team lost 1-0 to ten-man United at Wembley in the FA Cup final.

Continental adventures, like City's, had previously been disappointing: a loss to Panathinaikos on away goals in the 1971 European Cup, then early UEFA Cup exits to AC Milan (1975/76), Dukla Prague (1978/79) and Feyenoord (1979/80). In the Cup-Winners' Cup of 1984/85; however, UC Dublin, Slovan Bratislava and Fortuna Sittard were easily swept aside before the semi-final, where Bayern Munich were held 0-0 in Germany then beaten 3-1 on a famous night at Goodison. In the final in Rotterdam goals by Gray, Steven and Sheedy beat Rapid Vienna.

European Cup-Winners' Cup Final 1985: Everton 3 Rapid Vienna 1

Everton: Southall; Stevens, Van den Hauwe, Ratcliffe, Mountfield, Reid, Steven, Sharp, Gray, Bracewell, Sheedy.
Rapid Vienna: Konsel; Lainer, Garger, Brauneder, Weber, Kienast, Kranjčar, Hristic, Krankl, Weinhofer (Panenka 67), Pacult (Gröss, 60).

The Austrian team's star striker Hans Krankl described Everton as 'possibly the best side in the whole of Europe'. Yet the chance to put that proposition to the test was denied them two weeks later when Liverpool fans rioted at Heysel and all English teams were banned.

Salt was rubbed into Evertonian wounds a year later when Liverpool relieved them of the championship trophy by two points and beat them in the Merseyside FA Cup final 3-1 after the Blues had led with a goal by Gary Lineker, signed the previous summer from Leicester City as replacement for Gray.

Lineker's 38 goals that season plus six at the World Cup finals won him a move to Barcelona under Terry Venables but despite not replacing him, the Blues won a second First Division title in three years, nine points ahead of Liverpool with wide-men Steven and Sheedy their top scorers.

Kendall unexpectedly took off to manage Athletic Bilbao and successor Colin Harvey was unable to emulate his success, finishing fourth, then with Tony Cottee and Pat Nevin in the side, eighth and sixth; as well as losing the emotional post-Hillsborough FA Cup final to Liverpool 3-2 in extra time.

A poor start to the 1990/91 season got Harvey the sack, prompting an ultimately unhappy return for Kendall, who upset Manchester City by walking out on them after only 11 months.

* * * * *

As if to emphasise how Merseyside and Manchester were pulling away from the rest, in 1970/71 Burnley and Blackpool went down from the First Division, while Blackburn and Bolton both dropped into the third tier for the first time in their histories.

From third in the top division in 1966, **Burnley**, unthinkably, almost went out of the Football League altogether within 20 years. Although stuck for four seasons just below halfway, they were never in danger of relegation during that time, so the 1970/71 campaign under Jimmy Adamson was something of a shock for a squad that boasted Martin Dobson in midfield and Dave Thomas and Ralph Coates in attack.

Dobson missed the first 17 games with injury and without him only one of them was won and 11 goals scored. Half a dozen members of the victorious 1968 FA Youth Cup team were in the side but it was too early for some of them and by the finish they were seven points short of safety, having totalled only 29 goals. The fact that Blackpool's record was even worse was no consolation.

Coates left for Tottenham, bringing in a club record £190,000, and was replaced by the dynamic Welshman Leighton James, who soon became an international. Thomas followed Coates to London in October 1972, with Queens Park Rangers, and found his old club pipping his new one to the Second Division title by a point.

For two seasons back upstairs Adamson's attractive side were excellent, finishing sixth and reaching the FA Cup semi-final against Newcastle in 1974, then scoring more goals than anyone despite finishing only tenth. The 1974/75 campaign is more likely to be remembered, however, for an historic FA Cup defeat, 1-0 at home to non-league Wimbledon.

Dobson was sold to Everton early that season and James joined champions Derby the following autumn, a 5-1 home defeat by Wolves marking his final game and leaving the Clarets 20th. They continued to struggle and finished 21st, Adamson having resigned in January after a cup defeat at Second Division Blackpool led to scuffles in the dressing room.

This time there was no quick return, just a failure to make any impact under returning manager Harry Potts and then calamitous relegation to the Third Division. It came in 1979/80, following a terrible start and finish to the season with only six wins in-between times. Dobson and James had both returned to the club, as did 1960s hero Brian Miller as manager, able to lead a misleading title-winning campaign in 1981/82, in which attendances were initially below 4,000 – smaller than in the 19th century.

After promotion they lasted for only one season before going straight back down, accompanied by Bolton. Once again there were talented players in the side, including little midfielder Bryan Flynn, back from Leeds, a teenaged Trevor Steven and leading scorer Billy Hamilton, who had played regularly at the World Cup for Northern Ireland. They showed their capabilities by beating Coventry and Spurs to reach a League Cup semi-final against Liverpool, as well as the FA Cup sixth round, but were too easily distracted along the way.

Then in the second of two poor Third Division seasons they went down again in 1985 to the ignominy of the lowest tier. A team capable of beating mid-table Rotherham 7-0 was not in the bottom four until the end of March but an agonising six-day wait after the final match led to relegation when Swansea drew with Bristol City.

John Bond and John Benson, together again after Manchester City, had both failed to halt the slump, as did former United men Martin Buchan and Tommy Cavanagh. Then Brian Miller was back for the dramatic 1986/87 season.

It was the first in which the Fourth Division's bottom team would automatically drop into what was seen as the black hole of non-league football. Having come down by such a narrow margin with Orient, Preston and Cambridge United, Burnley were hardly expected to be contenders for such a fearful fate, quarter of a century after playing in the European Cup. Yet as the final day of the season dawned on 9 May they were bottom of the table, with the worst goal difference of the three contenders, knowing that not even victory at home to Orient would necessarily save them.

Earlier in the season the crowd at home to Colchester was 1,692. For the visit of Frank Clark's Orient, who needed a win to make the play-offs, more than 15,000 came and kick-off had to be delayed by 20 minutes to accommodate them. The day went Burnley's way with goals by Neil Grewcock and Ian Britton before late concern was caused by the London side pulling one back. Had they equalised, Burnley would have gone down; instead Lincoln lost and made the drop.

'The tension was unbearable and the atmosphere unbelievable,' reported *The Observer*. 'The team responded with a stirring performance when it mattered most.' By 1990 the Clarets were still a league club, but had finished in the bottom half of the lowest division three times in four years.

✳ ✳ ✳ ✳ ✳

The decline of **Blackpool** was as sad as Burnley's and even faster. Leaving the First Division with them in 1971, they were in the fourth tier ten years and six managers later.

A return to the top level in 1970 lasted only one season, as concerns about having scored so few goals in the promotion campaign were realised. A mere four games were won, two of which were in August. Les Shannon lasted as manager only until late October, when a 3-0 lead at home to Chelsea turned into a 4-3 defeat; under 9,000 watched the penultimate home match, a rare win against Crystal Palace, but more than three times as many turned out six days later for Manchester United's visit after Jimmy Armfield announced it would be his 627th and final game.

After considering his options and offers he decided to leap into management with Bolton (see next section) while Shannon's successor Bob Stokoe was soon lured back to the north-east to make his name nationally by winning the 1973 FA Cup with Sunderland's giant-killers.

Blackpool meanwhile unexpectedly won a trophy of their own, the 1971 Anglo-Italian Cup, topping the English group and winning the final 2-1 in Bologna with an extra-time goal by Micky Burns. They even reached the final again 12 months later, losing to AS Roma, who within two years would be European Cup finalists against Liverpool.

More mundanely they settled in the top eight of the Second Division and with three teams now going up, were twice not far away from promotion: two points behind surprise packet Carlisle in 1974 after losing the last game at Stokoe's Sunderland, and in 1977 level with Bolton, a single point behind Brian Clough's Nottingham Forest, who immediately went on to win the First Division title.

From there, however, Blackpool suffered a dramatic and controversial collapse to relegation. Before the home game with Blackburn in February 1978, striker Bob Hatton was presented with a silver salver for scoring three hat-tricks that season; he went out and scored four times in a 5-2 win over Rovers to put his team in seventh place but three days later manager Allan Brown was suddenly sacked after a row with club officials.

The board optimistically asked Bill Shankly to take over for the rest of the season, which he declined to do, and a disenchanted group of players won just one of their remaining 16 games and lost out in the tightest of finishes, with seven teams all clambering to safety just a point above them. Hatton's 22 league goals had been in vain.

Twelfth place in the Third Division confirmed how low the club's stock had fallen but amid a rapid turnover of managers – Stokoe returning briefly, then Stan Ternent and Alan Ball – the Seasiders sank even lower and in 1981 dropped into the lowest division for the first time, fully nine points from safety.

Two seasons into Fourth Division life, one home gate fell below 2,000 and the team finished in the bottom four, forced to apply for re-election after a deduction of two points for using an ineligible player.

Slowly things looked up under Sam Ellis, formerly assistant to Graham Taylor in Watford's rise through the divisions. He could not pull off a similar trick but did manage promotion within two years back to the Third Division with 12 unbeaten games over the new year and a strong finish.

After three seasons in mid-table and then a poor one in 1988/89 he was sacked by a board that now included the controversial figure of Owen Oyston, a local businessman who sold his chain of estate agents for a reported £37m. Ellis's seven years was a good stint at that level but the divisive Oyston family were to stay around for much longer. And by the summer of 1990 the club were back in the Fourth Division.

* * * * *

Blackpool's loss of Jimmy Armfield proved to be **Bolton's** gain, relegation with Blackburn in 1970/71 coinciding with his retirement as a player. Meticulous as ever in preparation, he watched their reserve team play and took a day to wander round the town before phoning Sir Matt Busby for advice and accepting the job.

When 40,000 came to Burnden Park to see Manchester City beaten 3-0 in the League Cup early in his first season, the potential was plain and 18 months later Wanderers were Third Division champions with a younger team in which the more experienced John Byrom, once of Blackburn, scored 20 goals.

The manager proved a born negotiator too, persuading Shankly to let him have winger Peter Thompson when Coventry City had offered three times as much as Bolton's meagre £15,000 budget. Times were hard and one victim was none less than general manager Nat Lofthouse, forced out because as Armfield put it, 'We were a Third Division side and couldn't afford the luxury of two managers.'

Happily, he returned in 1978, to what was a First Division club again. Such solid foundations had been laid that when Armfield was lured to Leeds in October 1974 after Brian Clough's calamitous 44 days in charge, Ian Greaves had them within a point of promotion in 1976 and 1977, then won the title in a close finish the next year.

Frank Worthington joined from Leicester and chipped in as second-highest goalscorer behind Neil Whatmore, with Sam Allardyce at the back, Peter Reid at his first club in midfield and Scottish international Willie Morgan on the wing. Blackburn was a nice place to seal promotion with Worthington's goal.

The top division was hard and after one season in the bottom six, Bolton were down again in 1980, winning only one game before March. Players like Whatmore (who ended the first of three spells by moving to Birmingham with 100 goals to his name) and Reid (Everton) proved too good to keep and in three more seasons they were bottom again and back where they had been ten years earlier, in the Third Division – taking Burnley with them.

Four more years and they followed their fellow Lancastrians into the lowest division.

That at least lasted for just one season, with John Thomas, back from Preston, getting the goals and Phil Neal, who joined from Liverpool in December 1985 with four European Cup winner's medals, busy as player-manager. Three wins and a draw from the last four games squeezed them into the last automatic promotion place

Although gates were only averaging 5,000, thousands more Boltonians followed them to Wembley in 1989 for the final of the Sherpa Van Trophy for Third and Fourth Division clubs, and saw Torquay beaten 4-1.

* * * * *

Blackburn were another club who endured some difficult times in the 1970s, before spending the next decade wishing and hoping in the Second Division and eventually finding the sort of benefactor any club would have wanted. Before then a trio of young managers who did well for them were snatched away by First Division clubs.

Accompanying Bolton down to the Third Division in 1971, they took two years longer to return, despite being only two points short in their second season. In 1974/75 they led the way as champions exactly 100 years after John Lewis and the founding fathers had brought the club into existence. Don Martin from Northampton Town led the scorers, Tony Parkes was well into his 12-year stint in midfield and the manager was Gordon Lee, who had joined in January 1974. Newcastle United noted his success and made an offer he felt unable to refuse.

A similar attraction lured away Jim Smith, not quite the bald eagle yet, after stabilising in the Second Division until March 1978, when Birmingham City snaffled him as successor to Sir Alf Ramsey. He was badly missed in 1978/79 when Rovers were much too far adrift before Duncan McKenzie arrived from Chelsea in March. Half a dozen wins from then on still left them bottom.

McKenzie stayed around for the Third Division and new player-manager Howard Kendall appeared 41 times to lead them straight back up with a moderate attack but the soundest defence. The following season was the same, Glenn Keeley and Derek Fazackerley presiding over a superb defence that conceded only 29 goals, but the 42 scored meant missing out on successive promotions on goal difference. Only five were scored in the last nine games, which included a crucial defeat by Swansea, who went up instead.

Kendall, coveted by Everton, became the third manager in six years to move on to greater things as Bobby Saxton (1985) and Don Mackay (1988) fell only a point short of going up. In both 1989 and 1990 they reached the play-offs, losing a two-legged final to Crystal Palace after winning the first 3-1 and then missing out in the semi-final to Swindon.

In the second of those seasons Simon Garner passed 150 league goals for the club. He was on his way out, but a man called Jack Walker was on his way in.

* * * * *

When Accrington were replaced by Oxford United in 1962, it was part of the Football League's significant 20-year shift away from struggling northern clubs to thriving areas further south. Gateshead (1960), Bradford Park Avenue (1970), Barrow (1972) and Workington (1977) also lost their places, to Peterborough, Cambridge United, Hereford United and Wimbledon respectively. The small consolation for the north was that when Southport were voted out in 1978 after three successive seasons in the bottom two, it was another Lancashire side, Wigan Athletic, who took their place.

Others on tiny gates like Rochdale, Tranmere and Stockport were frequently at the wrong end of the table and pleased just to preserve their status, as well as enjoy a little *Schadenfreude* when Burnley, Preston, Blackpool and Bolton briefly joined them in the murky depths.

Wigan aside, the one success story among the smaller clubs was that of **Oldham Athletic**, where former defender Jimmy Frizzell proved a more enduring manager than Ken Bates had a chairman. In 1970/71, the first of his 12 seasons in charge, the Scot lifted them from the bottom six to third place and promotion. The much-travelled Jim Fryatt scored 24 league goals and David Shaw was only one behind him.

Two seasons later in the Third Division the Latics were fourth behind Bolton and Blackburn, and a year later won the title with almost 19,000 turning up for the final home game. Back in the Second Division for the first time in 20 years, Frizzell's team had the huge bonus of two games against Manchester United, who had just been relegated. Maurice Whittle's penalty beat the Reds on a famous day with 26,384 inside Boundary Park and the return at Old Trafford was lost only 3-2 with almost 57,000 present.

Often only five or six points above trouble during the rest of Frizzell's reign, which ended in 1982, they appointed Joe Royle to his first managerial role. After a difficult second season in 19th place, they took off, reaching the top eight in 1986 and installing an artificial pitch identical to those at Preston and Luton. It inevitably brought complaints from opponents but none from Oldham supporters as Royle's team climbed to third place, narrowly losing the play-off semi-final to Leeds after finishing seven points above them.

Mixing it with teams like Leeds, Chelsea, Manchester City, West Ham and Newcastle in the league, they also had a historic run in both domestic cup competitions in 1989/90. First came the League Cup, going all the way to Wembley and a narrow 1-0 defeat by Nottingham Forest after demolishing West Ham 6-0 in the semi-final first leg; then in the FA Cup, there was a thrilling 3-3 draw with Manchester United at Maine Road, leading with Earl Barrett's goal and twice coming back to equalise, before losing the replay in extra time after a late equaliser by former United man and future manager Andy Ritchie.

Royle had assembled an exciting team and their greatest triumph was around the next corner.

* * * * *

Wigan Athletic, it will be recalled (Chapter 4), grew out of Wigan Borough in 1932. Despite regular applications to return the town to the Football League, it took 46 years to make it.

Playing at the same Springfield Park ground in red and white shirts, the new club joined the Cheshire County League, winning a hat-trick of titles from 1934–36 but not convincing anyone that they were better equipped than Wigan Borough to replace pre-war strugglers like New Brighton, Rochdale, Accrington or Southport.

Surprisingly dropped from the Cheshire competition after finishing bottom of it in 1947, they opted for the Lancashire

Combination, becoming champions at the first attempt and then three times during a successful decade in the 1950s. They were now playing in blue, apparently because of a shortage of red dye during the war.

In December 1953 what is still the highest crowd for a game between two non-league clubs at a non-league ground – 27,526 – watched Lancashire's other Latics beat Hereford 4-1 in the FA Cup, earning a third-round tie away to recent winners Newcastle. Against a team of six internationals, Wigan led 2-1 with quarter of an hour to play until Jackie Milburn equalised. The attendance was more than 52,000 and half that number packed Springfield Park for the replay, where the First Division club, who had refused to use the ground's 'crude' facilities and changed elsewhere, came through 3-2.

Jack Livesey, Bill Lomax and Jackie Lyon were the goalscoring inside-forward trio in a memorable run. It was still insufficient to help gain that desired Football League berth, the best opportunity having come when the two Third Divisions were expanded to 24 teams each in 1950. Wigan tied on the first and second votes for one of the places but missed out to Scunthorpe on the third. Although topping the non-league vote from 1952–54, they had missed their chance and under the 'old boys' system would have to wait.

Indeed, for a brief spell from 1959–61, they were arguably not even the biggest club in Wigan, Wigan Rovers in the Cheshire County League playing at a higher level. Returning to that league themselves in the 1960s, the Latics became founder members of the Northern Premier League in 1968, finishing runners-up to Macclesfield for the first two seasons, the second of them by a fractional disadvantage on goal difference.

In January 1971 the club's reputation under Gordon Milne was furthered when narrowly losing 1-0 to Colin Bell's goal for Manchester City in the FA Cup, then winning the league title. Two years later they went to Wembley for the first time, losing the FA Trophy Final 2-1 to Scarborough.

Applying to join the Scottish Second Division in 1972 was an expression of frustration at being confined to the non-league ranks when Hereford won the vote to replace Barrow; such a move would hardly have solved any problems for a club struggling again financially. In 1975 they were champions again and towards the end of the decade the Southern and Northern Premier leagues each sensibly decided to put only one club forward annually for election. In 1978 champions Boston United's ground did not meet the required standard so runners-up Wigan were nominated and after polling 26 votes, the same as Southport, beat them 29-20 on a second ballot.

With the local rugby league team suffering a rare trophy drought that lasted eight seasons, league football returned to the town at last, a goalless draw at Hereford on 19 August being followed by a 3-0 home defeat by Grimsby Town with 9,227 present. Three further losses had them bottom of the table but they rallied well to finish sixth and repeated the feat the following season, averaging over 6,500 in the first of them.

Ian McNeill, manager since 1976 in his second spell, was sacked in February 1981 and soon became assistant to John Neal at Chelsea. He returned with the London club to suffer a 4-2 League Cup defeat in his first season, which finished with player-manager Larry Lloyd having taken Wigan to a first promotion in third place. Only seven games were lost and 80 goals scored, 19 to Les Bradd in his first season since leaving Stockport and another 15 to the reliable Merseysider Peter Houghton.

At the higher level, Lloyd's team survived by a point, then he too was sacked at Easter 1983, club director Bobby Charlton briefly taking charge. In 1986 and 1987 the Latics finished fourth in successive seasons; only a point behind promoted Derby under Bryan Hamilton and beaten 12 months later in the new-fangled play-offs by promoted Swindon. Only in 1989 and 1990 did they drop back into the bottom half.

* * * * *

Bury, although unable to match the feats of neighbours Oldham, did at least spend more of the 1970s and '80s in the Third Division than the one below, albeit only just.

Narrowly relegated to the Fourth Division in 1971, they recovered from being the lowest-placed of all Lancashire clubs two years later to win promotion in 1974. It was only in fourth, but with 81 goals widely shared around and former England centre-half Peter Swan, once banned in a betting scandal, holding the defence together as captain in his only season at Gigg Lane.

There were six seasons back at the higher level, the best of them in seventh place under Bobby Smith. A quick turnover of managers, including the return of Bob Stokoe, did not prevent relegation in a close finish to the 1979/80 campaign and this time it took five years to get back, with a near miss in 1983 and success two years later. Martin Dobson was player-manager and the popular Mancunian Craig Madden passed 100 league goals for the club to earn a move to West Bromwich Albion.

Dobson finished playing in 1985 but stayed on as manager to see the Shakers consolidate again in the Third Division.

* * * * *

From a historical high of ninth in the Third Division in 1970, **Rochdale** managed three more seasons in the bottom half of the table before sinking back to the Fourth Division in 1974 with one of the worst records of any side ever. They won two games, one at Southend in September and one at home to Shrewsbury in January, which was the fewest of any team since 1900.

Drawing 17 times meant they avoided the lowest number of points, but another unenviable record was set in February when the crowd to see a home defeat by Cambridge was 588 (widely reported at the time as 450).

Walter Joyce kept his job for two more seasons and a long run in the bottom half of the lowest division extended until 1990. Several times the club had to apply for re-election and they were lucky to be reprieved after finishing bottom in 1978, when Wigan replaced Southport, and even more so two years later when only one vote ahead of Altrincham (see Non-league chapter). Over those three seasons they also had the lowest crowds in all four divisions, bottoming out at an average of 1,275 in 1977/78.

Staying out of the bottom four came to be regarded as something of an achievement and winning 20 games in 1989/90 with Terry Dolan now in charge seemed positively heroic. There was even the bonus of a club record run to the FA Cup fifth round that season, with highest-ever Spotland receipts from a crowd of 9,000 to see Northampton beaten before a 1-0 defeat away to eventual finalists Crystal Palace.

* * * * *

Tranmere were another club in the shadow of much bigger ones who oscillated between the Third and Fourth Divisions with no realistic hope of ascending any higher. What they had in contrast to some was a greater consistency of managers.

Ron Yeats, after the leaving of Liverpool in 1971, lasted three seasons as player-manager, making the most of his Anfield connections. Tommy Lawrence became a popular figure in goal, and signing Ian St John and Bobby Graham for a few games each in 1972/73 (St John broke a leg in training and retired) helped the team finish tenth. Both had left before a 1-0 League Cup win away to Arsenal the following season with Eddie Loyden's goal, giving Rovers the rare distinction for any club of a 100 per cent record at Highbury.

In 1974/75 Yeats was sacked and Rovers went down to the Fourth Division. John King, beginning the first of two long spells, took them straight back with 34 goals from Ronnie Moore as well as back down again in 1979. The former Northern Ireland international and Evertonian Bryan Hamilton took over as player-manager and was also given five years, the best of them in sixth place in 1985 before moving to Wigan.

Frank Worthington, once denied a move to Liverpool because of a failed medical, got a less glamorous opportunity on Merseyside as Hamilton's successor but spent two years in the bottom six and in May 1987 Rovers had to beat Exeter on the final weekend of the season, which they did 1-0, to ensure they were not the first club automatically relegated to the Conference.

King had returned to save them and then inspire the most successful period in the club's history. It began with the first of several Wembley visits (see next chapter), promotion in 1989 with Ian Muir prolific in attack and Eric Nixon from Manchester City a reliable goalkeeper, followed by fourth place in the Third Division and greater things to come.

* * * * *

Unlike Tranmere, **Stockport** found no managerial stability until Uruguayan Danny Bergara took over in 1989, becoming the 15th man in charge in 19 years. During that time they tried just about everything, including big-name novices (Mike Summerbee, Asa Hartford), lesser-known novices (25 year-old Alan Thompson), those much more experienced at higher level (Jimmy Melia) and lower (Jimmy Meadows and Colin Murphy, twice).

Nothing worked and during a 21-year spell in the Fourth Division, average gates that had reached 9,820 in 1967 dropped to little more than 2,000. A further concern was the introduction of automatic relegation to non-league football at a time when County were regulars in the bottom six.

Bottom from the start of the 1986/87 season until Boxing Day (and knocked out of the FA Cup by Caernarfon Town), they seemed the club most likely to make the drop and went to the bottom again in late March before clambering to safety with six wins in nine games under Murphy.

Bergara, who played mainly in Spain, married an English woman and worked as a youth coach before having seven months as manager of Rochdale. He immediately took County to the play-offs in 1989/90, with Brett Angell emerging as a significant goalscorer. Chesterfield proved too strong in the play-off semi-final but the club's fortunes were on the up at last.

The previous two decades had been mostly dismal, for all the excitement that 'Go-go County' Friday nights at Edgeley Park were supposed to engender. Local resident George Best brought some rare glamour by appearing in three home games in November and December 1975 for £300 a time; for the first one, when he scored the winning goal against Swansea, the crowd went up from a previous 2,789 to 9,220. He then decided Los Angeles Aztecs sounded more fun and more lucrative, and by the end of the season County were having to apply for re-election again, just like in 1972, 1974 and 1985. Fortunately they had enough friends to cast votes in their favour.

The Caernarfon defeat was just one of several by non-league opponents who relished meeting them in the FA Cup: Grantham Town, Blyth Spartans, Stafford Rangers and Telford United (twice) all took advantage.

Luckily there were no non-league teams in the League Cup and the competition did provide one memorable performance when drawn at home to Manchester United in 1978/79. Chairman Freddie Pye decided to concede ground advantage and Summerbee, player-manager at the time, made sure the team were up for the challenge in front of a crowd of more than 42,000 at Old Trafford. Playing far above themselves, County led 2-1 with ten minutes to play thanks to goals by Thompson's penalty and Terry Park but were the victims of two controversial refereeing decisions and conceded to Sammy McIlroy and a Jimmy Greenhoff penalty.

* * * * *

Southport, mirroring Stockport's fortunes for so long, left them behind for one season after topping the Fourth Division in 1973 under Jimmy Meadows; winning 7-0 away to Darlington at the start of the new year took them top and they stayed there.

They dropped back down with Rochdale immediately and after one season in mid-table began the disastrous spell that cost them their league status. With only the doomed Workington below them in 1976 and 1977 and crowds often less than 1,000 (780 was the worst) they found the clubs keen on further change after finishing bottom but one for a third successive year. Although Rochdale, who were seven points below them, escaped, Wigan beat them on a second ballot, Southport paying the penalty for having done little or no canvassing. More than half a century of league football was over.

The last home game had been a 1-1 draw against Huddersfield on 22 April 1978, watched by 1,465; a week later Fourth Division champions Watford beat them 3-2, Gary Cooper scoring their last Football League goal.

From there the Sandgrounders lost their way for 15 years after declining an option to join the new 'Fifth Division', the Football Alliance, on grounds of cost. By 1993, however, they were Northern Premier League champions and survived for ten seasons in the Conference, finishing third once and fourth twice. In 1998 under Paul Futcher they reached the FA Trophy final, taking 10,000 followers to Wembley for narrow defeat by Cheltenham Town.

A couple of spells in the Conference North were followed by a return as champions in 2010 to the fifth tier, where they stayed until 2017, relegated on gates of 1,110. The lack of canvassing to preserve Football League status while they had the chance almost 30 years earlier looked more costly with every passing year.

Interlude III

Non-league

Only Northern Nomads and Skem make Amateur Cup impression; Lancs Challenge Trophy a gateway to the Football League; but Altrincham left two votes short; South Liverpool's complex history; short-lived dreams of Manchester Central and Colne Dynamoes; upward progress of FC United rebels, Fylde and Salford.

FOR such a historically important football hotbed, it is surprising that Lancashire has not been more successful at non-league and amateur level. The most likely explanation is that because the north-west was so heavily involved in the spread and acceptance of professionalism from 1885, payment became regarded as an important part of the game for working men. Added to that was a general distrust of the London-based Football Association, the southern amateur clubs and all their works.

The lack of impact in 80 years of the FA Amateur Cup (1894–1974) is nevertheless remarkable. This prestigious tournament, which attracted several capacity gates of 100,000 when moved to Wembley after the Second World War, was dominated from its inception by clubs from the north-east like Bishop Auckland, Stockton and Crook Town and the south-east (Clapton, Dulwich Hamlet, Bromley, Hendon, Leytonstone). Those eight clubs alone won the trophy 36 times between them. Lancashire did so just twice.

First were the **Northern Nomads**, for whom occasional claims have been made of origins dating back to the early 1860s. As an old club programme points out, the actual date was the early 1900s. Based variously in Liverpool, Edgeley Park Stockport and at Fallowfield, they represented pure amateurism similar to that of the southern-based Corinthians, ideally 'the kind of amateur who does not mind paying a little for his sport'. Winning the Amateur Alliance competition in 1908/09 suggested they were the most prominent amateur side in the area, competing successfully in a league with teams from as far away as Grimsby, Hull, Leeds, Leicester, Rotherham, Sheffield and south Nottingham.

Anything but parochial, the Nomads also won an International Exhibition Cup in Brussels in 1911, a Challenge Cup in Bruges two years later, and regularly competed in the Welsh Amateur Cup, winning it in 1921 and four years later.

Then, in 1926, 12 years after losing the FA Amateur Cup Final to Bishop Auckland 1-0, came a triumph, in emphatic fashion. Again, they had to go far and wide for it, playing the semi-final at Highbury (Arsenal's stadium, not Fleetwood's), where Redhill were beaten 7-1; and travelling for the final to Roker Park, Sunderland, where Stockton, also much closer to home ground, suffered the same fate and the same scoreline. That score of 7-1 remains the joint-highest win in the final of the competition.

After the Second World War the Nomads played in the Mid-Cheshire League, and winning that in 1957 joined the Lancashire Combination Division Two, playing at Belle Vue, but disbanding in 1984.

Lancashire's only other FA Amateur Cup winners were the better known **Skelmersdale United**. Although dating back to 1882, the club's improved fortunes in more modern times coincided with 'Skem' becoming a designated new town in 1961.

A Liverpool County Combination side from 1909 until the early 1950s, they moved back to the Lancashire Combination, then the Cheshire County League and flourished. A first Amateur Cup final appearance came in 1967, when they held Enfield at Wembley in front of 75,000 but were beaten 3-0 in the Maine Road replay.

But in 1971 they were at Wembley again and beat Dagenham 4-1. Three times in five seasons they also took on Football League opposition in the FA Cup, losing to Scunthorpe (1967), Chesterfield (1968) and Tranmere (1971).

Members of the Northern Premier League from 2006, they suffered serious financial problems in 2015 and after being evicted from their home ground two years later were rescued by a ground-share with Prescot Cables.

As recounted in Chapter 1 the leading local clubs of the 1880s were prominent among the 40 entries for the inaugural Lancashire Senior Cup, before Darwen beat Blackburn Rovers in the first final. Those denied entry, or fancying their chances at a lower level, opted for the Junior Cup started in 1885, when a team called Bell's Temperance won it for the first two seasons. The executive committee of the LFA declared them ready for the Senior Cup, where unfortunately they were drawn away to the mighty Bolton Wanderers at Pike's Lane – and beaten 10-0.

Bell's Temperance soon disappeared but the Junior Cup was a useful pathway for clubs on the up like early winners Blackpool and Bury as well as lesser lights Oswaldtwistle Rovers and other winners during the 1890s: Kearsley (Bolton), Clitheroe, Chorley, Lytham, Hapton (near Burnley) and Skerton (on the River Lune in Lancaster).

A much more recent list of winners of the competition, now known as the Challenge Trophy, shows how important success has been to ambitious clubs, including as it does Wigan Athletic (eight wins from 1953 until joining the Football League in 1978), Morecambe (six wins from 1986–2004) and AFC Fylde (2011, 2013, 2014).

As well as the cup competitions, leagues were well established by the start of the 20th century. The Lancashire League began in 1889 and was subsumed in 1903 into the Lancashire Combination. Half a dozen of those clubs helped form the Third Division North when the Football League was expanded in 1921 (Chapter 4) but many others remained, including the runners-up that year Eccles United.

Post-war the Combination and Cheshire County League both attracted Lancashire clubs until a reorganisation brought the Northern Premier League into existence in 1968, with Altrincham, Hyde United, Fleetwood and Wigan Athletic joining from the Cheshire County League, while from the Combination came Chorley, Fleetwood, Morecambe and South Liverpool. At last the north now had a single competition to rival the Southern League, especially in the vital matter of gaining entry to the Football League. Meanwhile semi-professional clubs now had a shot at a Wembley final in the FA Trophy from the 1969/70 season, especially enticing as the FA Amateur Cup was brought to an end in 1974 when the FA abolished amateur status within the game.

The final bold step to launch a national non-league competition was taken in 1979 with the formation of the Alliance Premier League, to which **Altrincham** (founded 1891) were the area's only representatives, playing opposition as far away as Weymouth and Yeovil.

Backed by future Manchester City chairman Peter Swales, they were hopeful of following in the footsteps of Wigan, elected to the Football League the previous year, but never made it, despite the nearest of misses in 1980. As the first Alliance champions, they were the only challengers to the four Fourth Division clubs seeking re-election and missed out with 25 votes to Rochdale's 26. Later they would claim to have been promised two other votes, from clubs who failed to take part in the ballot – one of them allegedly after an especially long and liquid lunch.

The following year, champions again, their support dropped to only 15. It was nevertheless the club's best period, including FA Trophy wins in 1978 and 1986, and a whole series of impressive FA Cup performances. Everton (1975) and Tottenham (1979) were both held to draws at Goodison and White Hart Lane respectively and most famously Birmingham City, then in the top tier, were beaten 2-1 at St Andrew's in the third round of 1986 when an own goal by Robert Hopkins went past David Seaman; losing to York City in the next round was something of an anti-climax.

Lancashire's only other FA Trophy winners were unfashionable **Burscough**, who started life in the Liverpool County Combination in 1946, having grown out of green-shirted forerunners also known as the Linnets. Their Trophy triumph came in 2003, beating Tamworth 2-1 in the final. It was a disappointment that the game could not be played at Wembley, being rebuilt at the time, but Villa Park suited Burscough's manager, the former Aston Villa defender Shaun Teale.

No club has won the Lancashire Junior Cup/Challenge Trophy more times than **Chorley** with 18, most recently in 2015, 2016 and 2018. Having begun as a rugby club in 1875, they switched to the more sensibly shaped ball eight years later and have been FA Cup contestants too since the nineteenth century.

They were more than 100 years old when achieving their greatest feat in the latter competition, eliminating Wolverhampton Wanderers in November 1986. Wolves had fallen as low as the Fourth Division and it took three attempts, but the third game on neutral ground at Burnden Park was decisively won 3-0. The club's record attendance of 15,153 was then set in the next round, drawing 0-0 with Preston at Blackburn's Ewood Park.

Of other clubs to have won the Challenge Trophy but never reached the Football League, **Lancaster City** rank highest with half a dozen successes, to which might be added a couple more won by Skerton, their 19th-century forerunners in the ancient county town. Renamed from Lancaster Town when their home was awarded city status just before the Second World War, the club served in the Lancashire Combination for almost 60 years until 1970, but had to reform twice amid financial woes, in the 1980s and then 2007. In 2017 they won the Northern Premier League Division One to reach the Premier Division.

Other clubs with four Challenge Trophy wins include Turton, rapidly approaching their 150th birthday, Burscough, Skelmersdale and old rivals Marine and South Liverpool.

Merseyside's **Marine** (former Lancashire Amateur Cup winners) date back to 1894, taking their name from a hotel on the seafront at Waterloo, and have been at their Rossett Park home since 1903. FA Amateur Cup finalists in 1932, they suffered an unhappy day in London, losing 7-1 at Upton Park to Dulwich Hamlet, who therefore share the Northern Nomads record (see above) for record victory margin in the final.

Two years before the amateur/professional distinction was abolished in 1974, the most famous figure in Marine's history joined the club. Roly Howard took over as manager in 1972 and claimed a world record of 1,975 competitive games in the next 33 years.

During that time they were twice Northern Premier champions and knocked Barnsley (1972) and Halifax (1992) out of the FA

Cup, reaching the third round in the latter season. Less happily, the competition also brought an embarrassing 11-2 defeat at Shrewsbury in 1995.

The history of **South Liverpool** is a tortuous one, but appears to span four different clubs. The original side ran for about six years until 1900, playing as the name implied in the south of the city before losing their ground to works on the new railway at Dingle.

A works team, African Royal, was formed early in the century playing at Toxteth, but in 1910 took the name South Liverpool, joining the Lancashire Combination for 1911/12. They attracted a gate of more than 18,000 for Tranmere's visit in 1914 and later that year made a first unsuccessful application to join the Football League, repeated in 1921, after which a group of businessmen moved the club from a temporary home in east Liverpool to Wallasey, changing the name in June to **New Brighton** (see end of Chapter 4).

A new South Liverpool emerged in 1935, the Liverpool County FA ruling that New Brighton did not own the name, so the two clubs ran in tandem, playing each other in the Lancashire Combination after New Brighton left the Football League in 1951.

New Brighton folded in 1983 after a season without a permanent home ground. South Liverpool, forced to share for one season with Bootle in 1990/91, reformed, joined with Cheshire Lines, then de-merged and settled in the West Cheshire League, winning the title in 2015 and 2016. They count Jimmy Case and John Aldridge among their old boys.

Other winners of the Lancashire Challenge Trophy have included **Horwich Railway Mechanics Insititute** and their successors ten miles south **Leigh RMI**, who won it in 2003 during their five years as a Conference team. They resigned from senior football before re-emerging as Leigh Genesis. Other two-time winners with a long history include **Clitheroe** (founded 1877), and Rossendale United (1898–2011).

Colne Dynamoes (1963–1990) flared more briefly under millionaire chairman Graham White, their motto 'We Long Endure' proving illusory. Racing through the North West Counties League and Northern Premier in the 1980s on a wage bill large enough to attract players like double European Cup winner Alan Kennedy, and keen to share Turf Moor with Burnley, they were denied entry to the Conference in 1990 and dramatically folded. **Colne FC** replaced them in 1996, using the same ground.

Manchester Central (1928–32) were an equally ambitious and similarly short-lived outfit. Like Thames FC in London at exactly the same time, the club came into existence to occupy a large stadium in need of an extra sport. In this case it was the 45,000-capacity Belle Vue, short of one when Manchester City left Hyde Road but opted for Maine Road further south.

City and United having both deserted East Manchester, it was believed there was room for another club there with potential to join the Football League. Local heroes Billy Meredith and Charlie Roberts helped with trials and put together an experienced team that finished seventh in the Lancashire Combination and immediately applied to join the Third Division North, receiving only two votes.

Combination runners-up the following season, having beaten Mansfield Town in the FA Cup, before a crowd of 8,500 saw Wrexham win 1-0 in the next round at Belle Vue, they garnered 13 votes this time. That was still ten short as Halifax, who had severe financial problems, and regular supplicants Barrow were overwhelmingly re-elected. 'The Northern Section are making their competition a farce,' thundered the Manchester-based *Athletic News*.

In 1931 Central failed again, Chester being voted in to replace ailing Nelson, and when Wigan Borough dropped out after 12 games of the following season, Central applied in vain to take over their fixtures. They had strong support in the press and from Third Division North clubs but City and United, who had both suffered a heavy drop in attendances, did not welcome further competition and their formal complaint to the League was upheld. 'We shall get there before long,' promised chairman George Hardman, but in summer 1932 the club disbanded, just like Thames, who had at least reached the Football League for two seasons of struggle.

Much more recently, Morecambe (2007) and Fleetwood (2012) both succeeded in achieving that status via what is now called the National League (see Chapter 9). Hoping to emulate them are **AFC Fylde**, who changed their name from Kirkham and Wesham after winning the FA Vase in 2008 to better reflect their image as the self styled 'football team of the Fylde coast'. On a sharp upward curve since the late 1990s, they progressed through the divisions to reach the National League in 2017, under benefactor David Haythornthwaite, a former Blackpool supporter who tried unsuccessfully to buy that club from the Oyston family.

Salford City have also benefited from more than useful patronage, in their case from the better-known names of 'Project 92', namely the Manchester United old boys Nicky Butt, Ryan Giggs, Gary and Phil Neville, and Paul Scholes, who took over in 2014.

Founded in 1940 and known as the Ammies after a previous name of Salford Amateurs, they are now highly professional and relentlessly ambitious. In ten years from 2008 they progressed from step nine of the football pyramid to the National League, just one tier below the Football League.

Clubs they left behind included Chorley, Curzon Ashton and FC United of Manchester. **Curzon Ashton** emerged only in 1963 from a merger of two clubs humble in origin, Curzon Road Methodists and Ashton Amateurs. As a Cheshire League side they reached the FA Vase semi-final in 1979/80, joined the North West Counties League and then Northern Premier, challenging 2017 Challenge Trophy winners **Ashton United** (where Alan Ball started and Dixie Dean finished) as the strongest local club.

A move to the impressive Tameside Stadium, opened by Sir Alex Ferguson in 2005, was followed by reaching another FA Vase semi-final and then winning promotion back to the Northern Premier, knocking Exeter City out of the FA Cup and reaching new heights in the National League North in 2015. To do so they beat Ashton United, their elders but no longer their betters, on penalties in a replayed play-off semi-final.

FC United of Manchester crossed paths, and swords, with both Ashton clubs on an even swifter climb up the pyramid after their dramatic formation in 2005 by Manchester United supporters disenchanted with the Glazer regime. Owned by fans and playing in United's red and white, they brought new life and colour to a succession of leagues through which they were another club to swiftly progress.

Playing at Bury's Gigg Lane, they won successive promotions for three seasons, reaching the top division of the Northern Premier League. After losing in the play-offs for four successive years from

2011–14, they finally reached the National League North, where average gates returned to the original high of more than 3,000 – better than ten Football League clubs. Drawn away to Brighton in the FA Cup second round in 2010 they held the League One leaders 1-1 and had more than 6,500 at the televised replay. A 4-0 defeat ensured that any possibility of Manchester United's nightmare of having to play them was averted.

In 2015 they moved to their own home at Broadhurst Park, playing a reserve team from United's 1968 European Cup Final opponents Benfica in the opening game before 4,232 people.

Amid all this relentless ambition and social climbing, **Liverpool Ramblers** from Crosby go on their own sweet, old-fashioned way, declining to play any form of league football. In the 1880s they entered the FA Cup and Liverpool Senior Cup but these days play only friendlies. They did, however, boast an England international in George Dewhurst, who appeared against Wales in 1895, and claim to have assisted Liverpool engineer John Alexander Brodie with his design of football's first goal nets, after he was upset that Everton had a goal disallowed against Accrington.

Chapter 8

Fergie's Time (1991–2000)

*A whole new ball game as the 'big five' get the reform
they wanted – a breakaway league and lucrative TV
deal; Cantona's United do the Double, Beckham's United
the Treble; Hillsborough takes its toll on Dalglish before
he makes Blackburn champions of England; Goodison's
School of Science houses the 'dogs of war'; City 'not really
here' in third tier; Oldham's Royle progress; Bolton's
white hot years with Rioch; heady days for Tranmere
and Stockport; Wigan enter the DW era.*

I N the late 1980s, Everton, Liverpool and Manchester United,
along with Arsenal and Tottenham, were the self-styled 'big
five' pushing hardest for reform of the 92-club Football League,
which in their eyes essentially meant taking a larger share of the
revenue.

Once live televised matches, frowned upon for so long, became
accepted from 1983 onwards, it also became clear that here was
a significant form of income for the top clubs, especially if the
TV companies could be persuaded to bid against each other for
exclusive rights instead of operating as a cartel intent on keeping
the price down.

Those were the five clubs who in 1990 met Greg Dyke, the
chairman of London Weekend Television, over dinner, out of which
came an audacious proposal that would not only give them the

majority of live matches but could be under the umbrella of a new league altogether.

Knowing that the Football League would not sanction such a plan after more than 100 years of democratic existence, the plotters turned to the FA, who were much more receptive. Keen to capitalise on England's run to the 1990 World Cup semi-final, and subsequent much-needed improvement in the game's image, the governing body believed that the national team would benefit if they had greater control.

Thus the FA produced their 'Blueprint for the Future of Football', listing the future of the England team as a major priority and proposing that the Football Association Premier League would begin in 1992/93, with 22 clubs reduced to 18 by the time the country hosted Euro '96 four years later.

In fact they had created a monster that they would soon lose control of. The 'FA' tag was soon ignored and then quietly dropped altogether. 'We were guilty of a tremendous collective lack of vision,' chief executive Graham Kelly conceded in retrospect. In leaving the Football League's Lytham headquarters for Lancaster Gate in 1989, Kelly, a boyhood Blackpool supporter, had backed the right horse but was not strong enough to ride it.

Rick Parry, chief executive of Liverpool, was placed in charge of the new league, which quickly became an organisation of its own, run by the 22 clubs, whose priorities did not involve the England team or anyone other than themselves.

Just like in 1888, the north-west had six representatives; Everton, Liverpool, Manchester City and Manchester United being joined among the lucky 22 by Oldham Athletic and Blackburn Rovers, both timing their return to the big time perfectly by gaining promotion in successive seasons at the start of the decade.

They would also share the riches available from an astonishing £304m television contract. Cosy cartels had now been smashed with the entry into the market of satellite broadcasting, which to football's benefit saw the national sport as a driver of audience and subscriptions. Thus Rupert Murdoch's Sky Television pulled out all the stops to pip ITV, who had been favoured by a majority of the big five clubs but were outflanked by Tottenham chairman Alan Sugar, whose company just happened to make satellite dishes.

Tottenham's vote enabled Sky to gain the majority required among the 22 clubs, which also meant that although smaller audiences would view the games, attendances were less likely to be affected – the great concern about live league football ever since the failed experiment when Blackpool played Bolton all those years ago.

Now it was, to quote the publicity, 'A Whole New Ball Game'.

* * * * *

No club would enjoy the new era of English football or benefit more from the exposure than **Manchester United**. Alex Ferguson had been under pressure, but winning the 1990 FA Cup 'allowed us breathing space,' as he put it, in the much quoted quest to 'knock Liverpool off their (expletive deleted) perch'.

It was Arsenal and Leeds who did that first by winning the last of the old Football League championships in successive seasons at the start of the decade, while United continued to make solid progress. In 1990/91 they still sat one place behind fifth-placed Manchester City, having been deducted one point after a fracas with George Graham's Arsenal, but won the European Cup Winners' Cup.

As English clubs returned to European competition (though not the European Cup as Liverpool had an extra year to serve), United began in low-key fashion. Barely 28,000 turned out to see unknown Hungarian opposition Pécsi Mecsek beaten 2-0. Reaching the semi-final, they had the best of the draw in avoiding Barcelona and Juventus, and duly overcame Montpellier, despite a draw at Old Trafford, to qualify for a first European final since 1968.

It was staged in Rotterdam and went down as Mark Hughes's night, though he modestly admitted the first of his two goals in the 2-1 win over Barca should have been credited to Steve Bruce.

Leeds squeezed United out of a long-awaited First Division title by four points the following year but unwisely allowed Eric Cantona to cross the Pennines. Ferguson had lost out on Southampton's Alan Shearer, been turned down by Sheffield Wednesday for David Hirst and lost new signing Dion Dublin with a badly broken leg after only three games. Dublin likes to joke that he was the making of the modern United, his injury in autumn 1992 prompting Ferguson to buy the maverick Frenchman, who not only trusted him more than Howard Wilkinson but came to revere him as United went on to dominate the new Premier League.

They should have won five successive titles, unprecedented in English football history, from the start of the new competition in 1992, but were interrupted by Blackburn's dramatic success of 1995.

The League Cup, won for the first time in 1992 after defeat in the previous year's final to Sheffield Wednesday, was small consolation for not winning the title that year but maintained the record of at least one trophy per season from 1990's FA Cup, extended with a domestic Double in 1994. It could easily have been a Treble: United finished eight points clear in the league and won the FA Cup final 4-0 against Chelsea but Aston Villa denied them the League Cup by 3-1 in Ron Atkinson's revenge match, after Andrei Kanchelskis was sent off.

The 1994 team was one of Ferguson's favourites, one he said of 'winners … and bad losers'. The description was particularly appropriate for Roy Keane, snatched from under Blackburn's nose as heir to the equally dynamic Bryan Robson's midfield role.

In 1995, with Cantona suspended for eight months and narrowly avoiding prison after attacking a Crystal Palace fan at Selhurst Park, United could never quite catch Blackburn, even after Andy Cole scored five in the record 9-0 win over Ipswich. While Rovers were losing to a late goal at Liverpool on the final day, United failed to get the win they needed at Upton Park, where West Ham's traditional antipathy to them, dating back to the hooliganism days, encouraged their team, not far above the relegation fight, to give everything and draw 1-1.

Ferguson, to his credit, sent a handsome letter of congratulation to Kenny Dalglish, the manager who had denied him a title hat-trick.

No titles, just a runners-up double in league and FA Cup after losing the final to Everton (see below), led to what passed for a crisis at the club. Questions were raised about the manager, who had sold Hughes (reluctantly), Paul Ince and Kanchelskis (less so). To his fury the *Manchester Evening News* ran a poll asking whether he should be sacked: 56 per cent (a number not inconceivably bumped up by supporters of City and others) replied 'yes'.

A year later that majority was shamed by another Double, achieved by a younger squad featuring David Beckham, the epitome of practice making perfect, the Neville brothers, Nicky Butt and Paul Scholes as well as Ryan Giggs and Lee Sharpe. Cantona, who had to be talked out of retiring during his suspension, added one further title before retiring; United ended up seven points clear of Kevin Keegan's floundering Newcastle in 1997, before Arsenal and Arsene Wenger emerged as the team and the manager to challenge United and Ferguson.

'United against Arsenal was great for the game. It made the Premier League,' the Scot said on the occasion of Wenger's last visit to Old Trafford as Arsenal manager in 2018.

For four years in a row from 1998 the two clubs were the top two in the Premier League and in the second of them United had their best Treble chance yet. The Champions League, replacing the European Cup in 1992 to guarantee the biggest clubs more games, had been a source of frustration to England's most regular contestants. A semi-final in 1997 brought the bitter disappointment of defeat by Borussia Dortmund at home and away, and the following year Monaco inflicted an away goals victory with a 1-1 draw at Old Trafford.

The 1998/99 campaign began with a 3-0 defeat by Arsenal in the Charity Shield and required a change of assistant manager halfway through, Steve McClaren replacing Brian Kidd, who unwisely left to manage Blackburn. McClaren's first match was an 8-1 away win at Nottingham Forest but the season was exemplified by two key performances on successive Wednesdays in April.

In the most dramatic of FA Cup semi-finals at Villa Park, Roy Keane was sent off, Peter Schmeichel saved Dennis Bergkamp's last-minute penalty to keep the Treble hopes alive and in extra time Giggs intercepted a square pass by Patrick Vieira and raced away to score one of the great cup goals.

Gary Neville called it the best match of the 700-odd in his career and there was another epic seven days later. Travelling to Turin for the second leg of the Champions League semi-final at 1-1, United went 2-0 down to Juventus in ten minutes yet found the reserves of character, class and stamina to win the game and the tie. Keane was outstanding despite collecting a yellow card to put him out of the final.

The league title was clinched by a point on the final day, though only because Leeds had done United a rare favour the previous week by defeating Arsenal. Beating Newcastle with a degree of ease in the FA Cup final meant that a historic Treble depended on doing the same to Bayern Munich in Barcelona four days later.

Neutral opinion was that Bayern deserved the 1-0 lead they held going into added time, having also hit the bar and post. United's performance had been 'bereft of their usual verve and imagination', according to *The Independent*. What followed was described by the *Daily Mirror* as 'the greatest two minutes in the history of sport' as Beckham swung in successive corners that substitutes Teddy Sheringham and Ole Gunnar Solskjaer forced into the net. The astonishing turnaround prompted the most famous of Ferguson soundbites when he told ITV's post-match interviewer, 'Football … bloody hell!'

European Cup Final 1999: Manchester United 2 Bayern Munich 1

Manchester United: Schmeichel; G. Neville, Johnsen, Stam, Irwin, Giggs, Beckham, Butt, Blomqvist (Sheringham 67), Cole (Solskjaer 81), Yorke.

Bayern Munich: Kahn, Mätthaus (Fink, 80), Babbel, Linke, Kuffour, Tarnat, Effenberg, Jeremies, Basler (Salihamidžić 87), Jancker, Zickler (Scholl 71).

As with the 1994 side, Ferguson admired his squad's character and team spirit as much as their talent. The Premier League, the FA Cup and the Champions League could all very easily have been lost at various moments, but they had come through for each other. They followed up by losing only three league games for the second successive season and retaining the title by a huge margin of 18 points.

From the start of the 1990s United had won the Champions League, six Premier League titles, a European Cup Winners' Cup, Super Cup, World Club Championship, four FA Cups and a League Cup. There were still a few more where those came from.

* * * * *

Liverpool had been well and truly removed from their perch in a period of extended trauma. The toll would tell on everyone, but on Kenny Dalglish especially.

As if playing for those lost at Hillsborough and their families, they had done superbly to win the 1989 FA Cup Final and come within seconds of the Double, then regain the title the following season. In 1990/91 they reeled off 12 wins and a draw from the first 13 games, but then stuttered, notably in a 3-0 hammering at Arsenal. By the end of February, a seminal month, Arsenal had eased them off the top, the midfield had been disrupted if not destroyed by injuries to Steve McMahon and Ronnie Whelan, new signings David Speedie and Jimmy Carter were proving poor choices, and, worst of all, the manager had gone.

Dalglish, who had been at Ibrox in 1971 when 66 of his fellow Rangers fans were crushed to death, and at Heysel in 1985, was on the touchline and then the pitch at Hillsborough, knowing his son Paul was among the crowd. Later he attended up to four funerals a day, and midway through the 1990/91 season he was struggling to sleep and coming out in rashes. Just before one of the most dramatic of all Merseyside derbies, an FA Cup replay at Goodison drawn 4-4 on 20 February, Dalglish came to realise it was 'me as an individual who had a problem' and decided to resign. It had been 22 long months since Hillsborough but he finally understood that he was not over it.

The official announcement was made two days later, Ronnie Moran stepping up as caretaker, although Dalglish, like Shankly, came to regret that Liverpool did not wait a few months for him to return refreshed. Instead they turned in April to Graeme Souness, fed up with managing Rangers in a Glasgow goldfish bowl.

It was only a slight departure from the in-house progression, but although still perceived as a Liverpool man and believing in the one-for-all culture, the Scot had been away seven years in Italy and Scotland and picked up ideas of his own. Told by senior players that young ones didn't listen anymore and that it was no longer a self-policing dressing room, he made changes on and off the field – too many too soon as it turned out.

Despite winning 7-1 at Derby and 5-4 at Leeds under Moran, Liverpool lost the league title to Arsenal by seven points. Souness's first full season in 1991/92, with a much-changed squad, was barely redeemed by winning the FA Cup final against Sunderland, having beaten only one First Division team (Aston Villa) on the way. Sixth place in the league was the lowest since 1965. The manager meanwhile required a heart bypass operation and foolishly sold the story to *The Sun,* not forgiven on Merseyside to this day for its lurid front-page lies about Hillsborough.

Eighth place in 1993/94 was worse, although Robbie Fowler came through the ranks to add some much needed goals, and it was back to the boot room boys in January (the famed room itself having been demolished) when Roy Evans replaced Souness after a home defeat in the FA Cup to Bristol City. In the programme for that game John Barnes was forced to apologise for a newspaper article criticising Souness's 'abrasive manner'.

There was nothing abrasive about Evans and under his very different approach Liverpool finished fourth, third, fourth and third, won the 1995 League Cup and reached the 1996 FA Cup Final, where the men in white suits lost to Eric Cantona's goal for Manchester United.

Six European seasons in the 1990s brought little more success than a run to the Cup Winners' Cup semi-final in 1997, narrowly lost to Paris St Germain, but foreign influence was coming to the fore in English football. Gerard Houllier, a renowned Anglophile and Merseyphile, followed countrymen Arsene Wenger and Cantona into the Premier League, initially in tandem with Evans, who then fell on his sword to give the Frenchman full control.

Seventh place in 1999 while United fans crowed about their Treble was followed by fourth, with Emile Heskey the club's record signing at £11m, but there was still no return to the top table of European football. That was a couple of years off.

* * * * *

Across Stanley Park **Everton** in the '90s extended their record as a top-division club to 45 years and won an FA Cup, but had nothing else to boast about.

The temptation for Howard Kendall to return in November 1990 after his old midfield comrade Colin Harvey was sacked was understandable, although it ultimately added weight to the argument 'never go back', as well as making another return in 1997 all the more ill-advised.

Harvey quickly returned as assistant but the old magic had gone. For three seasons the Blues chugged along in mid-table with almost identical records, including a poor scoring return despite the best efforts of Tony Cottee and then Liverpool outcast Peter Beardsley.

Accused of poaching Mike Walker as manager from Norwich City midway through 1993/94, Everton had a hair's-breadth escape from relegation. Sitting in the bottom three places on the final morning of the season they went 2-0 behind at home to Wimbledon in 20 minutes and were still going down with nine minutes to play when Graham Stuart's shot somehow squirmed past goalkeeper Hans Segers for a 3-2 victory.

It was only a brief reprieve for Walker, sacked six months later with his team bottom of the table. Joe Royle, having taken Oldham Athletic to unexpected heights, was a popular choice and made the best possible start by beating Liverpool 2-0. Then he not only steered them up the table but reached the FA Cup final. Tottenham were brushed aside 4-1 in the semi-final and at Wembley the hot favourites United were caught cold when Swedish winger Anders Limpar led a swift counter-attack, Stuart hit the bar and Paul Rideout headed in.

FA Cup Final 1995: Everton 1 Manchester United 0

Everton: Southall; Jackson, Watson, Unsworth, Ablett, Limpar (Amokachi 69), Parkinson, Horne, Hinchcliffe, Stuart, Rideout (Ferguson 51).
Manchester United: Schmeichel; G. Neville, Bruce (Giggs 45), Pallister, Irwin, Keane, Butt, Ince, Sharpe (Scholes,72), McClair, Hughes.

Royle initially employed a more basic style, the former School of Science now housing the 'dogs of war,' named after Frederick Forsyth's novel about a group of ruthless cut-throats. Royle himself came up with the tag for his combative side but later felt it was over-used as the quality improved.

As FA Cup holders in 1995/96 they suffered an ignominious exit at the hands of Port Vale, and went out early in the Cup Winners' Cup, but recovered from a poor Premier League start to finish sixth with the added bonus of a 2-1 win at Anfield – one of only two in the '90s.

Andrei Kanchelskis was leading scorer after his acrimonious move from Old Trafford but he left during the following season, as did Royle in March after being refused permission to sign Tore André Flo. The Blues finished only two points from relegation and the following season under the returning Kendall was worse, requiring a draw at home to Coventry on the final day to send Bolton down instead.

Kendall was unsentimentally sacked and Walter Smith from Rangers became a more imaginative appointment without lifting a financially stricken club out of the lower reaches of the table. More encouraging was the departure of unpopular chairman Peter Johnson to be replaced by theatrical impresario and true Blue Bill Kenwright.

* * * * *

If ever there was a decade to sum up the riddle inside an enigma that was **Manchester City**, it was surely the 1990s. 'We're not really here' became the theme tune of disbelieving supporters for a period that began in fifth place in the Premier League, above Manchester United, took in Macclesfield and Wrexham, turmoil off the field and then the most dramatic of Wembley victories, before ending up back in the top tier.

Finishing two points ahead of United in 1990/91 despite Howard Kendall's mid-season defection to Everton turned out to be the last time they could look down on the oldest enemy for more than 20 years. With Peter Reid in charge and David White a regular scorer from the right wing, they were fifth again in 1992 then slipped to 9th and 16th as United began mopping up titles and Reid made way for Brian Horton.

Like Peter Johnson at Everton, chairman Peter Swales took most of the flak and there was great rejoicing in February 1994 when Francis Lee, once an all-round goalscoring hero, replaced him, inheriting what he called 'a desperate situation' financially. Redeveloping the Kippax Stand at a cost of over £15m would make it worse.

Unfortunately the new regime's first major football decisions, to concentrate on importing cheap foreign players, sack manager Horton and bring in Alan Ball (whose record hardly merited it) did not work. Even with Georgi Kinkladze one of the more successful imports, Ball's team took two points from their first 11 games of 1995/96, the last of which was a 6-0 defeat at Anfield, and it was an achievement to be in with a chance of staying up on the final day, when Liverpool were again the opposition.

City fought back heroically from 2-0 down to draw level, whereupon Ball 'heard a rumour' that relegation rivals Coventry were losing and told his players just to keep possession. Coventry, like Southampton, were actually drawing and the point that each took kept them both up but sent City down on goal difference.

In November 1995 Manchester was awarded the Commonwealth Games, the significance of which was not apparent at the time. City fans had more worrying things on their mind, which unthinkably got even worse. Ball resigned three matches into the 1996/97 season, having sold off some of the club's highest wage-earners. Dave Bassett accepted the job then changed his mind, and Steve Coppell lasted from 7 October to 8 November, citing a stress-related illness that has never been fully explained. Frank Clark was next in, in December, ten days after resigning at Nottingham Forest because of boardroom instability; the words 'frying pan' and 'fire' seemed appropriate, but he was optimistic. 'It certainly doesn't seem like the job from hell to me,' he said.

Going into 1997 City were 21st and although Clark lifted them to 14th he found the next season no easier. Losing to teams like Stockport and Bury was damaging psychologically and a home defeat by the Shakers in February put the team in the bottom three. Clark was sacked four days later and in his autobiography he decided after all that the chapter on his City experience should be called 'The Job From Hell'.

Within four weeks Lee had gone too but 11 months after leaving Everton, Joe Royle was unable to prevent the unthinkable, a further relegation. Typically, his team won the final game 5-2 at Stoke, sending them down as well, but Port Vale and Portsmouth also won away and, like QPR, escaped by a point.

Could things get any worse? Sitting 12th in the third tier at Christmas 1998 offered that possibility but from then things took an upward turn. A 6-0 win at Burnley was still capable of being followed by home defeat against Oldham but from late February City were in the play-off positions and finished third, scraping past Wigan 2-1 on aggregate to make the final against unfancied Gillingham, who they had beaten 2-0 away the previous month.

There were almost 77,000 at Wembley to see a final astonishing even by City standards: 0-0 after 80 minutes, then suddenly it was 2-0 to the Kent side; one goal was retrieved by Kevin Horlock and in the fifth minute of added time came an equaliser by Paul Dickov. To penalties it went and whereas all of City's history suggested inevitable defeat, goalkeeper Nicky Weaver saved two of Gillingham's to earn promotion.

An average attendance of 32,471 at Maine Road was the highest for 17 years, and 12 months later City had sailed through the First Division to win promotion behind Charlton with 23 goals from Shaun Goater. But losing the first Premier League game 4-0 away to the London side was unfortunately a reliable hint of what was to come.

* * * * *

In 1991 **Blackburn Rovers** finished 19th in the Second Division, four points off relegation. Four years later they were champions of England for the first time since 1914. If Kenny Dalglish, Alan Shearer and others deserve a share of the credit, the one person who made the whole thing possible was a local man of steel who had been a tax exile for two decades. Jack Walker, an old schoolfriend of club chairman Bill Fox, made £360m in January 1991 by selling his company to British Steel. He ended up spending more than a quarter of it on his local football club.

At the start of the 1991/92 season, with great things expected, Rovers took one point from three games. Manager Don Mackay was sacked, which proved to be good timing for Dalglish. Having rested for eight months after leaving Liverpool, the Scot was keen to return to football and thought he was about to do so with Marseille, only for the deal to fall through. Receiving the reassurance he needed from Blackburn about money being available for the squad as well as the stadium and the poor training facilities, he summoned Ray Harford as his coach but kept the loyal retainer and regular caretaker Tony Parkes and set to work.

On 12 October the new management team saw Plymouth beaten 5-2 in front of a modest 10,830 crowd. That had almost doubled by the February day when a hat-trick by David Speedie, proving more successful than at Liverpool, put Rovers seven points clear at the top.

Manchester City's Colin Hendry returned for a second spell at a cost of £700,000, Alan Wright came in from Blackpool for £500,000, Everton's Mike Newell was signed for £1.2m and Gordon Cowans cost £200,000 from Aston Villa, but nerves set in and only one win in a dozen games threatened hopes of even a play-off place.

They recovered just in time but were the lowest-placed of the play-off teams and went 2-0 down at home to Derby in the semi-final before coming through 5-4 on aggregate. Parkes led them out at Wembley, where Newell scored a penalty and missed one against Leicester to confirm promotion back after 26 years.

Signing Shearer, who rebuffed Manchester United, plus winger Stuart Ripley, Rovers were top of the new Premier League after five games. Shearer scored 14 goals in as many games but injured his cruciate at Christmas and missed the rest of the season, in which Liverpool were beaten 4-1 as Rovers finished fourth, top scorers with 68, as well as reaching the League Cup semi-final.

In the summer Roy Keane agreed a move to Ewood, then went to Manchester United instead, Ferguson having revenge for the Shearer signing and leaving Dalglish furious. Rovers got David Batty and Tim Flowers; then Chris Sutton for the sort of fee and wages that raised eyebrows and the Premier League inflation rate.

With Shearer back and rattling in 31 from 34 starts they beat Liverpool, United and Leeds and finished runners-up, ready for a sustained challenge. The cups were a let-down, above all defeat by the little known Swedes Trelleborgs in the club's first-ever European tie, but that did no harm to league ambitions.

When Rovers lost 4-2 at home to United in October 1994 they were only fourth but a month later were top and stayed there until the defining last day of 14 May. Ferguson deliberately chose to quote Devon Loch's famous slip when clear in the Grand National almost 30 years earlier and Blackburn did indeed stumble on the last day, losing 2-1 at Anfield as some Liverpool fans, desperate not to help United win the title, wore blue and white. It did not matter, thanks to West Ham's defiance at home to United.

Rovers were top scorers for the second time in three seasons, Shearer this time hitting 34 (including ten penalties) out of 80 and Sutton 15. Dalglish joined Brian Clough as the only manager since the war to win the title with two different clubs, yet he had already decided, 'I had had enough of the daily grind.' He handed the reins to Harford and became an ill-defined consultant, subsequently admitting the title 'director of football' was misleading.

Whatever the reasons, Rovers left new signings very late that summer, lost four of the first six games as champions and finished no higher than seventh, Sutton having been injured from October onwards. The Champions League campaign was a huge disappointment, symbolised by Batty and Graeme Le Saux fighting each other in defeat by Spartak Moscow.

'It was amazing how quickly it all began to unravel for us,' Le Saux wrote. Shearer's departure in the 1996 close-season for his boyhood club Newcastle was a serious loss, Dalglish was removed from even his consultant's role that August and Harford resigned after a League Cup defeat by Stockport that followed ten league matches without a win.

After a sixth place in 1997/98 under Roy Hodgson, with Sutton and Kevin Gallacher scoring 34 between them, the following season's poor form cost Hodgson his job and Brian Kidd was unable to prevent relegation with only one win in the last 14 games. Manchester United sent them down by drawing the penultimate game at Ewood en route to another title themselves.

* * * * *

It was an exciting time for **Oldham** who had not known many of them since finishing runners-up to Football League champions Everton as long ago as 1915.

Evertonian Joe Royle had made excellent progress since going straight into management with them in 1982 and the great cup runs of 1990 to the FA Cup semi-finals against Manchester United and the equally narrow League Cup final defeat by Nottingham Forest illustrated the potential which came to fruition in winning Division Two in 1991.

Andy Ritchie's 28 goals the previous season was the best haul since the days of Bert Lister, although in the promotion year the goals were shared around, the tall and versatile Ian Marshall from

Everton leading the list. The most crucial one, however, was scored by Neil Redfearn from a penalty with almost the last kick of the season to beat fellow contenders Sheffield Wednesday 3-2 after being 2-0 down, pipping West Ham to the title by a point.

Five teams had a better defensive record but none could match the 83 scored, 55 at home being the best Boundary Park had seen for 30 years. The Everton connections were numerous with Scottish striker Graeme Sharp joining from Goodison in 1991 and midfielder Mike Milligan going the other way and then returning. Both played an important role in avoiding relegation in the first two seasons back in the top tier since 1923, as did another Goodison recruit, Neil McDonald.

The first year was comfortable with nine points to spare in ensuring membership of the Premier League for its inaugural campaign. An away win at Maine Road was one of the highlights although Manchester United, on their way to the title, won an eventful Boxing Day game 6-3 at Boundary Park.

The second season was more fraught, ending in astonishing fashion with the Latics needing to win their last three games in the space of seven days – two of them against top six teams – and hoping Crystal Palace took no more than a point from their last two. The first of Oldham's treble was a stunning 3-2 success away to runners-up Aston Villa, which handed United the title; next Liverpool fell by the same score and then Southampton were beaten 4-3 as Palace went down to defeat by Arsenal.

Next season, however, it was a bad finish that did for them, no wins in the final eight games causing them to drop too far from an apparently safe position. There appeared to be a reaction to another epic FA Cup semi-final against United, which Oldham were winning with a goal by Neil Pointon (another old Evertonian) until Mark Hughes's volley in the last minute. United cruised through the Maine Road replay 4-1 and Oldham's star was dimming.

If anything gates of around 11,000 were a little disappointing so that players like Denis Irwin (to Manchester United) and defender Earl Barrett, who was capped by England before moving on to Aston Villa, could not be kept.

In November 1994 Royle could not resist the call from Goodison Park to replace Mike Walker and the Latics suffered two seasons in the lower half of the new First Division before dropping into the third tier in 1997. Two years later they were only a point away from a further fall. The great adventure was well and truly over but it had been wonderful fun.

* * * * *

Envious as they were of neighbouring Oldham's time in the spotlight, **Bolton** finally reasserted what they considered to be natural superiority in the mid-to-late 1990s, albeit by going up and then down in four successive seasons and with three high-profile managers in nine months.

The earlier years of the decade were spent attempting to escape from the third level, which Phil Neal could not manage but Bruce Rioch did at the first attempt, as runners-up to Stoke in 1992/93 as well as winning an FA Cup replay 2-0 at Anfield. It was the first of the giant-killings that also saw Everton (3-2) and Arsenal (3-1) slain in their own backyards in what became known as the White Hot Years of 1993 and 1994. The disappointment in the latter year was a quarter-final defeat by Oldham.

In 1995 they were in the Premier League via a dramatic play-off final against Reading, who were 2-0 up and then missed a penalty. Wanderers kept their nerve and won 4-3 in extra time with a goal by Fabian de Freitas.

Rioch was head-hunted by Arsenal, where he signed Dennis Bergkamp but lasted only one season as Arsene Wenger came in and Bolton's yo-yoing got going. It was straight back down in 1996, Roy McFarland having been given only six months in partnership with Colin Todd, who then took sole control. He won the First Division title the following season by a street with only four defeats and 100 goals scored. John McGinlay got 30 in all competitions, including a hat-trick in the 6-1 demolition of Tottenham in the League Cup.

On 25 April the Scot scored the last two goals at Burnden Park in a 4-1 win over Charlton before the move to a smart new £25m Reebok Stadium out by the M61 at Horwich, with a hotel included. Only four games were lost there the following season but away form was poor and on the final day a 2-0 defeat at Chelsea meant relegation on goal difference as Everton survived by scrambling a draw at home to Coventry.

Remarkably, it might have been another change of division 12 months later as Wanderers reached the play-off final on away goals against Ipswich but lost 2-0 at Wembley to Watford. Early in the following season Todd resigned after Per Frandsen was sold to Blackburn, Sam Allardyce arrived and a successful new era began.

* * * * *

Wembley may have seemed an unlikely second home for **Tranmere** but they became more regular visitors than Liverpool or Everton in the most exciting period in the club's history. It was a remarkable recovery from the financially stricken days of the 1980s and the Fourth Division's bottom six. After the Football League Centenary Tournament of 1988, Rovers were at the national stadium in successive weeks two years later; winning the Leyland DAF Cup Final by beating Bristol Rovers with Jim Steel's goal in front of more than 48,000 before losing the play-off final 2-0 to Notts County.

A year later Chris Malkin's goal won the play-offs against Bolton, who had finished five points ahead of them and so it was back to the second tier, only previously reached for one season in 1938/39.

John Aldridge, returning to Merseyside from Real Sociedad, signed up for the journey and was hugely influential in bringing crowds and publicity as well as goals. He scored regularly for the next eight years, latterly as player-manager when John King became director of football.

After one settling-in season at the higher level Rovers were three times in contention to reach the Premier League itself via successive play-off semi-final appearances. In 1992/93 they finished fourth but never quite recovered from going 3-0 down in half an hour of the first leg at Swindon, eventually losing 5-4 on aggregate.

Fifth the following year, they lost 2-1 on aggregate to David Speedie's late goal for Leicester. In 1995 it was fifth place again in another tight finish, but they were eliminated thanks to a decisive home defeat by Reading.

Amidst all that was the bitter disappointment of missing out on a League Cup final against Manchester United when Aston Villa knocked them out on penalties in the semi-final. They made up for it in the 2000 competition, going all the way to Wembley with wins over Premier League clubs Middlesbrough and Coventry, then 4-0 on aggregate in the semi-final against Bolton, only to bravely lose 2-1 to Leicester in front of more than 74,000. David Kelly scored an equalising goal after Clint Hill was sent off.

By that time they had also set a second club record by reaching the FA Cup quarter-final, beating West Ham, Sunderland and Fulham before a 3-2 home defeat by Newcastle. Aldridge, having retired from playing in 1998, with 164 goals for the club to add to his 64 at Liverpool, was a proud manager.

* * * * *

Blackpool and Burnley, in the top division together 20 years earlier, became used to meeting each other regularly in the third tier during the '90s. They began the decade even lower, both beaten in the 1991 play-offs and escaping together in 1992.

Burnley did so as Fourth Division champions, which made them only the second club, after Wolves, to win all four divisions. 'Spurred on by their formidable support at home and away, [they] were worthy champions,' opined the *Rothmans Football Yearbook*. Despite being overshadowed by neighbours Blackburn after Kenny Dalglish's appointment in October, they did their best to earn some headlines by winning nine games in a row before Christmas and finished six points clear at the top, Glaswegian Mike Conroy scoring 24 goals in his first season.

Jimmy Mullen stayed as manager for five years and in 1994 took them up again, winning the play-off final 2-1 against Stockport at Wembley, only to suffer immediate relegation from the second tier.

Bigger names in Adrian Heath and Chris Waddle took a turn in charge without success before Stan Ternent arrived in 1998, moving up from Bury and moving the Clarets up again as runners-up to Preston two years later. They won seven of the last eight games as local boy Andy Payton reached 27 goals.

* * * * *

Blackpool went back down to the lowest level that same season, after Sam Allardyce had begun his managerial career in England by having them close to promotion four years earlier. Missing the two automatic promotion places after being top with a month to play, they managed the unlikely feat of winning the play-off first leg 2-0 at Bradford City then nervously losing the home leg

3-0; 'folding like a deck of cards,' Allardyce said. He was sacked two weeks later, after Owen Oyston had been sent to prison for six years (serving three and a half) and his wife succeeded him as chairman.

Before Allardyce, Billy Ayre had survived four years under the Oystons, although forced to sell players like Alan Wright and Trevor Sinclair. The Seasiders lost the 1991 play-off final on penalties to Torquay after a 2-2 draw but were luckier the following year in another Wembley shoot-out, when defeating Scunthorpe. Their scorer in the final with his 35th of the season was Dave Bamber, back for his second spell at the club after leaving for Coventry in 1983.

Narrowly avoiding relegation in 1994 by beating Leyton Orient 4-1 on the final day, they fired Ayre and appointed Allardyce, who found that 'Bloomfield Road was falling to bits and the training ground was an abomination'. Neither would improve for some time, although increasingly disenchanted fans were given false hope at the end of 1998 when a new consortium offered the Oystons £18m, hoping to develop Bloomfield Road and move to a new ground. Karl Oyston replaced his mother in the chair but nothing came of the move.

Meanwhile, post-Allardyce, Gary Megson just missed the play-offs then headed off to Stockport, and Northern Ireland international Nigel Worthington was less successful from 1997 with two mid-table seasons before he and Steve McMahon shared stewardship of the relegation season of 1999/2000.

* * * * *

Before joining Blackpool, Allardyce had spent an unhappy time working as youth-team manager at **Preston** under one of the country's most controversial managers in John Beck. Anyone who believes the former England manager to be a devotee of direct play may not be familiar with the work of Beck, who took it to new extremes while lifting Cambridge United to the brink of the Premier League in 1992 on crowds of 7,000.

He insisted on players hitting passes to what he called 'Paradise Alley', the attacking area between the penalty area and touchline, from where wingers would be judged on how many crosses they put in. Deepdale's plastic pitch was less suitable for such tactics so

Beck had the corners heavily sanded, and after joining struggling North End in December 1992 he would still have saved them from relegation to the bottom division but for a disastrous finish, losing the final five games to go down by three points.

In his first full season they reached the play-off final, losing 4-2 to Wycombe, but by the end of 1993/94 his assistant Gary Peters had taken over for a second successive fifth-placed finish and another failure in the play-offs, losing to Bury. They had been helped by a 19-year-old Manchester United midfielder called David Beckham, hyped in the local paper as 'the new Bobby Charlton'. He played in five games without losing during March but was then summoned back to Old Trafford to make his Premier League debut.

The following season, helped financially by new owners, Peters led the club to the (new) Third Division championship as the country's highest scorers with 78 goals, 29 of them to Andy Saville, who had been signed from Birmingham City.

When Peters was moved to the club's Centre of Excellence in January 1998 after a bad run, his successor was David Moyes, a solid centre-half for several seasons. The following season he took North End to the play-offs, where they lost to Gillingham, who went on to the famous final against Manchester City.

Moyes was establishing a fine reputation, not harmed by a televised FA Cup tie at Deepdale in which Preston led the holders Arsenal 2-0 before losing 4-2. By the end of the decade he had taken them back into the second tier for the first time since 1974, winning the Division Two title by seven points from Burnley with a major goalscoring contribution from Jon Macken.

* * * * *

Stockport, like Oldham, found themselves reliving days of yore in the upper reaches of the second tier of English football. Danny Bergara, the Uruguayan who was one of the more unheralded foreign managers, was instrumental in laying the foundations from his appointment in 1989 until 1994.

He led them out of the Fourth Division in 1991, top scorers in the country with 84 as four players reached double figures. Winning eight of the last nine games, County missed the title by only a point.

Like Tranmere they became unexpectedly familiar with Wembley and as well as two Autoglass Trophy finals (1992 and 1993) were in the play-offs for three seasons running without success.

In 1992 they knocked out Stoke but lost the final to a late Peterborough goal after the 6ft 7in Kevin Francis equalised, in 1993 they lost the semi-final 2-1 on aggregate to Port Vale, and a year later came a 2-1 defeat to Burnley at Wembley after leading with Chris Beaumont's early goal before he and Mike Wallace were both sent off.

Bergara left before the end of a mid-table 1994/95 season but his assistant Dave Jones did even better. In 1996 County were close to beating Everton in the FA Cup, drawing at Goodison and then going down 3-2 to a late goal at home. The following year they won promotion with Bury as well as reaching the League Cup semi-final and a narrow 2-1 aggregate defeat by Middlesbrough.

Regarded as relegation favourites, they outshone the Shakers at the higher level by finishing eighth, which included beating Manchester City 3-1 in the first league meeting for 87 years. City went down but Stockport were there to welcome them back in 1999 and beat them again – this time at Maine Road.

All the while, however, there was an acknowledgment of the gulf in resources between County and many of those they were successfully mixing it with. 'Where are the good people of Stockport?' asked the match programme plaintively for the City game in November 1997, which attracted 11,351. Within a few years half that many would be a big crowd.

* * * * *

Oscillating up and down the Third Division in the eighties, **Wigan** were relegated in 1993 and suffered for a while with particularly poor attendances before returning and finding a new owner, new home and new hope.

In the relegation season a May Day crowd (in every sense) of just 1,432 saw a ninth defeat in 11 games and the following season under Kenny Swain they finished in the bottom four of the fourth tier. Swain departed with the team struggling early the following season and one crowd numbering 1,232, but the most significant change was in February 1995 when Dave Whelan, the Blackburn full-back who broke his leg in the 1960 FA Cup Final and was now a millionaire businessman, bought the ailing club.

Three seasons of steady improvement, the last two under former Norwich City manager John Deehan, had them promoted as champions in 1997. The 46 games produced 135 goals, 84 of them to Wigan, for whom Graeme Jones scored a club record 31. The free-scoring entertainment paid dividends: Fulham had the same number of points and a better goal difference, but under a temporary league rule – ironically pioneered by Fulham chairman Jimmy Hill – the number of goals scored was the deciding factor.

Whelan's influence helped secure three notable Spanish additions in Isidro Díaz, Jesús Seba and, most significantly for the future, Roberto Martinez. Inevitably christened the 'Three Amigos', they stayed together for only a year but Martinez became a mainstay of the team for six years with his cultured midfield play.

By 2001, when he left, they were regularly pressing for promotion to the second tier for the first time. For three seasons running from 1999 they reached the play-offs, Whelan having strengthened the squad and funded a move from Springfield Park to the new stadium, named JJB after his sportswear firm.

Just like Tranmere and Stockport, however, they found the play-offs tough, first losing by a single goal to Manchester City, then losing a final to Gillingham after leading with six minutes of extra time remaining, and going out 2-1 on aggregate to Reading with another pair of late goals. Whelan regularly changed managers but needed to be patient in waiting for the next step up. Winning the 1999 Auto Windscreens Trophy at Wembley against Millwall was a consolation of sorts.

* * * * *

Pipped 2-1 on aggregate in the 1990 Third Division play-off semi-final by Bolton, **Bury** had to drop into the bottom tier before climbing up two divisions in successive seasons.

From seventh place in 1991 they fell to relegation by two points the following year but were close to a return in 1995 and achieved it a year later. Delighted to see off Preston in the 1995 semi-final, having finished fully 13 points above them, they lost the Wembley final to Chesterfield 2-0.

Mike Walsh, manager since December 1990, was suddenly sacked only five games into the new season following a 5-0 home defeat by Plymouth and his assistant Stan Ternent won automatic promotion in third place. It confirmed Ternent's reputation as a doer of good works in the lower divisions.

With local benefactor Hugh Eaves bankrolling the club on modest gates, an even better season followed as Division Two champions ahead of Stockport, bringing a return to the second tier after 28 years.

Ternent left after a reasonable first season back, including victory over Manchester City at Maine Road, seeing greater potential at Burnley although they were one division lower.

By 1999 the clubs were in the same division, the Shakers having gone down with Neil Warnock as manager on number of goals scored as one of four teams on the same number of points.

* * * * *

Rochdale, back down in the bottom tier since 1974 and almost voted out in 1980, were at least mid-table for much of the 1990s. For that reason Dave Sutton and Graham Barrow were both given three-year spells in charge.

Sutton took over midway through the 1990/91 season after declining to join the departing Terry Dolan at Hull City, and was rewarded with one of the longer stints for a Dale manager. In his first and third full seasons they were close to a play-off place, having almost doubled attendances from the 1,400 average of the bleak mid-'80s, and record £80,000 signing Andy Flounders was decent value with 31 goals in two seasons.

Sutton left in November 1994 after a run of defeats, Graham Barrow arrived following his year in charge of Wigan but was always in the bottom half for his three seasons and in 1999 was succeeded by the more successful Steve Parkin.

Chapter 9

For richer, for poorer (2001–18)

City over the blue moon with Fergie's time up; Liverpool find title elusive but perform a miracle in Europe; Everton in neighbours' shadow still; Wigan's unique double; Venky's at Blackburn; Owen Coyle does the rounds; Holloway's Blackpool prove every dog has its day; Preston end play-off hoodoo; historic high for Rochdale but down, down for Stockport; Accrington back and making national news; Morecambe shrimps among the big fish; Fleetwood's impressive progress.

I N 2008 Professor John Samuels wrote a book called *The Beautiful Game is Over* which suggested, 'The winning of major competitions is now largely over for clubs from the midlands, north-east and most other parts of the country.'

Apart from the Football League Cup, one FA Cup success by Portsmouth and Leicester City's astonishing triumph in 2016 that analysis has been borne out ever since the Premier League began in 1992.

In 2003 Portsmouth's south coast rivals Southampton reached the FA Cup final and Newcastle United finished as high as third in the table, but that summer English football changed forever when Roman Abramovich, a Russian oligarch with enough money to make Jack Walker's millions look like small change, bought Chelsea and spent £210m on players in his first two years, as well as doubling the club's wage bill.

Manchester United quickly followed into foreign ownership with the Glazer family's takeover (2005) and soon Manchester City and Liverpool (both 2007) rushed down the same path.

* * * * *

Until football's new money arrived in the north-west, it was much the same old **Manchester City.** At the start of the century they were looking forward to moving into a new £110m stadium paid for by the lottery and Manchester taxpayers but could not afford any more yo-yoing if they were to fill it.

Joe Royle was sacked in May 2001 after two promotions and one relegation back to the Championship, to be succeeded by Kevin Keegan. Still charismatic at the time, despite his depressing experience with England, he became manager of the relegated team, chairman David Bernstein promising that the former Anfield hero would bring back the style and flair lacking for the past 20 or 30 years; Keegan, ever the optimist, suggested City would be challenging for the Premier League title within the five years of his contract.

It seemed conceivable as they raced to the top of the Championship in his first season with 108 goals and 99 points. Stuart Pearce was signed to become the dynamic dressing room leader Keegan wanted, Shaun Goater scored 32 goals in all competitions and Darren Huckerby 26. For the final Maine Road season there was a revival from the bottom three in mid-October with a 3-1 win over United that led to a top-ten finish. A crowd of 34,957 packed in for the emotional final farewell against Southampton; City lost, of course.

There had also been a boardroom split that resulted in Bernstein resigning in March, John Wardle replacing him, which was hardly ideal just before the big move. Keegan signed a number of unsuccessful foreign imports, spending nearly £50m in two years, and the club had debts of that region going into the new ground.

On 23 August 2003 an opening crowd of 46,287 saw the 1-1 draw with Portsmouth, a figure that offered good reason for a move even without the highly favourable terms; the average at the end of the season was 46,830, an increase of more than 25 per cent.

Other than that, it was a season that Keegan called the most disappointing of his managerial career. Despite ending with a 5-1 win over Everton to follow the 4-1 caper against United, City ended up in the bottom five, with only nine victories, plus a return to Europe via the Fair Play League which did not last long.

With little more money to spend, Keegan-watchers did not expect the manager to last long and sure enough he walked out early the following March after a home defeat by Bolton, saying that as with England he could do no more. Criticism had been based on the old charge of lacking tactical nous, the players wanting more training and work on set pieces. They responded well to Pearce, an obvious and cheap successor, but the way the team ran out of steam in his first season was a prelude to the extraordinary goal-shy second when Joey Barton was the top scorer with six and the last nine home games produced not a single City goal.

There had been regular talk of the need for investment in the club. Suddenly, dramatically, it came just before the start of the 2007/08 season. A former Thai prime minister called Thaksin Shinawatra, who had tried to buy into Liverpool in 2004 and was overthrown by the military two years later, took over City at a cost (for starters) of £81.6m.

Desperate fans were none too fussed about his political record. He sailed through the 'fit and proper person test' as most people without an actual criminal record did, and made a high-profile appointment in Sven-Göran Eriksson, which after an early 1-0 win over United to go top of the table ended in the ignominy of an 8-1 defeat by Middlesbrough and ninth position, while Old Trafford celebrated yet another title.

Eriksson's team scraped another UEFA Cup place via the Fair Play League but he was sacked anyway, and Wardle soon resigned, disgusted by the manager's treatment. Mark Hughes was appointed, a phlegmatic man for whom that would prove an essential quality.

Thaksin was back in Thailand facing corruption charges, and with £800m of his assets frozen, new investment was going to have to come from elsewhere. On 1 September 2008, an extended day for transfers as 31 August was a Sunday, Hughes was taking part in the club's annual golf day as news broke that a fabulously wealthy Abu Dhabi consortium led by Sheikh Mansour, brother of the country's ruler, had bought the club. A day of increasingly wild rumour concluded with the Brazilian forward Robinho arriving from Real Madrid for no less than £32.5m.

The new men were 'set to alter football forever', the *Sunday Times* suggested (although Abramovich could reasonably claim to have done that already).

The Times said they would go for Cristiano Ronaldo, Fernando Torres, Cesc Fabregas and Ronaldinho. City, being City, were in the relegation places by Christmas but a further £49m spent in January with Nigel de Jong costing £17m and Craig Bellamy £14m helped towards a tenth-place finish and a long UEFA Cup campaign eventually taking 14 games.

There was clearly going to be no let-up in the spending, which in the 2009 close-season extended to almost £100m net on players like Emmanuel Adebayor, Gareth Barry and, most controversially, Carlos Tevez from United via the company that part-owned him. 'Welcome to Manchester' provocatively proclaimed a huge City billboard on Deansgate with his picture on, prompting Sir Alex Ferguson to snort that they were 'a small club with a small mentality'.

In fact they were growing bigger, and fast. A Champions League place was the next target and sitting sixth in the Premier League in mid-December was not considered good enough. Before the home game against Sunderland leaks suggested Hughes's time was up and he departed with a 4-3 win to be replaced by Roberto Mancini, once a long-serving, elegant Sampdoria forward, who had been dismissed by Inter a year earlier.

He oversaw a narrow League Cup semi-final defeat by United, who later inflicted a severe blow by winning 1-0 at Eastlands. When Spurs repeated that result it meant the Londoners pipped City to the final Champions League place. Tevez finished the season with 29 in all competitions, and losses of £92.6m were declared, which did not prevent another £100m splurge topped by James Milner, David Silva, Yaya Touré and Mario Balotelli, all at £20m-plus.

Keeping up with United proved impossible after the first half of 2010/11 but there was joy and a trophy at last after Touré scored the only goal to beat them in the FA Cup semi-final and then repeated the dose against Stoke City in the final before two more league wins ensured third place.

From the start Abu Dhabi money had been spent on infrastructure as well as footballers. The training ground close to United's in Carrington was clearly inadequate and in December 2011 planning permission was given for a whole new campus based around the City of Manchester stadium. A sponsorship from the Abu Dhabi airline Etihad had been agreed, bringing in £350m over ten years and giving the stadium a new name.

Ferguson meanwhile raged at City's 'stupid money and silly salaries', and Arsenal's Arsene Wenger bemoaned UEFA's Financial Fair Play rules not being strictly enough enforced.

The transfer policy may have been hit-and-miss but at the prices City could afford there were bound to be plenty of the former. Sergio Agüero, the big 2011 signing at £37m with Arsenal's Samir Nasri, was a huge one from his two-goal debut as a 60th-minute substitute. If the Champions League campaign was unfortunate, ten points being worth no more than third position and a Europa League place, and the FA Cup brought a home defeat by United in the third round when Vincent Kompany was sent off in the 11th minute, the domestic league campaign was momentous, with an ending rivalled in the whole history of league football only by Arsenal's last-minute triumph over Liverpool 23 years earlier.

An astounding 6-1 derby victory at Old Trafford in October, three of the goals coming in added time, put City five points clear at the top but when Mikel Arteta's late goal beat them at Arsenal on 8 April they were eight behind their neighbours with six to play.

Wigan and Everton then did them favours by taking unexpected points from United and when the return derby brought a 1-0 City win with Kompany's header they were back on top on goal difference. The final day, just like 1968, had the Manchester pair level on points but City knowing a win at home to Mark Hughes's relegation-threatened QPR would give them the title.

When United's game at Sunderland finished in a 1-0 victory Ferguson's team were actually top, City trailing 2-1 against ten men and in line to receive nothing more than yet another cup for cock-ups. But in the 90th minute Edin Džeko headed in a corner to equalise and in the fourth of five minutes added time Agüero played a one-two with Balotelli and drove in his 30th goal of the season to make his new team champions of England.

'Over the blue moon' was the *Daily Express* headline. 'City have never done the easy things, but they never used to be able to make it this hard, this dramatic, this utterly confounding,' said the *Manchester Evening News*.

13 May 2012: Manchester City 3 Queen's Park Rangers 2
Manchester City: Hart; Zabaleta, Kompany, Lescott, Clichy, Y. Touré (De Jong 44), Barry (Džeko 69), Silva, Nasri, Agüero, Tevez (Balotelli 75).
QPR: Kenny; Onuoha, Hill, Ferdinand, Taiwo; Mackie, Derry, Barton, Wright-Phillips; Zamora (Bothroyd 76), Cisse (Traore,59).

Further losses of £194.9m seemed a small price to pay at that moment, although UEFA was taking a close interest in the club's affairs. A wage bill of £174m, which on its own came to far more than total income, was hardly sustainable.

In summer 2013 as FA chairman Greg Dyke delivered a lecture in London on 'the future of the England team', bemoaning only 32 per cent of Premier League players being qualified for them, City spent £75m on six new foreigners. Fernandinho aside, it was not a vintage crop. The owners wanted the European title and finishing bottom of a difficult group, losing the FA Cup final to relegation-bound Wigan and conceding the Premier League title to United brought Mancini the sack with two games still to play.

The Chilean Manuel Pellegrini, who had spent nine seasons in Spain without winning a major trophy, was the unexpected replacement, tasked with winning 'five trophies in five years'. For the sixth summer in seven years City were the country's biggest net spenders, and this time they timed their run perfectly past Liverpool, Arsenal and Chelsea by winning the last five games to reclaim the title.

In a busy season they scored 156 goals, 22 of them on the way to winning the League Cup and 19 in a run to the knockout stage of the Champions League before defeat by Barcelona.

Pellegrini could neither repeat the title win nor achieve the desired European success despite a semi-final against Real Madrid in 2016 and three months before the end of the 2015/16 season he was told that he was to be replaced by a less surprising figure. Ever since chief executive Ferran Soriano and director of football Txiki Begiristain arrived from Barcelona in 2012, the name of Pep Guardiola had been mentioned as a future target. In 2013 he left Catalonia with two Champions Leagues to his name but went to Bayern Munich to win three successive league titles. Now City had the man they had wanted all along.

His first season was not easy amid such huge expectations, dropping away after starting with six straight Premier League wins to finish third and losing out on away goals to Monaco in an eventful 6-6 Champions League knockout round tie and 2-1 to Arsenal in the FA Cup semi-final.

In 2017/18, however, City were the dominant side, going unbeaten in the league until losing 4-3 at Anfield in January (the 23rd game), winning the title with five games to spare and a record 100 points. The League Cup was a bonus, the Champions League a disappointment once more when stunned by Liverpool at Anfield again and going out 5-1 on aggregate.

That remained the great target. After being heavily fined in 2014 and had transfer restrictions imposed for breaking Financial Fair Play regulations, they still seemed to have the backing to achieve it eventually.

* * * * *

In May 2001 **Manchester United** won their sixth Premier League title in eight years with only Blackburn in 1995 and Arsenal in 1998 having finished above them, in each case by a single point. Yet there was great news for the 19 other clubs as in January Sir Alex Ferguson had announced that he would retire at the end of the following season.

Concerned ever since 1999 that it would be impossible to top the Treble season, he was also disturbed by United's reluctance to confirm there would always be a role for him at the club. Doing something else with his life after the best part of 30 years in management came to seem as attractive as walking away aged 60, remembering as he did how his father had died so soon after finishing work.

Yet within a matter of weeks, 'I knew I'd made a mistake,' he told BTSport in 2015. 'It was impulse, the heat of the moment.'

Fortunately for United, his immediate family knew it too and on New Year's Eve, his 60th birthday, they demanded that he tell the club he had changed his mind; only just in time, as England manager Sven-Göran Eriksson later admitted he had been offered the job and was keen to accept.

The team had been unusually erratic in 2001/02, capable of coming from 3-0 down at Tottenham to win 5-3 yet also of losing an unheard of five games out of seven in the autumn and dropping to ninth place. Yet by the time the about-turn was officially announced at the start of February they were well on the way to winning 12 games out of 13, and were eventually only deprived of the runners-up spot to Arsenal in the last couple of matches. New signing Ruud van Nistelrooy, his move from PSV Eindhoven delayed for a year by injury, came up with 36 goals, ten of them in a Champions League run that should have ended in a Hampden Park final but stalled on away goals the round before against Bayer Leverkusen.

The next year United had their title back, in David Beckham's farewell after falling out with the manager and agreeing to join Real Madrid. The Spanish side had knocked Ferguson's team out of the Champions League in the tie which so enraptured Abramovich that for the 2003/04 season and beyond United had to contend with the most serious of challenges from not only Arsenal but the west London club too.

For two years running Ferguson's team finished behind the capital pair in third place, despite having acquired dazzling teenager Cristiano Ronaldo and Wayne Rooney, and then in 2005/06 United were only runners-up as Jose Mourinho, the man brought in at Chelsea to replace Claudio Ranieri, won his second successive title.

In all, 2005 was an unhappy year and by October *The Times* was headlining 'Downfall of the United empire'. In May they had dominated the goalless FA Cup final against Arsenal but lost it on penalties, and the American Glazer family bought a majority shareholding in the club, using loans that incurred huge interest payments. A group of disillusioned supporters soon formed their own club, FC United of Manchester, instead (see Interlude III). In November George Best died aged 59 and Roy Keane, an Old Trafford fixture since 1993, left after criticising his team-mates in typically uncompromising fashion for an MUTV interview that had to be withdrawn.

Mourinho was not a man for compromise either. Early in the 2007/08 season he was gone from Chelsea, having beaten United 1-0 in the 2007 FA Cup final but lost the title to them. So Avram Grant was the London side's manager when they took on United in the first all-English Champions League final on 21 May 2008. It could have been the second in succession but the previous year Milan had knocked United out in the last four and went on to meet Liverpool.

Boosted by £70m of new signings in Tevez, Owen Hargreaves, Anderson and Nani, United reached the final with Paul Scholes's thunderous second-leg goal to earn a 1-0 win against Barcelona. At the unholy hour of 10.45pm Moscow time on a soaking wet night they took on a Chelsea side they had only pipped to the Premier League title on the final day of the season.

Ronaldo headed United into the lead from Wes Brown's cross but Frank Lampard equalised just before half-time. A revitalised Chelsea improved in the second half but there was no further scoring even after extra time. For the penalty shoot-out, beginning well after 1am local time, Chelsea were without Didier Drogba, sent off for striking Nemanja Vidić. They led 4-3 after Ronaldo missed, but John Terry famously slipped and put his shot just wide. After Anderson and Ryan Giggs scored, Nicolas Anelka had his shot saved by Edwin van der Sar and United were European champions again, 50 years after Munich.

'On a fraught, angst-ridden, rain-washed night, United prevailed over Chelsea,' wrote Simon Barnes in *The Times*. 'They did so by a hair, but victors are victors and losers are losers.'

Champions League Final 2008: Chelsea 1 Manchester United 1 (United won 6-5 on penalties)

Chelsea: Cech; Essien, Carvalho, Terry, A. Cole, Makelele (Belletti 120), Ballack, Lampard, J.Cole (Anelka 99), Drogba, Malouda (Kalou 92).

Manchester United: Van der Sar; Brown (Anderson 120), Ferdinand, Vidić, Evra, Hargreaves, Scholes (Giggs 87), Carrick, Ronaldo, Rooney (Nani 101), Tevez.

In the excitement of victory Ferguson announced that this United had the makings of his best-ever team. They duly completed a championship hat-trick in an eventful 2008/09 season of 66 games, winning penalty shoot-outs against Spurs in the League Cup final and Portsmouth in the Community Shield but losing one to Everton in the FA Cup semi-final, and, most importantly of all, losing their European title in the Rome final with Barcelona 2-0 as their manager criticised 'shoddy defending'.

Now City were pushing to join the big league too. In the summer of 2009, while Mark Hughes's net transfer spending was almost £100m, United in contrast made a profit of £67m, reluctantly losing Ronaldo to Real Madrid and Tevez to their neighbours.

Chelsea did the Double in 2010, winning the league by a single point from United, who claimed it back a year later to overhaul Liverpool with their 19th title. Dimitar Berbatov, who scored five in the 7-1 win over Blackburn, was leading scorer with 20 but was left out of the Champions League final, in which playing at Wembley proved insufficient advantage to overcome Lionel Messi and Barcelona, who this time won 3-1.

Beating Arsenal 8-2 the following August, then losing 6-1 at home to City two months later, were two of the most extraordinary results of even Ferguson's extraordinary career. Jockeying with their neighbours at the top of the table all season they eventually lost out in the stunning last-minute of it (see City section above).

How long would Ferguson go on? Only one more year, it transpired, though this time the announcement was kept until a few days before the end of the season. He would have loved another European title but Real Madrid ended that dream with a 3-2 aggregate win in the round of 16 after Nani was sent off in the second leg with United in front. Equally important, however, if not more so, was putting City in their place and regaining the title.

United were still a dozen points clear despite losing 2-1 to them at Old Trafford in April, and Robin van Persie regained his scoring touch in time to confirm the championship with his hat-trick at home to Aston Villa. Now the retirement could be made public, with two games to go, a home win over Swansea and then an astonishing 5-5 draw at West Bromwich Albion.

Conceding three goals in the last ten minutes was hardly the way to say goodbye but a mellowed manager could not find it in him to complain.

'Emotional, very emotional' was all he could manage for the media, though his 'football – bloody hell!' refrain would have done just as well.

Fergie's final haul from 26 years at the club was 38 trophies, comprising 13 league titles, five FA Cups, four League Cups, two European Cups, one each of the European Cup Winners' Cup, Super Cup, Inter-Continental Cup and Club World Cup, and ten Community Shields. He had his wish to become a director and ambassador and the good wishes when he suffered a brain haemorrhage in May 2018 were touchingly widespread.

In retrospect it was significant that Albion's draw in the final game was earned by a hat-trick from Chelsea loanee Romelu Lukaku. Before the Belgian striker could begin reviving United fortunes under Jose Mourinho, however, there was an uncomfortable period of three seasons under first the anointed one, Everton's David Moyes, then Louis van Gaal.

'Your job now is to stand by the new manager,' Ferguson told Old Trafford supporters after his last home game. He might have been sending a message to directors too but within a matter of months he could not argue against the decision to dispense with the successor he had endorsed.

A less excitable chip off the Glaswegian block, Moyes had secured only Marouane Fellaini and Juan Mata to revamp a squad whose deficiencies may have been covered up by that last title success. He hadn't realised how big the club was, Ferguson insisted, criticising United's play for its slower tempo.

Soon after going out of the Champions League to Bayern, Moyes departed, his final game, cruelly, being a 2-0 defeat at Everton. United finished seventh after four games under caretaker Ryan Giggs, who then announced his retirement with a club record of 963 appearances, 672 of them in the league.

Allowing for the ban on English clubs, it was the first time the club had failed to qualify for European competition since 1987, which should have helped van Gaal, the self-confident Dutchman with a much greater track record of success than Moyes, from Ajax to Barcelona and Bayern Munich, as well as the Dutch national team. United's squad was 'broken' he said but in two years he mended it only enough to finish fourth and fifth, signing off with an FA Cup final win over Crystal Palace, by which time the world knew he was on his way out and that Mourinho was coming in.

The total of 49 goals in van Gaal's second season was the first time United had ever scored less than 50 in the Premier League. Mourinho's side managed only 54 in finishing sixth as he lost out in the eagerly anticipated head-to-head with old adversary Pep Guardiola at City but salvaged the campaign by winning the Europa League against Ajax and the League Cup against Southampton.

His second season, with Lukaku replacing Zlatan Ibrahimović as the main striker, also involved playing second fiddle to Guardiola as runners-up to City's runaway champions as well as a frustrating FA Cup final defeat by Chelsea.

Few believed Mourinho was getting the best out of either Alexis Sánchez or the £89m Paul Pogba, and the 'noisy neighbours' of Ferguson's description were growing more boisterous by the year.

* * * * *

At the end of the 1989/90 season, **Liverpool** had won 18 league titles. Almost 20 years later they were still stuck on the same number and Manchester United, from being 11 behind, had overtaken them. Gerard Houllier, Rafa Benitez, Roy Hodgson, Kenny Dalglish in his second stint and Brendan Rodgers had perished in attempting to end the drought. The consolation for Benitez was in having contributed to the one accomplishment the Kop could crow about: five European Cups to the other Reds' mere three.

Houllier's memorial was the 2000/01 season, his third at Anfield, which he began without a trophy and ended with three. In the League Cup final, the first major event in Cardiff while Wembley was being rebuilt, his team needed penalties to see off Birmingham City from the division below, but they were more impressive in beating Arsenal from 1-0 down with Michael Owen's two goals to take the FA Cup, and then four days later in a roller-coaster UEFA Cup final against Alaves, eventually won 5-4 after extra time .

It seemed a prelude to greater things, like breaking the duopoly of United and Arsenal, who had held the top two positions in the

Premier League for four successive years. The following season, however, during which Houllier had heart surgery before returning to inspire an emotional Anfield victory over Roma, Arsenal held them off comfortably by seven points, and in 2002/03 Liverpool built a seven-point lead by November, then lost four games out of five and were never in contention again. They finished fifth, missing out on Champions League qualification to Chelsea on the final day, and Houllier signings from France like El Hadji Diouf carried the can.

He needed a big season in 2003/04 but despite moving up to fourth, the Reds scored only 55 goals and were 30 points behind unbeaten champions Arsenal. Houllier was replaced by Benitez, who inherited a Champions League team and became a hero for evermore in one match; or rather half a match.

On the manager's own admission Liverpool did not have a squad to become champions of Europe. Yet after a Premier League campaign with even fewer goals (52) than the previous year, ending below Everton in fifth place, they found themselves having beaten Juventus and Chelsea and in a Champions League Final in Istanbul against a clearly superior AC Milan squad.

At 2-0 down approaching half-time and with Harry Kewell already off injured, Benitez was wondering how he might rally his troops. Then Hernán Crespo scored again. The players walked off with their heads down, Jamie Carragher believing their main task was to prevent a massacre by five or six. In the dressing room Benitez silenced them, then announced a 3-5-2 formation for the second half with Didi Hamann, who most people thought should have started the game, to be brought on along with Djibril Cisse. It was gently pointed out that Liverpool would then have 12 men, though the feeling was that a round dozen would still not be enough.

Cisse would have to wait until the 85th minute, by which time, astonishingly, Liverpool were level. Defiant supporters bellowing 'You'll Never Walk Alone' lifted the players, as did the manager's exhortations not to let them down.

Gerrard, leading from the front, did what they desperately needed by heading an early goal and when Vladimir Šmicer (playing his last game for the club) added a second within two minutes the whole team believed again. Xabi Alonso's equaliser, following up his own penalty, meant Liverpool had scored three times in six minutes. Milan had almost all the best chances for the remaining hour – above all Andrei Shevchenko's double attempt somehow thwarted by Jerzy Dudek – against opponents who in extra time looked dead on their feet.

In the shoot-out, however, nerves got to Carlo Ancelotti's team first, missing their opening two kicks and losing by 3-2 when Dudek, replicating Bruce Grobbelaar's wobbly legs and windmill arms from 1984, defied Shevchenko once more.

Champions League Final 2005: Liverpool 3 Milan 3 (Liverpool won 3-2 on penalties)
Liverpool: Dudek; Finnan (Hamann 46), Carragher, Hyypia, Traore, Alonso, Luis Garcia, Gerrard, Riise, Kewell (Šmicer 23), Baros (Cisse 85).
Milan: Dida; Cafu, Stam, Nesta, Maldini, Pirlo, Gattuso (Rui Costa 112), Seedorf (Serginho 86), Kaká, Shevchenko, Crespo (Tomasson, 85).

There were dramas throughout what should have been a celebratory summer.

The question of whether Liverpool would be allowed to defend their European title, having finished only fifth in the league, was resolved, but they would have to start from the first qualifying round in early July. Chairman David Moores was coming round to the idea of selling the club and then Steven Gerrard, not convinced that Liverpool wanted badly enough to keep him out of Chelsea's clutches, handed in a transfer request to force their hand.

His gamble paid off and finally on 8 July Gerrard agreed to stay, four days before the opening Champions League match against little Welsh club Total Network Solutions. Gerrard celebrated with a hat-trick and rewarded the fans further (though not the one who had burnt a shirt outside Anfield) by saving the 2006 FA Cup Final.

The spirit of Istanbul was able to sustain all those who had experienced it and in Cardiff the skipper's thunderous shot in the last minute brought the score back to 3-3 against a surprisingly effective West Ham, who had earlier led 2-0. Once again Liverpool prevailed on penalties.

In February 2007 Moores made a fortune by selling to two Americans, Tom Hicks and George Gillett, but even with a few dollars more and signings like Fernando Torres at £26.5m, Liverpool were still unable to break what had become a United-Chelsea stranglehold. For three seasons all they could do was challenge Arsenal for third spot, the bonus being to make another Champions League final in 2007. After beating Chelsea on penalties in the semi-final, it was lost to Milan, whereupon Benitez walked round Athens and the hotel corridors for four hours with his chief scout and decided to make an impassioned plea through the media for greater and quicker investment.

'If we don't change things we will not be contenders,' was the message, but in November, when he wanted more planning for January purchases, the reply came back 'in capital letters' from Hicks, 'concentrate on coaching the team'.

That season the Reds finished fourth and reached the Champions League semi-final again but lost 4-3 to Chelsea. The following one, 2008/09, they led the Premier League at the turn of the year, prompting a strange 'facts' rant about Ferguson from Benitez, whose team finished four points behind United in second place despite winning 4-1 at Old Trafford and losing only two league games, at Tottenham and Middlesbrough.

A bad season in 2009/10 proved to be Benitez's last. Torres and Gerrard almost matched their combined 30 goals from the previous campaign, but had less support and the team dropped to seventh, the worst since 1999. A poor Champions League campaign condemned them to the Europa League where Torres's old club Atletico Madrid beat them on away goals in the semi-final after a 2-2 draw. Benitez departed 'disappointed, hurt and sad'.

As Roy Hodgson struggled in his first few months there was better news for supporters when the unpopular Hicks and Gillett finally sold up. Nothing had come of the new stadium they promised on taking over and debts stood at £350m when fellow countryman John Henry took over in October 2010, inheriting a team in depths unknown for many years: from 16th to 18th to 19th they went after defeats by Blackpool at Anfield and Everton at Goodison (in the first game after the sale).

The old chant of 'Dalglish' was being heard again. Hodgson got the Reds up to 12th place and would have been pleased to read in the *Sunday Times* on 2 January that 'Hodgson survives for rest of season'. In fact, he was sacked a week later after a 3-1 loss at his previous English club, Blackburn.

So fans got the man they wanted. King Kenny was back, just in time to lose an FA Cup tie at Old Trafford, watch Blackpool complete the double over them and endure an astonishing transfer window, buying Luis Suárez and the less successful Andy Carroll, after selling Torres to Chelsea for £50m. Dalglish soon had them up to sixth, where they stayed to the end of the season.

The new owners backed him in the summer to the tune of £46m spent on Stewart Downing, Jordan Henderson and Charlie Adam but there was trouble ahead. During United's visit to Anfield in October, Suárez was found to have used a racial insult to Patrice Evra, bringing an eight-match ban and £40,000 fine. In the return game the Uruguayan refused to shake Evra's hand; Dalglish, still true to the old principle of protecting his players, came out of it badly and had to apologise.

A few months later he was sacked after winning the League Cup (yet another success on penalties) but losing the FA Cup final to Chelsea after beating Everton in the semi, and finishing no higher than eighth.

Brendan Rodgers, arriving from Swansea, was undermined by a bad start to the 2012/13 season but rose from 18th to 9th before Philippe Coutinho and Daniel Sturridge were signed at the start of January and helped a push to finish seventh, after going out of the FA Cup to Oldham, and Suárez collected a ten-match ban for biting Chelsea's Branislav Ivanović. 'We're still the top club here [on Merseyside],' Rodgers insisted before the derby in which a goalless draw helped Everton stay above them in sixth place.

The following season should have brought that desperately desired first title since 1990. Top from the end of March to the start of May, Liverpool then lost 2-0 at home to a weakened Chelsea with Gerrard slipping over to let in Demba Ba for the first goal, and from 3-0 up after 79 minutes of a televised game at Crystal Palace they drew 3-3.

A fast finishing Manchester City came through to win it by two points, both teams passing 100 league goals with Suárez claiming 31 of Liverpool's. Defence essentially let them down when it mattered.

Rodgers needed to build on second place but was unable to keep Suárez, who went to Barcelona for £65m, spent on three Southampton players, Emre Can and controversially Mario Ballotelli. 'Sometimes you have to take a risk with people,' Rodgers said. But the team went backwards as goals dropped from 101 to a calamitous 52 and sixth place. Gerrard, top scorer with only nine (of which five were penalties), was briefly dropped and for once could not inspire the required Champions League revival. As 2014 turned into 2015, it was announced he was going to LA Galaxy, piqued at not having been offered a new contract the previous summer. His miserable last few months included an FA Cup semi-final defeat by Villa, a red card 38 seconds after coming on against United and a humiliating 6-1 defeat at Stoke in his last game, his 710th for the club.

Some thought Rodgers would go and he survived only until October, given just eight league games, of which Liverpool won three to lie tenth in the table. Jürgen Klopp was tipped early on as successor and arrived only four days later. Highly regarded throughout Europe for a bold approach, he had left Borussia Dortmund at the end of the previous season with two Bundesliga titles and a Champions League final to his name. 'Arsenal's football is a silent song,' he once said before Dortmund met them. 'I like heavy metal.'

By the end of the season he had the Reds making good music again, as away wins by 5-4 at Norwich (in the 95th minute) and 6-0 at Villa suggested. They reached the League Cup final, lost on penalties to City, and the Europa League final after knocking out United and Dortmund, only to be beaten 3-1 by Seville.

Thirty goals from 11 league games to start 2016/17 confirmed that excitement was back on the agenda, putting Klopp's adventurers briefly top, but it could not be sustained. However, fourth place got them back into the Champions League and a run all the way to the final after knocking out City. Alas, meeting Cristiano Ronaldo's Real Madrid in Kiev brought only tears for souvenirs, first from Mo Salah, taken off with an injured shoulder in the first half and then goalkeeper Loris Karius, whose two errors cost goals in a 3-1 defeat.

Salah's consolation was to break the Premier League record for a 38-game season with 32 goals and become Player of the Year as Liverpool finished third. Beating runaway winners City 4-3, then losing to bottom club Swansea a week later, however, summed up a lingering unpredictability not solved by paying £75m for a centre-half, Virgil Van Dijk.

Meanwhile there was a momentous result for the club off the field in April 2016 when the hearings into the Hillsborough disaster overturned the verdict of accidental death at the original inquest and decided that the 96 supporters were unlawfully killed.

The families had closure of a sort after 27 years and the citation for Dalglish's knighthood in June 2018 made his contribution clear, 'He selflessly made himself available to the families of the bereaved, attending most of the funerals, organising hospital visits and attending annual memorial services held at Anfield. He has been a steadfast supporter of the families.'

* * * * *

Everton remained in their neighbours' shadow for another long period, finishing above them only three times (2005, 2012 and 2013) in over 30 years from 1987 and enduring 17 derbies without a win from the start of 2011 to 2018.

Walter Smith's four years in charge ended in March 2002 after an FA Cup defeat at Middlesbrough and led to David Moyes being given his big chance after admired work at Preston. He immediately lifted them to seventh in 2003 (they had been third at one point) before missing out on a UEFA Cup place with a poor finish, and apart from an unexpected blip in the bottom four the following season, with only one away win all season and nobody – not even Wayne Rooney – reaching double figures, Moyes had returned them to being a top-six club.

In the summer of 2004 there were pessimistic noises from supporters after Rooney, outstanding at Euro 2004, was sold to Manchester United for £23m and Tim Cahill from Millwall was the only notable signing. Yet the Australian midfielder became leading scorer and on the back of a tight defence the Blues were in a Champions League place virtually all season and qualified, bizarrely, straight after a 7-0 defeat at Arsenal. Moyes was named LMA Manager of the Year.

The Champions League qualifying round draw was cruel, however, bringing a talented Villareal to Goodison to win both legs 2-1 and start their run to the semi-final.

From 2006/07 the Blues were in the top six for three more seasons, the finances improving sufficiently (and helped by a UEFA Cup fourth-round run in 2007/08) to allow for record signings like Andrew Johnson (£8.6m) and Yakubu Aiyegbeni (£11.25m), both of whom were leading scorers for a season with Cahill always chipping in from midfield.

There had been regular talk too of a new stadium, or even a ground-share with Liverpool if the local council would build it, and in 2009 proposals for a £78m project in Kirkby, eight miles from the city centre, were turned down to the delight of those supporters who had started a Keep Everton In Our City movement.

The Blues finished fifth again in 2009 and reached the FA Cup final by beating champions United on penalties in the last four. In the final Louis Saha set a record by scoring after just 25 seconds but Chelsea recovered to win 2-1.

With Manchester City now among the big spenders and Tottenham improved, the top eight became a more realistic aim. It was achieved in 2010, despite little investment in the squad, and starting with a 6-1 home defeat by Arsenal, and for the next four seasons too, including a fifth and sixth place.

Everton were never high scorers even before Saha left for Tottenham in January 2012, after which Moyes completed ten years at the club with another creditable seventh place, followed by sixth, ahead of Liverpool each time.

It was enough to earn the manager what turned out to be the poisoned chalice of the Old Trafford job. Roberto Martinez was a pleasing appointment from Wigan Athletic, bringing four players with him and finishing fifth in his first season. Romelu Lukaku, on loan from Chelsea, scored 15 league goals and doing the double over United for the first time since 1969 spelt the end of Moyes.

Signing Lukaku permanently for £28m did not have the same effect; he scored almost as many goals in a run to Europa League round of 16 as his ten in the Premier League, where Everton managed only 11th place after losing Ross Barkley and John Stones for long spells.

The 2015/16 season was most notable not for Lukaku's goals or a League Cup semi-final (lost to Manchester City) but for Iranian Farhad Moshiri taking almost a 50 per cent stake in the club and Martinez being sacked after a second successive 11th place.

Ronald Koeman came in after reaching the top six with Southampton and had Everton up to seventh as Lukaku scored 25 league goals before going to Manchester United for £90m, half of which was spent on Swansea's Gylfi Sigurdsson. With Rooney moving back the other way on a sentimental journey and Barkley also wanting to play in a similar position, the right blend was missing for a poor 2017/18 season. Koeman was soon sacked and Sam Allardyce proved an unpopular appointment despite lifting them from 13th when he arrived in December to eighth at the finish. He then made way for the man they originally wanted, Marco Silva.

Living next to Liverpool was as tough as ever.

* * * * *

From the bottom four out of 92 clubs in 1994 with gates of 1,300, **Wigan** were a Premier League club within 11 years. Along with Oldham's ascent in the previous decade it was one of the more unlikely stories and they survived eight years before the unparalleled achievement of winning the FA Cup and dropping out of the top tier inside four days.

Dave Whelan, owner since 1995, remained the force behind the club in the new decade, when they were initially contenders in the third tier despite the departures of Bruce Rioch and then Steve Bruce during a single season (2000/01).

Merseysider Paul Jewell took over in the summer of 2001 and after a settling-in season that included an FA Cup defeat at home to Canvey Island he led them to the title in 2003 with only four defeats and 100 points. Beating West Bromwich Albion, Manchester City and Fulham in the League Cup before a derby defeat by Blackburn suggested possibilities that were borne out with seventh place in the second tier, missing a play-off place in the final minute of the campaign, and then a triumphant 2004/05 as runners-up to Sunderland.

The Latics went unbeaten until November (17 games) and had a crowd of almost 20,000 to see elevation confirmed on the last day at home to Reading. Nathan Ellington and Jason Roberts were a formidable striking partnership with 45 league goals.

Despite selling Ellington to West Bromwich Albion and naturally being made favourites to come back down, they were never in trouble; sitting in second place at the start of November and winning eight away games (the fourth best in the league) to finish tenth. They reached the League Cup final too on a famous night at the Emirates Stadium when Roberts's last-minute goal in the semi-final beat Arsenal. Manchester United ran out 4-0 winners at Cardiff.

Tenth was the high point of the club's history but there were seven more Premier League campaigns. The first of them was survived by a single goal, when David Unsworth's penalty won the last-day game at Sheffield United, sending the Blades down instead. Jewell retired from the fray and full-back Leighton Baines left for Everton but 14th was another respectable finish for a low-scoring side after eight successive defeats brought Bruce back to replace Chris Hutchings.

He had them up to 11th in 2009, albeit with only 34 goals again, before leaving to join Sunderland and paving the way for former midfielder Roberto Martinez. The Spaniard could not find a goalscoring striker either and finished in the bottom five for two seasons running, the first of them including a 9-1 defeat away to Tottenham, who scored eight times in 40 second-half minutes.

The next two seasons were similar and led to an inevitable fate, with an unexpected twist. Staying up by winning five of the last six games in 2012, the Latics could not pull off the same trick a year later and went down three points short, ironically having scored more goals (47) than in any previous Premier League campaign.

The twist was provided by the FA Cup, in which beating only one other Premier League team (Everton) earned a place at Wembley, where Ben Watson's header in the last minute stunned Manchester City and won the club's first major trophy.

They returned to Wembley to lose to Manchester United in the Community Shield and enjoyed half a dozen low-key Europa League games (another first for the club) before Uwe Rösler, replacing the unsuccessful Owen Coyle, launched a run to the Championship play-offs (losing to 2-1 on aggregate to QPR) and the FA Cup semi-final, losing to Arsenal on penalties after beating Manchester City again. Still, however, nobody scored more than seven league goals.

The following season was a shock, as three different managers failed to prevent a return to the third tier. Rösler left in November and Malky Mackay in April, Gary Caldwell failing to pull off the Houdini act. There were only three home wins and this time the leading scorer (James McClean) had just six.

Chairman Whelan, a hard-nosed businessman who understood but hated football's mad-house finances, stood down that year, giving way to his 23-year-old grandson David Sharpe, who could not have had a more up-and-down (or down-and-up) reign.

At last a real goalscorer was found in Northern Ireland international Will Grigg, whose haul of 25 brought the League One championship in 2016, only to be followed by relegation again, then promotion straight back under Paul Cook with Grigg on fire once more.

* * * * *

Accompanying Wigan back to the upper two tiers in 2018 were **Blackburn**, one of many clubs suffering from ownership traumas. Jack Walker was ill from the start of the century and died in August 2000, but his trust continued putting in money until 2007, after which the disastrous decision was made three years later to sell to the Venky's group of poultry farmers.

In March 2000 Graeme Souness replaced Brian Kidd as manager and enjoyed 'four of my happiest years'. The 2000/01 season was dedicated to Walker and happily ended in promotion back to the Premier League as runners-up, beating Burnley 5-0 to complete the double over them and securing promotion at Preston.

Signing the gifted creator Tugay, who Souness knew from Turkey, they finished tenth and won the League Cup for the first time by beating Spurs 2-1 with goals from Matt Jansen (later to suffer a bad moped crash on holiday in Rome that left him in a coma) plus Andy Cole.

The manager had good characters in what he called a 'self-policing dressing room', something he had found missing at Liverpool. In the second season back Rovers were up to sixth place, reaching another League Cup semi-final that was lost to Manchester United (4-2 on aggregate) and returning to European football but losing to Celtic, for whom Chris Sutton scored at Ewood Park.

Souness was disappointed at having to sell Damien Duff and David Dunn for a total of £22.5m and after finishing in the bottom six in 2004, left for Newcastle – a bad move that put him off management for life.

Successor Mark Hughes, making an impressive start to a long career in Premier League management, then had Rovers sixth and seventh during his four-year spell, reaching FA Cup semi-finals, lost to Arsenal and Chelsea, in the other two seasons. Craig Bellamy, then Benni McCarthy and Paraguyan Roque Santa Cruz provided the goals, the latter soon following Hughes to Manchester City.

In 2007, however, the Walker trustees decided that the £97m spent by the man of steel and then his estate was sufficient, and declared that Rovers were for sale. Although the size of the club, its gates and the town were clearly below that of Lancashire's big four, it seemed an attractive proposition, especially once Sam Allardyce restored the team to the top half of the Premier League in 2009/10 as well as reaching an eventful League Cup semi-final, which was lost 7-4 over two legs to Aston Villa.

The purchase by Venky's for £23m in November 2010 broke new ground in taking ownership of an English club as far as India, though the firm's main interest appeared to be promoting international recognition for their brand.

The regime was shrouded in controversy from the moment Allardyce was dismissed three weeks later, and never recovered. A 7-1 defeat at Manchester United immediately after the takeover did not help him, but nor, he felt, did the influence of agent Jerome Anderson, whose client Steve Kean was promoted to become manager.

Rovers slumped to 15th and sold Phil Jones to United and by the following January supporters were staging a 24-hour protest outside the ground with Kean's team well on the way to relegation. Yakubu's 16 goals could not keep them up and it was a home defeat by Wigan that confirmed the drop, along with Bolton.

The 2012/13 season was an extraordinary one of four managers, one outstanding signing and tumbling from top of the table to a relegation fight, all played out against growing supporter unrest with the owners. Kean led them to the head of the table after half a dozen games and they were still third when he resigned in late-September after a fan boycott and the appointment by Venky's of a 'global football adviser', Shebby Singh.

New signing Jordan Rhodes from Huddersfield had notched up the first of his 27 league goals and continued to do so as three more managers – Henning Berg, Michael Appleton and Gary Bowyer – arrived before the end of the season, which ended only four points clear of relegation. Bowyer did a reasonable job in difficult circumstances, finishing eighth and ninth over the next two years, but was sacked in November 2015, Paul Lambert seeing out the season and Owen Coyle being sacked on the way to demotion to the third tier a year later.

At last there was some better news for supporters as Venky's hinted that they might sell and Tony Mowbray, one of the more popular appointments, returned the team to the Championship in 2018. Then the owners released a statement saying the club was 'more united on and off the pitch than it has ever been'. Promotion or not, many begged to differ.

* * * * *

After playing second fiddle to old rivals Blackburn during the Jack Walker years, **Burnley** finally joined them in the Premier League for one season in 2009, but unlike their neighbours, they were able to return. In 2018 they even made it back into Europe after a wait of 51 years, having been one game away from going out of the Football League in that time.

There was only one season together in the Championship, 2000/01, before Rovers ascended, leaving the Clarets seventh, one place outside the play-offs for the first of two successive seasons. The second one was particularly anti-climatic after Stan Ternent had them top of the table until a 5-1 drubbing at Manchester City in late-December. Ternent was manager for a six-year period, ending in 2004 when they dropped to 19th despite Nathan Blake's 19 goals.

Steve Cotterill could not bring about any great improvement in three seasons, although his side knocked Liverpool out of the FA Cup in 2005, but Owen Coyle began his rounds of four local clubs with promotion back to the top tier in 2009 after an absence of 33 years.

The Clarets beat Sheffield United at Wembley in the play-off final with Wade Elliott's goal in what should have been a second trip that season to the national stadium; in January's League Cup semi-final Coyle's team were minutes away from retrieving a 4-1 first-leg deficit to knock out Tottenham. Had away goals counted after 90 minutes as in European football, they would have done so.

With only £3m striker Steven Fletcher as an expensive addition, they became the first promoted team to win their opening four home games in the Premier League, claiming champions Manchester United and Everton as the first two victims. At the turn of the year, however, Coyle outraged supporters by moving to Bolton, the one English club he had played for.

From 14th place and already on the slide, Burnley continued to slip and in winning two games out of 27 were relegated with a 4-0 defeat at Liverpool. They had lost 17 of 19 away games and conceded 82 goals.

There were three moderate Championship seasons before Sean Dyche, appointed the previous October when Eddie Howe returned to Bournemouth, led a promotion charge in 2013/14. Despite having sold strikers Jay Rodriguez and Charlie Austin in successive seasons, Burnley had in Danny Ings and Sam Vokes a pair of well-matched forwards who contributed 41 goals between them, while the ever-present Tom Heaton in goal had the division's best defensive record. Staying second from early-February, they beat Wigan to confirm promotion with two games to spare.

Again it was a one-season stay, Vokes missing much of the campaign with a knee injury and Ings managing only 11 of the mere 28 total. At a crucial stage of the season Burnley scored only one goal in nine games as they came straight back down.

But sensible husbandry of finance built up over two Premier League campaigns, together with parachute payments, meant the Clarets were nevertheless on a reasonable footing and could even afford to splash out on the right player, who turned out to be Brentford striker Andre Gray. He scored 23 times as they finished the 2015/16 season undefeated after Boxing Day and Championship winners ahead of Middlesbrough.

Even so, to qualify for the Europa League two years later was a remarkable feat and another tribute to Dyche. Winning away to champions Chelsea on the opening day, and drawing at Anfield and Old Trafford, they were seventh almost all season, the highest finish since 1974.

* * * * *

The Burnley supporters who labelled Owen Coyle 'Judas' for walking out on them in 2010 – he preferred 'Moses', for having led them to the PL (Promised Land and Premier League) – were delighted to see **Bolton** join them back in the Championship in 2012 and then sink further.

In his first full season he had Wanderers in 14th place, and lost an FA Cup semi-final 5-0 against Stoke City, but in his next they were relegated by a couple of points after losing a half-time lead, again against Stoke.

That season the FA Cup campaign was remembered for a potential tragedy. The quarter-final tie on 17 March at Tottenham had to be abandoned after midfielder Fabrice Muamba suffered a cardiac arrest and almost died. He recovered but apart from a brief appearance in a testimonial match never played again.

Supporters were losing faith with Coyle and after dropping to 18th in the Championship with a run of results that started in defeat at Burnley, he was sacked. Dougie Freedman lifted them to seventh but worse was to come under Neil Lennon, who finished 18th, faced a transfer embargo and then left in March 2016 before relegation to the third tier was confirmed.

What had been bubbling under all this time was concern about the club's finances. Local businessman Eddie Davies, 'Lord of the Manor of Farnsworth', had ploughed money into the club since joining the board in 1999 but run up heavy losses. Debts were £64m in 2009 and a staggering £163.8m by 2013, having lost more than £50m in a single year. All that kept the club afloat was Davies's promise not to call in his loans of a reported £170m.

He finally escaped in March 2016, becoming honorary president, in the week the club faced a winding up order in the high court. A consortium fronted by Dean Holdsworth took over but within a year the former striker was in dispute with chairman Ken Anderson.

Promotion back to the Championship was seen as financially imperative and Phil Parkinson achieved it in second place, a healthier crowd of 22,590 seeing them home. Equally important was staying there, helped by the transfer embargo being lifted in September 2017. It was still a dreadfully nervous finish on the final day of the season; with three minutes to play Bolton were losing 2-1 at home to Nottingham Forest and going down but goals from Adam Le Fondre and 38-year-old Aaron Wilbraham kept them up.

'Never before in the storied existence of Bolton Wanderers have emotions lurched so violently from despair to unbridled joy, as they did on Sunday afternoon,' reported the local *Evening News*.

* * * * *

Extremes of despair and joy were hardly unknown to **Blackpool** followers in the new century.

From relegation back to the bottom tier in 2000, they rose to the Championship seven years later and then to the Premier League itself in 2010 for a brave season that so nearly kept them there. After that, alas, the only way was down, back whence they came in the space of five short years, and it all played out amid familiar dramas in the boardroom and beyond.

Owner Owen Oyston was out of prison by the time of relegation, followed by an immediate return engineered by Steve McMahon as manager, when Leyton Orient were beaten 4-2 in the Cardiff play-off final. McMahon stayed for three seasons, which included two further Cardiff victories in the Football League Trophy (2002 and 2004).

Simon Grayson, moving up from the reserve team and first-team caretaker, also did a three-year stint, which was successful enough to earn him a promotion to Leeds United. Under him in 2006/07 the Seasiders rose from the bottom four of League One in September to finish third and were again successful in the play-offs, beating Oldham in the semi-final and then Yeovil at Wembley.

Grayson kept them up at the higher level with two points to spare after dropping from 12th to 19th over the last dozen games, then moved on to to Elland Road in December 2008, which brought the inimitable Ian Holloway to the seaside for the following season.

There was some apparently encouraging news at last off the field when the Latvian businessman Valeri Belokon, introduced to the club by Oyston in 2006, made sufficient money available for Holloway to break the club's transfer record by paying Scottish champions Rangers £500,000 for midfielder Charlie Adam. It was almost twice as much as they had ever paid before and proved superb value when the Scot led the goalscorers and helped cajole an entertaining team all the way to the Premier League.

On the final day of the normal season they edged Swansea out of contention by a point, then saw off Nottingham Forest 6-4 in a typically high-scoring play-off semi-final and defeated Cardiff 3-2 at Wembley with more than 82,000 spectators seeing five goals before half-time. Brett Ormerod, in his second spell at the club six years on from his first, scored what proved to be the crucial one.

'Every dog has its day and today it's woof day, I just want to bark,' was the sort of quote that endeared the madcap manager to the media and to underdogs of every kind. Like most play-off winners, Holloway's team were made favourites for relegation, not least because their average gate of 8,611 at a ground with only two permanent stands had been the second-lowest in the Championship. Up among the big boys, however, they played out a memorable season, encapsulated in the first two results – a 4-0 win at Wigan followed by a 6-0 defeat at Arsenal.

At the turn of the year they were eighth, having beaten Liverpool 2-1, but repeating that result in January was one of only three successes in the second half of the campaign. Even on the last day they raised hopes by taking the lead at Old Trafford, only to lose 4-2. Adam and DJ Campbell were among the top dozen scorers in the Premier League, but conceding 78 goals was too many. 'We had a go and we shocked 'em a little bit,' Holloway said of the final game, though he might have been talking of the season as a whole.

Even though he was concerned about how few players would stay, he managed to recruit the ever-reliable Kevin Phillips, who scored sufficient goals (16) to earn another Wembley visit, only for the play-off luck to run out; West Ham won 2-1 in the final and the manager decided he could do no more and left for Crystal Palace.

From there it was a slippery slope. Michael Appleton stayed for only two months and Paul Ince went from one extreme to the other, presiding over the Seasiders's best-ever start in 2013/14, then getting one point from ten games and the sack.

Staying in the Championship by two points, they were rock-bottom the following year and in 2015/16 went straight through League One back to the bottom division, before a happier 2017. Under Gary Bowyer there was another exciting play-off semi-final, won 6-5 on aggregate against Luton, then a 2-1 victory in the final over Exeter City.

Crowds were 50 per cent down at 3,456 because of a supporters' boycott, but later in the year the Oystons finally agreed to put the club up for sale. That followed a high court judgment that Owen and Karl were guilty of 'illegitimate stripping' of the club in moving almost £27m out of it. The money, and more, had to be paid to Belikon, who was by that time banned – unlike the Oystons – under the English Football League's feeble owners and directors test. With all that going on and the future as cloudy as ever, a mid-table place in League One reflected well on Bowyer.

* * * * *

From being champions of the Second Division (the third tier) in 2000, **Preston** continued to enhance the reputation of manager David Moyes, being one game away from going through to the Premier League. That was the all-Lancashire play-off final, lost 3-0 to Bolton, who to be fair had finished nine points ahead after doing the double over them.

Another promotion challenge then earned Moyes his big move to Everton, after which Craig Brown's team sat in the middle of the table for two seasons and a third successive Scottish manager, the combative Billy Davies, had them to the play-offs two years running. In 2005 they beat Derby 2-0 on aggregate but lost the final by the only goal to West Ham, and the following season went out 3-1 in the semi-final to Leeds.

With Paul Simpson replacing Davies, who left for Derby, there should have been a third successive tilt at the play-offs in 2007 but after sitting second for a long time, North End finished a point short. Consolation of a sort was provided by David Nugent, who scored 15 goals, becoming their first player since Tom Finney to win an England cap.

Portsmouth paid £6m for him and without his goals, Preston's form cost Simpson his job. In 2009 Alan Irvine had them back in the play-offs for the third time in five seasons, narrowly beaten 2-1 by Sheffield United in the semi-final, but Irvine and then Darren Ferguson both paid for poor first halves of a season with dismissal. The latter's sacking infuriated Sir Alex Ferguson, who recalled the loan players his son had borrowed from Manchester United.

Phil Brown could not prevent relegation from the Championship after a dreadful run of six points from 14 games and it was a struggle for two seasons down in League One. Peter Ridsdale replaced Maurice Lindsay, the former Rugby Football League chief executive, as chairman and Simon Grayson did better as manager following his four years at Leeds.

For two seasons he steered them to the play-offs and, best of all, ended the long run of nine failures (a record) at that crucial stage. Blackburn native Joe Garner scored 18 and 25 goals respectively in the two campaigns and although the first ended in a 4-2 semi-final defeat by Rotherham the second brought emphatic triumphs over Chesterfield (4-0 in the semi-final) and then Swindon, also 4-0 with a Wembley hat-trick by Jermaine Beckford.

Back in the Championship the Whites were a model of mid-table consistency, twice finishing 11th and after Grayson was lured to Sunderland, Alex Neil continued the honourable tradition of Prestonian Scots with a seventh place, only missing out on yet another play-off venture on the last day.

* * * * *

As the rich got richer, the poor were always likely to do the other thing. So if holding on to Football League status seemed a modest achievement for near-neighbours Bury, Oldham and Rochdale, they would note that Stockport County and Tranmere Rovers failed to do so; while Accrington made a romantic return, Morecambe and Fleetwood arrived, and AFC Fylde and Salford City became contenders to emulate them.

Bury sank back into the lowest division (2002) under Andy Preece, just missed the play-offs (2003) then settled into the lower half of the table. In 2007 they had a narrow escape under former Manchester United junior Chris Casper, ending up four points from automatic relegation; in the same season any hope of a financial boost from the FA Cup ended when they were disqualified from the competition for fielding an ineligible player in their 3-1 second-round replay win over Chester City.

Chester took the prize money instead and went on to play Ipswich in the third round.

In 2009, however, just short of automatic promotion, the Shakers made the play-offs, leading Shrewsbury until the 88th minute of the second leg then losing on penalties. Two years later under Alan Knill there was no mistake, a strong campaign ending in second place with 27 goals from Ryan Lowe, who established a club record by scoring in nine successive games.

In two years they were back down but two further seasons brought promotion again. Lee Clark got them to safety in 2017 but the following season included an embarrassing 3-0 FA Cup defeat at home to non-league Woking, chairman Stewart Day criticising a lack of 'fight, passion and desire'. Relegation ensued once more, nine points clear at the bottom and a full 15 from safety.

* * * * *

Oldham had a new owner from 2001 in Chris Moore, whose talk of Premier League football within five years brought back memories of Ken Bates's wild optimism. He quickly got rid of managers Andy Ritchie and then Mick Wadsworth but gave Iain Dowie sufficient financial support to get into the third tier play-offs in 2003, losing 2-1 on aggregate to Queens Park Rangers.

Familiar financial problems led to administration the following October and prompted Dowie to leave for Crystal Palace, lifting the London side to the play-offs and the Premier League in a remarkable run from 21st place.

Meanwhile Oldham were taken over by Simon Corney, a Londoner working in New York City, and two American colleagues. Brian Talbot's best achievement as manager was knocking Manchester City out of the FA Cup in 2005 with a goal by Mancunian Scott Vernon, but John Sheridan was more successful than Talbot or Ronnie Moore. His team were sixth in 2007, well beaten by Blackpool in the play-offs, and eighth the following year.

Two points above relegation in 2010 after the briefest of returns for Joe Royle the previous year, they had to wait until 2013 for another taste of glory. Two goals from lanky striker Matt Smith beat Liverpool 3-2 in the FA Cup fourth round and he then grabbed a last-minute equaliser at home to Everton and scored in a 3-1 defeat in the Goodison replay before moving on to Leeds.

Only three points clear of relegation as Lee Johnson replaced Paul Dickov that season, the Latics stayed in the bottom half of the third tier for nine years in all but went down in the last of them, drawing at Northampton while Rochdale won to stay up.

Corney ended his 14 years at the club as Moroccan Abdallah Lemsagam set out on the long road to restoring former glories.

* * * * *

Sending Oldham down to League Two on the last day of that 2017/18 season by beating top-six side Charlton was a rare triumph for **Rochdale**, whose main achievement was survival as a Football League club.

At that point they had played more seasons than anyone else (90) without ever having climbed out of the bottom two divisions. From 1974 to 2010, 36 successive seasons was the most of any team without escaping from the bottom division and from 1970 until 2001 they set another unwanted record (albeit soon beaten by Coventry City) for never finishing in the top six.

Yet still there were glimmers of hope and pride, not merely at the despair of local rivals. Following promotion at last, in 2010, came a ninth place finish in the third tier that equalled the best in the club's history (from 1969/70) and was then beaten by one place in 2015.

After Steve Parkin walked out in November 2001 to take over at Barnsley, John Hollins, the former Chelsea and England international, was the manager who made the top five in 2001 to earn a play-off place, only a point away from automatic promotion and ending in narrow failure against Rushden & Diamonds. The Dale drew 2-2 away but lost a 1-0 lead in the home leg watched by more than 8,500 people.

That season youngsters Paddy McCourt, who later played for Celtic, and Lee McEvilly became the club's first-ever internationals when capped by Northern Ireland.

Hollins, negotiating a new contract, received a fax saying the club were pulling out and discovered that Paul Simpson was taking on the demanding role of player-manager. The Dale were soon back in the bottom six with crowds below 3,000 again, despite a record-equalling run to the FA Cup fifth round in 2003, beating Preston and Coventry but losing to Wolves.

In December 2006 Keith Hill, a Boltonian who played for the club for five seasons from 1996, started the first of two spells that qualify him as arguably the club's best manager. In his first full season his side finished fifth and beat Darlington in the play-off semi-final with almost 10,000 at Spotland, but lost the final 3-2 to Stockport in a first-ever Wembley appearance.

In the next two seasons they first reached the play-offs again, losing to Gillingham, then won promotion at last, scoring 82 goals. Chris O'Grady and Chris Dagnall contributed 42 between them and Hill's men would have been champions but for a series of late defeats.

Like Parkin before him, Hill moved on to Barnsley, and by the time he returned in January 2013 the Dale were back in League Two again, John Coleman from Accrington having been unable to keep them up the previous season.

Fifteen months later Hill had them promoted again, having knocked Leeds out of the FA Cup, and eighth place in 2015, followed by tenth and ninth, represented a historic high in terms of consistency.

If the 2017/18 campaign required a goal by double cancer survivor Joe Thompson to keep them up and demote Oldham, it was a season also notable for national exposure in holding Tottenham 2-2 in the FA Cup fifth round and then taking thousands of supporters to Wembley for the midweek replay, lost 6-1 and also televised live.

* * * * *

What **Stockport** would have given for the modest achievement of hanging on in the Football League. From eighth place in the Championship and beating Manchester City, they were in the Conference North within 15 years.

Five mostly enjoyable years in the second tier had ended ingloriously in 2001/02, bottom with only half a dozen wins, and 102 goals conceded, leaving them fully 22 points behind the rest. Oddly it also included another victory over champions-elect City, this one in the last few minutes, met with particular glee by supporters who had reacted furiously to owner Brendan Elwood's proposal to move to Maine Road when City left.

In summer 2003 the real problems began when the club was sold to Brian Kennedy, looking for a nice home for Sale Sharks rugby club, who duly moved in at Edgeley Park. Sammy McIlroy became manager but the 2004/05 campaign was another horrendous one, with again only six wins and 26 points meaning bottom spot.

By 2005 financial alarm bells were clanging. The Supporters Trust took over ownership without the financial wherewithal to find heavy rental payments and a 6-0 defeat at Macclesfield on Boxing Day had County rooted to the bottom. Chris Turner gave way to former stalwart Jim Gannon for the first of three spells in the hottest of seats as an end to more than 100 years of league football seemed inevitable. Remarkably they survived on the last day by holding champions Carlisle in front of a five-figure Edgeley Park crowd.

The upturn continued under Gannon and from January to March 2007 even took in a run of nine league matches without conceding a goal, the best of any club in league history. It was quite a start to the professional career of Wayne Hennessey, the future Wales goalkeeper on loan from Wolves.

The following year they were promoted with a play-off win over Rochdale at Wembley in front of over 35,000 but, financial bonus or not, money problems worsened. Despite improved gates averaging over 6,000 the club went into administration in April 2009. They avoided relegation despite the automatic ten-point deduction but Gannon, who had turned down the chance to join Brighton, was made redundant, later joining Motherwell.

A consortium led by the former Manchester City striker Jim Melrose began negotiations that came to nothing and with no money for players there was a new low in 2009/10 in five wins from 46 games, 25 points and inevitable relegation back to the lowest tier.

In June a new consortium the '2015 Group' took over but the team went from bad to even worse under first Paul Simpson and then Ray Mathias, bottom again after conceding 191 goals in two seasons, and doomed to eviction from the Football League berth gained in 1900. A 2-0 defeat by Crewe on 30 April sealed their fate and a week later 5,027 turned up for the wake, at home to Cheltenham. Leading scorer Greg Tansey did at least salvage a 1-1 draw with his last-minute penalty.

Any optimism garnered from that and the appointment of former Liverpool and Manchester City man Dietmar Hamann failed to last much beyond the summer. Hamann resigned in November after another failed takeover, Gannon returned as director of football and manager until January 2013, but the Blue Square Premier, as the Conference/National League was known at the time, provided no quick fix.

In 2011/12 with Fleetwood Town's promotion illustrating the changing of the guard, Stockport struggled in the lower reaches. Bottom but one at Christmas, they finished 16th only by virtue of winning five of the last seven games. County had the third highest crowds, averaging 3,676.

They needed a similar finish the following season but could not manage it and were relegated to the Blue Square North in 21st place, four points below old adversaries Southport, who had beaten them 4-3 at Edgeley Park. Ryan McKnight, the youngest CEO in football at 30, was held responsible for the latest catastrophe, after putting Swiss-born Bosnian Darije Kalezic, a man with no experience of English football, in charge of the team. (Kalezic lasted 55 days, McKnight 16 months).

From 14th place in 2013/14 at the sixth level of English football there did at least appear to be a recovery. The following year County were in the top half of any table for the first time since 2008, issuing a document called 'Moving Forward' which set out ambitions for the next five years. Returning to the Football League by 2020 was soon looking improbable, although they were taking small steps in the right direction: ninth in 2015/16 with the popular Gannon returning, three points off the play-offs a year later and then qualifying for new extended play-offs in 2017/18, losing 1-0 at home to Chorley in front of more than 6,000.

It all represented an improvement on moving backward, and downward.

* * * * *

Like Stockport, **Tranmere** found themselves victims of the decision that from 1987 there should be automatic relegation from the Football League, which from 2003 became two clubs. Rovers, exiled in 2015, four years after Stockport, suffered only three seasons below stairs, but it was still a heavy fall from all those Wembley trips round about the time the 1980s gave way to the '90s.

Relegated to the third tier after finishing bottom in 2001, they were close to the play-offs in 2003 and 2004 in a period that included the excitement of two more FA Cup quarter-finals. In the relegation season it took in performances utterly at variance with league form by winning 3-0 away to Everton, beating Southampton 4-3 with a hat-trick by Paul Rideout after being 3-0 down at half-time and going down only 4-2 at home to eventual winners Liverpool.

That best-ever run was equalled three years later, losing a replay at home to Millwall before a strong league finish to climb to eighth place. John Aldridge had left in 2001 and Brian Little was in charge when Rovers were third in 2005 but went out on penalties to Hartlepool.

Ronnie Moore came close but not close enough in his three seasons from 2006, finishing ninth, eleventh and seventh but John Barnes, appointed in the summer of 2009, took just seven points from 11 games and was replaced by popular physiotherapist Les Parry. From bottom in mid-November with crowds below 5,000 he led a revival that finished spectacularly with survival on the final day by winning 3-0 at doomed Stockport.

Moore returned briefly and less successfully, and from being top of League One in January 2013, Rovers found themselves out of the Football League little more than two years later.

The fall was so sudden as to be far less predictable than Stockport's. In 2013/14 they lost four of the last five games to go down to League Two by only three points. They might have been expected to make a challenge to return but instead went straight through it and out of the league, after losing 12 of the last 15 games under Micky Adams.

'Tranmere Rovers: 'Where did it all go wrong?' asked the *Liverpool Echo*, citing long-term under-investment; 'high turnover in managers, (especially Ronnie Moore's dismissal after minor betting infringements); gambling on rookie manager Rob Edwards in that final season; too many short-term signings; and 'a fragile dressing room'.

The one positive, the paper said, was having committed new owners in former midfielder and FA chief executive Mark Palios and his wife Nicola. They were rewarded three long years later after finishing runners-up twice. The first play-off final was lost 3-1 to Forest Green Rovers but the second brought a dramatic win, beating Boreham Wood after having left-back Liam Ridehalgh sent off in the first minute.

* * * * *

For **Accrington Stanley** to take so long to return their town to league football was a warning to any club dropping out of the 92-club league and yet a beacon of hope too.

Having dropped out mid-season in 1962, disbanded four years later and reformed as 'Accrington Stanley 1968', it took almost 40 years to recover that status but was all the better received, while promotion to the third tier as champions in 2018 made the club headline news nationally. The one concern, though it made the achievement all the more romantic, was that they were still doing it on tiny crowds.

The newly reformed club joined the Lancashire Combination (Chapter 6) and slowly fought their way back up the football pyramid, via the Cheshire County League, north-west Counties League, Northern League and Northern Premier, where as champions in 2003 with 100 points they were well and truly back in the game.

The manager was John Coleman, appointed in 1999 and destined to stay until 2012, then return in further triumph. In 2003/04 he had them tenth in the Conference and confident enough to become full-time professionals again.

In 2005/06 they stormed to the title by 11 points, Paul Mullin dropping from his regular 20 goals a season but with the team's 76 more widely shared. Stanley were unbeaten from mid-October until defeat at Southport at the end of March, yet still had only the eighth highest average crowd of 1,895.

League football returned with the short visit to Chester on 5 August 2006. One win in the opening seven games was a useful reminder that the new status would not be easily preserved. The League Cup offered some confidence, however, with a 1-0 win over Nottingham Forest and then a goalless draw away to Premier League Watford (which was followed by a 6-5 defeat on penalties), and they wound up 20th but comfortable after a strong finish. Mullin was their top scorer once again.

Derbies with Bury and Rochdale drew crowds of 3,000 but the overall average was only 2,260 – fewer than in the final league season of 1961/62. Eight of the next ten campaigns saw them finish in the bottom half of the table, the exceptions bringing play-off semi-finals lost to Stevenage (2011) and AFC Wimbledon (2016).

Coleman left for Rochdale in 2012 but lasted only a year and returned in September 2014 after brief spells at Southport and Sligo Rovers. At last a breakthrough came in 2018, as champions by five points from Luton Town, Billy Kee scoring 25 goals. Only ninth at the halfway stage, Stanley came on strong and beat Lincoln 1-0 in the penultimate game with the highest crowd at the Wham Stadium (formerly the Crown Ground) of 4,753 present, as well BBC and ITV news cameras.

It was a happy story and average crowds had crept up to almost 2,000, yet the fear that finance would remain a problem had been highlighted the previous year by chairman Andy Holt, who said the club expected to lose £500,000 most seasons. 'The EFL is like a starving peasant begging for scraps off your table, Premier League,' he said. 'When you do things for the game, you've got to look at the entire game you can't just deal with them in isolation. They generate all the cash and they need to get some of it spread about.'

* * * * *

The season that Accrington won the League Two championship, only one club had smaller crowds. That was **Morecambe**, thrilled to be a Football League club but with only a couple of exceptions finding it hard going.

The Shrimps were founded in May 1920 and played their first competitive game at home to Fleetwood, who 90 years later would follow them into the league and provide their most local derby.

In the Lancashire Combination they played at the local cricket club ground at Woodhill Lane, then Roseberry Park, which became Christie Park after the club president, where they remained until 2010.

Although winning the Lancashire Combination as early as 1925, the big steps forward began in the 1960s. In 1961/62 they beat a Football League club for the first time in the FA Cup, seeing off Chester 2-1 away with Gordon Howarth's winning goal. In the next round Weymouth's visit set a ground record for Christie Park of 9,383.

Further cup success came by winning the 1968 Lancashire Senior Cup Final against Burnley, and then going to Wembley six years later to beat Dartford 2-1 in the FA Trophy final.

331

Finishing third in the inaugural Northern Premier League season of 1968, they did so again three times in a row at the start of the '90s as a prelude to promotion. In 1994/95 they made it as runners-up to Marine, whose ground was not good enough to step up. John Coleman, later such an influential manager at Accrington, was top scorer with 31 goals, plus 15 in the cups.

Coleman may have developed his taste for a long, stable stay at one club from his manager at Morecambe, Jim Harvey, who served from 1994 to 2006. Taking them into the Conference in 1995, he saw gates rise from 750 to 1,100 in a consolidatory first season that included demolishing Altrincham 7-0.

Runners-up in 2002/03, they hoped to accompany Yeovil into the Football League but lost on penalties to Dagenham & Redbridge. Two years later Harvey suffered a heart attack during a game and Sammy McIlroy took over as caretaker. Harvey, expecting to return the following season, was sacked instead.

The former Manchester United man was therefore in charge when the Shrimps joined the bigger fish as Football League members in 2007. Squeezing past York City in the play-off semi-final, they beat Exeter at Wembley 2-1 with Danny Carlton's late goal watched by a crowd of over 40,000.

League life began with a goalless draw at home to Barnet on 11 August 2007, ending up in a respectable 11th place and average gates of 2,812, as well as an enjoyable introduction to the Football League Cup with away wins at Preston and Wolves. Paul Mullin arrived from Accrington to score some useful goals and in 2010 they reached the play-offs, only to suffer a record defeat when losing the first leg of the semi-final 6-0 to Dagenham. The home leg, a 2-1 win, was the last game played at Christie Park and most seasons in the new ground on Christie Way have been a struggle.

McIlroy left after a drop to 20th place in 2010/11, since when they have also been 21st and 22nd, surviving a return to non-league football only on the last day of 2017/18 with a 0-0 draw at Coventry that suited both teams, while Barnet made a valiant but vain attempt to escape.

They had made Accrington their biggest rivals, failing frustratingly to beat them in the first 16 meetings since going up in 2007. Then Fleetwood arrived for a derby a little closer to home.

* * * * *

Folding twice and reforming before making the Football League after 104 years, **Fleetwood Town** are another club who stand as an inspiration to others.

The original Fleetwood club ran from 1908 to 1976, for most of that time in the Lancashire Combination and briefly boasting a young Frank Swift, born down the coast in Blackpool, between the posts. They set a ground record of 6,150 for the 1965 FA Cup tie against Rochdale and joined the new Northern Premier League in 1968, along with Morecambe, Wigan, Altrincham, South Liverpool and Chorley, but by 1975 were finishing bottom and after doing so for the second successive season folded amid financial concerns.

Fleetwood Town emerged as a phoenix club in the Cheshire League and had an FA Vase final to their name in 1985 and were well placed in the Northern Premier by 1991, but went to the wall five years later.

Fleetwood Wanderers emerged, becoming Fleetwood Freeport under a sponsorship deal, and reverting to Fleetwood Town in 2002. Under local businessman Andy Pilley they made good progress on a more solid basis with successive promotions in 2005 and 2006, and by 2008 had won the Northern Premier League to reach the Conference North.

In the first season at the higher level Micky Mellon came in as manager, initially while still coaching youth teams at Burnley, and his side pulled in over 3,000 for an FA Cup second round defeat to Hartlepool.

The following season they made the play-offs and came through by beating Droylsden and Alfreton Town to stand one step from the Football League. With sufficient financial muscle to make all the playing staff full-time, the self-styled Cod Army enjoyed another fine season in 2010/11 but were well beaten in the play-off semi-final by AFC Wimbledon, 8-1 on aggregate after a 6-1 drubbing in the second leg.

In August 2011 they signed a bright young striker from FC Halifax Town named Jamie Vardy, who proved a sensation with 31 goals, propelling them to the title and the Football League. In the FA Cup third round they received a dream draw at home to neighbouring Blackpool of the Championship, who won 5-1 and immediately offered £750,000 for Vardy, scorer of the Fleetwood goal.

Town held out for £1m and got it from Leicester City at the end of the season, setting a record for a non-league player. They should have set another record by beating Crawley's 105 points but failed to win any of the last four games and had to settle for 103, with 102 goals.

Crowds peaked at almost 5,000 for Wrexham's visit in April and on 18 August 2016 there were 3,624 to see a first Football League game at home to Torquay, drawn 0-0.

Replacing Vardy and his goals was not easily done and at the end of a mixed season the ambitious Mellon had departed, former Preston and Burnley stalwart Graham Alexander was in charge and a much-changed team were 13th in the table, having done the double over Morecambe.

In 2014 Alexander's side finished fourth and beat Burton Albion at Wembley to win the play-offs and reach League One on crowds of under 3,000. Allowed one full season in which they finished tenth, he was dismissed the following September and Steven Pressley, after keeping them up in 19th place, finished 2016/17 on the verge of the Championship, fourth in the table after winning at places like Sheffield United and Coventry but squeezed out by the only goal of the play-off semi-final against Bradford City.

It was impressive progress on the lowest crowds in the division.

* * * * *

So in 2012 Fleetwood Town had joined the Football League and five years later were playing against fellow Lancastrians Blackburn Rovers, who had been founder members of it 124 years earlier and won the FA Cup three times even before that. Fleetwood finished only two places below their nearest neighbours Blackpool, another of the great names of English football.

It was a reflection of the democracy of the game, although no one was suggesting they would ever rub shoulders with the giants of Manchester and Merseyside. Burnley, once down in the Fourth Division and almost out of the league altogether, were doing so again but the task for the likes of Fleetwood, Morecambe and Accrington on their tiny gates was just to keep competing at the highest possible level.

Lancashire football, as this book has attempted to show, has much to be proud of, not least in its range. In United and City, Liverpool and Everton, the north-west had four of the top 20 richest clubs in the world in 2018, with 15 major European trophies between them. But as the turf wars continue, the survival of so many representatives among the country's 92 senior clubs, with others pushing to join them, should not be overlooked as an achievement worthy of celebration too.

Appendix I

Top Lancashire club each season by league position
(Football League First Division from 1888/89; Premier League from 1992/93)

1888/89 **Preston North End (1st)**
1889/90 **Preston North End (1st)**
1890/91 **Everton (1st)**
1891/92 Preston North End (2nd)
1892/93 Preston North End (2nd)
1893/94 Blackburn Rovers (4th)
1894/95 Everton (2nd)
1895/96 Everton (3rd)
1896/97 Preston North End (4th)
1897/98 Everton (4th)
1898/99 Liverpool (2nd)
1899/00 Manchester City (7th)
1900/01 **Liverpool (1st)**
1901/02 Everton (2nd)
1902/03 Liverpool (5th)
1903/04 Manchester City (2nd)
1904/05 Everton (2nd)
1905/06 **Liverpool (1st)**
1906/07 Everton (3rd)
1907/08 **Manchester United (1st)**
1908/09 Everton (2nd)
1909/10 Liverpool (2nd)
1910/11 **Manchester United (1st)**
1911/12 **Blackburn Rovers (1st)**
1912/13 Manchester United (4th)

1913/14 **Blackburn Rovers (1st)**
1914/15 **Everton (1st)**

1919/20 Burnley (2nd)
1920/21 **Burnley (1st)**
1921/22 **Liverpool (1st)**
1922/23 **Liverpool (1st)**
1923/24 Bolton Wanderers (4th)
1924/25 Bolton Wanderers (3rd)
1925/26 Bury (4th)
1926/27 Bolton Wanderers (4th)
1927/28 **Everton (1st)**
1928/29 Liverpool (5th)
1929/30 Manchester City (3rd)
1930/31 Manchester City (8th)
1931/32 **Everton (1st)**
1932/33 Everton (11th)
1933/34 Manchester City (5th)
1934/35 Manchester City (4th)
1935/36 Preston North End (7th)
1936/37 **Manchester City (1st)**
1937/38 Preston North End (3rd)
1938/39 **Everton (1st)**

1946/47 **Liverpool (1st)**
1947/48 Manchester United (2nd)
1948/49 Manchester United (2nd)
1949/50 Manchester United (4th)
1950/51 Manchester United (2nd)
1951/52 **Manchester United (1st)**
1952/53 Preston North End (2nd)
1953/54 Manchester United (4th)
1954/55 Manchester United (5th)
1955/56 **Manchester United (1st)**
1956/57 **Manchester United (1st)**
1957/58 Preston North End (2nd)
1958/59 Manchester United (2nd)
1959/60 **Burnley (1st)**
1960/61 Burnley (4th)

1961/62 Burnley (2nd)
1962/63 **Everton (1st)**
1963/64 **Liverpool (1st)**
1964/65 **Manchester United (1st)**
1965/66 **Liverpool (1st)**
1966/67 **Manchester United (1st)**
1967/68 **Manchester City (1st)**
1968/69 Liverpool (2nd)
1969/70 **Everton (1st)**
1970/71 Liverpool (5th)
1971/72 Liverpool (3th)
1972/73 **Liverpool (1st)**
1973/74 Liverpool (2nd)
1974/75 Liverpool (2nd)
1975/76 **Liverpool (1st)**
1976/77 **Liverpool (1st)**
1977/78 Liverpool (2nd)
1978/79 **Liverpool (1st)**
1979/80 **Liverpool (1st)**
1980/81 Liverpool (5th)
1981/82 **Liverpool (1st)**
1982/83 **Liverpool (1st)**
1983/84 **Liverpool (1st)**
1984/85 **Everton (1st)**
1985/86 **Liverpool (1st)**
1986/87 **Everton (1st)**
1987/88 **Liverpool (1st)**
1988/89 Liverpool (2nd)
1989/90 **Liverpool (1st)**
1990/91 Liverpool (2nd)
1991/92 Manchester United (2nd)
1992/93 **Manchester United (1st)**
1993/94 **Manchester United (1st)**
1994/95 **Blackburn Rovers (1st)**
1995/96 **Manchester United (1st)**
1996/97 **Manchester United (1st)**
1997/98 Manchester United (2nd)
1998/99 **Manchester United (1st)**
1999/00 **Manchester United (1st)**

2000/01 **Manchester United (1st)**
2001/02 Liverpool (2nd)
2002/03 **Manchester United (1st)**
2003/04 Manchester United (3rd)
2004/05 Manchester United (3rd)
2005/06 Manchester United (2nd)
2006/07 **Manchester United (1st)**
2007/08 **Manchester United (1st)**
2008/09 **Manchester United (1st)**
2009/10 Manchester United (2nd)
2010/11 **Manchester United (1st)**
2011/12 **Manchester City (1st)**
2012/13 **Manchester United (1st)**
2013/14 **Manchester City (1st)**
2014/15 Manchester City (2nd)
2015/16 Manchester City (4th)
2016/17 Manchester City (3rd)
2017/18 **Manchester City (1st)**

Total: Manchester United 34, Liverpool 32, Everton 17, Manchester City 14, Preston 9, Burnley 5, Blackburn 4, Bolton 3, Bury 1.

League champions (59): Manchester United 20, Liverpool 18, Everton 9, Manchester City 5, Blackburn 3, Burnley 2, Preston 2.

Appendix II

Lowest Lancashire club each season by league position
(Football League First Division from 1888/89; Second Division from 1892/93; Third Division North from 1921/22; Fourth Division (or equivalent) from 1958/59)
*Denotes left league

1888/89 Burnley (9th)
1889/90 Burnley (11th)
1890/91 Accrington (10th)
1891/92 Darwen (14th)
1892/93 Bootle (8th)
1893/94 Ardwick (13th)
1894/95 Manchester City (9th)
1895/96 Darwen (9th)
1896/97 Darwen (11th)
1897/98 Darwen (15th)
1898/99 Darwen (18th)*
1899/00 New Brighton Tower (10th)
1900/01 Stockport County (17th)
1901/02 Stockport County (17th)
1902/03 Burnley (18th)
1903/04 Stockport County (16th)*
1904/05 Blackpool (15th)
1905/06 Blackpool (14th)
1906/07 Blackpool (13th)
1907/08 Blackpool (15th)
1908/09 Blackpool (20th)
1909/10 Burnley (14th)
1910/11 Stockport County (17th)

1911/12 Stockport County (16th)
1912/13 Blackpool (20th)
1913/14 Blackpool (16th)
1914/15 Stockport County (14th)

1919/20 Stockport County (16th)
1920/21 Stockport County (22nd)
1921/22 Rochdale (20th)
1922/23 Southport (17th)
      Stalybridge Celtic (resigned)*
1923/24 New Brighton (18th)
1924/25 Tranmere Rovers (21st)
1925/26 Southport (20th)
1926/27 Accrington Stanley (21st)
1927/28 Nelson (22nd)
1928/29 Accrington Stanley (18th)
1929/30 Nelson (19th)
1930/31 Nelson (22nd)*
1931/32 Rochdale (21st)
      Wigan Borough (resigned)*
1932/33 New Brighton (21st)
1933/34 Rochdale (22nd)
1934/35 Southport (21st)
1935/36 New Brighton (22nd)
1936/37 Tranmere Rovers (19th)
1937/38 Accrington Stanley (22nd)
1938/39 Accrington Stanley (22nd)

1946/47 Southport (21st)
1947/48 New Brighton (22nd)
1948/49 Southport (21st)
1949/50 Southport (16th)
1950/51 New Brighton (24th)*
1951/52 Accrington Stanley (22nd)
1952/53 Accrington Stanley (24th)
1953/54 Rochdale (21st)
1954/55 Tranmere Rovers 19th)
1955/56 Oldham Athletic (20th)
1956/57 Tranmere Rovers (23rd)

1957/58 Southport (23rd)
1958/59 Southport (24th)
1959/60 Oldham Athletic (23rd)
1960/61 Accrington Stanley (18th)
1961/62 Southport (17th)
          Accrington Stanley (resigned)*
1962/63 Stockport County (19th)
1963/64 Southport (21st)
1964/65 Stockport County (24th)
1965/66 Rochdale (21st)
1966/67 Rochdale (21st)
1967/68 Rochdale (19th)
1968/69 Rochdale (3rd)
1969/70 Oldham Athletic (19th)
1970/71 Stockport County (11th)
1971/72 Stockport County (23rd)
1972/73 Bury (12th)
1973/74 Stockport County (24th)
1974/75 Stockport County (20th)
1975/76 Southport (23rd)
1976/77 Southport (23rd)
1977/78 Rochdale (24th)
          Southport (23rd)*
1978/79 Rochdale (20th)
1979/80 Rochdale (24th)
1980/81 Tranmere Rovers (21st)
1981/82 Rochdale (21st)
1982/83 Blackpool (21st)
1983/84 Rochdale (22nd)
1984/85 Stockport County (22nd)
1985/86 Preston North End (23rd)
1986/87 Burnley (22nd)
1987/88 Rochdale (21st)
1988/89 Stockport County (20th)
1989/90 Burnley (16th)
1990/91 Rochdale (12th)
1991/92 Rochdale (8th)
1992/93 Rochdale (11th)
1993/94 Wigan Athletic (19th)

1994/95 Rochdale (15th)
1995/96 Rochdale (15th)
1996/97 Rochdale (14th)
1997/98 Rochdale (18th)
1998/99 Rochdale (19th)
1999/00 Rochdale (10th)
2000/01 Rochdale (8th)
2001/02 Rochdale (5th)
2002/03 Rochdale (19th)
2003/04 Rochdale (21st)
2004/05 Bury (17th)
2005/06 Stockport County (22nd)
2006/07 Bury (21st)
2007/08 Accrington Stanley (17th)
2008/09 Accrington Stanley (16th)
2009/10 Accrington Stanley (15th)
2010/11 Stockport County (24th)*
2011/12 Morecambe (15th)
2012/13 Accrington Stanley (18th)
2013/14 Morecambe (18th)
2014/15 Tranmere Rovers (24th)*
2015/16 Morecambe (21st)
2016/17 Morecambe (18th)
2017/18 Morecambe (22nd)

Total : Rochdale 27,Stockport 18, Southport 12,
Accrington Stanley 11, Blackpool 8, Burnley 6, Bury 6, Tranmere
6, Darwen 5, Morecambe 5, New Brighton 5, Oldham 3, Ardwick/
Manchester City 2, Preston North End 1, Accrington 1, Bootle 1,
New Brighton Tower 1, Wigan Athletic 1.

Select Bibliography

Allardyce, Sam *My Autobiography* (Headline, 2015)

Armfield, Jimmy *Right Back to the Beginning* (Headline, 2004)

Barclay, Patrick *Sir Matt Busby* (Ebury Press, 2017)

Benitez, Rafa *Champions League Dreams* (Headline, 2012)

Butler, Bryon *The Football League 1888–1988 – The Official Illustrated History* (Queen Anne Press, 1998)

Butler, Bryon *The Official History of the Football Association* (Queen Anne Press, 1991)

Calley, Roy *Blackpool: The Complete Record 1887– 2011* (Breedon, 2011)

Cawley, Steve and James, Gary *The Pride of Manchester* (ACL & Polar, 1991)

Charlton, Sir Bobby *My Manchester United Years* (Headline, 2007)

Clark, Frank *Kicking with Both Feet* (Headline, 1999)

Collett, Mike *The Complete Record Of The FA Cup* (Sports Books, 2003)

Conn, David *Richer Than God* (Quercus, 2012)

Crick, Michael *The Boss* (Simon & Schuster, 2002)

Curry, Graham and Dunning, Eric *Association Football* (Routledge, 2015)

Dalglish, Kenny *My Liverpool Home* (Hodder & Stoughton, 2010)

Dewhurst, Keith *Underdogs* (Yellow Jersey, 2012)

Dunphy, Eamon *A Strange Kind of Glory* (Heinemann, 1991)

Ferguson, Sir Alex *My Autobiography* (Hodder & Stoughton, 2013)

Finney, Tom *My Autobiography* (Headline, 2003)

Gerrard, Steven *My Autobiography* (Bantam, 2006)

Giles, John *A Football Man* (Hodder & Stoughton, 2010)

Gobel, Ray and Ward, Andrew *Manchester City: A Complete Record* (Breedon, 1993)

Hardaker, Alan *Hardaker of the League* (Pelham, 1977)

Hodgson, Derek *The Everton Story* (Arthur Barker, 1979)

Holt, Oliver *If You Are Second, You Are Nothing* (Macmillan, 2006)

Hugman, Barry *Football Players Record 1946–84* (Rothmans, 1984)

Inglis, Simon League *Football and the Men Who Made It* (Willow Books, 1988)

Inglis, Simon *Soccer in the Dock* (Collins Willow, 1985)

Inglis, Simon *The Football Grounds of Great Britain* (Collins Willow, 1987)

Jackman, Mike *Blackburn Rovers: A Complete Record* (Breedon, 1990)

James, Gary *The Manchester City Years* (James Ward, 2012)

Keane, Roy *The Second Half* (Orion, 2014)

Kelly, Richard *Keegan and Dalglish* (Simon & Schuster, 2017)

Kelly, Stephen *Bill Shankly* (Virgin, 1996)

Kelly, Stephen *Gerard Houllier, The Liverpool Revolution* (Virgin, 2011)

Law, Denis *The King* (Bantam, 2003)

Lee, Eddie and Simpson, Ray *Burnley: A Complete Record* (Breedon, 1991)

Lovejoy, Joe *Bestie* (Sidgwick & Jackson, 1998)

Marland, Simon *Bolton Wanderers: The Complete Record* (Breedon, 1992)

Matthews, Stanley *The Way it Was* (Headline, 2000)

McCartney, Ian *Manchester United 1958–68: Rising From the Wreckage* (Amberley, 2013)

Meek, David and Tyrell, Tom *Manchester United in Europe* (Coronet, 2002)

Metcalf, Mark, Bugby, Tony and Millman, Leslie *Bright Red: The Liverpool-Manchester United Matches* (Amberley, 2012)

Metcalf, Mark *The Origins of the Football League: The First Season 1888/89* (Amberley, 2013)

Morrison, Ian and Shury, Alan *Manchester United: A Complete Record* (Breedon Books, 1992)

Motson, John and Rowlinson, John *The European Cup, 1955–80* (Queen Anne Press, 1980)

Onslow, Tony *The Forgotten Rivals, A History of Bootle Football Club* (Countryvice, 2005)

Pead, Brian *Liverpool: A Complete Record* (Breedon Books, 1986)

Pythian, Graham *Shooting Stars: The Brief and Glorious History of Blackburn Olympic* (SoccerData, 2007)

Robinson, Michael (ed.) *English Football League and FA Premier League Tables 1888–2011* (Soccer Books, 2011)

Rollin, Jack *Soccer at War 1939–45* (Headline, 2005)

Ross, Ian and Smailes, Gordon *Everton: A Complete Record* (Breedon Books, 1993)

St John, Ian *The Saint* (Hodder & Stoughton, 2005)

Shankly, Bill *Shankly* (Arthur Barker, 1976)

Souness, Graeme *Football My Life, My Passion* (Headline, 2017)

Stiles, Nobby *After the Ball* (Hodder & Stoughton, 2003)

Summerbee, Mike *The Autobiography* (Century, 2008)

Sutcliffe, C.E and Hargreaves, F. *History of the Lancashire Football Association 1878–1928* (Yore Publications reprint, 1992)

Tabner, Brian *Through the Turnstiles* (Yore, 1992)

Tate, Tim *Women's Football: The Secret History* (John Blake, 2016)

Tyler, Martin *Cup Final Extra!* (Hamlyn, 1981)

Williams, John and Hopkins, Stephen *The Miracle of Istanbul* (Mainstream, 2005)

Young, Percy *Bolton Wanderers* (Stanley Paul, 1961)

Young, Percy *Football on Merseyside* (Stanley Paul, 1963)

Young, Percy *Manchester United* (Heinemann, 1960)

Rothmans Football Yearbook, 1970–2002

Sky Sports Football Yearbook, 2003–2018

Select Webography

www.11v11.com

www.bbc.co.uk/sport/football

www.dickkerrladies.com

www.donmouth.co.uk

www.european-football-statistics.co.uk

www.fchd.info

www.footballandthefirstworldwar.org

www.footballgroundmap.com

www.historicalkits.co.uk

www.thefootballarchives.com
www.managerstats.co.uk
www.nonleaguematters.co.uk
www.soccerbase.co.uk
www.soccer-history.co.uk
www.southportfc.net/complete-history-of-southport-football-club/
www.spartacus-educational.com
www.tranmererovers-mad.co.uk
www.tranmereroverspast.wordpress.com
www.wikipedia.org
www.youtube.com
League club official websites and national newspaper websites.

Main Index to Clubs